EAST ASIAN HISTORICAL MONOGRAPHS

General Editor: WANG GUNGWU

The Rural Economy of Pre-Liberation China
Trade Expansion and Peasant Livelihood
in Jiangsu and Guangdong, 1870 to 1937

EAST ASIAN HISTORICAL MONOGRAPHS

General Editor: WANG GUNGWU

The East Asian Historical Monographs series has, since its inception in the late 1960s, earned a reputation for the publication of works of innovative historical scholarship. It has encouraged a generation of scholars of Asian history to go beyond Western activities in Asia seen from Western points of view. Their books have included a wider range of Asian viewpoints and also reflected a stronger awareness of economic and socio-cultural factors in Asia which lay behind political events.

During its second decade the series has broadened to reflect the interest among historians in studying and reassessing Chinese history, and now includes important works on China and Hong Kong.

It is the hope of the publishers that, as the series moves into its third decade, it will continue to meet the need and demand for historical writings on the region and that the fruits of the scholarship of new generations of historians will reach a wider reading public.

Other titles in this series are listed at the end of the book.

The Rural Economy of Pre-Liberation China

Trade Expansion and Peasant Livelihood in Jiangsu and Guangdong, 1870 to 1937

David Faure

HONG KONG
OXFORD UNIVERSITY PRESS
OXFORD   NEW YORK
1989

Oxford University Press

Oxford New York Toronto
Petaling Jaya Singapore Hong Kong Tokyo
Delhi Bombay Calcutta Madras Karachi
Nairobi Dar es Salaam Cape Town
Melbourne Auckland

and associated companies in
Berlin Ibadan

First published 1989
Published in the United States
by Oxford University Press, Inc., New York

British Library Cataloguing in Publication Data
Faure, David
The rural economy of pre-liberation China:trade expansion
and peasant livelihood in Jiangsu and
Guangdong, 1870 to 1937.
1. China. Rural regions. Economic development,
history
I. Title
330.951
ISBN 0-19-582707-4

Library of Congress Cataloging-in-Publication Data

Faure, David.
The rural economy of pre-liberation China:
trade expansion and peasant livelihood in Jiangsu and Guangdong,
1870 to 1937 / David Faure.
p. cm — (East Asian historical monographs)
Bibliography: p.
Includes index.
ISBN 0-19-582707-4 : $37.50 (U.S. : est.)
1. Kiangsu Province (China) — Economic conditions. 2. Kwangtung
Province (China) —Economic conditions. 3. Kiangsu Province (China) —
Commerce. 4. Kwangtung Province (China) — Commerce. 5. Kiangsu
Province (China) — Rural conditions. 6. Kwangtung Province (China)—
Rural conditions. I. Title. II. Series.
HC428.K5F38 1989
330.951'136—dc20 89–8658
CIP

Printed in Hong Kong by Calay Printing Co., Ltd.
Published by Oxford University Press, Warwick House, Hong Kong

Contents

Tables

Figures

Measurements

1 *mu* = 0.06144 hectare
1 *shimu* = 1.085 *mu*
1 *picul* = 100 catties = 60.50 kg.
1 *shi* = 103.55 litres

Acknowledgements

THERE are many people to thank for help and encouragement over the more than ten years that, on and off, went into this book. Marion J. Levy Jr., Gilbert Rozman, and Roberta Cohen were my dissertation advisers at Princeton University and I owe to them my graduate training and a start on the problem that led to this book. Chuan Hansheng and Ramon Myers were most encouraging at a crucial time in my career. James Hayes provided the opportunity to conduct field research in the villages of the New Territories. Susan Mann's request for an article several years ago forced me to formulate my argument at a time when I might have preferred to abandon the research altogether. Then I must thank all the many librarians at the following institutions for locating and providing source materials: Princeton University Library, the Harvard Yenching Library, the Library of Congress, Chicago University Library, the University of British Columbia Library, the Hoover Institution, Zhongshan University Library, Zhongshan Tushuguan (Guangzhou), the provincial branch of the Zhongyang Tushuguan (Taibei), the Chinese University of Hong Kong Library, and Hong Kong University Library. I must also thank the Harvard Yenching Foundation for providing research funds for the purchase of source materials at an early stage of my research, and the Commonwealth Fellowship Commission for a Commonwealth Fellowship for my sabbatical in 1982 to 1983. I stayed at Clare Hall during that year, where I wrote a complete first draft of this book, and I am grateful for its hospitality. Just as this book was in draft form, I also benefited from extensive discussion on its subject matter with Philip C.C. Huang, James Lee, R. Bin Wong, and others during a term's stay at the University of California, Los Angeles, in 1987. A short visit to the University of British Columbia during that term also provided the chance to present my argument in a seminar and for some challenging discussions with Edgar Wickberg, while a visit to Pittsburgh made it possible for me to meet Thomas Rawski, and, through his kindness and generosity, read his manuscript on the Republican economy which is highly relevant to my subject. Kathryn Bernhardt, Leo Goodstadt, Patrick Hase, Ho Hon-wai, Philip C.C. Huang, Ramon Myers, Helen Siu, and Gilbert Rozman kindly read the manuscript and offered many valuable opinions for which I am very grateful. Tables

6.6 and 6.8 and parts of Chapter 6, moreover, have been published previously in my article in *Modern China*, and I am grateful to its editors and publisher for permission to reproduce them in this book.

Work on this and other books and papers at times made strenuous demands on my family life. I am grateful to my wife and children for accepting them without question. To them I dedicate this book.

1

Introduction

China's Agrarian Problem

One of the most absorbing and controversial subjects in modern Chinese history is what is often described as China's agrarian problem. Before 1949 this problem was the poverty of China's rural population and how it might be alleviated. Its causes were manifold. Consensus is expressed among students of China's economic history over such causes as the short supply of high-yielding farmland for the size of China's population, the periodic destruction wrought by adverse weather, insects, and floods, the technological backwardness of Chinese agriculture measured by the standards of the twentieth century, and the shortage of capital for agricultural improvements, both on the farm itself and in large-scale projects. It is generally accepted that these are hindrances to development that must ultimately be overcome by technological progress. Where students of Chinese economic history have been unable to agree is in the area that may loosely be described as the social structural factors of economic development, which include, in particular, such factors that might bear on technological backwardness and widespread poverty as inequitable land distribution, tenancy relationships, and uneven access to opportunities generated by trade expansion. On these issues, opinions are polarized into two camps. What may be described as the pessimistic school argues that from the middle of the nineteenth century the economic well-being of the majority of China's peasants continuously deteriorated, owing primarily to inequity in land distribution and the increase in trade. The opposing argument, which I shall refer to as 'optimistic',[1] rejects as a point of fact the idea that the Chinese peasant's standard of living had declined and argues that, quite the contrary, it improved in some places. The role of trade is not clearly spelled out in this argument, but it would be consistent with this position to argue that over the period when trade did increase, it did not lower but raised rural income. This debate has been carried on since the 1930s and is far from settled in the current literature. It is at the heart of any discussion on the evolution of modern Chinese Society.[2]

The Pessimistic Case and a Critique

The epitome of the pessimist's argument, and to this day, its principal documentation, is the massive *Sources of Modern Chinese Agricultural History* published in 1957.[3] The selection of documentary extracts for inclusion in its three sizable volumes, and the titles under which they are arranged, suggest that the pessimist's argument is made up of six components. Firstly, it is argued that the inroads made by trade from the mid-nineteenth century accelerated the commercialization of the rural economy and the destruction of its self-subsistence. Secondly, foreign imports directly competed with Chinese rural produce, and some major products, such as sugar and hand-spun yarn, lost out almost completely in the process. Thirdly, throughout the period under consideration, the market shifted against the rural producer, as prices received by farmers declined while those paid by them increased, as did farm rent. Fourthly, even the successful export of certain rural products over several decades, such as silk, cotton, and tea, was a mixed blessing, for cyclical variations that characterized the international market introduced periodic depressions into export-oriented areas. Fifthly, as the rural economy declined, landlords, urban entrepreneurs, and capitalists, all of whom had benefited from the newly expanded foreign trade, gradually bought out the small owner-cultivators, raised rents, and dislodged tenants, and these activities began a process whereby owner-cultivators lost their independence and were transformed into tenants, while tenants lost their rights over rented land and became landless labourers, so that, in consequence, the proportion of tenants in the total rural population increased. Sixthly, political repercussions, related directly to the extension of foreign interests in China, took their toll on the rural economy as successive governments raised taxes to augment their income and as internal wars disrupted production, destroyed farmland, and delayed much needed construction projects. Natural disasters and banditry followed, bringing in their wake famine and further disruption. A vicious circle was created in which poverty generated more poverty.[4]

At first sight, most of these assertions appear quite factual, and it would seem that the historian need merely test them against the records to see if they are accurate. Did, for instance, the rural standard of living increase or decline? Did any changes bring the standard of living of some groups below the subsistence level? Was tenancy, measured in terms of the proportion of tenants within a population, rising or falling? Evidently, these basic points must first be established by reference to the factual records if they are to be explained. Nevertheless, as anyone familiar with Chinese economic history would realize, establishing these elementary facts is often the heart of the research problem. Before going further, it is important, therefore, to appreciate the difficulties embedded in the records.

The fundamental difficulties related to the available sources for an empirical study of the historical development of China's rural economy from the mid-nineteenth century to the 1930s are twofold. Firstly, some of the essential facts may now be established only to the extent that contemporary field research was carried out, but field research came late to China. From the 1920s field studies became quite common: before that they were as good as non-existent.[5] Longitudinal comparisons that rely primarily on data collected in the 1920s and 1930s shed little light on such questions as the proportion of the population that were tenants or the long-term changes in the rural standard of living.[6] In search of answers to their questions, researchers looking at the earlier period resort to a plethora of incidental references that include county gazetteers, official reports, travellers' tales, and the newspapers. Even though these are valuable sources of information in their own right and highly informative on matters related to short-term trade fluctuations or provincial finance, none of them is comparable to the field research of later years as sources on rural conditions. The student of China's rural economy, therefore, tends to know a good deal about the 1920s and 1930s but very little about earlier decades, and opinions on the performance of the economy from the 1870s on tend to be heavily influenced by its record in the 1920s and 1930s. Secondly, detailed though some of the later reports are, these field studies are far from being unbiased records of observation. To begin with, many are no more than general impressions obtained from brief excursions to the countryside; but even the best consist primarily of opinions solicited from local informants and not of direct observation. Allowance must therefore constantly be made for sampling and interviewing biases. Moreover, the researchers of the 1920s and 1930s were themselves highly influenced by contemporary emotions. For most of these years, China was being invaded by Japan, Chinese agriculture suffered disastrously under the world depression, and the Nationalist government newly established at Nanjing committed much more of its meagre budget to military expenditures against the Chinese Communist Party than to programmes that might have helped to alleviate the poverty of the country's peasantry. The field research of the 1920s and 1930s was designed for the most part to reveal and document these current issues rather than the underlying structural changes that had originated perhaps half a century earlier. Consequently, the student who searches in these reports for confirmation that the peasantry had suffered readily finds it, but the one who wants to document long-term structural changes should obviously be on his guard.[7]

It is perhaps unfair to criticize the *Sources* thirty years after its publication for taking a simplistic stance on a complicated historical problem. However, the criticism has to be made because it is far from clear that proponents of the pessimistic argument have come round to the view that the *Sources* is dated. On the contrary, it seems to me that it is a major weakness in the current literature that gross generalizations that sometimes amount to little more than unfounded claims are made on the basis of crude impressions. It is surprising that even such a careful historian as Albert Feuerwerker would argue quite categorically:

While it is certain that rural living standards between 1870 and 1911 did not improve, there is no conclusive evidence that population growth and declining average farm size were accompanied by a drastic secular fall in the peasant standard of living.

The statement carries weight, even though it is made in a context that borders between a non-committal and an anti-pessimistic stance, and even though it is unsubstantiated.[8] Ralph Thaxton, who relates the breakdown of the peasant's 'moral economy' in the Shanxi-Hebei-Shandong-Henan border region in the early twentieth century to 'immoral landlordism', rests his subsistence estimates on two unqualified statistics, namely that most peasants tilled 3 to 10 one-*mu* plots and that 'the land usually gave 100 to 150 catties per *mu*.'[9] More recently, in his grossly oversimplified adaptation of the 'world system theory' to the case of southern China, Alvin Y. So attempted to account for social changes in Shunde county from the mid-nineteenth century to the 1930s in terms of the rise and decline of the silk trade.[10] However, it is the *Sources* that is most guilty of uncritical selection of contemporary evidence without qualification or caution. Its treatment of J.L. Buck's surveys, the most comprehensive in the 1920s and 1930s, is a case in point. It reproduces copiously Buck's statistics, but omits those of Buck's conclusions that do not side with the pessimistic view.[11] It is not an overstatement to charge that the *Sources* consciously suppresses evidence that counters its argument.

Aside from the question of documentation, the pessimist's case may also be disputed point by point. The first and perhaps most central issue, that trade expansion destroyed the self-subsistence of the Chinese farmer from the mid-nineteenth century, is easily exaggerated. Trade did expand and make an inroad into the local economy, but the critical geographic areas which were to see the greatest impact of trade expansion were precisely those in which commercialized agriculture had been firmly entrenched for centuries.[12] The next issue, that the effects of competition from foreign imports were necessarily detrimental to the rural economy, is not by any means established. It is true that imported yarn in some localities displaced hand-spun yarn and that some agricultural products did indeed lose to foreign competition, sugar being a notable example. However, such losses must be balanced against the market expansion for other products that was brought about by trade increase, and in neither cotton nor silk, the two products that have been most closely studied by historians, is there a clear record of one-sided gain or loss by the Chinese peasant producer.[13] The third issue, that the terms of trade might have shifted against farm products, is founded on a mistaken interpretation of Republican price studies, for they do not show that prices shifted against the farmer until the 1930s. The fourth issue, that cyclical depressions necessarily accompanied trade expansion, is as obvious as it is trite. The question to ask, certainly, is not whether farmers who produced for export might have been better off without them, but whether over a period of time, they were not better off in spite of them. Again, except for references to the depression of the 1930s, the question is largely unexplored in the literature on the Chinese rural economy.[14]

Fifthly, questions concerning tenancy, rent, and tax are also easily misunderstood. In general, it may be observed as a point of departure that the surveyors of the 1920s and 1930s considered such questions within a very narrow definition of land relationships that dealt only with alienable land rights. As a result of this narrow view, the farmer was categorized on the basis that he was either an owner-cultivator, a part-owner, or a tenant. However, it is becoming increasingly clear from several areas of research that the holding of alienable rights in itself says little about economic status or the ability to gain from the market. Anthropological field studies of village communities in Taiwan and Hong Kong show, for instance, that alienable land rights formed only a part of a wide range of land rights in the village, and that the settled villager did not only need to rent or own land, but he needed also the right of residence, access to market, the right of exploitation of common land, and protection by the lineage or village, which sometimes extended to protection against eviction or rent and tax increase.[15] Studies conducted on rent records in the lower Changjiang (Yangzi) River area and in northern China have also drawn attention to the need to recognize different types of landlord.[16] Along a different line, an interesting debate has developed between Ramon Myers and Philip C.C. Huang on the ability of small farms to take advantage of commercial opportunities in the development of cash-crops.[17] The issue of the landlord-tenant relationship in China is, therefore, one that is under considerable review at present, and on which no definitive conclusion has been reached.

Finally, if variations in market factors and tenancy arrangements are taken into account, then, given the size and geographic diversity of China, the recognition of regional differences should be a matter of paramount importance in any discussion of China's rural economic development. Yet, although the details offered in the *Sources* imply an acknowledgement of regional variations, the pessimist's argument in general places much greater emphasis on a hypothetical common experience that was shared by all of China than on regional distinctions. In so far as the pessimist identifies the growth of international trade as a prime mover that led to the impoverishment of the rural population, this position is quite untenable. The size of the country, the varied terrain, and the segmented economy alone imply that the effects of international trade must have varied in a major way over space and time. Certain crops, such as rice, silk, cotton, sugar, and tobacco, came to be increasingly linked to an international market, while other products, including many handicrafts, remained largely sold within China, free from foreign competition. How a region was affected by the growth of international trade depended very much, therefore, on the commodities they produced. Moreover, in addition to regional variations that may be traced directly to trade, the local effects of political changes, especially those that led to wars of various scales, must also be taken into consideration. Wars, however, affected local economies in ways that are not always predictable. While disruptions to transport and production must be noted, it should also be expected that shortages in one area could lead to increased demand in another even if only on a short term basis. Until regional studies are conducted and their findings seriously assessed, any discussion of the performance of the overall Chinese rural economy as a whole must be grossly simplified.

There are, therefore, serious shortcomings in the pessimist's view of the involvement of the Chinese rural economy in international trade. The question then arises if the optimistic position provides a stronger guideline for an overview of this problem. To see if it does, and because the optimistic viewpoint is no less nebulous, it is necessary to broaden the debate.

The Current Pessimist–Optimist Debate

At the heart of the pessimist's point of view are two allegations directed against the expansion of trade which can be more precisely stated in the context of arguments concerning Third World economic development. The first is the allegation that the expansion of trade, especially international trade under capitalist constraints, produces a dependent economy which is 'locked into' a supplier-purchaser relationship with an industrial economy, and that the terms of trade are set to its disadvantage. The second is that under these terms a dual economy develops in the dependent economy which magnifies income disparity between rich and poor. Both allegations are strongly associated with the Marxist tradition.[18] In recent years, under the general rubric of the 'moral economy of the peasant', the claim has also been made that trade expansion breaks down the social insurance ('moral economy') that village society provides, leaving peasants vulnerable to the whims of the capitalist market. However, this position is really no more than a variation of the Marxist viewpoint.[19]

Non-Marxist development economists have produced a wide range of answers to the Marxist position. It is recognized that one of the social constraints placed on raising productivity in agriculture is the lack of capital, but it is argued that this does not mean that available capital is inefficiently used within the knowledge and skill available to the farmer. That high rent may stifle opportunities for improvement is often referred to, and the solution advocated is some degree of land reform, but not to the extent that the market may be substituted by state allocation. It is also widely accepted that agricultural advances must proceed only as an integral part of overall economic modernization, and that ultimately, it is not agriculture on its own, but modernization in all spheres of the economy, that would alter the standard of living.[20] As long as the farm is looked upon as an independent unit of operation, and the farmer as a free agent capable of making decisions in the light of market conditions, it makes sense to argue that given proper aid, he may, by improving his skill and his awareness, bring about improvements to his standard of living.

A deep chasm, of course, divides the two positions, the disagreement ranging from broad ideological standpoints to observations of facts and standards of measurement. It is not true, however, that the two positions are totally exclusive. A widely accepted revision of particular relevance to the discussion of the Chinese experience is the concession by the non-Marxists that even as overall income increases in the process of development, the gap between the haves and have-nots may well widen. Following from this, they have to acknowledge that the transfer of income from the haves to the have-nots, whether defined as a social or geographic sector, is not automatic. The shift in focus from the *absolute* standard of living to the *relative* standard of living does not really alter the terms of the debate, but it focuses the question on the relative size of the underprivileged in the overall population and how their absolute standards had changed over time.[21]

All this should prompt a study of China's rural economy, but does not really do much more than that. Given the best of all worlds, there must be many reasons to think that the independent farmer will or will not be able to improve his lot, but the task of the historian is to see if he did, given the specific conditions of the particular time that is being researched. These positions are too remote from the Chinese economic historian's sources to provide very much more than very general research guidelines. It is for the historian to sift through contemporary reports, learn the intricacies of the sentiments and awareness of the people who wrote them, collate them, read between the lines until he can distinguish between an observation and an accompanying opinion, to arrange these same reports into an order that can put these general positions into a meaningful context within Chinese history. This is why a study such as Alvin Y. So's, which refuses to come to grips with the records, is so disappointing, and it is also why the very few studies that have managed to demonstrate how contemporary records might bear upon these general issues are such important landmarks in our understanding of the situation. The *Sources of Modern Chinese Agriculture* was one such landmark. It appeared in the 1950s when for the first time the events of the 1930s ceased to be regarded as news and came to appear as history. Since its publication, the most important discussions of the problems of the Chinese rural economy before 1949 are the studies of Ramon Myers and Philip C.C. Huang. Both works relate to the provinces of Shandong and Hebei in north China.[22]

In the provinces of Shandong and Hebei, the flourmill and the spinning mill, both introduced into China from the West in the late nineteenth century, had made a considerable impact on wheat and cotton farming. Changes were also brought about by the introduction of the railway, another product of contact with the West. As improved internal communications linked the rural areas to the treaty ports, as more wheat was fed into the flourmills, as the cotton acreage expanded, and as other developments followed, such as the introduction of Japanese-made looms sold on credit, or the cultivation of American tobacco on contract under the close supervision of foreign tobacco companies, a *prima facie* case can be made that the rural economy in these two provinces was gradually being drawn into the world market.[23]

Just how the process of commercialization affected the standard of living of farmers in Shandong and Hebei is the crucial and controversial issue crystallized in Myers' and Huang's works. Myers, who drew his material primarily from the field research of the 1930s and 1940s, argued that, on the whole, commercialization brought increased opportunities to the rural areas. Farmers were fast to seize these opportunities, and therefore, although population increased while cultivated acreage did not, and although there were few improvements to farm technology (and these few, such as the introduction of American cotton seed, were not highly significant), villagers maintained their standard of living. Random disturbances (for example, the weather) and local conditions affected individual villages, but Myers could detect no general trend that might have systematically impoverished wide tracts of the countryside. On the contrary, he found that the proportion of tenant households did not increase, that as farms became smaller initially (a result of population increase without concomitant increase in agricultural land), yield also increased. Despite these changes, there was no change to the mode of farm operation. As household income increased, farmers might buy more land, but yield declined beyond an optimum that might be farmed by the individual family, at which point the farmer would have invested in non-farm activities and leased out the land that his own family found less profitable to farm. What kept back the rural economy was technological backwardness, not rural socio-economic relationships.[24]

Huang, who analysed much the same material that Myers had used and attempted to integrate different points of view into his study, stressed the uneven returns from land and labour that were reaped by rich and poor farmers. Huang agreed that commercialization brought little structural development, but he argued that by the late nineteenth century, small family farms in Shandong and Hebei had reached a stage of diminishing returns. As small farmers could no longer increase yield by extra labour input, the only resource available to many small farmers, it was the larger 'managerial farms' — farms operated with hired labour — that made much more efficient use of the land. By implication, 'managerial farms' stood in a more advantageous position to exploit opportunities offered by commercialization and would have expanded at the expense of small family farms. As Huang proposed in a central argument of his book, as the 'managerial farms' prospered, as small family farms lost out in the competition, and as more farmhands were hired, a 'semiproletariat' of hired labourers developed. Whatever benefits commercialization brought were, therefore, unequally shared. The rural class structure that resulted from small farms being incapable of holding on to sufficient farmland to gain a subsistence living led to greater inequity.[25]

In the works of Myers and Huang, as these summaries of their arguments show, we have in a nutshell the development debate, with Myers stressing the overall rise in income without documenting in detail how it was distributed, and with Huang making the case for an increase in income disparity, without dispelling — and in parts, accepting — the possibility that overall income might have risen. In some ways, they complement each other, although to conclude that the two positions do not conflict is, of course, to force the issue. In the absence of precise measurement, the idea of income disparity is, however, a vague one. Huang gives the impression that the population of the social stratum that, despite the opportunities for commercialization, did not rise out of a low standard of living, was substantial. The general tone of Myers' work tends to support the inference that the spread of the income from trade expansion was more extensive. The heart of the pessimist-optimist debate, therefore, is not to relate changing trade patterns to social differentiation in a general sense, but to reassess the magnitude of income change and the extensiveness of such change within defined populations and geographic areas. The task requires some numerical precision in the discussion of matters related to income changes, and China being a large country, a regional focus that can take account of local variations and experiences. This book seeks to provide one such regional study, and it chooses as its subject two provinces that were most susceptible to the influence of trade expansion from 1870 to 1937.

Jiangsu and Guangdong

The provinces of Jiangsu and Guangdong are essentially administrative units and not geographic divisions. They include some of China's

Figure 1.1 Jiangsu Province

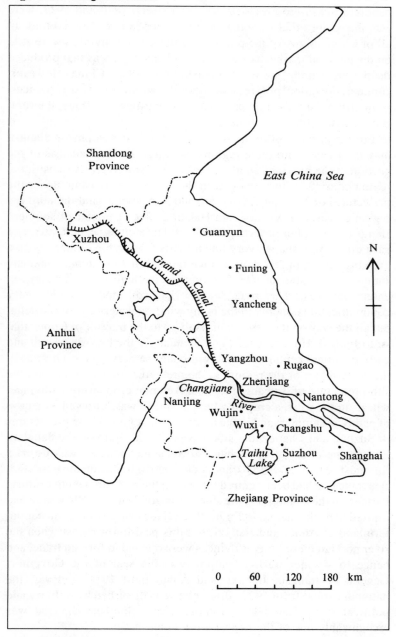

most fertile farmland and the largest cities, and the most developed handicraft/cash-crop regions, which, between 1870 and 1937, were also the regions that were the most involved in international trade in all of China. Many of the products of these two provinces were sold on the national market as well as abroad, and the areas that produced them were among the most prosperous in all of China. However, commercialization progressed unevenly within the two provinces. Away from the areas that produced for long-distance trade, the rural economy was little developed.

For the purpose of discussing its economic development, Jiangsu may be divided into three regions. Southern Jiangsu consists of the portion of the province south of the Changjiang River. A transitional region consists of the area that in the Qing dynasty came under the prefectures of Yangzhou, Huai'an, and Tongzhou;[26] and the northern region consists of Xuzhou and Haizhou. The character of southern Jiangsu, the region of fertile farmland, large cities, handicrafts, and cash crops, was shaped very much by its favourable climate, with a growing season of 287 days, annual rainfall of 1,148 mm., and mean summer temperature of 26.8°C. Moreover, it is here that the Changjiang enters the sea. The river leaves rich soil and provides easy communication not only in the many winding waterways of the delta, but all the way on the main river itself up to the interior of China, that is, to Jiangxi, Hunan, Hubei, and Sichuan. In the late nineteenth and early twentieth centuries, two crops could be harvested each year. In the eastern part of the region, in the prefecture of Songjiang and the sub-prefecture of Taicang, the most common crops were cotton and wheat. In the west, a crop of wheat in spring was followed by a crop of paddy in summer; and in the centre of the region, in the prefectures of Suzhou and Changzhou, silk was produced. Here on the delta are located the cities of Shanghai and Suzhou. Shanghai was China's foremost seaport after 1870, and took over from Suzhou the important rice trade that had been centred there until the mid-nineteenth century. Farther up the Changjiang are Zhenjiang and Nanjing. Zhenjiang had aspired to be the main port for northern Jiangsu and for the substantial farmland of Anhui and Jiangxi, but this position was lost when the river ports in these latter provinces were opened to foreign trade, and hence to steamer traffic. Nanjing was the seat of the Governor-General of Jiangsu, Jiangxi, and Anhui until 1911, and was the national capital from 1927, although it was disturbed by military and political turmoil in between those years. Southern Jiangsu was recognizably one of the richest areas in all of China.[27]

Running north–south across the part of Jiangsu north of the Changjiang was the Grand Canal. Before 1870, this served as the main north-
south waterway from Beijing to the Changjiang provinces and on it
were located cities whose importance within the province was second
only to those of southern Jiangsu.[28] These cities, Yangzhou, Huai'an,
and Xuzhou, had a somewhat checkered history from 1870 to 1937.
The shift of the north-south traffic from the Canal to the coast from the
mid-nineteenth century reduced their importance, which only Xuzhou
partly regained when the Tianjin–Pukou Railway was opened in 1911,
and the Long–Hai Railway in 1925.[29] Xuzhou continued to suffer from
military turmoil until 1927, none the less, for the railways were
essential for troop transport.

Within this area north of the Changjiang marked contrasts may be
detected between what has been referred to above as the northern
region and the transitional region, although, in any case, the entire
area was poorer than the south. The soil along the Grand Canal from
the Changjiang until some point halfway up the province, across
Yangzhou and Huai'an prefectures, is fertile. This is the *lixiahe* (inner
river) area, made up of river deposits from the Huaihe and land
reclaimed from the lakes. This area was the most productive of the
transitional region.[30] To its north and east, however, fertility declines
rapidly on calcareous or saline soil, and to its north, the climate
becomes harsher. Temperatures become more extreme, the growing
season shortens, and rainfall slackens towards the northern region:
Yangzhou in the transitional region has a mean January temperature
of 3.76 °C, a July temperature of 30.13 °C, and an annual rainfall of
869 mm., while Peixian county in the northern region has a mean
January temperature of 0.7°C, a July temperature of 23.8°C, and an
annual rainfall of 642 mm.[31] In the late nineteenth and early twentieth
centuries, the *lixiahe* area grew paddy and wheat, while the land to its
north and east grew wheat, sorghum, beans, and cotton which was
introduced in the early 1900s, but little paddy. It should also be noted
that the entire territory north of the Changjiang was liable to flood,
partly because the Huaihe River had no direct outlet to the sea, and
partly because the gradient of the territory was low and water could
not be controlled readily. Droughts and locusts were also common
throughout this area. Yet another drawback to development was the
lack of water transport in areas away from the canal. Without inland
waterways, the most common means for the transport of goods was the
wheelbarrow, pushed along dusty roads by human labour, and the cart,
drawn by oxen or donkeys. The *lixiahe* region resembled the south,

but the northern region, with little rice, subject to frequent floods, and dependent on poor land transport, was more similar to northern provinces such as Shandong and Hebei.

In contrast to Jiangsu, Guangdong presents greater climatic and topographic unity.[32] The province has a tropical climate, is frost-free in all areas for almost the entire year, and is capable of producing three crops annually.[33] The deltas and valleys of the Zhujiang (Pearl) and the Hanjiang rivers make up the bulk of the cultivated land of the province. The Zhujiang is much the larger of the two rivers, and its tributaries, the Xijiang (West), the Beijiang (North), and the Dongjiang (East) rivers form the main arteries of the province. In the nineteenth and early twentieth centuries, the Xijiang was navigable by sailing junks and steam launches as far upriver as Yunnan Province, and the Beijiang and Dongjiang were navigable for a hundred miles. The Hanjiang, however, was barely navigable by such boats, although it was used by smaller craft.[34] On all sides of these river basins except the sea coast are mountain ranges dividing Guangdong Province from Jiangxi, Fujian, and Guangxi. To the south lies Hainan Island, potentially fertile, but barely developed even as late as the 1930s.[35] Paddy and sweet potato were the main staple crops of the whole of Guangdong, but export crops were grown in various counties. Silk was produced principally in three counties in the Zhujiang delta. Sugar-cane was grown and sugar was extracted by an indigenous process in parts of the Zhujiang delta and the Hanjiang delta. Tea came from the hilly land bordering the valleys. Tobacco, palmleaves, and fruit were among other crops grown in scattered localities. The major cities in the province were Guangzhou and Hong Kong at the mouth of the Zhujiang, and Shantou (Swatow) at the mouth of the Hanjiang. It was through these ports that cash crops were exported. Floods were not uncommon: they might be caused by excessive rainfall or the collapse of one of the many dykes on the rivers. Occasional droughts were also brought about by irregularities in the monsoon. Disasters always mattered where they occurred, but compared to damages wrought by the Huaihe River in Jiangsu and farther north, those in Guangdong were relatively insignificant.

Something should also be said by way of introduction about administrative and political development. Between 1870 and 1911, the imperial government maintained a centralized administration in the provinces, including Jiangsu and Guangdong. As historians know well, the force of the imperial regime upon local autonomy was always mediated by local recruits at the *yamen* (seat of the magistrate), the

Figure 1.2 Guangdong Province

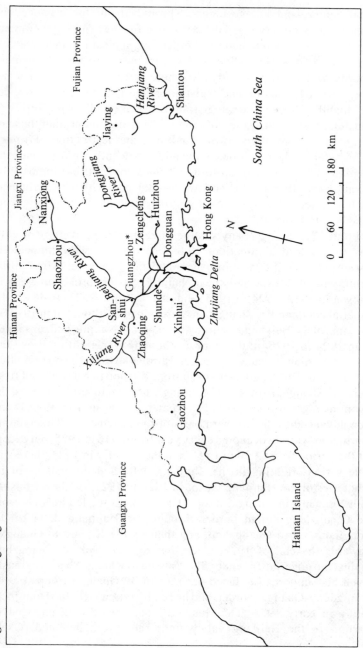

Fujian Province

Jiangxi Province

Hunan Province

Nanxiong

Shaozhou

Guangxi Province

Hanjiang River

Shantou

Jiaying

Dongjiang River

Huizhou

Zengcheng

Guangzhou*

Dongguan

Hong Kong

San-Beijiang River shui

Xijiang River

Bei-Jiang River

Zhaoqing

Shunde

Xinhui

Zhujiang Delta

Gaozhou

South China Sea

N

0   60   120   180   km

Hainan Island

*Incorporating Nanhai and Panyu.

local gentry, and village elders. Through them, for instance, the county magistrate collected the taxes specified by central government regulations and maintained local order, but in most instances, he had neither the manpower, military or civil, nor the necessary documentary records to act independently. Nowhere were such records needed more seriously than in land registration and land-tax collection, but the inability to enforce registration when land ownership was transferred, the registration of land under names other than those of the *de facto* controllers of the land, and the destruction of *yamen* records during the rebellions of the mid-nineteenth century, made the keeping of accurate and up-to-date land records all but impossible. Taxation was, therefore, negotiated through men with local influence. Such a system of government by proxy sheltered local power from outside interference.[36]

From 1912 to 1927, any vestige of centralized government gave way to war-lord domination. Two consequences were immediate: disruption by military skirmishes, and tax increases. After initial fighting in 1911, especially near Nanjing, warfare broke out again in Jiangsu in 1913, 1924 to 1925, and then again in 1927. In 1911 the imperial commander, Zhang Xun, retreated to Xuzhou, but in 1913, in the name of the Beiyang war-lords, he captured Nanjing and ransacked it. In 1924 to 1925, in the Jiangsu-Zhejiang war, fighting broke out first in Songjiang, near Shanghai, and armies advancing and retreating disturbed the full length of Jiangsu from Xuzhou to Nanjing and from there to Shanghai. In 1927, fighting once again broke out as the Guomindang's northern expedition entered Jiangsu from Jiangxi and then advanced to the northern parts of the province. In Guangdong, continuous warfare occupied every year from 1916 to 1925, but except for the period from 1920 to 1921, and then briefly in 1923, there was little serious fighting in the Zhujiang delta and the valleys of its tributaries or the Hanjiang basin. In 1920 to 1921, in his skirmishes with Yunnan and Guangxi troops, Chen Jiongming led his men from the Guangdong-Fujian border through the Hanjiang delta to the Dongjiang, on to Guangzhou, and then up the Xijiang to Guangxi. Towards the end of 1922, Chen, having marched on Guangzhou against the government under Sun Yat-sen to which he had previously given his support, was faced once again by Guangxi troops on the Guangdong-Guangxi border, and he finally retreated to the Dongjiang valley in early 1923. The Guangxi troops were then engaged in warfare in the Beijiang valley until they were defeated. Chen, meanwhile, remained on the Dongjiang, where intermittent fighting occupied 1924 and 1925.[37]

Continuous fighting among armed groups in the war-lord era obviously disrupted the economy. Fighting disturbed production and trade, eroded business confidence, and heightened the need for local armed protection. As local groups armed themselves, their conflicts tended also to be more disruptive. Such local conflicts would be reported in the newspapers and government reports as banditry or local feuds, along with genuine cases that might be more properly described in these terms. The war-lord era was consequently one of deterioration of local order all over Guangdong, including the Zhujiang and the Hanjiang basins.[38] Moreover, the war-lords needed financing, and there was a tendency for them to increase taxes or to issue poorly backed currencies. In fairness, it should be noted that tax increases had begun in the late Qing, and although a sizeable literature accuses the war-lords of raising the land tax, it is far from obvious how they could have done so, the war-lords not having records of land registration that were any better than the imperial government's. More likely, they resorted to accessible sources of finance, for example, charges on goods in transit, on shops and businesses in towns and cities, surcharges on gambling, opium, and prostitution, and, again, the circulation of inflated currencies. The literature also confuses direct requisition of human labour and property in war with taxation: soldiering, like banditry, might be disruptive to some communities, but must have added income to others.[39]

Compared to the previous decade, the ten years from 1927 to 1936 were peaceful ones in both Jiangsu and Guangdong. Peace was disturbed only by the Japanese invasion of Shanghai in 1932, and then by the outbreak of war in 1937. Under at least a nominally unified government, provincial administration was restored in 1931. The Revised Law for the Organization of Provincial Governments provided for a senior official to be appointed to both Jiangsu and Guangdong, as well as to Nanjing and Shanghai, which were among six cities that became autonomous. Within the provinces, except for a limited number of cities that were governed directly by the provincial government, Guangzhou and Shantou among them, the county to which a magistrate was appointed remained the unit of administration. The subject of county administration was the focus of much debate. Attempts were made to streamline it, requiring county magistrates to submit budgets for approval, to institute local registration, and at least in principle, to allow some local representation and autonomy. Electoral representation was not formally put into practice, but the informal involvement of local leaders in administration that had been the common practice since imperial times continued.[40] Where reforms did come about apparently was in land registration. Serious attempts were made to register newly cultivated land, and some counties were, under central government direction, required to conduct land surveys.[41] Considerable improvements were made in railway and road building, and a farmers' bank was established, also under central government direction. Given time, some of the economic projects started by the Nationalist government might have yielded results, but with the outbreak of the Sino-Japanese War at the end of the decade, any improvement that might have arisen from them was short-lived.[42]

This brief introduction into the provinces of Jiangsu and Guangdong neither characterizes their experience from the 1870s to the 1930s as unique in China, nor attempts to draw from it generalizations that may be applicable to the rest of China. To see why a study of these two provinces should have relevance for the experience of China as a whole, in full consideration that the local study is ultimately only a portion of the fabric that makes up the whole, it is necessary to delineate the case being studied.

Delineating the Test Case

Essentially, the development experience of Jiangsu and Guangdong is of interest to the China historian because it illustrates the fundamental changes brought to the rural economy by transportation improvement, industrialization, and the growth of international trade. It was not an experience that was shared by all of China, but it was one that was repeated to varying extents in numerous provinces, and inasmuch as the social consequences of economic changes are given pride of place in contemporary interpretations of modern Chinese history, an accurate description of this experience is an integral part of a China historian's task. The intricate relationships between trade expansion and peasant livelihood must, therefore, be clearly identified and documented, and the experience of Jiangsu and Guangdong is relevant precisely because in these two provinces we have some of the best documentation available to reconstruct some of these relationships.

The improvement in transportation from the late nineteenth to the early twentieth century was due primarily to the introduction of the steamer and the railway. In China, they made an immediate impact in areas they served, but they did not affect all areas equally or in the same way. The steamer was useful especially on the China coast and in international traffic. Its impact was greatest along the Changjiang and the Zhujiang rivers, particularly in their delta areas. However, away from these areas, overland, it was the railway that noticeably improved transportation, and for most of the period considered in this book, the impact of the Beijing–Hankou Railway, the earliest major railway built in China, stood out above any other overland transportation improvement.[43] Quite aside from these improvements in transport, industrialization was beginning in some of China's major cities in the late nineteenth and early twentieth centuries. These new industries, among which cotton spinning and food processing (rice and wheat milling) were major items, were concentrated in the coastal cities, especially Shanghai. Trade expansion under these circumstances was very uneven. It was more limited in Guangdong than in Jiangsu. In Guangdong, it made little headway beyond the delta areas of the Zhujiang and Hanjiang rivers. However, in Jiangsu, trade expanded in the areas to the north of the Changjiang that were connected to the North China Plain as well as in the Changjiang delta. Much of this difference may be explained with reference to the wider adoption of cotton farming in Jiangsu, for export-oriented crops were largely absent in those parts of Guangdong outside the delta areas. Cotton had long been grown in parts of the North China Plain. It was grown more extensively by the late nineteenth century in response to overseas demand, and more extensively yet in the twentieth century when it was needed to supply the mills in Shanghai and nearby cities.

The impact made by the extension of cash crops in the late nineteenth and early twentieth centuries could conceivably have varied according to the extent to which the areas that adopted these cash crops had previously been exposed to cash cropping. For parts of Guangdong and Jiangsu, the impact was one of degree of commercialization. The delta areas had long been used to producing for the market, and the development of the late nineteenth and early twentieth centuries may be seen as an intensification of such activities. For other areas, however, the impact was new: the coastal areas of Jiangsu came to be developed as newly reclaimed land was settled, the settlers being attracted by the profit that cotton growing might bring. The change that came over such an area was, therefore, not only quantitative but qualitative. Yet there were many areas, even of Guangdong and Jiangsu, that remained largely untouched by the increasing trade, parts that remained removed from the main transport routes or easy access to the new industrial centres. The commercialization of the

Chinese countryside was a continuous process of transport and industrial development that broke down the seclusion of local economies. That, of course, for pessimist as for optimist, is the gist of economic and social change since the middle of the nineteenth century.[44]

This approach to the problem assumes that changes introduced in the farm economy were induced by the involvement of the farm in the market. A major portion of this book, therefore, traces how price changes over the years might have affected farm income, how the trade in different farm produce rose and fell, and by how much farm income might have been changed by the adoption of different cash crops on the farm and by fluctuations in their prices. In the increasingly integrated international market of the late nineteenth and early twentieth centuries, trade volumes and prices changed in response to national and international conditions.[45] They seldom arose from local conditions within Jiangsu and Guangdong.

While this book seeks to shift the focus of debate on peasant livelihood in China to prices and trade volumes, it must also directly attack two arguments that arose out of the debates of the 1920s and 1930s that saw other factors as more important determinants of livelihood. These arguments are, firstly, that the adoption of cash crops undermined the production of food crops, thereby leading to food shortages, and, secondly, that income distribution in the Chinese countryside can be meaningfully explained in terms of landlord-tenant relationships. It will be shown in this book that both arguments are fallacious. Evidence will be produced to show that the first argument misconstrues the nature of food imports into China, and that the second does not take into account the complications introduced into landlord-tenant relationships by several institutions commonly found in Chinese rural society. Three of these institutions will be singled out for discussion; they are the villager-outsider distinction associated with the question of settlement rights, the corporate structure of land holding, and the persistence of permanent tenancy. In general, it may be said that the stress on landlord-tenant relationships had too readily taken for granted the landlord's ability to collect rent from their tenants or to raise it. When the complications of rent collection and rental charges are taken into consideration, the landlord-tenant distinction may be reduced to being one of a set of factors that bore on income distribution, but not a determining one. Although some of these features of landlord-tenant relationships have long been known in the literature, I believe the discussion of landlord-tenant relationships here offers interpretations applicable to parts of China other than

Jiangsu and Guangdong that have up to now not been taken into account by historians.

It should be pointed out that the argument as presented here sidesteps the ideological issue of whether trade is preferable to communal self-subsistence. It is not for the historian to decide if the people he studies should prefer one end or another. Nor is it my object to be drawn into the question of whether China's rural inhabitants would have chosen the particular ways of life offered by increased trade had they understood all their ramifications, even if such a question could be answered. The task that is set for this book is to explain how the increase in trade, particularly international trade, might have affected rural livelihood in China. The history of popular ideology is an interesting subject in its own right, but I am more concerned in this book with economic realities. It should also be pointed out that no part of this book seeks to alter the view that the Chinese rural economy in the late nineteenth and the early twentieth centuries was poor. It does, however, try to distinguish the changes introduced by trade expansion from long-established practices in the treatment of the poor that were ingrained in local custom. Trade expansion provided opportunities for those destitute people who were displaced from their villages. Had there been more trade, they would have had more opportunities to survive. As it was, rural China was poor not because there was excessive trade, but because there was not enough of it.

2

Sources of Change

THE years from 1870 to 1937 were tumultuous ones for the Chinese economy, as they were for the economy of the rest of the world. The 1870s saw the beginning of the 'second' industrial revolution, which introduced the age of steel and of the chemical industries, and which came when China had yet to acquire the products of the 'first' industrial revolution, that is, the steam engine, the spinning mill, and the railway. This was also a period of unprecedented growth in world trade and shipping, facilitated by economic growth and the development of the intercontinental telegraph. Like other countries, and not only those of the Third World, China was rapidly affected by these major world changes. Some of these changes are selected for discussion in this chapter as, obviously, they provide essential background for an understanding of China's rural economy in this period.

Transport

Probably in no other field did change come so rapidly and lead to so much development from 1870 to 1937 in the whole of China, not only in Jiangsu and Guangdong, as in transport. The use of steamers in international trade from the 1860s, the opening of the Suez Canal in 1869, the building of railways in China from the turn of the century to the 1930s, were most important developments. Motor roads were built in the 1920s and 1930s, but they never equalled the railway or the steamer in the transport of goods.[1]

In the days before the steamer, the clipper ship took 120 days to reach England from China, and it carried 1,000 tons of cargo. When the Blue Funnel Line was launched in 1865, the steamer carrying 3,000 tons of cargo took 77 days to make the same journey. When the Suez Canal was opened, the distance that the steamer had to travel to reach England was reduced by 4,500 miles. By the 1870s, the fastest ship of the Blue Funnel Line could travel to England from China in 50 days. Most of the ships belonging to its competitors took only 45. By 1882, the fastest ship could do it in 29 days. Not surprisingly, freight charges fell. During the 1860s, they fell from £8 to £4 per ton, and by

1878 they were about £1.15s. per ton. At this juncture, the major shipping companies began to regulate their charges by the conference system. Prices stabilized and were undoubtedly higher than they might have been had a free market continued to prevail. However, the long-term trend to 1913 shows a steady decline in freight charges. Increased capacity and lower freight must have helped to promote China's overseas commerce, as they benefited commerce the world over in the second half of the nineteenth century.[2]

The steamer was introduced into China at a time when for some centuries north-south traffic had depended on inland routes. The lack of major development in these routes is well illustrated by the fact that the same travellers' guidebook was reprinted with few alterations from the early Qing to the nineteenth century. According to this book, the *Show Me the Way Hither* (*shiwo zhouxing*), the principal north-south long-distance routes in Jiangsu were land routes. The Grand Canal, which would seem to have been the obvious route to take from Suzhou to Beijing, was listed only as one among many alternatives. Even then, suggestions were given to the traveller to begin his overland journey at numerous points before the end of the Canal, for instance, at Yangzhou in Jiangsu, or in Qingxian county in Hebei Province.[3] The Canal was not recommended because it was unreliable. In a year of drought, it could be too shallow, or in winter, frozen solid. In any case, there would have been much waiting at various junctions where the water levels had to be adjusted. If all went well, the Canal offered a faster journey, but interruptions must have been frequent for the twenty-one day overland journey from Pukou, outside Nanjing, to be suggested as a viable alternative.[4]

From Guangzhou, travel to the north was faced with extra difficulties. Firstly, the mountain ranges between Guangdong and Jiangxi, or Fujian, had to be crossed on foot. Secondly, while the remainder of the journey could be covered almost entirely by boat, the traveller had to travel up to the source of one river system and then cross the mountains to the source of another, so that whether he was travelling north-south or vice versa, a substantial portion of the journey was against the current in shallow upland streams. From Foshan, near Guangzhou, the upstream journey to Nanxiong took fifteen days. It was another day's journey to cross the mountains, and about a month's to reach Pukou. An accident-free journey from Foshan to Beijing would thus take at least two months.[5]

This lengthy journey time was sharply reduced once Western ships travelling along the coast became available. A Western sailing ship in the 1870s, travelling along the coast from Shantou, could reach Tianjin in fourteen days and Niuzhuang in eighteen, suggesting a Guangzhou–Beijing journey time of about sixteen days. A steamer in the 1930s could travel from Shanghai to Guangzhou in four days, to Qingdao in two, and Dalian in three, suggesting a Guangzhou–Beijing journey time of just one week. When the Beijing–Hankou and Hankou–Guangzhou railways were completed, it took a day and a half to reach Hankou from Beijing and two more days to reach Guangzhou.[6]

The use of Western coastal shipping had an equally marked effect on available trading tonnage. In terms of capacity, the largest river junks could carry approximately 1,000 to 2,000 *shi*, a capacity equivalent to 1,000 to 2,000 piculs (approximately 100 tons) of grain, and an ocean-going junk could only carry up to 5,000 *shi*. A small sailing ship of Western design, none the less, could carry 500 tons, or 8,400 piculs, and a larger one twice to three times this amount. Most of the steamers that plied the Changjiang in the 1860s drew approximately 1,000 tons, while the total non-Chinese shipping reaching Hankou in 1901 amounted to just over 2,000,000 tons, or the equivalent of 16,800 junk-journeys from Shanghai to Hankou (that is, if large river junks of 2,000 *shi* were used).[7] As for the railway, in 1919 alone, the Shanghai–Hangzhou– Ningbo line carried 494,000 tons of goods, and the Shanghai–Nanjing line carried a total of 1,352,000 tons. The combined total would be equivalent to the capacity of 12,000 large river junks.[8] A short railway ran from Guangzhou to Sanshui by 1903. The Beijing–Hankou line was completed in 1906, the Shanghai–Nanjing line in 1908, and the Hankou–Guangzhou line had been completed as far as Shaozhou by 1913. The Kowloon–Canton Railway (linking Hong Kong and Guangzhou) was completed in 1912, the Tianjin–Pukou line in 1913, the Shanghai–Hangzhou–Ningbo line in 1916, and the Long–Hai line that connected Xuzhou and Haizhou in northern Jiangsu by 1925. In addition, a short line was built to join Shantou to Chaozhou city and another at Xinning, both in Guangdong, in 1906 and 1909 respectively. By the late 1920s, the major cities of Jiangsu and Guangdong were connected to the railways, even though the networks were not yet unified.[9]

There is no question that the steamer and the railway were technologically superior to the river- or sea-going junk, but it is a matter of some dispute whether the immediate impact of their introduction into China was substantial. The question is a complex one. To resolve it, it would be necessary to take into account differences in freight charges between different modes of transport, with the different transit times, storage and handling charges, losses due to handling and shipment, and so on all considered.[10] Such complexities are largely unresearched in Chinese economic history. The impression is none the less clear that neither the steamer nor the railway replaced the junk, but that marked changes were rapidly introduced. The river-junk trade, up the Changjiang and on the Zhujiang or the Hanjiang, did not lose out to competition, partly because portions of these rivers were not navigable to steamers and partly because junk freight charges were kept low.[11] In fact, an innovation from the 1880s, the steam launch, which took river junks in its tow, opened new possibilities to the traditional traffic on the rivers.[12] In contrast, the steamer did replace the sea-going junk, for the junk fleets at the coastal ports, especially in Guangdong, gradually diminished.[13] Overall, there must have been an increase in traffic, even though, as Rhoads Murphey has pointed out, the increase would have been smaller than is indicated by the shipping figures of the Maritime Customs as these would have included also shipments that had been transferred from the junk trade to the steamer trade.[14]

The Telegraph

In 1869, the telegraph line that linked China to Europe was completed. In the next two decades, it was extended to most major cities in China, especially in provinces such as Jiangsu and Guangdong that were opened to external trade.[15] Its impact was immediate, as the *North China Herald* noted in its 'Retrospect of 1871':

This year the opening of daily telegraphic communication with London has introduced, or at least made general, the entirely new custom of selling early seasons silk 'to arrive'. The facility of doing this, and of quickly closing and as quickly repeating transactions, has increased the already severe competition here, and has also had the effect of hurrying forward the greater part of the season's supplies in the first two or three months, and of so strengthening the hands of Chinese holders during the remainder of the season that prices have since ruled even more considerably over London rates than in previous years. On the other hand, while rapidity of communication has diminished the chance of large profits, it has also lessened the risk of heavy losses, and tended to reduce the trade to a system of regular shipments for full or partial commissions.[16]

Such changes were soon lamented by officials of the Maritime Customs:

In old times business was done in Shanghai by men having command of large capital, who brought heavy consignments here and stored them till there was a chance of sale, or they bought goods and sent them home to find a market. Now a very large and increasing amount of foreign produce is bought on commission, orders being conveyed abroad by telegrams and the total price and rate of exchange being settled before the order is despatched. Similarly, the silk trade is largely done now on orders from Europe, and purchases from the Chinese merchant are not completed until the finance of the transaction is definitely arranged and the laying-down cost calculated to a fraction of a penny. The daily or hourly fluctuations of exchange may have made this necessary, but the system entails consequences anything but desirable. It facilitates the carrying on of trade with small or almost no capital: it promotes a sharpness in business and a keenness in competition which tend to make getting business a more important consideration than how it is got; and it renders it necessary, too, for us Customs people to be far more watchful of frauds than in days when Chinese trade was confined to men of more means and making larger profits, to whom there was not the same temptation to take advantage of us as when business is done on a fine margin not exceeding 2^1/$_2$ per cent.[17]

Between the lines, the change that is depicted in these two passages amounts to no less than a commercial revolution. Business had developed from a stage when the agent purchased and stocked with his own capital on his own risk, to purchasing, with little stocking, only when orders had been received, using bank capital.[18] The telegraph had made this possible by shortening the time lag in communications between the wholesale market in China and the retail market in Europe and the United States. Purchase on direct order from the Western merchant's home markets reduced the risks he had to face, and the orders themselves became the collaterals for bank credit.

The extension of credit by banks must not be confused with the use of bills in the place of specie as media of exchange. It was a characteristic of China's rural marketing that although the banks came to be drawn into long-distance trade, hard cash and silver continued to be paid for goods at the rural markets and in the villages. Huge quantities of precious metal, in the form of silver dollars and copper cash, were sent to silk-producing areas every season for the purchase of silk, for instance, even though the banks were directly involved in making the metal available.[19]

It is not clear to what extent bank credit came to be generally used outside the export trades. Another passage in the Maritime Customs' reports indicates that the telegraph had some effect on the rice trade in Wuhu, that exported this commodity to the lower Changjiang and to Guangdong.[20] None the less, there is no indication that rice was purchased through bank credit, and there is no corroboration for this passage in the reports from other treaty ports.

The Modern Mint and Currency Devaluation

Not all technological innovations were beneficial to trade: modern equipment for minting coins was at least partly responsible for bringing the currency to almost total collapse. The machinery had been introduced into China at an unfortunate time, when the central government was losing its grip over its senior provincial officials, and when it was faced with huge expenditures for military reforms and indemnities. It could have raised the land tax, the mainstay of government revenue, but in the aftermath of the Taiping rebellion, provincial officials, with the approval of the central government, were finding it easier to raise revenue from transit taxes (the *lijin* or *likin*) and direct impositions on the urban population. The major difference between these new taxes and the land tax was that they bypassed the webs of entrenched power relationships long established in the villages and which had been strengthened by the official permission granted to villages to arm themselves in the policy pursued during the Taiping era known as the *tuanlian* (local defence corps).[21] The modern mints, from the 1880s, offered similar advantages. The mints were controlled by provincial officials, and the provincial treasury could derive an income from them free from interference by any village headmen. The size of the income, obviously, depended on the extent to which the provincial mint was prepared to debase the coinage.

The experiment that ushered in the runaway inflation of the 1930s was the opening of the Guangzhou mint in 1889. It is possible that Governor-General Zhang Zhidong, who initiated it, did not in those early days view the mint as essentially a revenue-raising device. The object of the enterprise was to produce Chinese silver dollars that would take the place of the Mexican dollar that commanded a slight premium over silver 'shoes' (ingots). The Guangzhou mint's early silver dollars were known to be of a high quality, and apparently the mint did not make a profit out of them.[22]

However, besides silver dollars, the Guangzhou mint also produced silver subsidiary coins and copper cash. To appreciate the significance of these new coins, it is important to understand that in China's dual currency system, silver was generally used in long-distance and bulk trade, while copper cash was used in the rural and retail trade. There were some exceptions. In Suzhou city, for instance, silver dollars were also generally used in daily purchases. None the less, in most places, the cultivator would have sold his produce at the local market for cash with which he would then have bought his supplies, even though as the same produce he had sold for cash moved along the marketing network it would eventually be sold in large quantities for silver by the wholesalers. The new coins must, therefore, be understood as being designed for circulation in different markets. The silver subsidiary coinage, in particular, was meant to overhaul the copper coinage and it produced consequences that the builders of the first mint probably did not expect and certainly did not fully comprehend.

Zhang Zhidong was transferred out of his Guangdong-Guangxi governor-generalship in 1890, the year the new coins were issued. Transferred to the governor-generalship of Hunan-Hubei, he soon established a mint at Wuchang, and issued silver coins there that were largely shipped into the lower Changjiang. The success of these coins as a source of revenue prompted other provincial governors to start their own mints. As silver coins were produced in astronomical numbers, a slow inflation gathered momentum. This was, however, complicated by the price of silver on the world market, which had since the 1870s been steadily declining, and, therefore, also contributing to price increases. As silver depreciated in value while copper did not, the value of copper coins noticeably rose. This had the effect of increasing the cost of minting copper cash and of producing a shortage of cash on the market. As a result, the new mints had ample excuse to venture into manufacturing a new copper coinage, again grossly debased, using as raw material traditional cash that they withdrew from the market. As it was market practice to recognize the metallic content and not the nominal value of the coins, the net result of the new issues was to bring about the devaluation of both the silver and the copper coinages at the same time, causing panic in the market, both in the bulk trade and in the local retail trade. China was, in this way, left without a stable currency just as monetary stability was most needed.

The central government sought to bring the provincial mints under its control in 1906 but had little success. Any semblance of central control disappeared after the revolution of 1911, and local mints continued to issue debased silver and copper coins. To compound monetary confusion, paper notes came to be issued in large volumes. The introduction of paper currency in the late Qing and the early Republican periods is a complex subject. It represents in part an attempt to modernize the currency, in part a means of forcing loans out of businesses by the war-lords, and in part the reaction of local traders to debasement. Without a central bank until the 1930s, no government in China had within its means the ability to stabilize the monetary

Table 2.1
Exports of Local Produce from Jiangsu and Guangdong, 1883, 1904, and 1924

| | Total Value (millions) | | | | | |
	Current Hk.Tls.	1913 Hk.Tls.	Major Items (mill. hk.tls.)			
A. From Jiangsu*			Silk	Cotton	Rice	Flour
1883	24.4	59.7	14.8	4.0	3.0	—
1904	94.0	100.9	38.7	26.4	5.3	2.0
1924	418.5	296.7	62.7	124.3	0.6	24.0
B. From the Zhujiang Delta†			Silk	Tea	Sugar	Tobacco
1883	17.1	41.8	10.1	1.3	1.0	0.2
1904	67.3	72.5	31.6	1.3	0.7	2.3
1924	120.6	85.8	62.6	1.1	0.2	3.1
C. From Shantou				Tea	Sugar	Tobacco
1883	7.8	19.1		0.1	6.0	0.4
1904	14.7	15.7		0.1	6.0	0.9
1924	20.9	14.8		—	2.8	1.0

Notes: * Total exports from Shanghai, Nanjing, Zhenjiang, and Suzhou.
    † Total exports from Guangzhou, Jiulong, Gongbei, Sanshui, and Jiangmen.
    The index for the construction of values in 1913 Hk.Tls. is taken from Ho
    (1930). Exports of silk include silk products, those of cotton include cotton
    products, and those of rice include paddy.
Source: MC, trade reports.

system. As governments over-issued and banks defaulted, by the 1920s monetary confusion reigned.[23]

Trade Expansion and Agricultural Change

Despite monetary confusion, trade grew. The only figures that we have concerning its growth are the Maritime Customs', which are presented in Table 2.1.

The shortcomings of the Customs' statistics must first be pointed out. The Maritime Customs Service operated only in the treaty ports, and therefore its records did not cover the overall national trade. The statistics were also distorted by the gradual expansion of the Customs organization as more ports were opened to Western trade, as it tightened its control over the junk trade, and as Chinese merchants abandoned the junk for the steamer. Moreover, the peculiarities of the export regulations introduced by the treaties with Western countries left other distortions that must be taken into account. For instance, trade between Hong Kong and its immediate hinterland in China showed on Customs records, but not that between Shanghai and its hinterland unless the trade passed *en route* through another port opened to foreign trade.[24] To make matters more complicated, Chinese goods were shipped into Hong Kong for subsequent re-export back into China so that they might, fraudulently, be counted as imports. Such duty-dodging attempts would not be readily apparent in the Customs statistics. Also to be considered are internal changes in statistical procedures within the Customs Service, of which little is known. It is known, however, that some time in the 1880s, the Service adopted reporting in CIF rather than in FOB price terms, and for this change allowance must be made in reading Customs statistics.[25]

Table 2.1 is designed to provide a general impression of export developments in Jiangsu and Guangdong from the 1870s to the 1920s. The 1930s have been excluded from it because the Great Depression from 1929 made this decade a peculiar one in the general trend of development and its effects can be more precisely discussed separately. Part A of Table 2.1 shows that allowing for inflation, the export of local produce from Jiangsu ports (Shanghai, Suzhou, Nanjing, and Zhenjiang) increased fivefold from 1883 to 1924. The practice of the Maritime Customs was to count as local produce all goods exported from any port that had not previously paid duty at another Chinese port, and these figures include, therefore, not only exports from Jiangsu itself, but also goods sent from other provinces along the Changjiang for export from the Jiangsu ports. However, it must be noted that as the railway was built and as more ports on the middle and upper Changjiang were opened to Western trade, a substantial portion of the goods that had previously been exported direct, in Maritime Customs terms, from Jiangsu ports, were included in the reports of those ports outside Jiangsu from which they were shipped. The increase in exports from within Jiangsu province, therefore, should be considerably larger than is indicated by the Customs statistics. Changes in administrative arrangements, too, had their effects, especially in the rice trade. Until 1911, Shanghai was the principal exporter of tribute rice to the north, even though the product was collected largely outside Jiangsu. The collapse of the Qing government brought this traffic to a conclusion, and with it a marked decline in the figures in the Customs' rice-export statistics from this port.[26]

In all, four products constituted the bulk of Jiangsu exports to other provinces in China and to foreign countries: silk and silk products, cotton and cotton products, rice and paddy, and flour. With the exception of rice and paddy, the export values of all these products increased over the years. The increase in silk and silk products exports was the most lasting. However, cotton and cotton products clearly outperformed silk in the twentieth century, and flour also became more established. The export of cotton products and flour was created by the development of industries in the cities of Jiangsu, especially in Shanghai, Wuxi, and Tongzhou. Grouping cotton with cotton products in the table, in fact, blurs the development. Until 1904, Shanghai exported raw cotton, but from 1904 to 1924, the export of machine-spun cotton yarn increased while that of raw cotton sharply declined. By 1924, 77 per cent of the export value of this group consisted of yarn while little raw cotton was exported.[27]

The stimulus this increase in exports provided for the south Jiangsu countryside may be documented. In Jiangsu, before the mid-nineteenth century, mulberry was grown and silkworms were raised largely in the vicinity of Suzhou city. Under the stimulus of the expanding export demand, these activities extended to Wuxi and other counties in nearby Changzhou, and on a smaller scale to Zhenjiang, Jiangning, and Xuzhou, with Wuxi becoming the largest exporter of cocoons and silk from Jiangsu.[28] The growing of cotton was also extended from the traditional cotton-producing counties in Songjiang and Taicang to the coastal counties in the transitional region, and in northern Jiangsu, that is, in Tongzhou, Chongming, Haimen, Rugao, Dongtai, Yancheng, and Funing. Because wheat had been grown as a staple in most of Jiangsu long before power machinery made possible the development of the flour-milling industry, the effects of export increase cannot, as in the case of cotton or silk, be traced by the spread of the crop to new regions of production. None the less, the phenomenal increase in the export of flour, and the further details provided in Table 2.2, should put to rest any doubt that the export trade might not have made an impact on the amount of Jiangsu-produced wheat entering the flour market. As the table shows, from 1900 to 1929, except for 1907 and 1911, the net quantity of flour exported (exports less imports) from Shanghai far exceeded the amounts of flour that could have been obtained by milling imported wheat. Actual production of wheat for trade in Jiangsu must, of course, be set at higher levels than are

Table 2.2

Imports and Exports of Wheat and Flour, Shanghai, 1900–1929

('000 piculs)

	Wheat Imports			Wheat Exports	Flour	
	From Abroad	From Chinese Ports	Flour Equivalent		Imports	Exports
1900	—	7	5	568	49	92
1901	—	3	2	751	58	190
1902	—	34	26	779	37	217
1903	—	1	1	525	25	326
1904	2	171	130	200	34	528
1905	—	260	195	124	36	742
1906	65	50	86	188	100	891
1907	928	44	729	110	439	544
1908	—	301	226	35	53	753
1909	—	140	105	84	120	1,335
1910	—	36	27	27	138	1,166
1911	1	768	577	3	350	635
1912	—	494	371	53	312	991
1913	—	293	220	20	132	1,492
1914	—	376	282	11	94	1,860
1915	—	1,272	954	21	109	2,927
1916	—	1,748	1,311	1	110	2,747
1917	5	2,279	1,713	4	164	2,983
1918	—	2,757	2,068	—	185	4,429
1919	—	2,370	1,778	18	140	5,080
1920	—	1,498	1,124	54	182	5,896
1921	68	778	635	8	231	4,685
1922	832	413	934	3	632	2,226
1923	2,213	79	1,719	—	106	2,769
1924	4,663	983	4,235	222	719	5,666
1925	587	1,563	1,613	196	126	6,576
1926	4,066	506	3,429	10	250	7,493
1927	1,646	978	1,968	—	181	6,186
1928	790	345	851	114	244	6,355
1929	5,464	617	4,561	˙ 32	257	7,267

Note: Flour equivalent = wheat imports × 0.75.
Source: MC, trade reports.

indicated in the table, as Shanghai itself was a major consumer of flour. Much of the wheat consumed by the milling industry came from the lower Changjiang .[29]

Parts B and C of Table 2.1 present, respectively, figures for export growth in the Zhujiang delta (including exports from Guangzhou, Jiulong, Gongbei, Jiangmen, and Sanshui) and Shantou. The two regions are separately tabulated because their exports differed substantially. Export figures from Hainan Island have been omitted altogether because these constituted yet another variation but were numerically of little significance in the overall exports of Guangdong.[30]

The export trade did not develop in Guangdong as successfully as it did in Jiangsu. Between 1883 and 1924, the inflation-weighted value of the total export of local produce from the Zhujiang delta only doubled, while that from Shantou actually declined. None the less, because silk occupied half of the overall export from the Zhujiang delta, in the several silk-producing counties noticeable changes did come about. Mulberry growing and silkworm rearing, naturally, became more extensive, but more than this, in some areas, they grew from supplementary occupations into specialized primary farm activities. Most notably, in Shunde, a form of land use known as the 'mulberry dykes and fishponds' came to be adopted. Under this regime, 40 per cent of the farmland that had been formerly put to paddy was converted into fishponds, the mud excavated from the fields being spread over the remaining 60 per cent, thus forming the 'dykes' that were put to mulberry. This was a highly efficient form of land use, for the ponds were drained and deepened every year, and a fresh coating of rich and fertile pond mud was added to the embankment. This combination of fish raising and mulberry growing came to be adopted in Shunde during the 1860s, and into the 1920s it was in this county that this pattern of land use was concentrated. This was one of the very few areas in China where silkworm rearing and mulberry growing were conducted to the exclusion of grain cultivation.[31]

As well as silk, tea and sugar were also regarded as promising exports from Guangdong in the 1860s and 1870s. Sugar alone constituted 77 per cent of the total export of local produce from Shantou in 1883, and sugar and tea together 13 per cent of that from the Zhujiang delta. Both products, however, proved to be disappointing. By 1924, the value of the export of tea and sugar from the Zhujiang delta and that of sugar alone from Shantou declined to 1 per cent and 13 per cent of the overall export of local produce respectively. No replacement was ever found for them. The largest single agricultural export from the Zhujiang delta in 1924, aside from silk, was tobacco, but it amounted to no more than 2.5 per cent of exported local produce. In Shantou, fruits came to occupy 12 per cent, and tobacco 4.8 per cent of this total.

A large assortment of other products was also exported, each of which forming only a minuscule percentage of the overall total, including eggs, live animals, feathers, groundnut oil, lard, meat, rice wine, sugar-cane, vegetables, bamboo and bamboo products, charcoal, firewood, timber, woodware, bags, bricks and tiles, pottery, fans, firecrackers, incense sticks, paper, and cassia. Some of these items were evidently shipped to Hong Kong and consumed by the urban population there. Similar exports to Shanghai would also have been registered by the Customs Service had similar diplomatic conditions applied. If this imbalance in the Customs' statistics is taken into account, despite its rather rapid start in the 1880s and 1890s, exports from Guangdong, in fact, fared rather poorly compared with those from Jiangsu.[32]

A large number of export products, totalling 58 million Haikwan taels (literally 'Customs tael', the standard currency quoted in foreign trade) in 1924, spread over the entire province of Guangdong, represents very little trade at the end of half a century of export development. It is even less if one also takes into account the likelihood that a substantial portion of this trade was gained by regions that were readily accessible to the cities. Most of Guangdong could not have benefited greatly from direct foreign trade. Jiangsu, in contrast, with its cotton, wheat, and rice, in addition to silk, proved to be a more diversified economy, where developments could have been more far-reaching.

Emigration

Yet another source of change that affected the rural economy in parts of Jiangsu and Guangdong was emigration. The effects that may be traced to it are more obvious in Guangdong than in Jiangsu, for in that province, apart from emigration to the cities, a large number of people also went abroad, largely to work as indentured labourers. However, migration to both the cities and overseas was consequential.

Precise statistics are not available. Overall, between 1900 and 1938, it has been estimated that the population of the larger cities in Guangdong increased from 2.7 to 3.8 million, and that in Jiangsu from 2.8 to 6.2 million; while emigration overseas from Guangdong averaged well over 100,000 each year.[33] As the population of Jiangsu stood at approximately 35 million in the 1930s, and that of Guangdong stood at 30 million, these figures imply emigration of well over 10 per cent of the population in both provinces. For a better appreciation of the figures, however, it should be realized that in Jiangsu, most of the urban expansion may be traced to the increase of population in Shanghai and Nanjing, and that in Shanghai it incorporated a substantial number of migrants from other provinces.[34] Moreover, population growth probably resulted from the shift in economic importance from Suzhou to Shanghai in the years from 1870 to 1911, and was accelerated in the 1910s and 1930s by political turmoil. Even so, what statistics are available of Shanghai's population composition suggest that the lower income groups included a large portion of migrants from the counties located near the city and from the poorer parts of northern Jiangsu.[35] In Guangdong, the urban growth occurred in Hong Kong, Shantou, and Guangzhou (in this order of importance), and the influx was drawn principally from the hinterlands of these cities.[36] Emigrants overseas, however, were largely recruited by agencies that operated from Hong Kong and Shantou, and these drew from long-established social networks that were based on family connections. The counties that supplied the largest number of overseas migrants were the ones that were located in the west of the Zhujiang delta near the Portuguese colony of Macao, the counties near Shantou, and the poorer counties located in the highland area to the north of the Hanjiang basin. Some of these counties reported exceptionally high population density in the 1920s and 1930s, and emigration might have, in the short run, helped to alleviate the pressure on land .[37]

The more lasting effects of emigration, however, came from the flow of income into the countryside from the cities and from overseas countries. Again, the evidence in Jiangsu is quite obscure, but it is almost certain that first and second generation settlers in Shanghai and Nanjing remitted part of their incomes back to the villages. None the less, such remittances are noted only incidentally in the records and apparently made no impression on the field surveyors of the 1920s and 1930s.[38] In contrast, incomes derived from outside the village were commonly noted in surveys conducted in Guangdong. Chen Ta, who in 1934–5 made a comparative study of villages from which emigration took place (and other villages where it did not) in Shantou and several localities in Fujian Province, noted the importance of overseas remittances. He found that his sample of households from the emigrants' villages received over 75 per cent of their monthly income from remittances, whether the household income totalled 15 dollars or 230 dollars. It should not be surprising, then, to see that, on average, they received a larger monthly income and spent a slightly smaller proportion it of on food and a larger proportion on their houses.[39] The overall income remitted from abroad was very large, even though not all of it was destined for the rural areas. In its decennial reports in 1902-11, the Maritime Customs estimated that remittances sent to Jiangmen, in the Zhujiang delta, amounted to 4 million Mexican dollars per annum, and those to Shantou amounted to 21 million. These figures should not be regarded as unlikely if it is noted that quite a few estimates of remittances from Chinese people working overseas quote the national total at over 100 million dollars per year.[40]

Farm Technology

Where changes were slow was in farm technology. Among the more successful applications of modern technology in Jiangsu and Guangdong were the steam filature, the rice mill, and the flour mill, and it is characteristic that none of the three was adopted as a part of farm operations. They were introduced in much the same way as the spinning mill, the sugar refinery, or the cigarette factory was introduced into China. Each was a private entrepreneurial enterprise, producing for an expanding market with recognized success at an early stage, and was taken up almost immediately. These new industries made a tremendous impact on some areas of agricultural production, but innovation stopped with the factories and was not extended to the farm.

The difficulties encountered by attempts to improve the quality of Chinese silk are too well known to need more than the barest description here.[41] The silkworm was susceptible to the disease known as pebrine, which was responsible not only for waste but also for poor quality silk. The disease could be detected by microscopic examination and healthy eggs could be isolated. In Japan, egg farmers were strictly controlled by government to ensure that the eggs sold to silkworm rearers were free of pebrine. In China, although silkworm rearers also bought their eggs from specialized egg farmers, and so one might have thought that similar control could have been instituted, it was not, and egg sheets were sold that included sick as well as healthy eggs. As a result, Chinese silk cocoons were of a lower quality than those from Japan. A weak government and lack of central direction could have been the causes of such inefficiency, but one might also wonder why Chinese egg farmers did not introduce the method on their own initiative, and why silk reelers, especially the operators of the larger filatures, who were not unaware of market opinions, did not initiate the necessary improvements and reap what could have been certain profit. It was not because the Chinese egg-farmer could not recognize the importance of raising healthy worms that he did not adopt what seemed to Western observers and Western-trained scientists to be the obvious remedy. The Chinese egg farmer by tradition had another remedy, one that required spraying the eggs with hot water, thereby killing the weaker eggs and leaving the strong ones to survive.[42] His method was not nearly as effective as Pasteur's application of the microscope, and therein lay his ruin. However, how could the relative weakness of his method be demonstrated to him? To call his adherence to his traditional method 'conservatism' prejudges his rationality, to think that government control could have altered it underestimates the size of the problem.

Technological transfer could also be unsuccessful because the specific conditions required for implementation might not be readily recognized. The introduction of American cotton is a case in point. Enthusiasm for the American species came early, its longer fibre compared to that of the Chinese variety being recognized as necessary for machine-ginning. Attempts to introduce American cotton into Jiangsu, however, met with little success, but not because of the lack of enthusiasm. Backed by senior officials and the late Qing central government, and then by Zhang Jian, the entrepreneur and cotton-mill owner of Nantong, American seeds were purchased and distributed to farmers. However, since the seeds were not acclimatized and were propagated without adaptation to traditional methods, except on the newly reclaimed land of Nantong, the cotton that was grown degenerated rapidly into myriad varieties of low quality hybrids. It was not until the 1920s, when experimental stations were established under expert personnel to study and advance cotton farming, that American varieties were reintroduced into Jiangsu.[43]

The most successful technological imports were the ones that provided the most immediate cost savings. The use of machine-spun yarn in the place of hand-spun yarn in the production of native cloth comes readily to mind, and the steam filature follows as another example. In the mulberry-growing areas of the Zhujiang delta, imported chemical fertilizers came to be accepted in the 1920s. By 1922, there were ten fertilizer stores in the town of Yongqi (Shunde county) and in the next year, there were sixty-eight such stores.[44] A ready market for filatured silk or home-woven cloth contributed to their success. The employment of women workers in connection with the steam filature, moreover, blended closely with rural marketing and the traditional division of labour. Labour-saving devices, on the other hand, found little favour. The mechanical water pump was introduced into some villages, for instance, but most continued with traditional water-drawing devices.[45] In these cases, the point must be borne in mind that villagers had plenty of labour at their disposal, and the cost of purchasing such a device could not be offset by any reduction in labour costs, thus leaving the traditional device as the most cost-effective.[46]

Traditional Agriculture in a Changing Environment

Overall, the developments in transport and communications, the growth of trade, and the increase in emigration imply that between 1870 and 1937 the rural areas of Jiangsu and Guangdong were integrated into the wider economy in and beyond China to a greater extent that they had ever been before. However, without changes in farm technology or organization, the changes that were introduced were met by farmers who continued to practise traditional agriculture. The farm continued to be run as a household enterprise, and farm operations continued to be characterized by features well known to students of traditional agriculture, such as high labour intensity, high per-unit area yield, intense use of available resources, and low per capita return from farm production. How traditional agriculture faced up to the challenges introduced by development is very much the subject of the following chapters, but to conclude this discussion on sources of change in the period under consideration, it is useful to review briefly how the lack of change in farm operation may provide an alternative statement of the pessimistic position. Although this alternative statement will not be taken further in this book, it should not be readily dismissed.

The point to note is that the changes introduced from 1870 to 1937 were largely external to farm operation. Even when cash crops were adopted, they were cultivated by farmers who made use of traditional skills and who continued to manage their farms in the traditional manner. Fei Xiaotong's study of Kaixiangong village in Wujiang county, southern Jiangsu, in 1936, brings out this aspect of cash-crop farming poignantly. Fei stressed the efficient use of land in the village, exemplified in a fine balance between the number of adult men in the village and the acreage available for cultivation. He also noted that farming was conducted as individual, not group, work. As he described it:

The use of the hoe in cultivation has made most of the work very individualistic. Group work yields no more than the sum total of individual efforts. It also does not increase efficiency very much.[47]

The farmers worked within their households, the men being aided by the women and children during the busy seasons. Otherwise, group work was needed chiefly in drainage and irrigation. The village that Fei studied was divided into a number of drainage units, the one that he described consisting of 336 *mu* of land. The annual drainage of the fields was conducted by fifteen teams of workers provided by households that held land (it is not clear from Fei's description whether they owned or rented the land) in the drainage area. All positions of management on the pumping teams, including the post of chief manager, were rotated among the members. The organization was apparently very effective, but as Fei noted:

The collective responsibility of drainage has made the introduction of the modern pumping machine difficult, because it requires the unanimous consent of the whole *cien* [drainage unit].[48]

What is traditional about this form of agriculture is that its methods were founded on principles that were passed down from generation to generation in the farming community and that had evolved without the aid of the experimental tradition that was introduced into agriculture in the late nineteenth and early twentieth centuries. The interest in raising productivity in China in the 1920s and 1930s that, in China, originated in the universities, welfare institutions, and the Chinese government, called into question the efficiency of relying on these traditional skills to improve yield, but the agricultural research that was conducted at the time made little immediate impact.[49] In the villages of Henan district, in the suburb of Guangzhou city, the only agricultural implements used were traditional, and farmers who found chemical fertilizers less effective than natural fertilizers continued to fertilize their crops with human and animal manure.[50] In these villages, technical expertise in farming was supplied by hired workers who were hired to manage the farm, and the expertise that they supplied was traditional.[51] In Kaixiangong, it was the chief manager of the drainage teams who had the authority to determine when to begin or to stop draining the fields.[52] Except for the new varieties of seed popularized in the 1920s and 1930s, and the slow start made by chemical fertilizers in some parts of Guangdong, farm technology in the twentieth century was no different from that of the nineteenth.

The argument has been put forward by the pessimists, not without justification, that the small scale of operation that characterizes Chinese farms was not conducive to the introduction of modern agricultural technology. Chen Hansheng stated this line of argument emphatically:

Small peasants' property excludes by its very nature the development of the social powers of production of labour, the social forms of labour, the social concentration of capital, cattle raising on a large scale, and a progressive application of science.[53]

It should be noted that the question at issue is not whether small farms were efficient in the use of resources by traditional farming methods, but whether they could absorb modern methods of agriculture that would increase their efficiency. Given the nature of our sources, this is hardly a question that can be taken very much further. However, it is a useful reminder that the period in which trade expansion made its impact was also one in which agricultural technology might have been transformed, and that there was a considerable time gap, in China, between the impact that was made by trade expansion, and that made by technological changes in agriculture. In hindsight, agriculture in Jiangsu and Guangdong from 1870 to 1937 would appear to have been characterized by this technological gap.

In other words, technological change could have followed the opportunities provided by the expanding market between 1870 and the 1930s, but for most of this period, it was as yet insignificant. It is possible to argue that technological change could have occurred faster, or that the Chinese government might have been more active to promote it, but it is hard to see this order of events could have been altered.

3

Did Trade Expansion Undermine
Subsistence?

IN the 1920s and 1930s, the argument gained currency that as rice was imported in large quantities from abroad, firstly into Guangdong, but in the 1930s also into Jiangsu, grain was being displaced by such cash crops as mulberry, cotton, or tobacco. In particular, Guangdong was singled out as a province where the production of *food*, rather than rice, fell short of demand, and statistics were gathered to corroborate this view.[1] These alarmist views were unjustified and arose from a serious misunderstanding of the rural economy.

Crop Distribution

For one thing, this argument goes against all available source materials on crop distribution. An example of such materials is reproduced in Table 3.1, which comprises provincial statistics gathered by the central government from a national survey of farms and crops between 1929 and 1931, and breakdowns for the localities reported by J.L. Buck from his national survey conducted between 1927 and 1933. In the 1930s, as always, grain was by far the most commonly cultivated crop in Jiangsu and Guangdong. In none of the localities that Buck surveyed, with the exception of Jieyang (Guangdong) and one locality in Yancheng county (Jiangsu), did the acreage devoted to grain fall much below 70 per cent of the total crop acreage. Where it did fall below this percentage, the shortfall was made up for by the cultivation of legumes, oilseeds, or tubers. In Jieyang, the low percentage of the cultivated acreage devoted to staple food crops was due to the cultivation of sugar-cane, and in Yancheng, to the cultivation of cotton, both of which were grown as cash crops. The acreages devoted to cash crops in these two localities were quite exceptional, as may be seen in the small proportion of the provincial crop acreages devoted to them (see the first line under both Jiangsu and Guangdong in Table 3.1). Grain, legumes, oilseeds, and tubers together occupied 92 per cent of the total crop acreage of Jiangsu and 98 per cent of that of Guangdong.[2]

Table 3.1

Percentage of Crop Area Devoted to Principal Crops, c.1930

	Grain	Legumes	Oilseeds	Grain and Seed Interplanted	Fibres	Tubers and Roots	Fruit	Vegetables	Trees	Others	Unknown
Jiangsu	72.6	15.6	1.9	—	8.0	2.3	—	—	—	—	—
Southern:											
Jiangning	77.7	20.9	0.4	—	0.1	0.5	—	0.1	—	0.3	—
Changshu	75.9	1.8	14.0	—	8.1	—	—	—	0.2	—	—
Kunshan	69.1	5.5	3.1	—	6.6	—	—	1.0	—	14.4*	—
Wuxi (1)	82.2	—	—	—	—	—	—	—	14.7	3.1	—
Wuxi (2)	85.1	—	—	—	—	—	—	0.5	14.2	0.1	0.1
Wujin (1)	78.3	9.0	0.8	0.5†	0.7	0.1	—	1.0	3.9	5.0	—
Wujin (2)	86.6	8.0	—	—	0.1	—	0.7	0.1	5.1	0.1	—
Wujin (3)	98.4	0.5	—	—	0.6	—	—	0.1	0.2	0.2	—
Transitional:											
Funing	41.0	33.3	0.1	25.5‡	—	0.1	—	—	—	—	—
Huaiyin	63.3	16.5	7.5	—	—	12.3	—	0.4	—	—	—
Yancheng (1)	2.2	—	—	—	97.8	—	—	—	—	—	—
Yancheng (2)	99.9	—	—	—	—	—	—	0.1	—	—	—
Yancheng (3)	53.8	—	—	—	—	—	—	0.6	—	45.6#	—
Yancheng (4)	100.0	—	—	—	—	—	—	—	—	—	—

Jiangdu	86.0	14.0	—	—	—	—	—	—	—	—	—
Taixian	79.9	19.1	0.1	—	0.1	0.5	—	0.3	—	—	—
Northern:											
Guanyun	64.3	22.6	—	10.6†	1.4	—	0.5	—	0.4	—	—
Guangdong	89.9	2.9	1.2	—	0.4	4.3	—	—	—	1.2	—
Zhujiang delta											
Zhongshan	97.4	—	—	—	—	—	—	2.5	—	0.1	—
Xijiang											
Gaoyao	89.2	—	0.2	—	—	3.9	1.4	4.2	—	0.9	0.3
Beijiang											
Qujiang	90.1	—	2.4	—	0.2	5.8	—	0.3	—	0.9	0.3
Hanjiang											
Chao'an	63.3	0.4	—	—	0.2	5.7	30.0	—	—	0.4	—
Jieyang	39.1	—	5.1	—	—	22.7	—	5.6	—	27.5	—
North and west											
Nanxiong	50.0	0.5	13.7	—	—	14.7	—	5.1	—	15.3	0.7
Maoming	50.7	9.0	11.0	0.1**	0.1	20.2	2.2	—	5.0	1.5	0.2

Notes: * 12.2 per cent given to *astragalus sinensis*.
     † Grain interplanted with legumes.
     ‡ 13.2 per cent being grain interplanted with legumes, 12.3 per cent legumes interplanted with oilseeds.
     # Not specified.
     ** Grain interplanted with oilseeds.

Sources: Provincial totals from Alfred Kai-ming Chiu (1933), pp. 501–501H, quoting *Statistical Monthly*, 1932; other figures from J.L. Buck (1937b), pp. 172–3.

These percentages agree with other reports of acreages devoted to such cash crops as mulberry, cotton, tobacco, or sugar.[3] In Jiangsu, the total mulberry acreage in the 1930s amounted to 1,000,000 *mu*, cotton 10,000,000 *mu*, while tobacco and sugar-cane were not widely grown. In Guangdong, the mulberry acreage in the 1920s amounted to 1,600,000 *mu*, tobacco in the 1930s to 70,000 *mu*, and sugar-cane 670,000 *mu*. These figures compare with an overall cultivated acreage in Jiangsu of 90,000,000 *mu* and in Guangdong of 42,000,000 *mu*.[4] Moreover, descriptive accounts on the distribution of the major cash crops suggest that few areas specialized in their production. In much of the silk-producing district in southern Jiangsu, with the exception of parts of Wuxi county, mulberry was grown on the side of paddy fields. The silk farmers that Fei Xiaotong studied in Kaixiangong (Wujiang, Jiangsu) were also rice farmers whose custom was to reserve a year's food supply at each harvest.[5] In the Zhujiang delta, only in Shunde county was mulberry growing a specialized activity. In this county mulberry occupied as much as 70 per cent of the total farm acreage, cultivated under the land-use pattern known as 'mulberry-dykes and fish-ponds'.[6] In nearby Panyu, well known for its fruit exports, Chen Hansheng reported that, in 1933, 68 per cent of all farmland in ten villages surveyed was planted under rice, and in two villages in which fruit was obviously the dominant crop, rice still occupied from 27.5 per cent to 37.8 per cent of the farm acreage.[7] It should always be remembered that crop rotation alone would have required the farmer to grow food crops along with industrial cash crops. The rotation for cotton required that wheat be grown in one out of every three years, and, for sugar-cane, that another crop, such as rice, tubers, or groundnuts be planted for two to three years after a crop of cane. As cane could grow for two or three years, for every six years or so, a staple food crop would have been planted for half the time.[8]

Yet another source of error is the severe under-reporting of supplementary food crops, chiefly roots and tubers. It is well documented that roots and tubers, especially the sweet potato, were important sources of food, and for this reason the figures in Table 3.1 should be suspect. In Xuzhou, northern Jiangsu, the sweet potato was reported as constituting 30 per cent of the annual food intake in one study, and 20 per cent in another, which also noted that it was the principal staple for four months of the year.[9] In Guangdong, a study of a representative diet reported that rice formed only 66.48 per cent of an average person's food intake, while the sweet potato formed 22.7 per cent.[10] In the county-by-county study conducted by Zhongshan

University's School of Agriculture in the 1920s, the sweet potato was reported to be second only to rice as a staple food in numerous counties.[11] Food production in Yangshan, a Beijiang River county, was described in the following terms:

Rice is not produced in sufficient quantities to satisfy consumption, and corn, sweet potatoes, and taro must be used for food. Hence, supplementary food crops are the principal sources of food in this county. In some districts such as Gaofeng, Tongshan, and Jiangkou, paddy is not grown at all, and it is said that many people have not tasted rice for several decades.[12]

Even Sihui county, located in an area that would not have been unduly infertile, produced only eight months' supply of rice each year, and depended on sweet potatoes and other supplementary crops for four months.[13]

The under-reporting of supplementary food crops may also be demonstrated by comparing county-by-county reports in two separate provincial studies in Guangdong, one of which was conducted by the National Reconstruction Committee of the province in 1937 and the other by the Bureau of Agriculture and Forestry, possibly also in the 1930s.[14] The National Reconstruction Committee's survey was conducted by a team of nine commissioners over a few months, and the preface to the report noted the hurry in which they had to work as well as the suspicion with which local people regarded them. Unfortunately, a comparable statement on the information gathering by the Bureau of Agriculture and Forestry cannot be made, as my source for its statistics is totally silent on such matters.

Two features in these reports are outstanding. First, among 86 counties on which the National Reconstruction Committee provides information, 14 are quoted production figures that are identical to figures of quantities of crop sold. The same anomaly may be noted in reports concerning crops other than sweet potato in these counties, including paddy. Second, the reports in the two surveys are highly inconsistent. Out of the more than 80 counties for which statistics are quoted in both surveys, only 15 are not given figures that do not vary by 50 per cent or more. None the less, the paddy statistics in the two reports are much closer, only 19 counties being quoted figures that vary by more than 25 per cent.[15] An explanation for the discrepancies may be found if it is remembered that Republican acreage statistics were supplied by local informants. The proximity of the paddy statistics must, therefore, reflect closer agreement among informants over the acreage devoted to paddy than to sweet potato. This is understandable when paddy was planted on the more fertile land of the village, that would at least nominally be liable to tax. The sweet potato, on the contrary, was planted as a 'catch' crop as well as on wasteland and the land devoted to it was not considered essential cultivated land. The surveyors of the 1930s were therefore given wild guesses when they asked for its acreage. These acreages would not have been reported at all had they not been specifically asked for.

A Statistical Assessment of Food Sufficiency

The argument that cash crops displaced food crops to the extent that food was insufficient in the more commercialized provinces also goes against the statistics on yield, acreage, and population that were introduced in its support. These are problematic statistics to draw on for any argument, but, with care, it is possible to show that they do not support this position.

Yield

The easier part of the problem is how much was grown per unit area. In Table 3.2, yield approximations are listed according to prefectures. The method by which these figures are compiled should be noted. It should be understood that the figures are not mechanical averages derived from the survey reports. Instead, values have been entered into this table in a two-step procedure. In the first place, average yields are determined for the Suzhou area and the Zhujiang delta on the basis of survey and other reports. Secondly, with these averages as benchmarks, values are assigned to other localities that reflect variations in geographical conditions and the survey reports of the 1920s and 1930s. The method is not altogether satisfactory, but it provides an effective way of incorporating what is known of the geographical conditions with yield estimates as calculated from the survey statistics.

The benchmark incorporated into Table 3.2 that allows some confidence is the upper limit of average yields in Suzhou and the Zhujiang delta. Gu Yanwu, the late Ming scholar, and Zhang Lixiang, the author of the *Bunongshu*, both writing in the seventeenth century, Bao Shichen, the eminent scholar of the statecraft school in the first half of the nineteenth century, and Tao Xu, a small landlord writing in the 1880s who owned land near Suzhou city, all consistently reported that 3 *shi* of paddy (approximately 300 catties) per *mu* or more was considered a good average yield. Moreover, reports of yields amounting

Table 3.2
Yield per *mu* of Major Grain Crops (catties per *mu*)

	Paddy	Wheat	Sorghum
Jiangsu			
Southern:			
Jiangning	250	80	—
Suzhou	375	80	—
Songjiang	325	80	—
Taicang	250	80	—
Changzhou	375	100–150	—
Zhenjiang	300	120	—
Transitional.			
Huai'an	250	90	50
Yangzhou	300	120	132
Tongzhou	220	90	—
Haimen	80	90	—
Northern:			
Xuzhou	80	90	80
Haizhou	80	80	80
Guangdong			
Zhujiang delta:			
Guangzhou	250–400	—	—
Xijiang:			
Zhaoqing	200–400	—	—
Beijiang:			
Shaozhou	230–350	—	—
Dongjiang:			
Huizhou	250–400	—	—
Hanjiang:			
Chaozhou	250–450	—	—
Xijiang highland:			
Luoding	100–300	—	—
Beijiang highland:			
Lianzhou and Nanxiong	230–350	—	—
Hanjiang highland:			
Jiaying	150–450	—	—
Western highland:			
Gaozhou and Leizhou	150–450	—	—
Hainan Island:			
Qiongzhou	150	—	—

Note: For standardization procedures and comparison of sources see Appendix.
Sources: See Appendix, Tables A.1–A.3.

to far more than 300 catties per *mu* are by no means uncommon in twentieth- century surveys.[16] A benchmark value of 375 catties per *mu* has consequently been entered in the table for Suzhou and Changzhou, that is, in the heartland of southern Jiangsu. In the New Territories of Hong Kong, on the fringe of the Zhujiang delta, villagers recall that the yield on the best land amounted to 4 piculs of paddy per harvest, and on average land 2.5 piculs.[17] On experimental farms in Dongguan county (Zhujiang delta) in the early 1900s, paddy yields were reported to have reached 400 catties per *mu*.[18] These reports have also been taken into account in the table.

The figures quoted in Table 3.2 are probably still on the high side, especially for southern Jiangsu. However, estimates that are very much lower than these would hardly be consistent with yields reported in field research.[19]

The areas with the highest yields must have been the well-watered and warm deltas of the Zhujiang, the Hanjiang, and the Changjiang rivers. Yields declined in areas farther away, being lowest, on average, in the uplands of Guangdong and to the north in Jiangsu. In the Guangdong uplands, yield declined to between 100 and 300 catties per *mu*, while in the northern parts of Jiangsu, to as low as 80 catties per *mu*.

Population and Cultivated Acreage

Estimates of population and cultivated acreage taken from official reports are presented in Table 3.3. The cultivated acreage figures were reported by the central government, checked, and corrected against other reports by J.L. Buck. Buck's checking procedure was as follows. The central government statistics were reduced to percentages of cultivated land in each county — total county area statistics having also been published by the central government — and these percentages were checked by his investigators on the basis of their 'studies and travelling experience'. It is not clear what the phrase might refer to, but it did not include information gathered directly from county governments and the farm surveys, even though he derived indicators from these sources with which he further corrected overall regional statistics. In the case of Jiangsu, he made no correction of the county statistics. In that of Guangdong, he corrected only the entries for Chao'an and Jieyang counties. None the less, he noted,'owing to the general under-reporting of crop areas, percentages [of cultivated land to total county area] were usually too low.'[20] Central government

Table 3.3
Population and Cultivated Acreage, *c*.1930

	Cultivated Acreage (mu)	Population c.1920	Urban Population c.1920	Rural Population per 1,000 mu
Jiangsu				
Southern:				
Jiangning	4,398,000	1,877,000	330,000	352
Suzhou	5,794,000	2,618,000	418,000	380
Songjiang	4,344,000	3,021,000	1,600,000	327
Taicang	4,317,000	1,640,000	40,000	371
Changzhou	6,583,000	3,048,000	325,000	414
Zhenjiang	4,323,000	1,845,000	390,000	337
Transitional:				
Huai'an	13,940,000	4,507,000	260,000	305
Yangzhou	12,988,000	5,619,000	340,000	406
Tongzhou	8,849,000	3,191,000	115,000	348
Haimen	1,608,000	635,000	—	395
Northern:				
Xuzhou	14,174,000	3,684,000	230,000	244
Haizhou	10,366,000	2,076,000	70,000	194
Guangdong				
Zhujiang Delta:				
Guangzhou	13,661,000	9,630,000	2,509,000	521
Xijiang:				
Zhaoqing	4,609,000	3,047,000	162,000	626
Yangjiang	402,000	464,000	—	1,154
Beijiang:				
Shaozhou	2,332,000	782,000	60,000	310
Dongjiang:				
Huizhou	5,150,000	3,188,000	—	619
Hanjiang:				
Chaozhou	4,564,000	4,607,000	625,000	872
Xijiang highland:				
Luoding	955,000	866,000	—	907
Beijiang highland:				
Nanxiong	877,000	375,000	40,000	382
Lianzhou (Lianxian and Yangshan)	837,000	580,000	30,000	657
Lianzhou (Lianshanxian)	531,000	44,000	—	83

Table 3.3   (continued)

	Cultivated Acreage (mu)	Population c.1920	Urban Population c.1920	Rural Population per 1,000 mu
Hanjiang highland:				
Jiaying	989,000	1,516,000	40,000	1,492
Western highland:				
Gaozhou	2,302,000	2,516,000	—	1,093
Leizhou	1,390,000	670,000	—	482
Hainan Island:				
Qiongzhou	4,100,000	2,252,000	100,000	525

Notes: Guangdong data exclude Chiqi and Nan'ao. Rural population = total population − urban population.

Sources: J.L. Buck (1937b) pp. 23–4, 26–7, quoting from *Statistical Monthly*, January and February 1932 and incorporating his own corrections; Zhu Kezhen (1926), pp. 98–100; *Guangdong jingji nianjian 1940*, pp. C2–10; Milton Stauffer (1922), pp. *lxxxviii–lxxxix*, with the following corrections: Suzhou 300,000, Yangzhou 120,000, Taizhou, Xinghua, Huai'an, Qing-jiangpu 50,000 each, Shaozhou 30,000, Guangzhou 1,123,000, Shantou 125,000.

estimates, in all likelihood, would have resembled tax-registered acreages, which would have been under-reported. In any case, they would not have included acreages on which supplementary food crops, such as the sweet potato, were grown. It is not unreasonable, therefore, to consider that these reports were on the low side.[21]

The population figures, as should be expected, are equally problematic. Republican population statistics are neither census nor registration enumeration. Except for the 1908 census figures, which as Ho Ping-ti has shown are highly unreliable, no one has found for any provincial or national series how the raw figures from which estimates were made were enumerated. Consequently, in his analysis of the historical development of the Chinese population from the Ming dynasty down to the 1950s, Ho Ping-ti discounted altogether the Republican estimates.[22] Economic historians of China who require an estimate for the Republican period to satisfy their research interests resort either to provincial figures of unknown origin or figures that are ultimately traceable to the 1908 census. The criterion they employ for the acceptability of their reworked figures has been that they are compatible with earlier Qing registration records and the 1953 census, with the proviso that little is known of the tremendous changes in population that must have occurred during the Taiping era (1850s and 1860s) and the Second World War.[23] Basically, the Republican population figures are employed because there is no alternative. They are difficult to interpret, for not only are they faulty, but their errors may also be quite systematic.

For many reasons, therefore, the population figures as quoted on Table 3.3 justifiably arouse scepticism. None the less, it may be noted that the Jiangsu figures were reported by the Post Office in 1920, which we may presume were gathered from local informants through postmasters, and that the total provincial population of 33.8 million accords reasonably well with the Jiangsu government's estimate in 1931 of 35.8 million, or the central government National Agricultural Research Bureau's 35.2 million in the late 1920s; or the 34.9 million for the early 1930s derived by Liu and Yeh on the basis of Wilcox's estimates drawn largely from the 1908 census; or with the 38.1 million (excluding the population of Shanghai) reported in 1953.[24] The Guangdong figures are reports compiled by the Guangdong provincial government for 1928 to 1931. None of the sources that quote these Guangdong statistics gives any indication as to how they were collected, but they probably originated from county reports. The provincial total of 30.5 million as noted in Table 3.3 may be compared with the imperial government's figure of 25.7 million in 1840, the National Agricultural Research Bureau's 31.3 million in the late 1920s, Liu and Yeh's 34.0 million estimated for the early 1930s, or the 32.8 million in the 1953 census.[25]

As the object here is to consider the question of food sufficiency in rural areas, an attempt must be made to isolate the urban population total from the overall figures. However, again, the delineation of the urban population is by no means a simple issue. Obviously, the population of the largest cities such as Shanghai or Guangzhou should not be confused with the rural population if only because one would not under normal circumstances expect their food supply to be derived from their immediate rural vicinity alone. However, urban characteristics can also be detected in the larger markets and towns, especially in that a substantial portion of their population would not have derived their principal income from farming. None the less, in the absence of detailed records on the components of the market populations, where one should draw the line on the hierarchy of rural markets, county cities, and treaty ports to distinguish the rural from the urban can be quite arbitrary. In Table 3.3, the solution to this problem is to account only for the population of the larger towns and cities, using a list compiled by the Protestant Missions in 1918, corrected for obvious errors.[26] The list is far from complete, but it seems that the source tends to exaggerate the populations of those cities that are noted. On balance, compared to Gilbert Rozman's estimates on the mid-nineteenth century and 1953, the urban population figures given in the table probably overstate. Not, however, by very much: if Rozman's figures are used as a basis for comparison, they overstate by no more than 2 to 3 per cent.[27]

When the weaknesses of the statistics are considered, some of the estimates of rural population density in Table 3.3 should raise suspicion. It is difficult to accept that the most densely populated areas included the Hanjiang highland and the western highland in Guangdong, given the poor soil conditions and low productivity. It is much more likely that these estimates reflect highly under-reported cultivated acreages. However, although the estimate for the Hanjiang delta area is also extreme, a high population density in this part of Guangdong is well documented and credible. That the valleys of the Xijiang and Dongjiang rivers show a higher density than the Zhujiang delta probably again reflects shortcomings in the urban population figures: little allowance has been made to take account of the city and market-town populations on the Xijiang and the Dongjiang, but the population of Guangzhou and the major market towns in the Zhujiang delta have been accounted for. In Jiangsu, the areas with the densest population are in the southern portion of the province, as one would expect.

Food Sufficiency

The estimates of Tables 3.2 and 3.3 may now be reworked to provide some indications of food sufficiency. The results are noted in Table 3.4. This table does not pretend to be more than a rough basis for comparing the reported statistics: it is not the precise statement that the use of statistics often suggests. To compile the table, it is assumed that in Jiangsu two crops were gathered every year, being made up of a combination of paddy, wheat, or sorghum, and in Guangdong, also two crops, of paddy. A reduction of 10 per cent is introduced to allow for seeds and 30 per cent for milling.[28] It is also assumed that all cultivated land was put to the major grain crops. This last assumption biases the results obtained, but is introduced none the less because, firstly, the reported acreages in any case do not include those put to supplementary crops; secondly, the acreages occupied by industrial cash crops in most counties would have been quite low; and thirdly, industrial crops would, on the whole, have fetched a higher income than could be derived from grain.

In effect, therefore, Table 3.4 represents a model for the hypothetical situation in which all reported cultivated land was put to grain crops. It shows that had all cultivated land, as reported, been devoted to paddy, wheat, or sorghum, most places in the Jiangsu or Guangdong countryside would have produced more than enough for a narrowly defined minimum, which may be taken to be 400 catties of grain per annum.[29] The only exceptions would have been those places that produced less than 300 catties of grain per *mu* per annum (parts of transitional Jiangsu and Hainan Island in Guangdong) or the ones where extraordinarily high population density has been recorded (Jiaying, Luoding, Yangjiang, and Gaozhou in Guangdong). Both the very low yields and the high density are suspect.[30] More credible is the low but not inadequate per capita food grain available for Jiangning, the rice-producing areas of northern Jiangsu, the Hanjiang delta, the Dongjiang valley, and Lianzhou. These areas had enough for subsistence, but hardly anything to spare. With the exception of the Hanjiang delta, these were not major producers of export industrial crops, and consequently they probably had few means to make up for grain shortages. The areas with the highest per-capita grain yields, on the contrary, were the ones with large cash crop exports, for instance, Suzhou, Songjiang, Changzhou, and the Zhujiang delta. This imbalance in crop production was quite fundamental to the economic structures of the two provinces being considered.

How much cultivated land would have had to be kept for food crops in southern Jiangsu and the Zhujiang delta in order to bring average per capita grain yield to subsistence level? The question may be answered by expressing 400 catties as a ratio of the food grain per capita estimated in Table 3.4. In most counties in southern Jiangsu (Suzhou, Songjiang, Changzhou, and Zhenjiang), this would have been slightly over 50 per cent, while for Jiangning it would be 67 per cent and for Taicang 71 per cent. In Guangzhou, it works out to be 51 per cent. In other words, with the exception of Jiangning and Taicang, up to 50 per cent of the available cultivated land that might be devoted to grain crops had to be diverted to industrial cash crops before a

Table 3.4
Food Sufficiency in Rural Jiangsu and Guangdong, c.1920

	Yield per mu × 0.9 (catties)	Population per 1,000 mu	Food Grain Per Capita × 0.7 (catties)	Number of Counties Short of		Industrial Crop
				(1) Rice*	(2) Wheat*	
Jiangsu						
Southern:						
Jiangning	297	352	590	2(6)	0(6)	—
Suzhou	410	380	755	1(4)	1(4)	silk
Songjiang	365	327	781	5(7)	1(7)	cotton
Taicang	297	371	560	5(5)	0(5)	cotton
Changzhou	450	414	761	3(6)	2(5)	silk
Zhenjiang	378	337	785	3(4)	1(5)	—
Transitional:						
Huai'an	306	305	702	0(3)	0(6)	—
Yangzhou	378	406	652	3(7)	2(6)	—
Tongzhou	279	348	561	2(3)	0(3)	cotton
Haimen	153	395	271	n.a	n.a.	cotton
Northern:						
Xuzhou	153	244	439	1(1)	0(8)	—
Haizhou	144	194	519	3(3)	0(4)	—
Guangdong						
Zhujiang Delta:						
Guangzhou	585	521	786	4(9)	n.a.	silk

Xijiang:						
Zhaoqing	540	626	604	2(8)	n.a.	—
Yangjiang	540	1,154	328	n.a.	n.a.	—
Bejiang:						
Shaozhou	522	310	1,179	0(5)	n.a.	—
Dongjiang:						
Huizhou	585	619	662	1(9)	n.a.	—
Hanjiang:						
Chaozhou	630	872	506	6(9)	n.a.	sugar
Xijiang highlands:						
Luoding	360	907	278	2(2)	n.a.	—
Beijiang highlands:						
Nanxiong	522	382	957	1(2)	n.a.	—
Lianzhou‡	522	657	556	1(2)	n.a.	—
Lianzhou†	522	83	4,402	n.a.	n.a.	—
Hanjiang highlands:						
Jiaying	540	1,492	253	3(4)	n.a.	—
Western highlands:						
Gaozhou	540	1,093	346	0(3)	n.a.	—
Leizhou	540	482	784	0(1)	n.a.	—
Hainan Island:						
Qiongzhu	135	525	180	n.a.	n.a.	—

Notes: * No. of counties with information in parentheses.
† Lianshanxian.
‡ Lianzhou and Yangshan.
Sources: Tables 3.2 and 3.3; *Zhongguo shiyezhi: Jiangsusheng*, pp. 36–7 and 77–8; Guoli Zhongshan daxue nongke xueyuan (1925, 1929, 1933).

physical shortage would develop. Few places in southern Jiangsu or the Zhujiang delta concentrated on these crops to such an extent.[31]

What Table 3.4 highlights is the fallacy that population pressure or the displacement of food crops by industrial cash crops could have necessitated grain imports. Instead, it would seem that the areas that suffered from population pressure or land shortage were not the ones that could have afforded to import grain, while the ones that did were not as short of grain. Grain was imported, not because food was short, but because income from export crops had raised the standard of living, and because grain, especially rice, was preferred to the sweet potato or other supplementary food crops. In years of poor harvest, no doubt, these areas also imported out of necessity, but for most years, they imported out of choice.[32]

Some corroboration may be found for this interpretation from contemporary reports on county rice and wheat movements (see columns under 'number of counties short of (1) rice, (2) wheat' in Table 3.4). It is not clear how these reports were compiled in the first place, but it seems likely that they incorporated commonly held knowledge within the grain trade at the county level. The reports for Jiangsu, for instance, indicate that Nanhui county consumed all the rice and 70 per cent of the wheat that was locally produced, and Songjiang 40 per cent of the rice and all the wheat. What happened to the portion of wheat not consumed in Nanhui is not made clear in the report, but the rice left over from consumption in Songjiang was exported to Shanghai. On the other hand, for Guangdong, the reports state that Nanhai county produced only enough rice for four or five months' consumption each year, and that Zengcheng exported 8,000,000 to 10,000,000 catties of rice per year. This is just the kind of information one would expect to be common knowledge among county grain merchants. The reports are not exact, therefore, but are not baseless.[33] From Table 3.4, it may be seen that of the six counties in Jiangning for which reports are available, two were short of rice but none short of wheat. Again, in the Zhujiang delta, of nine counties for which reports are available, four were short of rice. What is significant is that although grain availability per capita in Taicang, Tongzhou, Xuzhou, and Haizhou was low, rice was imported, but not wheat. In Gaozhou (Guangdong), rice was short, but not imported. That rice, rather than wheat, should be imported in northern Jiangsu, suggests that it was taste rather than need that governed food imports (rice being more expensive than wheat), and in Guangdong, the areas that imported rice, including Jiaying, would have been places that could afford to do so.

Periodic Shortages

Periodic shortages were regular features of rural society in Jiangsu and Guangdong. They were of two sorts. Firstly, an annual shortage set in every year that was apparent from a steady increase in food prices.[34] In most Chinese cities, charity institutions organized relief to cover the winter shortage. The more serious shortages were, however, irregular, arising from flood, drought, or locusts, and worst when these disasters came in several successive years. Between 1870 and 1937, Jiangsu faced six spells of famine, chiefly in the north. In 1876–7 famine in northern Jiangsu was caused by dry weather and locusts. It is not clear what the cause of the 1897–9 famine, also in the north, was: it seems that poor harvests had been reaped in several successive years, and that in 1897 the harvest was damaged by heavy rain. In 1906–7 Xuzhou and Huai'an were affected by floods caused by overflow from the lakes that linked the Huaihe river to the Grand Canal. Extensive flooding was again reported in Jiangsu in 1911 and 1912. It was reported that 2,300 square miles were inundated in three areas: a small portion of the Jiangsu-Anhui border where the Huaihe had overflowed, northeast of Huai'an where the rain had been excessively heavy, and on the Jiangsu-Shandong border, owing to overflow from rivers that drained into the Grand Canal. In 1921, another flood from the Huaihe affected the whole of northern and transitional Jiangsu. In 1931, came the unrivalled disaster: the Changjiang and the Huaihe both flooded, and the Canal burst its embankment in about fifteen places. In southern Jiangsu, 43 per cent of the farmland was flooded, and in the transitional region and northern Jiangsu, 53 per cent. In 1935, the Huanghe (Yellow River) overflowed, flooding 1.6 million *mu* in north Jiangsu.[35]

Like Jiangsu, Guangdong was susceptible to the vagaries of nature, but disasters did not hit with nearly the same force. Droughts that resulted from rain shortage were common, but tended to be local and less lasting, and the floods that resulted when the tributaries of the Zhujiang burst the dykes that held them back did not match the intensity of northern Jiangsu floods.[36]

There are no indications that floods and drought became any more common with the growth of trade. It was geography more than any other factor that determined their occurrence. Famines were common in northern and transitional Jiangsu, rare in southern Jiangsu and Guangdong. They accentuate the stark poverty of the subsistence economy of the north in contrast to the relatively well-off south, but neither province was really located in China's famine region, which lay slightly to the northwest of Jiangsu.

Conclusion

It is quite another question whether any sector of the population in Jiangsu or Guangdong was so poor that it did not produce enough for its sustenance. This is a subject that will be looked into in the the following chapters. This chapter has shown that the argument that the increase in grain purchase might be due to sheer necessity in Guangdong misreads the evidence. Did cash cropping undermine subsistence? In the sense that it produced an income with which to purchase a preferred foodstuff, it probably did. However, in this case, the increase in grain consumption in Guangdong was, in all likelihood, not a sign of impoverishment, but of rising prosperity.

4

Inflation

THE immediate impact that trade expansion made on the rural economy in Jiangsu and Guangdong from 1870 to 1937 came from two sources: changes in price and changes in trade quantities. Both were related in the long term to currency value as well as supply and demand. This chapter, therefore, begins the discussion on the impact of trade expansion by examining the course of price inflation in this period, and later chapters will examine the mechanisms for trade, the record of the major commodities traded, and the income that trade might have brought to the farmers.

The inflation that lasted from the last decade of the Qing dynasty to the 1930s is well documented,[1] but its effects, especially in its earlier years, are insufficiently noticed in the current literature. It was caused by the depreciation of silver in the international market, over which successive Chinese governments had no control, and the debasement of the coinage, which they pursued as a conscious and consistent policy. Such effects varied from locality to locality, and an accurate description of them requires a deeper appreciation of the regionalization of China's monetary system than the current state of our knowledge allows. None the less, it was one of the most important factors that shaped the Chinese rural economy before the Second World War, and it must be given the prominence that is its due.

Currency Debasement

In the nineteenth and early twentieth centuries, in Jiangsu and Guangdong as in most of China, cash was used for the purchase of goods and the payment of taxes, but in most places rent was paid in kind, and payment for services, even when quoted in money, incorporated major components that were not monetary. Cash, therefore, was widely used, but not all payments were settled in cash.[2]

By the 1870s, the silver dollar was the most common medium of exchange in the large cities, such as Guangzhou, Shantou, Suzhou, or Shanghai. It was also used commonly, along with copper cash, in their suburbs and in areas that had strong links to international trade.

Elsewhere, the copper cash was more common. Paper notes were also circulated, but they did not alter the bimetallic basis of the currency, for they were denominated in either copper or silver.[3] For most of China, including Jiangsu and Guangdong, bimetallism prevailed, and local custom determined the choice between copper and silver. Taxes were quoted in silver, but were almost invariably paid in copper. In the larger cities and in long-distance trade, prices were quoted in silver by weight, its fineness being determined by strict local regulations. In the rural markets and in local trade, they were quoted in copper cash, usually expressed in thousands, and settled in strings that were only nominally a thousand cash each. Given the proliferation of local standards, China cannot by any means be considered in the late nineteenth century to have had a unified monetary system, even though silver and copper cash remained the common elements of exchange throughout the market economy.[4]

The exchange rate between silver and copper cash regulated all spheres of pricing in the market. This rate was subject to no external control. It floated according to the supply and demand of both currencies in the local markets. After the cocoon harvest, for instance, silver dollars had to be shipped inland to the silk-producing areas to pay for silk, and the exchange rate in Shanghai would adjust in favour of the silver dollar. Eventually, the silver dollars accumulated in the silk-producing areas would find their way back to the coastal cities, through payments made for rent and tax and purchase of goods, and this inflow would bring the price of silver down.[5] A similar cycle may be observed in the rice-growing areas, which needed a substantial volume of copper coins for the payment of land tax after harvest.[6] Cash was received through the sale of the crop, and was delivered to the county governments, which eventually deposited it at the city banks, whence it flowed back to the rural areas. Where rural produce was exported to foreign countries, naturally, the situation was further complicated by the exchange rate between China's currencies and the international medium of exchange, which for most of the period under consideration was gold. A decline in the gold price of silver had the same effect on China's foreign trade as the devaluation of China's currency. However, unless the price of copper declined with it, the initial effects of such devaluation were absorbed by China's silver sector, that is, largely by the urban population, with the exception of southern China where silver also circulated in the countryside. Any variation in the exchange rate between gold and silver, or between silver and copper cash, was immediately apparent in the silk trade. As rice exports increased, it was obvious also in the rice trade.

The considerable remittance between the countryside and the county city, and among county cities, that is implied in the monetary process, was served by native banks.[7] They were small in scale in comparison to the foreign or foreign-style banks that were active in the external trade and in servicing the Chinese government's internal as well as international debts. Normal banking business provided the linkages between the native banks, the foreign-style banks, and the foreign banks. The exchange rates of copper cash to silver, of silver dollars to specie, of the Haikwan tael (which from the mid-nineteenth century until the 1930s was the standard currency quoted in foreign trade) to foreign currencies, and inter-bank lending rates were quoted daily in Shanghai as regular banking activities.[8] These daily quotations, greatly facilitated by the development of the telegraph, reverberated throughout the monetary networks. Fluctuations in the exchange rates in Shanghai sent tremors rapidly throughout the country, just as periodic needs for silver or copper cash in the countryside were reflected in Shanghai rates.

The basic trends in the currencies of Jiangsu and Guangdong are listed in Table 4.1, and they illustrate fully the extent of the inflation that China faced from the 1870s to the 1930s. The table traces the two principal components of monetary trends in China, which were the price of silver relative to gold and the value of the coinage produced from 1895 onwards. From 1872 to 1911, the price of silver relative to gold declined on the international market (column 1), during the First World War it rose, and immediately after the war again it declined. This continuous decline was brought about fundamentally by increased world supply of silver and the demonetization of the metal. However, as China continued to use silver as its principal medium of exchange in the cities, its decline in value was equivalent to the involuntary depreciation of China's currency relative to all major Western currencies. As Table 4.1 demonstrates, the Haikwan tael declined from US$ 1.32 in 1882–6 to US$ 0.57 in 1927–31 (column 2).[9]

Changes in the international price of silver affected the silver/ copper cash exchange within China. From 1872 to 1906, the silver dollar, which maintained a fairly constant rate of exchange to the Haikwan tael (column 10), exchanged steadily for fewer cash (column 4). The silver price of copper (column 3) apparently had little to do with the silver/cash exchange rates, for as the dollar exchanged for fewer cash from 1872 to 1891, the price of copper was declining. It probably mattered more that in these years the copper cash was undervalued in relation to its copper content, that is to say, the amount

Table 4.1
Currency Fluctuations in Various Localities in Jiangsu and Guangdong, 1872–1936

	(1) Price of Silver (pence/oz.)	(2) U.S. Dollar/ Haikwan Tael	(3) Price of Copper (hk.tls./picul)	(4) Cash/Silver Dollar, Ningbo	(5) Cash/Silver Dollar, Wujin
1872–6	57.5	—	16.49	1,213	—
1877–81	52.5	—	15.63	1,141	—
1882–6	49.4	1.32	14.12	1,144	—
1887–91	44.6	1.19	13.55	1,086	—
1892–6	33.0	0.88	19.99	1,064	—
1897–1901	27.5	0.72	28.04	927	—
1902–6	26.8	0.69	30.50	902	1,027†
1907–11	25.5	0.68	30.49	936*	1,244
1912–16	27.2	0.71	—	—	1,339
1917–21	48.8	1.14	—	—	1,350
1922–6	32.2	0.81	—	—	2,074
1927–31	21.9	0.57	—	—	2,906**
1932–6	19.1#	—	—	—	—

Table 4.1 (continued)

	(6) Cash/10-cent Silver, Wujin	(7) Copper Dollars/ Silver Dollar, Ningbo	(8) Discount for Subsidiary Silver Coins, Ningbo (per cent)	(9) Subsidiary Coins/100 Hong Kong Dollars, Guangzhou (dollars)	(10) Silver Dollars/ Silver Dollars Tael
1872–6	—	—	—	—	0.751
1877–81	—	—	—	—	0.736
1882–6	—	—	—	—	0.734
1887–91	—	—	—	—	0.731
1892–6	—	—	—	—	0.740
1897–1901	—	—	—	—	0.743
1902–6	96†	108‡	8.44	—	0.740
1907–11	112	122	10.81	—	0.744
1912–16	119	132	11.92	112	0.733
1917–21	121	134	9.51	107	0.727
1922–6	171	177	15.76	124	0.723
1927–31	239**	279	13.76	130	0.724
1932–6	—	308††	20.47††	—	—

Notes: * 1907–9.   ‡ 1906 only.   ** 1927–8.   † 1905–6.   # 1932–4.   †† 1932–5.

Sources: (1) Shiyebu yinjia wujia taolun weiyuanhui (1936), pp. 4–5; (2) T.R. Bannister (1933b), p. 171; (3) Yang Duanliu (1962), pp. 224–5; (4), (7) and (8) Yinxian tongzhi (1935), *shihuozhi* pp. 210–34; (5) and (6) L.L. Chang (1932), p. 502; (9) Ou Jiluan and Huang Yinpu (1932), p. 282; (10) Zhongguo renmin yinhang Shanghai shi fenhang (1960), pp. 608–9.

of copper that could be extracted from the cash exchangeable for a silver dollar was greater than the amount of raw copper that could be purchased for a silver dollar. As a result, substantial quantities of cash were melted down to obtain the metal. The consequent removal of cash from circulation increased its value relative to the silver dollar.[10] However, the depreciation of the silver dollar relative to copper cash continued only until 1906. Thereafter, a silver dollar exchanged for an increasingly larger number of cash (columns 4 and 5). It was, of course, in the 1890s that the Western mints introduced into China in the 1880s took their toll. They produced cash of a lower copper content, which rapidly displaced the standard cash that was in use. They also produced a new copper subsidiary coinage, which depreciated almost immediately upon its appearance (columns 6 and 7). This was followed by a silver subsidiary coinage which also depreciated (columns 8 and 9). As one should expect, the debasement of the currency ushered in price inflation.[11]

Prices

The prices of rice, silk, cotton, and various other items are given in Tables 4.2 to 4.5, and they serve to illustrate the inflation experienced in various sectors of the economy. These items have been selected to demonstrate the effects of the inflation on staples, exports, and imports, which were not identical.

Table 4.2 lists the price of rice as quoted in silver dollars. It can be seen from this table that the price in Shanghai between 1872 and 1931 increased continuously in four stages. From 1872 to 1896, it ranged between 1.90 and 2.40 dollars per picul. It reached 3.40 dollars in 1896, the year of the Sino-Japanese War, and remained at this level, averaging 3.30 to 3.80 dollars, until 1906. In 1907, it advanced to almost 5.00 dollars per picul, and until 1919 hovered around the annual average of 4.70 or 4.80 dollars. However, it further advanced to 6.50 dollars in 1921, a year marked by severe rice shortage, averaged 8.00 dollars from 1922 to 1926, and 9.20 dollars from 1927 to 1931. The advances were sudden: in 1896 war fever overshadowed dearer rice, but in 1907 food riots followed, and in 1921 considerable public outcry broke out over the suspicion that the increase had been due to exports to Japan. Comparison with Table 4.1 should also show that the years in which the price of rice advanced coincided with sharp changes in the silver/copper exchange rate. In the five years after 1895, the dollar exchanged for 13 per cent less copper cash. In 1907

Table 4.2

The Price of Rice in Shanghai and Guangzhou, 1872–1931

	Shanghai (dollars/picul)[†]	Guangzhou* (dollars/picul)
1872–6	1.90	—
1877–81	2.20	—
1882–6	2.10	—
1887–91	2.10	—
1892–6	2.40	—
1897–1901	3.30	—
1902–6	3.80	—
1907–11	4.70	—
1912–16	4.80	5.80
1917–21	5.30	6.70
1922–6	8.00	9.50
1927–31	9.20	10.55

Notes: * Local rice, to 1929 only.
   [†] Converted from dollars/*shishi* at 150 catties per *shishi*.
Sources: Zou Dafan, Wu Zhiwei, and Xu Wenhui (1965); Zhang Shantu (1930), pp. 101–18.

the depreciation of copper cash was beginning to be felt and the upturn in the silver/copper cash exchange rate was noticeable, while in 1921 the silver subsidiary coinage rapidly depreciated by some 40 to 50 per cent after a rather stable period from 1912 to 1926.[12] Between 1928 and 1931, commodity prices were also inflated by vast silver imports into China, of which more will be said.[13]

The close relationship between prices and currency depreciation is vividly brought out in newspaper reports. Contemporaries noticed the impact of the debasement both on the silver/copper exchange rates and on prices, even though they recognized that price changes might also be due to other causes. The following is a small assortment of these observations.

26 February 1896, Jiangyin [south Jiangsu]: The variation of the cash market has been so continuous and often so rapid that the natives have become much perplexed, the lowest figure being 850 cash per dollar. Up to the 1st of November last almost all prices in the stores were given in dollars and cents, now prices are wholly in cash.[14]

16 April 1908, Xuzhou [north Jiangsu]: This end of the province . . . is still groaning over the depreciated currency. The settled customs and rules for wages that have probably existed for hundreds of years are hopelessly overturned.[15]

4 December 1909, Xuzhou: The depreciation of the copper cash is an ever present subject of conversation among the common people. Most of them do not appreciate the real cause of the rise in price of all the necessities of life. That wages have not risen in keeping with the depreciation in the currency is well known by all. Five years ago one dollar gold exchanged for 1,680 cash. At that time the wage of a carpenter or mason was 140 cash per day. Now gold exchanges for more than 3,100 cash while carpenters get only 160 cash per day. Very little figuring will show how great is their loss. A silver dollar sold then for 840 cash while now it brings 1,420 or more. The carpenters and day labourers in general have been trying to obtain another rise in price, but have been blocked, so I am told, by the officials who are unwilling that the price of labour should rise. The only exception allowed is in the case of stone masons who now get 100 cash per day. The price of silver seems very high in comparison with what it is elsewhere. The Chinese say that the explanation lies in the suppression of the opium crop, which in this part of the country was done thoroughly. Formerly silver came in for the purchase of opium, and the city was known as an exporter of silver. Now silver is always in demand at a premium.[16]

13 May 1910, Suqian [north Jiangsu]: Grain riots continue in the district south of Suchien [Suqian]. There is similar trouble in North Anhui, Wuhehsien [Wuhu] and Kwoyanghsien [Guoyang] . . . The rioters have generally confined themselves to taking grain. The magistrate was present on several occasions and helplessly allowed the robbery, but promptly suppressed the taking of other property . . . It seems to an observer that the real difficulty is in the depreciated currency. The 'foreign mill', buying wheat before harvest, and the yamen runners extorting fees from brick kilns that were 'burning so much of the poor people's fuel', were only incidents. The fact is that the margin between the best wage and a starvation wage has vanished. The people feel that they have a right to live, and feel that they are doing a commendable thing in thus repaying the 'extortionate' holders of the stores of grain.[17]

14 September 1912, Guangzhou: The paper money has been forced upon the merchants by the authorities, but it has struggled in vain to establish its currency, being rejected even at only 70 per cent of its face value in some instances. From this source, many quarrels have arisen.[18]

7 January 1913, Shantou: Our currency, in the matter of the small coins, is a puzzle. The ten and twenty cent pieces from the Canton mint are never regarded as exchangeable at their face value for dollars. In at least one part of the country they will not be accepted at all, their place being taken by coins

from Hunan. In the same region the copper coinage is wholly debased. Elsewhere, there is an admixture of cash good and bad; but there every cash without exception is counterfeit, prices in cash being quoted at twice what they are in Swatow [Shantou]. But no one seems to complain. [19]

3 January 1914, Guangzhou: The condition of the current notes of this province is worse than it has ever been. Today they will only pass at a depreciation of something like 35 per cent. [20]

28 November 1914, Xuzhou: During the first week in November the silver dollar went into hiding and simply could not be coaxed out. The price in coppers had risen rapidly from 131 in early August to the unprecedented figure of 145 ... Then on or about November 8 a few dollars appeared but were eagerly snapped up at the old prices. And by the time that full news of the surrender [of Qingdao to Japan] was in, the hoarders had begun to unload. The price dropped day by day until now it stands at 139 with further drops expected every day.[21]

30 October 1915, Xuzhou: For the first time in many years this northwestern section of Kiangsu [Jiangsu] can boast of a good harvest. The wheat was fairly good, the kaoliang splendid and the bean crop equally good. While no single crop has beaten records, the average is unusual. It is interesting to observe that the adjustment of prices of all kinds, that became inevitable on the introduction of the 10-cash pieces ten years ago, has just about worked itself out in all lines. If there occurs nothing further to depreciate the currency the country will now have a fair chance to recuperate. The depreciation of currency took something over two years to reach its bottom level, and ten years have been occupied in the slow adjustment. For example, wages of carpenters, masons and stone cutters ten years ago were 140 cash a day, now they average 240. Flour averaged thirty- thirty-five cash, now it is rarely below 60.[22]

Stability did not last many years. As noted, prices rose sharply in 1921 amidst rumours of large volumes of rice being exported to Japan. Later reports show that inflation continued.

31 October 1925, Suqian: Prices are terribly high, and the autumn crops in low lying grounds were inundated. People, therefore, are looking forward with fear to famine conditions when the spring comes. The dollar is changing for 2,930 and as the exchange rate rises the price of everything also rises. Coal is very nearly double the price of this time last year. Our last magistrate, who has just left, fixed the price of wheat at 2,500 cash per *teo* [*dou*]; but he too has been succeeded by a new magistrate and the price has gone up.[23]

8 December 1928, Shantou: As if the tremendous number of debased twenty-cent 'silver' coins in circulation here were not enough to stagger a long-

Table 4.3
Silk Prices, 1872–1931 (hk.tls./picul)

	Shanghai White, Hand-reeled	Guangzhou White, Hand-reeled	Shanghai White, Filatured	Guangzhou White, Filatured	Overall Exports White, Filatured
1872–6	404	342	—	—	—
1877–81	328	263	—	—	—
1882–6	294	252	—	—	—
1887–91	312	315	—	—	—
1892–6	319	341	565[†]	367[‡]	422
1897–1901	392	339	669	396	465
1902–6	539	537	795	602	645
1907–11	493	531	822	627	684
1912–16	448*	547*	725*	622*	694
1917–21	—	—	—	—	835
1922–6	—	—	—	—	1121
1927–31	—	—	—	—	923

Notes: * 1912–15.
        † 1894–6.
        ‡ 1895–6.
Sources: MC (1917), p. 204; T.R. Bannister (1933b), p. 189.

suffering public, word has just been received that the Canton authorities have now lifted the ban on the exportation of 'silver' coins from Canton as from December 1. Inverted commas are used advisedly inasmuch as the silver contained in most of the 13th year twenty-cent coins represents only a fraction of what it should amount to . . . The exchange shops buy these debased coins in bulk at a discount of 40 per cent or so and then pass them over the counter, a few at a time, thus deliberately cheating the public.[24]

Many more reports may be cited to illustrate the disturbances caused by the introduction of silver coins in the early 1890s, the copper coins towards 1900, and their continuous debasement.

In a later chapter, it will be explained that until the 1930s Shanghai depended for its supply of rice on its hinterland. The discussion so far, therefore, pertains primarily to commodities wholly produced and consumed in China. The price of rice in Guangzhou, also listed in Table 4.2, suggests that inflation ran the same course there as in Shanghai, even though Southeast Asian rice was imported in vast quantities during the entire period under consideration. However, the price of silk, as one might expect, could have taken a somewhat

Table 4.4

Prices of Imported Commodities, 1882–1931 (hk.tls/picul)

	Rice	Flour	Indian Yarn	Japanese Yarn
1882–6	1.12	3.26	21.63	—
1887–91	1.14	3.04	18.82	—
1892–6	1.58	2.85	18.13	18.93
1897–1901	2.11	3.49	20.04	21.73
1902–6	2.80	3.75	24.56	24.93
1907–11	3.54	4.05	25.96	25.07
1912–16	3.39	4.43	25.88	25.07
1917–21	3.88	4.59	46.94	48.56
1922–6	4.55	4.88	47.81	58.38
1927–31	5.54	5.52	61.95	61.82

Source: T.R. Bannister (1933b), p. 179.

different course, the commodity being produced primarily for export and so its price being determined to a large extent by the overseas market. The relevant data are presented in Table 4.3.

Table 4.3 gives the prices in Haikwan taels of hand-reeled and filature silk in Shanghai and Guangzhou from 1872 to 1916 as well as overall prices from 1892 to 1931. The main trend of development should be clear: firstly, throughout the period from 1882 to 1926, silk prices rose steadily, and subsequently declined; and secondly, as filature silk commanded a higher price than hand-reeled silk, the shift in the market from the hand-reeled to the filature variety (see Chapter 6) meant that, on the whole, the unit price commanded by silk continued to increase, even when the price of filature silk declined temporarily between 1912 and 1916. However, to understand the implications of this table, it is also important to take into consideration the complications posed by currency conversions, both from Haikwan taels into US dollars, and from Haikwan taels into copper cash or silver subsidiary coins. From 1892 to 1926, the price of silk in US dollars rose 2.46 times, closely matching the increase of 2.68 times as reckoned in Haikwan taels. From 1922 to 1931, when the decline as reckoned in Haikwan taels amounted to 18 per cent, its equivalent price as reckoned in US dollars dropped by 42 per cent. This is to say that silk prices within China had been protected substantially by currency depreciation. Within the silk-producing areas, copper cash was more commonly used in the nineteenth century and silver subsidiary coins in the 1920s. Between 1892 and 1911, as the Haikwan tael price went up by 62 per cent, its price in copper cash advanced by only 43 per cent. Between 1902 and 1926, as the Haikwan tael price advanced by 74 per cent, the price in silver subsidiary coins advanced by 85 per cent. From 1922 to 1931, the Haikwan tael price dropped by only 18 per cent, and the silver subsidiary coinage price by 19 per cent. In other words, in terms of spending power, the income of silk producers derived from each unit weight of silk sold between 1902 and 1926 almost doubled.

As would be expected, the prices of imports also rose as silver depreciated, and this trend is shown in Table 4.4. The increase in the price of imported rice (395 per cent between 1882 and 1931) fully matched that in Shanghai (338 per cent in the same period; see Table 4.2).[25] Price increases in imported flour and yarn came only in the 1890s, although the silver depreciation had begun two decades earlier. Reference to Table 2.2 will show that the increase in the price of imported flour between 1900 and 1929 was accompanied by increasing Chinese exports of the commodity. In the same period, substantial progress was also made in the production of machine-spun yarn within China.[26]

Tables 4.2, 4.3, and 4.4 have been drawn up primarily from data gathered in the cities. They may be checked against Table 4.5, consisting of statistics gathered by Zhang Liluan in the 1930s from shop accounts in six market towns in Wujin county, south Jiangsu.[27] The table shows that the price of rice in these market towns followed closely its price in Shanghai (Table 4.2), although it was marginally lower.[28] The prices of salt and kerosene, that would have been imported into Wujin, rose by a proportion similar to the rise in the price of rice between 1907 and 1929, the years for which data are available. The price of yarn rose less sharply than the prices of other products shown in the table. By the 1910s, yarn was produced in Shanghai, and would have provided a cheaper alternative to imported yarn. Land prices rose considerably more than the other items.[29]

Zhang's original report was designed to compare changes in the prices of commodities purchased by farmers and those sold by them. By comparing statistical averages, he came to the conclusion that prices received by farmers rose less sharply than prices paid by them up to approximately 1920, and thereafter the trend reversed until 1930. While a reversal in the terms of trade for the farming sector in the 1930s is well documented, Zhang's argument concerning the 1920s is misleading. In fact, without doubt, he underrated the

Table 4.5
Prices in Wujin Market Towns, 1892–1931

	Rice (dol./picul)	Salt (dol./catty)	Yarn (dol./bale)	Kerosene (dol./tin)	Land (dol./mu)
1892–6	2.60*	—	—	—	—
1897–1901	2.90	—	—	—	—
1902–6	3.40	—	—	—	—
1907–11	4.30	4.40	3.60	1.20	—
1912–16	4.60	5.00	3.50	1.50	44.10
1917–21	4.70	6.10	5.40	1.40	56.20
1922–6	7.50	6.70	5.40	1.80	86.10
1927–31	8.60	9.90	5.30	3.50	141.70

Notes: * 1894–6.
Source: Zhang Liluan (1933), pp. 213–15.

improvement of farm income from rising prices, for in his calculations he had not weighted the various items of income and expenditure according to the farm budget. The 63 items that made up his expenditure index, for instance, included many that would not have occupied a large proportion of overall expenditure. It should also be noted that his data pertained to a primarily cereal-growing county: mulberry and silk were not counted in his income index. The averages, in fact, cloud the most outstanding feature of his statistics, that is, that the price of rice produced in Wujin increased more rapidly than most other items noted and with it the price of land advanced. That land value should increase is an indication that farming had become more, not less, profitable.[30]

The continuous inflation from the 1890s to the 1920s was broken towards the end of the 1920s. In the first place, the price of silk, under competition from rayon, had declined in the international market.[31] With the onset of the world depression, from 1929, it reached almost total collapse. Chinese silk that sold for US$ 6.43 per pound in 1926 fetched US$ 4.96 in 1929, and US$ 1.53 in 1933. Prices continued to decline into 1934, and only slowly recovered in 1935 and 1936.[32] Secondly, the onset of the depression affected the prices of other commodities, and the experience of Jiangsu and Guangdong was further aggravated by the movement of silver abroad. Some indications of these trends are provided in Table 4.6.

As Table 4.6 shows, the price of silver in US dollars declined rapidly between 1928 and 1931. As it declined on the international

Table 4.6

Silver Movements and Prices, 1928–1937

	Price of Silver* (US cents per ounce)	Movement of Silver (net)	
		Shanghai into Country ($ mill.)	Imports into China ($ mill.)
1928	60.10	n.a.	160
1929	52.00	58	159
1930	38.80	32	101
1931	31.50	53	68
1932	27.60	−143	n.a.
1933	34.80	−82	−14
1934	48.80	n.a.	−280
1935	65.40	n.a.	−289
1936	47.30	n.a.	−290
1937	45.80	n.a.	−398

Notes: * Average of high and low prices in New York.
† For Shanghai and Guangzhou, 1926 = 100; for Nanjing rice, 1922 = 100; for Nanjing general, 1930 = 100.

Sources: C.F. Remer (1933), p. 203; Shiyebu yinjia wujia taolun weiyuanhui (1936), p. 53; Dickens H. Leavens (1939), pp. 212 and 303; 'Index numbers of wholesale prices' (1937), p. 722; 'Wholesale price indexes in Canton' (1935), p. 217; MC, Nanjing 1922–31, p. 625.

market, China, the last major silver-standard country at the time, received vast imports of the metal from abroad. The increase in the quantity of silver in circulation, not only in Shanghai, but also in rural areas, for a substantial quantity was transported inland, brought about a sharp increase in wholesale prices. The general price index in Shanghai rose from 101.7 points in 1928 to 126.7 points in 1931, the price index for cereals, amidst reports of poor harvests, climbing from 89.6 points in 1928 to 110.3 in 1930, and declining to 94.4 in 1931. The price of rice in Nanjing went from 147.5 points in 1928 to 236 in 1930, and dropped to 214.3 in 1931, while in Guangzhou it went from 97.6 points in 1928 to 113.4 in 1930, and 102.1 in 1931. The silver inflow into the country did not last. By 1932, as the international price of silver reached its nadir, and as Chinese exports, especially silk, no longer fetched silver from abroad, the flow of silver into China stopped abruptly. By 1933, the price of silver had begun to improve. By mid-1934 the United States Silver Purchase Act firmly re-established the price of silver, and it was thus exported in large quantities from

	Price Indices in Major Cities[†]				
	Shanghai General	Shanghai Cereals	Nanjing Rice	Nanjing General	Guangzhou Rice
1928	101.7	89.6	147.5	n.a.	97.6
1929	104.5	97.2	205.0	n.a.	103.5
1930	114.5	110.3	236.0	n.a.	113.4
1931	126.7	94.4	214.3	106.1	102.1
1932	112.4	81.7	n.a.	100.8	95.5
1933	103.8	69.6	n.a.	92.1	84.2
1934	97.1	69.1	n.a.	80.6	74.9
1935	96.4	80.0	n.a.	80.3	n.a.
1936	108.2	92.7	n.a.	84.8	n.a.
1937	n.a.	n.a.	n.a.	n.a.	n.a.

China. The movement of silver into and out of China, and then into and out of the Chinese countryside into Shanghai, brought momentous results.[33]

These results will be further explored in Chapter 6, but a broad view can again be given in terms of prices. Reference to Table 4.6 will show that the Shanghai general price index dropped from 112.4 points in 1932 to 103.8 points in 1933, 97.1 in 1934, and 96.4 in 1935. As Chapter 6 will show, rice produced in the Changjiang delta had by now come under foreign competitition and the price index for cereals dropped from 81.7 points in 1932 to 69.1 in 1934; thereafter, it rose to 80.0 points in 1935, the year in which protective import tariffs were imposed. In Nanjing, the general price index decreased from 100.8 points in 1932 to 80.6 in 1934, and rose to 84.8 in 1936. In Guangzhou, the price of rice dropped from 95.5 points in 1932 to 74.9 in 1934. A general depression had set in, which was well noted in the contemporary literature.

Rent, Usury Interest, and Tax

Statistics are abundant on the issues of rent, usury interest, and tax, and, as noted, they are all highly problematic. Contemporaries who collected data on these issues accepted too readily reported statistics, and did not take into consideration the institutional arrangements under which rent, interest, or tax were collected. Some of these arrangements will be examined in Chapters 7 and 8, so this section will be restricted to the course of monetary changes. However, it is useful to remember that even in the most commercialized areas, many transactions were conducted without the use of money, and the effects of monetary changes on such matters as rent, interest, and tax were, therefore, limited.[34]

In Jiangsu and Guangdong, between 1870 and 1937, rent was paid either in kind or in money. Payment in money, however, was common practice over only small portions of Jiangsu and Guangdong. As late as the 1930s, J.L. Buck reported that in 20 localities surveyed by him in Jiangsu, over 80 per cent of the rented farms in 16 localities paid rent in kind, and in 7 localities surveyed in Guangdong, close to 100 per cent of the rented farms of two localities, 70 per cent of two more, and 50 per cent of one, paid rent in kind. Rent payment in kind was a long-established practice, and it did not give way easily to rent payment in cash .[35]

Where rent was paid in kind, it was paid either as a fixed measure of a crop, or as a share of the produce. In either case, village practice was to maintain the appearance that acknowledged standards were applied without change. Rent increases under such arrangements were not obvious. Rent could be raised, for instance, by converting a share crop rent into a fixed crop rent. It could also be raised by reducing the allowance normally made to take account of unfavourable harvest conditions. It was not uncommonly raised by changing to a larger grain measure in rent collection. None of these changes is easily detectable in any systematic way in historical records. We have isolated examples of the change-over from share-cropping to fixed crop rent but no evidence that the change was widespread. As for the reduction of the allowance for rent payment, because contemporary surveyors did not distinguish between the quota rate and actual payment, short of reconstructing actual rent received from landlords' accounts, we are now no longer in a position to describe the trend of its development. I doubt if it could have varied systematically over the several decades from 1870 to the 1930s, for the actual amount collected as rent was less a function of the harvest than of active negotiation between landlord and tenant. Where the landlords came to be more efficient in rent collection, they changed over to collection in cash, and this change is well documented.[36]

Rent could be collected in cash through a process of fixed crop rent commutation, or through a fixed money rent. Commuted rent was apparently uncommon in Jiangsu and Guangdong before the mid-nineteenth century.[37] In the past where money had been charged, it was charged as a fixed rent, and usually only on land held by institutions such as charity bodies or county schools. Fixed money rent continued into the twentieth century. However, after the mid-nineteenth century, first in the neighbourhood of Suzhou, and then in a wider area, the fixed crop rent was commuted to cash, according to a scale that was published every year by the landlords' associations, often with the approval of the local magistrates. The rates of commutation enforced in Suzhou from the 1870s to the 1920s can be established quite clearly from rent-collection records that have survived and are summarized in Table 4.7. The increase in rent introduced by changes in the commutation rates, as can be seen, quite clearly accompanied the changes in the price of rice in Shanghai.[38] Because commuted values for rent are given in copper cash before 1912 and in silver dollars thereafter, and cash depreciated considerably in the 1920s, standardizing the commutation values in terms of copper cash in Table 4.7 gives quite a deceptive impression of rent increase. Although we know that rent was commuted at a rate that was higher than the price of rice, it none the less increased only slightly more rapidly than the price of rice.[39]

As Chapter 8 will argue, the spread of rent commutation was related to the growth of more efficient means of rent collection by the landlords. Before 1911, such rents were enforced primarily within the Suzhou vicinity. In the 1920s and 1930s, they were reported in Shanghai, Kunshan, Songjiang, Wuxi, Wujin, Yixing, Haimen, and Jingjiang, all in southern Jiangsu. In Changshu, it was noted in 1934 that the change had come within the previous ten years. In Wujiang, Fei Xiaotong reported that the rate decided by the landlords' union was not the market price of rice but an arbitrary rate. One suspects, however, that with the spread of the practice of commuting rent to cash, the commutation rate was not always enforced with the landlords' collective backing as in Suzhou. In Wuxi, for example, where commutation was reported to be less common than in Suzhou or Changshu, commutation rates were decided by individual landlords,

Table 4.7
Rent and Tax in Southern Jiangsu, 1872–1929

	Rent (cash/shi)	Tax (cash/shi)	Price of Rice (dol./picul)
1872–6	2,243	3,632	1.90
1877–81	2,402[1]	3,492	2.20
1882–6	n.a.	3,432	2.10
1887–91	n.a.	3,392	2.10
1892–6	2,202[2]	3,752	2.40
1897–1901	2,825[3]	4,132	3.30
1902–6	3,292	4,912	3.80
1907–11	5,463[4]	6,923*	4.70
1912–16	5,970*	6,694*	4.80
1917–21	5,751[6]*	6,752[5]*	5.30
1922–6	11,912[7]*	10,368[5]*	8.00
1927–9	26,221[8]*	n.a.	8.80

Notes: 1. 1877–9.
   2. 1893.
   3. 1899–1901.
   4. 1907–10.
   5. Excluding surcharges levied on grain tax.
   6. 1917–18.
   7. 1922–3.
   8. 1927–8.
   * Estimated from quotations given in silver dollars.
Sources: Ihara Hirosuke (1967), p. 99; Muramatsu Yūji (1970), p. 726; *Chuansha xianzhi* (1936), p. 8/23b; *Shanghai xian xuzhi* (1918), pp. 6/20b–21a; Zou Dafan, Wu Zhiwei, and Xu Wenhui (1965).

while in Kunshan, Qiao Qiming's report in 1926 — while the price of rice was still rising — noted that landlords demanded payment in cash when the price of rice was high, and payment in grain when it was low.[40]

In Guangdong, Chen Hansheng writing in 1936 noted that rent commutation was spreading, but it is clear from his account that the practice was as yet uncommon.[41]

It has to be stressed that rent commutation was enforced only in those areas where landlords had become better organized. The introduction of cash cropping was in itself an insufficient condition to bring about the practice. Even in Wuxi, the village of Lishe charged a fixed crop rent from paddy fields and a fixed money rent from mulberry land.[42] In the Shanghai suburbs, where cotton farming dominated and rent was paid in cash even on paddy land, it was charged as a fixed sum.[43] The reclamation companies that encouraged commercial cropping accepted a rent that was known as the 'guaranteed three piculs' (*yibao sandan*), which consisted of a picul of cotton, one of wheat, and one of beans for every 1,000 *bu* (approximately 4.16 *mu*). Some companies demanded a fixed money rent that was paid after the early harvest of supplementary food crops and a share of the crops after the second harvest of cotton. Only in the late 1920s and 1930s did they accept commuted rent in the place of the crop for the second harvest.[44] In Guangdong, fixed money rent was the rule in the silk-growing parts of Shunde county. It was commonly accepted in Zhongshan, Xinhui, Nanhai and Taishan, counties that either produced substantial quantities for export or received considerable income from overseas remittances. Elsewhere, fixed money rent was found in those areas that produced for export, even when they fell within counties in which payment in kind was common. Such areas included parts of Chao'an given to fruit growing, of Guangning to bamboo, or Panyu to fruit, peanuts, or vegetables.[45]

The records are unclear, but it seems that as commercial crops became more common, commuted rent took root in areas where long-term or permanent tenancy predominated, while fixed money rent was demanded where tenants on short-term leases were required to pay their rent before harvest. It is not totally clear under what circumstances these short-term leases were introduced; the reports that note the varieties of tenancy describe them as alternatives to the down-payment (*yazu*) that usually implied the transfer of some form of permanent tenancy.[46] Payment of rent before cultivation, like a down-payment, protected the landlord from the risk of rent default. However, unlike a down-payment, it did not confer recognition of long-term tenure and effectively bypassed the right of the tenant to a reduction of the rent in the event of poor harvest.[47] Lack of information prevents a detailed discussion of the practice. It should, none the less, be noted that this form of rent collection became prevalent at a time when farmers were reported to be selling their crops before harvest. A speculative and eager market for export crops, such as silk or cotton, made it attractive for agents to contract with farmers for the purchase of their crops at an early date. The reports of the 1920s and 1930s unanimously condemned such practices as varieties of usury, but that should not obscure the possibility that payment of rent in advance of harvest would have complemented the sale of the crop before harvest.[48]

Something should also be said about the level of rent, but this is a thorny subject that should not be considered in isolation from farm income and expenditure patterns as they evolved in the late nineteenth and early twentieth centuries. The issue is much more complex than either contemporaries or later students have recognized. In general, it may be said with some confidence that over most of Jiangsu and Guangdong, a nominal crop rent prevailed that amounted to approximately half the produce of the major grain crops. The rate applied whether rent was collected as a share of the produce, or as a fixed amount of the grain crop. In the richer areas of south Jiangsu, this fixed rate amounted commonly to one *shi* of grain per *mu*, and in the Zhujiang delta, to two or more *shi*. Occasional references during the late Qing and the Republic indicate that a reduction of 20 per cent in this nominal rate was quite common, and no change in the practice of reducing rent at the time of harvest may be detected in the records where rent continued to be collected on the basis of this fixed crop rent.[49] Rent increase followed commutation as the price of rice increased, as Table 4.7 has shown.

In the cases where a fixed money rent was paid, evidently, the level of the rent cannot be meaningfully interpreted unless it can be equated to the rural prices of essential commodities, such as grain or the principal cash crops. Unfortunately, the reports that are available do not always provide information on prices at the localities where the fixed money rents are reported. From the isolated cases that can be reconstructed, it seems, none the less, that fixed money rents varied enormously. It is clear from gazetteer reports, for instance, that where it was charged on land that was owned by public institutions, it was quoted at a rate that was substantially lower than the crop rent charged on privately owned land.[50] On the other hand, the Tonghai Cultivation Company in Jiangsu sought unsuccessfully to introduce it at a level that was designed to reflect the value of traditionally accepted fixed crop rents in the region within which it reclaimed land. At the first meeting of its directors in 1911, it was recognized that the 'guaranteed three piculs', the traditional crop rent, amounted to between 6,000 and 12,000 cash for each 1,000 *bu* of land, equivalent to about 4 *mu*. The traditional fixed money rent in the region, however, amounted to only between 3,200 and 6,000 cash. The company adopted an incremental rent to be collected after the autumn harvest that varied from 2,200 cash for the first year of cultivation to 8,800 cash for the eighth year and thereafter. This autumn rent was further supplemented by a spring rent that amounted to approximately 0.60 dollars per 1,000 *bu* in the late 1920s or early 1930s.[51]

The same unevenness may be detected in the fixed money rent in Guangdong. In fact, Chen Hansheng summed up the situation quite precisely:

Where the rent in grain is prevailing, cash rent is not so high as rent in grain. For, in such a place, cash rent is collected only from non-irrigated lands, of lower productivity; the amount of this cash rent is sometimes 15 per cent less than the rent in grain. On the other hand, where the rent in cash is more common, as in the districts of Pan-yu, Sin-hwei, Nan-hai, Shun-teh, and Chung-shan [Panyu, Xinhui, Nanhai, Shunde, Zhongshan], the rent in grain is lower than the cash rent, sometimes by 10 per cent.[52]

Chen's observation concerning the prevalence of fixed money rent on non-irrigated land is borne out by the surveys of the Zhongshan University School of Agriculture in the 1920s.[53] His own research shows that money rent became more popular in counties that adopted cash crops. As non-irrigated land tended to be low-yielding, while cash crops were adopted for their profit, it would seem that the fixed money rent was found either as a remnant of a traditional practice which offered a lower rent, or was introduced with cash cropping. It would be reasonable to argue, therefore, that in areas where fixed crop rent prevailed, fixed money rent was collected at below the crop rent, and where the money rent was prevalent, it was above it.

Price fluctuations introduced complications into contemporary reports on fixed money rents. In the heyday of the silk industry, mulberry land in Shunde fetched a high rent. In Howard and Buswell's survey conducted in 1924, rent per *mu* was quoted at between 12 and 40 dollars,[54] at which time the median price of local rice in Guangzhou was quoted at 9.52 dollars, and Guangdong exported 42,000 piculs of silk worth 59.7 million Haikwan taels. At the time of the Zhongshan University School of Agriculture's survey in 1927, the rent of good mulberry land was quoted at 15 to 30 dollars per *mu*,[55] while economic conditions had not substantially changed. The median price of local rice in Guangzhou for that year was quoted at 11.22 dollars, and the silk export stood at 43,000 piculs, worth 60 million Haikwan taels. In 1934, when the median price of local rice in Guangzhou stood at 8.00 dollars, and silk exports at 27,600 piculs worth only 9.5 million dollars *fabi* (approximately 6.10 million Haikwan taels),[56] Chen Hansheng reported that rent on mulberry land had dropped 50 per cent from the commonly charged 20 to 25 dollars per *mu*.[57] In terms of the median price of local rice in Guangzhou, these figures imply that in 1924 an equivalent of 1.3 to 4.2 piculs was charged, in 1927, 1.3 to 2.7 piculs, and in 1934, 1.3 to 1.6 piculs. In terms of the price of rice, therefore, rent charged on mulberry land remained remarkably constant. Fixed money rent on mulberry land, it would seem, followed quite closely the trends of commodity prices.[58]

Less material is available on the rent charged on cotton land in Jiangsu, but the little that is reported indicates a fairly low rate of rent being demanded where it was collected as a fixed sum of money. In Haimen and Chongming, where rent was at its highest in the 1930s, 56 dollars was charged for 2,000 bu (8.32 mu). At the time, the income derived from cotton reaped on this much land amounted to 150 dollars. Several years later, the cotton income had declined to 120 dollars, and the rent to 52 dollars. This would have been equivalent to a fixed crop rent that amounted to one-third of the main crop, a low rent by average southern Jiangsu standards.[59]

In short, it is highly doubtful if payment of rent in money, as a fixed sum or a commuted rate, substantially raised the rent beyond increases that might be justified by increases in commodity prices.[60] As commuted rent was charged on land that was used for paddy-farming, it would seem that it led to steeper rent increases than the fixed money rent that was introduced into profitable export-oriented cash crops.

Closely related to the question of tenancy and rent is the equally complex subject of usury. Again, like tenancy and rent, any detailed examination of the subject is seriously hampered by the lack of precision in the reports of the 1920s and 1930s. In their enthusiasm to condemn usury, contemporary commentators seldom made allowance for the different social implications of different forms of rural credit. They noted that farmers borrowed for incidental celebrations such as weddings and funerals, that they borrowed in times of bad harvest, or to tie over the period before the grain harvest when the supply from the previous harvest had been exhausted, that they borrowed also to pay their rent, to buy seeds, or to pay their gambling debts, that they obtained credit from shops, and that not a few received loan subsidies from their ancestral trusts. However, the reports left it totally unclear if credit extended by relatives, fellow villagers, usurers, shops, money-lending societies, and lineage trusts was retrieved by the exertion of similar pressures. It is not clear if all these different bodies demanded collateral for loans, or the same type of collateral, if loans were repaid, or if mortgages were frequently foreclosed. At a time when prices were increasing, a rise in interest rates should only be expected, but from the reports of the 1920s and 1930s, it is unclear if the interest charged departed substantially from the 30 per cent per annum that was commonly required in the late nineteenth century or earlier. These reports demonstrate that a high proportion of farmers had borrowed, but leave us with little whereby to appreciate why credit was extended to them and at what risk it was extended.

The straits of many among the farming population of Jiangsu and Guangdong need not be underrated for us to see that a substantial volume of short-term credit was by tradition integrated into the regular workings of the rural economy. It should not be far-fetched even to argue that much of it was an extension of rural savings. Farmers did not keep spare cash in their own houses, and the same shops and money societies that accepted savings offered credit. The one report that we have of redemption at pawnshops — the report relates to Yixing county in south Jiangsu — shows that in 1931 and 1933, 80 to 85 per cent of jewellery pawned was redeemed.[61] Some long-term mortgages may also be explained as well-established economic practices. The evidence is overwhelming that farmers who sold land seldom sold it outright. Instead, it was sold with the provision that it might be redeemed. The practice of selling land with a provision for redemption comes close to and has often been interpreted as mortgaging, but it should be clear that much of the land so mortgaged was never redeemed. Much of what appears as land mortgaging in the reports of the 1920s and 1930s should not, therefore, be considered to be substantially different from land sale, the act of mortgaging being part of the process of selling.[62]

A major part of money lending was also made up of credit extended for trade. In Wuxi, grain sellers loaned rice to silkworm rearers in the spring on condition that it would be repaid after the sale of the first cocoon crop.[63] In Nantong (transitional Jiangsu) and Tongshan (north Jiangsu), machine-spun yarn was loaned at interest.[64] Sugar-cane dealers in Guangzhou loaned cane seedlings, fertilizer, bamboo supports for the cane during the windy season, and money for farmers to pay their rent. In Chao'an, dealers in Shantou and the 'leading families' of the county granted loans to growers of mandarin oranges two to three years before the trees bore fruit. In Maoming, pig dealers loaned money on the credit of pigs raised.[65] Chen Hansheng, who noted some of these practices in his report, summed up the conditions for usury very perceptively:

Evidently, there is a limit to what may be pawned by the peasants, and that is why, when these people are too poor, usury itself cannot flourish. To continue rural exploitation, usury capital must work hand in glove with its twin brother, trade capital. In Kwangtung [Guangdong], numerous dealers of unhusked rice, of fruit, of sugar, and of pigs, extort from the peasantry a huge profit through both price and interest.[66]

And he continued on the next page:

The peasant in Kwangtung runs to the bosom of the usurer as a child might run to his grandmother, asking for a favour, helpless and naive. He runs to him not only with his agricultural products such as rice seedlings, unhusked rice, mulberries and cocoons, pigs and cows, and fruit of all kinds as securities, but also often with his daily necessities, like clothing, furniture, and the house in which he lives. In every village, there are always several families pawning out their agricultural implements. In almost every district there is the pawning as well as selling of children . . . Only as a last stand in the desperate struggle, do the owner peasants resort to mortgaging their land. Personal properties can be replaced, more children can be bred; but land is hard to get back once it has been lost.[67]

Studies in the 1920s and 1930s acknowledged the importance of usury in the provision of trading credit, but bemoaned the high interest demanded by creditors. When the Farmers' Bank was established in 1927 in Jiangsu with the avowed purpose of assisting the peasants to bypass the usurers, it was found that one of the major operational problems was that farmers were unwilling to mortgage their land, and that they had little in the way of household property that could be offered as security. The solution adopted was to permit peasants to mortgage their crops and their draught cattle.[68] The moral dilemma of usury was insoluble: when the household was the work unit, no distinction could be made between its operating capital and its sustenance.

Some portions of the money that found its way into usury originated in the city. It is important, however, to set the discussion on usury and rural indebtedness in the context of the 1930s. In the 1920s and early 30s, with increasing prosperity in the rural areas and silver flowing in from the cities and from abroad, credit had probably become more readily available. The sudden contraction in 1934 would, therefore, have been quite noticeable and painful, and it was this that would have linked the sense of crisis in the countryside to rural indebtedness.[69]

Yet to be considered is the level of rural taxes, an issue shrouded in as much complexity as rent or usury interest. Like rent, tax might be raised by pegging it to a level determined by the rate between silver and copper cash or other forms of the currency. Unlike rent, in the late Qing and the Republic, surcharges might be imposed by fiat. Again, as in rent collection, in addition to official dues, tax collectors demanded fees that were not included in the official scales. In tax collection, such extra-legal charges were common and substantial, but quite incalculable. However, as these charges were heavy even in earlier years, and as contemporaries from the 1870s on did not make as serious an issue of them as of official increases, it is likely that, as a percentage of the official taxes, they were not increased beyond traditionally accepted levels.[70]

Table 4.7 provides the rate of commutation for the grain tribute that was charged in the counties of Chuansha and Shanghai and reflects the rate of exchange commonly demanded in southern Jiangsu. I have chosen the rate of commutation for the grain tribute rather than that for the land tax for inclusion in the table because it was the higher of the two. However, it can be seen from the table that its increase followed closely that of the price of rice: compared to the level of 1872–6, by 1922–6 the price of rice in dollars had increased by 5.3 times while the grain tax commutation calculated in copper cash had increased by only 2.9 times. Of this kind of comparison, more will be said in the next section, but it should be noted that contemporaries who complained of tax increases seldom made these simple comparisons.[71]

Much more intangible is the question of the increase due to new impositions. These began with the *lijin* (inland transit tax) introduced during the mid-nineteenth century rebellions, and were expanded by a series of supplementary taxes introduced from the last years of the Qing that included a house tax, a fuel tax, charges for the issue of public documents, a rice tax, a commercial brokerage tax, and a meat and wine tax. It should be noticed that most of these taxes were imposed on the city and town population.[72] The charges that were tied to the land tax were initially quite small, and when they were increased in the 1910s and 1920s, they barely made up for tax losses incurred by depreciation, since the commutation rates remained unchanged from the levels of the early years of the Republic (see Table 4.7). A study into supplementary charges in Juyong county (south Jiangsu), for instance, shows that while these charges amounted to 5 per cent of the standard taxes in 1911, they had risen only to 12 per cent in 1923 (in which period the price of rice had risen by 70 per cent.)[73]

Supplementary charges increased significantly from roughly 1926 onwards. The increase that was imposed varied from county to county. In Chuansha (south Jiangsu), it was due to the collection of taxes in advance that began in 1924. The advance of 50 cents for each *shi* of rice was to be repaid by that of 1.50 dollars in 1925, and then by 3.00 dollars in 1926 and 1927, and by 1.50 dollars again in 1928.[74] In other counties in Jiangsu, between 1928 and 1931, additions of up to three times the scheduled tax were collected.[75] In Gaoyao (Guangdong), under various pretexts, 30 per cent was added to the land tax in 1924, 15 per cent in 1925, and more than 30 per cent again in 1928.[76]

These various tax increases should also be considered with attempts to register cultivated land primarily in Republican years. In the middle of the nineteenth century, the turbulence of the rebellions destroyed long-standing land registration records at many county *yamen*, in both Jiangsu and Guangdong. The decline in the amount of land tax collected and the shift towards an increase in revenue from import duties was an indication of the central government's inability to enforce its land tax demands. By the last years of the Qing, some effort was made to register newly reclaimed land in the Zhujiang delta. Several attempts were made for the same purpose in early Republican years, even though no government was sufficiently powerful to enforce detailed registration. In the late 1920s and in the 1930s, however, efforts at registration were apparently much more successful. They add corroboration to the impression that land tax might actually have declined in the late Qing, increased slowly in the early years of the Republic, and then risen sharply from the late 1920s on.

A Comparative Perspective

For a comparative perspective of changes in prices, rent, and tax from the 1870s to the 1930s, Table 4.8 summarizes the statistics presented in Tables 4.2 to 4.7. The table demonstrates the rapid increase in price of the two major crops sold by farmers of southern Jiangsu and the Zhujiang delta, that is, rice and silk. The price of rice increased from 40 to 183 points (4.5 times) between 1872 and 1931 as reckoned in silver dollars, and that of silk, after an initial decline from 90 to 70 points (20 per cent) between 1872 and 1891, recovered to 110 points by 1911, and thereafter increased to 162 points (47 per cent since 1911) by 1926. The prices of imported commodities also increased substantially in the same period. The prices of machine-spun yarn and kerosene, however, both fell behind the increase in the prices of rice and silk up to 1926. Rent calculated in copper coins increased at a slightly faster rate than the price of rice between 1872 and 1926, but fell behind it when reckoned in silver. It was between 1927 and 1931 that rent increased at a rate that was noticeably faster than that of the price of rice.[77] Land tax commutation also rose, but much more slowly than rent or the price of rice. Until 1926, it is doubtful if the pattern

Table 4.8
Relative Prices, Southern Jiangsu, 1872–1931

	Rice*	Silk†	Silk‡	Yarn#	Kerosene#	Rent		Tax		Land#	
						1	2	1	2	1	2
1872–6	40	90	—	—	—	38	37	54	51	—	—
1877–81	46	73	—	—	—	40	41	52	54	—	—
1882–6	44	66	—	—	—	n.a.	—	51	52	—	—
1887–91	44	70	—	—	—	n.a.	—	51	55	—	—
1892–6	50	71	61	—	—	37	41	56	62	—	—
1897–1901	69	88	67	—	—	47	59	62	78	—	—
1902–6	79	120	93	—	—	55	71	73	95	—	—
1907–11	98	110	99	103	80	92	99	103	111	—	—
1912–16	100	100	100	100	100	100	100	100	100	100	100
1917–21	110	—	120	154	93	96	95	101	100	128	127
1922–6	167	—	162	154	120	200	129	155	100	302	195
1927–31	183	—	133	151	233	439	202	—	—	696	321

Notes: * Shanghai only.
    † Handreel only.
    ‡ Overall prices.
    # Wujin.
    1. As reckoned in copper currency.
    2. As reckoned in silver currency.
Source: Tables 4.2–4.7

would have been substantially different had supplementary charges also been counted. The high profitability of land holding is apparent in the price of land, which rose from 100 points during the 1912–16 period to 321 during the 1927–31 period.[78]

Comparative prices are difficult to ascertain for the period from 1931 to 1937. Table 4.9 presents statistics that were reported from Wujin county alone, but the depression that they indicate was felt in all of the export-oriented areas of Jiangsu and Guangdong. Prices received by farmers between 1930 and 1934 dropped by 42 per cent (from 217 to 125 points). Among the items that farmers sold, rice alone halved (dropping from 240 to 117 points) in the same period. The prices of goods paid by farmers did not decline by nearly as much, the difference between the high of 1930 (186 points) and the low of 1934 (140 points) being only 25 per cent. Land values responded quickly to price changes, dropping 48 per cent (from 410 to 214 points) between 1930 and 1933, but taxes did not, for they dropped only 22 per cent (from 156 to 121 points) between 1930 and 1933, and

Table 4.9

Relative Prices, Wujin, Southern Jiangsu, 1930–1936*

	Rice	Prices Received by Farmers[†]	Prices Paid by Farmers	Tax	Land
1930	240	217	186	156	410
1931	168	177	177	147	347
1932	163	165	170	156	328
1933	117	125	142	121	214
1934	150	152	140	171	223
1935	182	172	151	107	248
1936	165	179	166	—	—

Notes: * Rice and land prices and taxes are quoted in dollars in the sources, with no apparent adjustment for monetary changes in late 1935. Units for prices received and prices paid by farmers are not specified, but by the 1930s these prices were probably also quoted in dollars. The base period (value = 100) for these figures is 1910–14.

    † For cereals only.

Sources: Lewis and Wang (1936a), p. 87; Ko (1937), Raeburn and Ko (1937a), pp. 255–6.

31 per cent (107 points) between 1930 and 1935. This must have been a period of considerable hardship, following close behind a long period of increasing prosperity.[79]

5
Rural Marketing

THE question must be asked as to how inflation that was generated in the cities could be transmitted to the rural economy. The answer depends very much on one's view of the operation of the rural markets.[1] The author of a study on Huaxian (Guangdong) published in 1935, for instance, stated:

The merchants can manipulate prices, because each market might be separated from another by more than 10 *li*; and the market meets once every five days, so if goods are not sold on one market day, the seller has to wait for five days to go to another market farther away. But most farmers selling grain have urgent needs, and they have to sell even if prices are low.[2]

The passage implies that operators in a market could control prices with little regard for competition from other markets. This view was quite commonly held by the writers of the 1920s and 1930s, and if true, must mean that farmers might not have benefited directly from price increases in the cities.

To understand this view of the restrictive rural market, it is necessary to appreciate that much of the social research of the 1920s and 1930s was directed at government policies, and the research on rural marketing and credit in Jiangsu, in particular, supported the provision of rural credit through co-operatives backed by the National Government and the newly established Jiangsu Farmers' Bank. The reports sought to demonstrate the weakness of the cultivator in the rural markets: he had to sell when prices were low and buy when they were high, and buying on credit, he mortgaged much valued property and paid a high rate of interest. If credit could be provided by government, he would have been in a much better position to take advantage of market forces. Valuable as these reports were as contemporary social criticisms, they were written from a point of view that supported an institution extraneous to local marketing, and they paid little attention to indigenous ideas or practices. To find out if rural marketing was dominated by a privileged minority, or if in a relatively unrestrictive way it provided opportunities for competition among the majority of producers, it is necessary to ask who, among the rural producers, traded at the market, what institutions were employed in rural marketing, and how well integrated the markets were with the cities. It is the object of this chapter to explore these issues.[3]

Sources for a Marketable Surplus

In our limited knowledge of decision making on the farm, Fei Xiaotong's observation that the peasant produced first for subsistence needs and sold only his surplus stands out as a useful guiding principle.[4] To this may be added Philip C.C. Huang's observation that it was the small farm that would be forced to accept greater risk in its cropping pattern by devoting a greater proportion of land to cash crops.[5] The two statements are complementary if a distinction is made between cash crops that could also serve as staple foods and those that could not. The pattern would then seem to be that the farm that had more rice to sell would tend to be the one with the larger per capita production, but that small farms were prepared to abandon the priority they gave subsistence when industrial cash crops fetched a substantially better price than grain. Some evidence in support of these generalizations is presented in Tables 5.1 to 5.3.

The statistics reproduced in Table 5.1 illustrate the position of the larger farms in the sale of rice, in a village in which rice was the principal cash crop.[6] It can be seen that the larger farms sold more than 40 per cent of their grain produce, but the wonder must be that the small farms had any grain to sell at all. In the Songjiang villages from which these statistics are reported, the small farms of less than 4.9 mu on average were operated by households that averaged 4.1 persons. The total yield of grain of the 12 grain-selling households operating farms in this class amounted to only 98.51 shishi, equivalent to 9,457 catties. This amount was sufficient for 16 persons' subsistence for one year. The same 12 households rented practically all the land they farmed, for which they paid a cash rent, and the sale of farm produce would have been needed for rent payment. Significantly, the larger farms retained a larger volume of grain per capita.

Other than sale by cultivators, a substantial volume of rice that was sold on the market must also have originated as rent. No direct observation of the sale of rental rice is available: on the whole, no information is available on the uses to which landlords put their income. Some idea of the magnitude of available grain for the market may be obtained, however, by measuring the gap between food requirement of landlord households and the rent they received. The

Table 5.1

Rice Sold by Farm Households in a Songjiang Village, c.1941

Farm size (mu)	Number of Households*	Household Size (persons)	Paddy Harvested (shishi)	Proportion of Harvest Sold (per cent)
Below 4.9	12	4.1	98.51	26.4
5.0–9.9	17	4.0	249.66	49.3
10.0–14.9	13	5.1	290.28	41.7
15.0–19.9	8	4.8	246.03	46.3
Above 20.0	3 .	7.7	177.44	41.7

Notes: * Of the households selling grain, the number of households surveyed in the below 4.9 mu class was 16, the 5.0–9.9 mu class 18, and the other classes identical to numbers entered here.

Source: Mantetsu Shanhai Jimusho Chōsashitsu (1941), pp. 39 and 174–5.

Table 5.2

Landlords' Holdings and Likely Food Supply, Jiangsu, c.1930

	Number of Households	Population (persons)	Land Farmed (mu)	Land Rented Out (mu)	Yield Per Mu (catties)
Peixian	2	11	nil	110	153
Yancheng	1	6	7	26	306
Qidong	2	9	48	117	297
Changshu	2	16	21	69	410

Source: Nongcun fuxing weiyuanhui (1934), pp. 11–12. Totals of paddy and wheat yields for Xuzhou, Huai'an, Taicang, and Suzhou from Table 3.2, less 10 per cent for seeds.

relevant statistics, taken from the Jiangsu Rural Rehabilitation Commission's survey of 1934 and measured against the yield estimates noted in Table 3.2, are summarized in Table 5.2. It should be noted that the landlords recorded in the survey were not the super-rich that owned hundreds or thousands of mu. On average, these landlords held far less than 100 mu, and most maintained farms comparable in size to those of the 'rich peasants'. On the basis of yield estimates earlier derived, the two landlord households in Peixian would have required 41 mu to maintain their 11 household members at subsistence. If it is assumed that the rent received from their 110-mu holdings amounted to one-third of the overall grain produce, the rent would have barely

Table 5.3

Household Size, Labour per *Mu*, and Product Sold on Mulberry Farms
in Wuxi, 1941

Farm Size (mu)	0.99 and below	1.00–2.99	3.00–4.99	5.00–6.99	7.00 and above
Number of farms	8	40	22	3	2
Household size (persons)	3.63	3.30	3.91	4.67	7.50
Household labour (persons)	0.93	0.87	0.94	1.20	0.85
Hired labour (days)	3.63	8.15	38.38	3.30	—
Labour/*mu* (persons)	1.77	0.48	0.29	0.21	0.12
Percentage of farm devoted to mulberry	72.00	32.00	15.00	13.00	14.00
Cocoon sold (catties)	17.00	21.80	21.38	24.67	45.50
Mulberry sold (catties)	137.50	66.75	13.64	—	—

Source: Mantetsu Shanhai jimusho chosabu (1941a), Tables 2 and 13.

covered their subsistence needs.[7] With the 11 *mu* they themselves cultivated, however, they would have at hand just enough grain, with the produce of 5 *mu* to spare. The Yancheng landlord, who held considerably less land, would have been in a similar position but for the seven *mu* that he farmed, even though he reaped higher yields. The two landlords of Qidong would have been considerably better off, for they would have had enough to spare from the acreage they themselves cultivated and all their rental grain could have been sold. The Changshu landlords would have just covered their subsistence needs with the grain they themselves grew, and like the Qidong landlords, could sell all the grain received as rent. So far, account has not been taken of the possibility that landlords, especially the smaller ones, might also have substituted part of their preferred rice diet with cheaper grain, such as wheat or sorghum, or other supplementary crops, such as the sweet potato or soya bean. If this possibility is taken into consideration, the amount of grain that landlords could sell might even be larger.

The advantages of large farms are also apparent in the sale of industrial cash crops. In Table 5.3, which summarizes survey data gathered in Wuxi, it may be seen that on the whole, again, the larger farms supported the larger households and devoted to cultivation less labour per unit area. However, it was the small farms that devoted a greater percentage of the farm area to mulberry and the large farms that produced a greater amount of silkworm cocoon for the market. Even then, they sold more mulberry leaves than the large farms. would have produced it for their own consumption, and it was the small farms that tried to stretch their limited resources to full use that took mulberry to the market.

The limited evidence that is available, therefore, argues quite obviously that large and small farms did not enjoy equal access to the market. While large as well as small farms were able to sell significant portions of their produce, by virtue of having more to sell, the large farms stood to have more to gain when prices rose, and by spreading their acreage more evenly among a number of crops, stood better protected during any sudden downturn in the market. However, if this is true, and if rent contributed to a substantial portion of the products that entered the market, it would follow that many who sold their farm produce in the markets were not powerless in the bargaining process. This is a view of the market for which more evidence can be produced in support, as will be apparent below when the institutions of the rural market are described.

Institutions of the Rural Market

The best description we have of rural marketing in Jiangsu or Guangdong is Fei Xiaotong's discussion of trade at Kaixiangong, in which he presented the view that the rural market was much more open than many of his contemporaries would have accepted. At this village, pedlars and local stores imported goods from outside, but even more than they, 'agent boats' bought and sold on the villagers' behalf at the market. There were four such boats in the village, that made the two-and-a-half-hour journey to the market every day, even when they received no orders to buy or to sell. Apparently, from Fei's descriptions, orders to buy were usually placed with these agents for sundry items used in the household, and the agents executed these orders without charging the villagers a commission, for they were given occasional presents by the shops in the market. Their major business, however, came from selling on the villagers' behalf. With their intimate knowledge of the market and established connections with collectors of rural produce, they advised the villagers on packaging and accompanied them as they sold their goods. The market where villagers traded by tradition was Zhenze, a well-known town in the silk-producing area in southern Jiangsu located four miles from Kaixiangong village. The villagers could also have gone to Tai-miao-chiung (*sic*), that specialized in trade among the islands on Lake Tai. Trade with Tai-miao-chiung was insignificant, and Fei concluded that Zhenze had 'monopolized' nearly all the rice trade of Kaixiangong village. Clearly, however, the shops of Tai-miao-chiung could have offered the agents presents just as those of Zhenze did, and the trade had thus resulted from conscious choices. In the marketing of silk, significantly, a boat used to ply between Kaixiangong and Shengze, another well-known silk market, 12 miles from the village, but then it lost in competition to Zhenze.[8]

Obviously, transport determined to a large extent whether villagers could have had access to more than one market. Kaixiangong was located on an estuary and river transport was relatively easy. In regions that depended more on land transport, such as in northern Jiangsu, villagers might have had fewer choices. Even then, that some competition must have existed is apparent in the much larger number of markets in that region than in southern Jiangsu for the same cultivated acreage.[9] Likewise, in the highland areas of Guangdong, the market on average served a smaller number of villagers than in the river valleys and the delta areas.[10] The possibility cannot be ruled out that some villages were dominated by single markets, but most villages in Jiangsu and Guangdong would have been within travelling distance, by normal village marketing standards, of several markets.[11]

To argue that transport determined access, however, is not to argue that geography did. To understand the competitiveness of rural marketing, it is important to realize that even though markets seem to have sprung into existence in response to geography, they were opened, consciously and ostensibly, by groups of local people, with the aim of trade.[12] It was in the interest of market organizers to promote trade, and to this end to construct an infrastructure to facilitate buyers and sellers. The entrepreneurship required in the opening of a market is well brought out in the biography of one Wu Zhangfen in the Shunde gazetteer. Wu, a successful merchant who failed six times in the county examination, donated generously to local projects during the Guangxu and Xuantong periods:

To take advantage of the [local] geography, he established a market by the waters, and set up trading areas for mulberry, fish, cocoon, and vegetables. He *established regulations and invited merchants hither* . . . [italics added][13]

The regulations established would have included, for instance, a standard measure to be used in the market, the importance of which can be illustrated by another gazetteer biography:

Li Huixiang . . . sailed to Dianbai, and his boat capsized in a storm. He returned to his [native] village to set up a rice shop. He did not follow the cunning practices that were popular, but tried to be fair. Whenever village people disputed over rice measures, they used his measure as a standard.[14]

Having a standard measure in one market did not imply that all standard measures agreed. Irregularities from one market to another were commonplace, each market having its own standards.[15]

To attract merchants and to expand trade, however, required more than regulations. Market operators had to ensure that transport was available. In Kaixiangong it was provided by operators of ferry boats who were given the status of agents by the market shops. Elsewhere, the ferry boats were often provided by market owners. In Gangtuntao market in Funing county (north Jiangsu), a gentry lineage in 1892 channelled the river into the vicinity of the market.[16] Descriptions of markets in the Qingyuan gazetteer of 1937 note for the larger markets the presence of shops, pawnshops, charity societies, gun towers, newspaper reading rooms, dealers' associations, police stations, and easy access by river and motor road.[17] Besides the provision of transport facilities, market owners had to provide protection from extortion by petty government officials, from bandits, and, after 1911, from soldiers. The silk markets in the Zhujiang delta made use of boats that were heavily armed which sailed in convoys for fear of pirates who attacked not only the boats, but sometimes also the markets themselves.[18]

Details of market operation are rarely recorded in historical sources, and it was not a subject of enquiry that interested the surveyors of the 1920s and 1930s. Occasionally, the gazetteers note facets connected with the subject, but gazetteer entries are brief and usually disconnected. Detailed case studies are needed if we are to understand how the rural market functioned as a place for trade, and only in the New Territories of Hong Kong, through research into local history, have some of these cases been reconstructed. The result suggests the apparent anomaly that markets were dominated by local groups that contributed to their infrastructures, but that their domination did not imply control over the marketing region. Local groups competed for control of the markets and considerable competition could be generated especially in times of economic development.

Xigong (known locally as Saikung) was a small market town in the New Territories that began possibly towards the early twentieth century from a few shops on the shore of a coastal inlet. It was not the only inlet where shops were located: the boat people moored in these inlets and shops were found in several of them. Records from the nineteenth century suggest that small as these commercial operations were, they were not truly local. The shops at nearby Liangchuanwan (Leung Shuen Wan) that were far more important than the shops at Xigong came under the protection of a member of the junior gentry at Nantou, the county city. These shops supplied the fishing and transport boats. It is not clear if, in these early days, the fishermen sold their catches to them. The main fishing markets were a short distance away, at Dabu (Tai Po) and Yantian. None of these markets can be said to have enjoyed a monopoly.[19]

Outside the New Territories of Hong Kong, I know of only two case studies that concern market operations in Jiangsu and Guangdong. While neither furnishes the details that may be documented from research in Hong Kong, they provide sufficient information to demonstrate that the practices documented there were by no means confined to that small area alone. For this reason, they deserve rather careful examination.

Qiao Qiming's study of Chunhua *zhen*, outside Nanjing city, in the summer of 1930 or 1931, is primarily an attempt to map some readily observable social relationships among villages in the vicinity of the town. The study does not address the question of who owned the markets. Moreover, because it concentrates on the territory served by a single town, it does not even demonstrate very clearly where other markets were located from which competition might come. What it does demonstrate is the scale of business conducted by the shops in the town, and the web of social relationships founded upon the basis of common worship at earth-god shrines and temples, that complemented the commercial functions of the shops, and no doubt, even though no reference was made to them, also those of the pedlars. Both are important aspects to take into account in any discussion of market operations.[20]

According to Qiao, Chunhua *zhen* was a town of 1,805 people, who, besides operating 68 shops, also farmed 1,750 *mu*. In total, the shops employed 175 people. In other words, they were tiny: the six grain stores that employed altogether 21 people, and the seven general stores that employed 17, would hardly have had a staff to manage the accounts, let alone enforce a monopoly. Farmers came to the grain stores in the morning with small baskets of rice and wheat that they sold for cash. The shops also offered loans and so at harvest time the shopkeepers had to go into the countryside to collect debts owed to them. The largest shop was the carpenter's, that employed eight people, and this was followed by the single pawnshop, that employed six. The pawnshop, the grain stores, and the general stores together claimed half the daily business volume in the town (411 out of a total of 777.50 dollars). The other shops provided what may be considered essential services: they included clothiers, ironsmiths, herbalists, butchers, barbers, beancurd makers, teahouses, and restaurants.

Near the town were 56 villages, 41 of which traded at the town. The total population of the 41 villages amounted to 12,083. Of these, 20 had fewer than 200 inhabitants and were visibly less well endowed. Few of the ancestral halls, temples, rice mills, tea-houses, or private schools that Qiao has recorded were located in them. However, scattered in the larger villages were 30 general stores, 39 rice mills, and 21 tea-houses. Qiao does not make the point, but it seems common practice for rice millers to purchase rice from farmers as well as mill on consignment, and it is probably not far-fetched to suppose that they would have had an intimate knowledge of business conducted within the neighbourhood. They would have been linkages within the commercial network that any attempt at monopoly would have had to deal with.

On the important role played by religious unions in the smooth running of village affairs, Qiao is quite specific. Since the Taiping Rebellion, 48 villages in the neighbourhood had formed defence unions that had annually taken part in celebrating a ten-day festival at a temple located near, though not in, the town. The 48 village unions were known locally as the 48 *she*, each *she* being formed around worship at a temple or an earth-god shrine. In one village that Qiao quotes as an example, the *she* was made up of 48 families, divided into six groups. Annual worship at the *she* temple was organized by headmen drawn from these groups on the basis of equal representation. The village also held an annual celebration at its earth-god shrine, on which occasion the communal affairs of the village might also be discussed. These worship unions, therefore, represented social bonds that served more than religious purposes. Unfortunately, Qiao gives no indication of the power relationships among the villages in the neighbourhood. However, the near coincidence of the marketing territory and the territory defined by inter-village alliance exemplified in worship at the temple conforms very closely to observations made in Hong Kong's New Territories.[21]

The other study of a market that merits close examination is Daniel Harrison Kulp's on 'Phenix Village', near Shantou, Guangdong.[22] Kulp describes the village as consisting of 'a total of a hundred and ten buildings, large and small, of which thirty shops make up the business section'. The population of this village in 1919 amounted to 650 people, although it is not clear if this is the number of villagers alone or if it also includes the shopkeepers. Nevertheless, the relationship between the village proper and the shopping area is described in terms that are quite precise. The village consisted of people of a single surname who had settled at the site for nine generations. They had built the shops and started a market in order to compete for business with nearby Tan Village. Tan Village enjoyed a major geographical advantage: it was located at a lower point on the river, and in the dry season, it was at Tan Village that boats had to stop. Kulp's very brief description of Tan Village suggests that it was relatively more prosperous than Phenix. Tan also had a larger population. Why in these circumstances Phenix Village sought to build its own market is not clearly explained. Kulp claims that Tan Village had itself been started in competition with another market three miles away and Phenix Village followed when it saw that its own villagers who traded at Tan could just as well trade in their own village. That Phenix Village was not poor possibly had some bearing on the decision: in 1918, 55 members of the village were living abroad. That the village could afford to build the 24 shops and a road leading through them suggests that it had ready capital at its disposal.

As the owner of the market, Phenix Village benefited primarily from the rent received from the shops. Three of the shops were not rented in 1919, and of the remaining 21, only five were operated by people who were members of the village while the others were operated by outsiders. The five shops operated by Phenix Village members sold 'dry goods', rice, food, medicine, and opium. One can detect the exertion of a sense of monopoly in the distribution of these trades, for theirs were the only rice and opium shops in the market. However, they also illustrate precisely the restrictions on monopolies exerted by market owners: they would have had no control on the operation of similar stores in nearby Tan Village. In addition to food and medicine, the outsiders also sold beancurd, paper, pork, cakes, dyes, and coffins. It was also an outsider who was the market barber. Kulp notes the important part in business transactions played by the middlemen. An isolated reference to the 'captain of the ferry', who might be asked by village women to buy cloth at Shantou on their behalf, suggests that, like Kaixiangong, the village ferrymen served in some of these middleman roles.

As a lineage village, the natives of Phenix ordered themselves as members of kin-groups. They maintained ancestral halls, schools, and graves, and also a temple at which only members of the village were allowed to worship. Just outside the village was another temple, 'shared with two other villages in the immediate vicinity'. At this temple were held annual celebrations in honour of the temple gods in which only villagers were allowed to take part. In contrast to such exclusiveness in village affairs, Kulp notes the first signs of what he calls 'civism' in the relationship between the village and the market. He makes it very clear that as outsiders, the shop operators had no right in the management of village affairs, and yet because they were involved in the economic well-being of the village and because they came to know about village affairs through gossip, they were able to influence opinion. His study leaves open the question of how the market itself was managed, but there should be little doubt that an entrepeneurial interest on the part of both market owners and shopkeepers was present.

While our sources leave much to be desired, it seems quite clear from these two cases and from the Hong Kong research that the conditions for trade had to be created out of the political framework of the countryside. What the charges of monopoly have failed to acknowledge, therefore, is that the need for trade was recognized and integrated into the local political framework in rural China. Trade was not unfettered, but then, neither was it encased within monopolist control.[23]

Market–City Connections

Trade could proceed when standards had been established and when transport and protection had been provided. However, the development of trade required the establishment of networks of commercial relationships that went far beyond the rural markets. The successful rural market served more than its immediate marketing area: it needed to be linked to regional, national, or even international trade.

We have no idea, for any market in Jiangsu or Guangdong, how much of its trade catered to local consumption and how much of it consisted of exports to, or imports from, places beyond its immediate marketing region. Much firewood that was sold at rural markets must have been locally consumed, for example, but some market towns, especially in northern Guangdong, exported considerable quantities to the major cities. Much herbal medicine was probably also locally consumed, but some localities might acquire a reputation for various items that came to be sought after in the regional or national market. Most handicrafts, such as the making of farming implements and furniture, bricks and tiles, would have been local services, but the grass-cloth and lace of Chaozhou, the paper of Dongguan, the incense of Huizhou, the pottery of Yixing, and the cotton yarn of Songjiang were local products that enjoyed a long-standing national reputation.[24] In the silk industry, while cocoons were invariably exported to towns that had facilities for reeling, the mulberry market catered for local consumption.[25] Rice was partly locally consumed and partly shipped into the regional markets, its regional price always having considerable bearing on its local market price.[26] Riots occasionally broke out when regional shortages caused price increases locally as local consumers sought to prevent its export.[27] Within these networks of trading relationships that stretched across markets and cities, far from dictating the terms of trade to the regional markets, local shops were dictated to by custom and prevailing conditions that varied from trade to trade and from time to time.

In the rice trade, for instance, of which several excellent reports from the 1930s are available, most villages in rice-surplus southern Jiangsu were simply not many removes from the principal urban markets. Nanjing was one of these markets; it imported for its own consumption and exported to other cities. Close to 200 rice importers were established in this city. About half of them specialized in importing from distant suppliers, who brought their supplies to Nanjing in boats, but almost an equal number specialized in collecting from 'rural occasionals' (xiangshao) who arrived overland from the vicinity. These 'rural occasionals' had come from the rural markets. Some had collected grain from farmers, and husked and milled it before taking it to Nanjing on mules, in motor cars (the report being written in 1935), or by human carriers. Unlike the boats, they were not required to go through agents or grain measurers to make their sale, no doubt because they sold in small quantities.[28] In Zhenjiang, purchase from the vicinity was conducted by 17 companies, who owned capital that amounted to only 500 to 600 dollars, their operations being much smaller than the grain stores that collected from sailing junks. There, 'farmers' arrived every morning, carrying their grain baskets, which they emptied into specially made wicker baskets provided by these companies. They left the grain on display in front of their shops, where they would be approached by buyers. Buyer and seller would themselves negotiate the price, but the shops would arrange to transport it for the buyer, collect payment on the seller's behalf, and charge a commission for its work. The shops not only waited for 'farmers' to come in on their own accord, they also dispatched their own agents to the countryside to collect grain.[29] In Songjiang, where the rice merchants were primarily engaged in collecting directly from the countryside for export, one of the rules established by the rice merchants' association was directed against competitive bidding. At the market of Fengqing, samples of grain were examined a day before sale was concluded. The extra day allowed rural agents, or 'farmers', to offer the produce to several prospective buyers, and competition resulted from the practice. The rice merchants' association therefore ruled that when a price had been offered and the sale agreed upon, other dealers were not to compete. The rule was none the less found to be ineffective.[30] In Wuxi, by far the biggest rice market of the several discussed here, 56 rice dealers operated in 14 large markets, collecting rice for export to the city. Additionally, farmers could also sell directly to the shops located in the city. Those who lived nearby could take their grain into the city individually. Those who lived far away grouped together to charter a boat to carry their grain. Similar to the 'agent boats' discussed by Fei, these boats also sold grain on the farmers' behalf.[31]

A crucial institution in the rice trade at the cities was the warehouse, crucial not only because of its obvious storage function, but also because of its function in providing the documentation that was needed for bank credit. In the 1920s and 1930s, the combination of the bank, the warehouse, and the machine mill dominated the urban rice market.[32] In Nanjing, the warehouses were run by the banks, the large rice dealers, and the mills. They charged a rent for goods deposited with them, and also offered loans using the same goods as collateral. In 1935, Nanjing warehouses offered credit that amounted to 70 per cent of the value of the stored grain at an interest of 1.2 per cent per month. These loans were ultimately advanced by the banks to the warehouses.[33] Similar arrangements were made by warehouses at Zhenjiang and Wuxi. The Wuxi warehouses we know to be recent developments, the first warehouse having been set up only in 1863. By 1936, there were 26 warehouses.[34] In Songjiang, probably the most rustic of the several rice markets discussed here, bank loans were apparently less common except for handling remittances and commercial notes needed in selling rice to Shanghai. However, Songjiang rice dealers also accepted deposits of money on which they paid interest, and which they used to finance their trade. Rice dealers in Songjiang also borrowed from one another at an interest rate determined by their guild, the rate in 1935 being 1.2 per cent per month.[35] How limited these warehouses were except perhaps in a few major cities may be illustrated by the situation in Changshu (south Jiangsu), a major rice exporter. There were four warehouses in this county in the 1930s, charging 1 per cent interest per month, 0.2 per cent for insurance, and 0.2 per cent handling charge. However, one of these made loans worth only 80,000 *yuan*, and the other three 50,000 *yuan* each in 1933.[36]

The warehouse was apparently an institution that had developed in the more inland cities in southern Jiangsu, acting as intermediary between the banks and rice dealers. In Shanghai, rice dealers borrowed directly from banks on the strength of their own credibility.[37] In Guangzhou also, rice dealers borrowed from banks at rates that varied between 20 to 30 cents per 1,000 dollars per day and 8 to 9 dollars per 1,000 per month in the 1930s. Most of these loans were not secured, but some were raised against goods stored in warehouses.[38]

Without a better knowledge of the role of traditional banks in the rice trade prior to 1870, we cannot be certain if the substantial borrowing from the modern banks by the warehouses implies a considerable credit expansion. We must also leave aside the question of how much this development was due to the introduction of the machine mill, the cessation of government rice transport to the north in the Republican era, and the rise of modern banking in China. None the less, in the wheat-flour milling industry, some evidence is available to show that much credit was generated in the growing industrialization of flour milling. The relevant material is contained in documentary compilations relating to the Rong family of Wuxi.[39]

The Rong family opened its own bank in Shanghai in 1896. It was an old-style bank that specialized in remittances to and from Wuxi, and which dealt mainly with its own branch offices there and in other county cities. The bank made its profit by taking advantage of exchange-rate differences in these various places, by circulating newly minted debased coins, and by sponsoring the Rong family's investments in local businesses, including the purchase of cocoons for sale to the silk factories in Wuxi. The family set up its first machine flour mill in 1900 in Wuxi, when the price of wheat flour had increased substantially as a result of the Boxer turmoil. The flour-milling business did not succeed immediately. The mill was among the first to have been set up with native capital, and its product was not readily accepted in Wuxi. Moreover, the price of wheat was rising, partly as a result of coinage debasement and partly because of increased demand created by the new machine mills; and in a market dominated by imported flour, the increased costs could not be recovered. In 1908, the seven native machine mills in Shanghai and Wuxi came to an agreement to meet every day to fix a price for their wheat purchases. It is not clear if the agreement had very much effect, but it may have had, for the wheat trade was smaller than the rice trade and the flour mills were major consumers. In later years, when the Rongs' mills had become more successful, they could themselves control the prices of their purchases, as they could also turn to imports when local prices were high. However, in 1908, the Rongs' business was facing its first financial crisis. Its flour in these early years did not sell smoothly, and in that year, the family's bank had lost heavily in its speculative investments. The family was not daunted. The two brothers, Zongjing and Desheng, who were in control after their father's death, sold the bank, mortgaged much of their land holdings, bought new machinery on credit, and raised new capital to open another mill in Shanghai. These efforts bore fruit during the First World War, when flour prices rose and foreign competition dropped. More mills were opened after the war, and the Rongs conducted a thriving milling industry well into the 1930s.

The Rongs' mills bought wheat through their own local offices. Each local office had a small staff of two to three people, whose expenses were paid by the head office. The head office instructed them through the telegraph when and how much to buy and at what price. The local office, on instruction, bought from local grain stores, which in turn bought from dealers who collected wheat from the countryside. The local office paid by bills drawn on seven days' credit on their head office in Shanghai. Their bills were supported by local native banks and were readily accepted by the grain stores. In this way, bank credit was drawn into the process of wheat purchasing, even though it stopped at the level of the stores, for the country dealers and farmers had to be paid in ready cash.

Even in their heyday in the 1920s, the Rongs did not by any means enjoy a monopoly of wheat purchasing. In direct competition with them were other flour mills, the number of which had grown substantially in the 1920s, and the grain stores. Some of the grain stores were well capitalized, and they collected not only for the flour mills, but also directly for the urban markets.[40] In 1921, commodity exchanges were set up to deal in wheat flour and supplementary foods, including wheat. The trend of development thus allowed more, not less, competition among the major purchasers.[41]

The sharp division between the regional trade that was supported by bank credit and the collection at local markets, for which farm produce was paid for in ready cash, is also apparent in the silk trade. Here, the mulberry market was the least regulated of the various types of market in which traditional marketing practices dominated. Buyers and sellers met, made use of the scales provided by the markets, and conducted their transactions without third-party involvement. Some credit was extended by the markets to the buyers, so that farmers were always paid immediately. The sources that financed this local credit are unclear, but when the low costs involved are considered, it is possible that market operators provided it out of their own capital. In the cocoon market, however, bank credit becomes obvious, for the sums involved are substantial. In the 1920s, a public cocoon market in Guangdong might conduct 100,000 dollars' worth of business annually.[42] Their connections with the Guangzhou banks were overt, but details of their financial dealings are quite unclear.[43] In Shanghai alone, the annual expenditure in the late 1920s on cocoons by the steam filatures amounted to 14 to 15 million dollars, of which 6 million was borrowed from native banks. The silk filatures, which directly owned the cocoon warehouses that purchased cocoons, were considered to be modern enterprises, and the warehouses were regarded as being more 'scientific' than the public markets. In Shanghai, banks made loans to them under strict conditions: the banks despatched their own agents to the countryside to pay directly for the cocoons at the places of purchase, and the cocoons were then shipped to Shanghai under their supervision and stored at appointed warehouses.[44]

It is an indication that bank credit did not advance into the farming communities that a large volume of coins, both copper and silver, was

shipped to the silk districts at every season.[45] Bank credit stopped at
the cocoon markets, and the markets or the filatures on their own
responsibility and at their own risk, extended credit to silk farmers.

The extension of bank credit was a matter of controversy in the
1930s over the establishment of rural co-operatives. On the one hand,
all schools of thought agreed that attempts must be made by the
government to alleviate rural economic hardship by extending credit
and encouraging agricultural improvements. On the other hand, charges
were made that credit extended by banks had not been designed to
benefit the cultivators. For one thing, interest rates remained high: not
infrequently, the co-operatives charged 10 per cent per annum. For
another, the banks accepted agricultural produce as security only
when it was stored in recognized warehouses, and the amounts that
were loaned were tied to the market value of the produce. In times of
low prices, bank credit was naturally reduced, and because the banks
supervised the warehouses, they also maintained greater control on
the products stored therein than market operators at traditional rural
markets. The terms for credit, therefore, seemed unnecessarily harsh
to some critics. Moreover, in the exercising of authority, questions of
personality and abuse inevitably arose.

None the less, some of these co-operatives highlighted two shortcomings of the traditional rural markets that should be noted. In the
traditional market, the producer was more removed from the trading
networks, of which the cities formed major parts, than he needed be
had a co-operative been organized. Moreover, the rural market as it
was traditionally organized was a poor instrument for quality
improvements. It was a flexible institution that recognized local
power divisions, that encouraged trade in small quantities, that collected
local produce for the wholesale trades, that successfully reflected
price changes in the main centres of trade, and that allowed the
intrusion of bank credit; but, market operators were slow in seeking
new technologies that might be introduced into the villages to raise the
quality of agriculture. As these technologies became increasingly
important, especially in cotton and silk farming, government and
academic research institutions put their support behind attempts to
reform rural marketing practices, such as the organization of the co-
operatives. In the silk industry in Jiangsu, a virtual monopoly was
developed that was controlled by the well-positioned Xue family.[46]
None the less, most of these reforms came in the 1930s, far too late to
bring about much effect before 1937.

Conclusion

On the basis of the material summarized here, there is not very much on which one may build a case for the lack of competition in rural markets. Rural marketing was not a well-controlled process. It was one that involved innumerable small dealers handling small quantities. It was also one that placed the farmers many removes from the final consumers of their produce. However, because it was competitive, it would have reflected readily price changes in the cities. If anything, the fragmentation of the marketing process, not a monopolistic tendency, was the weakness of the rural economy. It was a very difficult setting in which to introduce new technological skills, as the many Western merchants who wanted higher quality silk and cotton learned.

6

Cash Crops and Trade: Successes and Failures

TEXTBOOKS argue that China was 'opened' in the mid-nineteenth century to Western cultural, diplomatic, and commercial intercourse. As far as the last is concerned, the generalization is misleading. China had been involved in international trade for centuries before 1850, and if by 'opening' is meant increase in trade volume, then not only was China 'opened' in the second half of the nineteenth century, but so were Europe and the United States. World trade grew twentyfold between the beginning and the final years of the nineteenth century.[1] The new manufacturing industries, modern means of communication and transport, the banks, and the expansion of knowledge, combined to elevate world trade to a magnitude hitherto unknown in human history. What matters, of course, as the pessimists correctly point out, is that China was drawn into the current as a producer of raw materials and a consumer of manufactured goods, and this was an imbalance that would only be corrected by industrialization in China. For China's rural economy, however, involvement in international trade meant opportunities for economic gain that were limited only by China's ability to compete in the international market place. As it happened, China did not compete well, but that does not mean that the rural economy did not benefit from trade expansion while it lasted.

To 1929

The world depression which began in 1929 had a significant impact on China's rural economy. This section, therefore, considers the history of the major cash crops and handicrafts only up to that year, while the next section continues with developments in the 1930s.

Cotton, Yarn, and Cloth

The impact of manufactured yarn, both imported and locally produced in China's cities, on hand-spinning and weaving is well known. In summary, in the 1820s and 1830s, when imported yarn was first introduced into the Chinese countryside, it badly affected hand-spinning. However, manufactured yarn did not at any time totally replace hand-spun yarn. Firstly, imports were unevenly distributed in the provinces. Imports into Guangdong from the 1870s to the 1910s far outweighed imports into Shanghai, and probably not until Chinese spinning mills began to operate, from the 1890s on, was its effect fully felt in Jiangsu. Secondly, even in areas that consumed manufactured yarn, hand-spun yarn continued to be used. It found a ready market in particular varieties of hand-woven cloth that combined the manufactured and the hand-spun product. Moreover, because manufactured yarn was very much cheaper than hand-spun yarn, it gave a strong impetus to the development of the hand-weaving industry. Far from causing unemployment in the countryside, therefore, the introduction of manufactured yarn gave rise to some prosperity.[2]

The production of yarn required a constant supply of cotton (see Table 6.1) which was extensively grown in the Songjiang area in Jiangsu before 1870. Between 1870 and the 1890s, it was exported to Japan, where the manufacturing of yarn took root earlier than in China. After an initial decline, the price of cotton rose in the mid-1880s, catching hand-spinners in the pincers of rising costs for raw materials and falling prices for the finished product that had to compete with foreign imports. However, the ready market for cotton supported the extension of the crop. By the early 1900s, coastal land formerly reserved as salt fields was reclaimed for cotton cultivation by the reclamation companies. Meanwhile, the rise in the price of rice from the 1890s matched that in the price of cotton, with the result that cotton cultivation tended to remain concentrated on the saline soil that was unsuited for paddy. The cultivation of cotton grew phenomenally in the 1920s, for the consumption of the Jiangsu spinning mills alone rose from 961,000 piculs annually in 1917–21 to 5,084,000 piculs annually in 1927–9. Although imports rose from 1,131,000 piculs to 3,346,000 piculs, the excess of consumption over imports in Jiangsu alone totalled 1,738,000 piculs.[3] Cotton farmers, like all farmers, suffered from the vagaries of the weather, but they suffered no serious trade fluctuations from the 1910s up to the 1920s. Moreover, if import prices are a guide, the price of raw cotton rose by more than 50 per cent between the 1910s and the 1920s. So, although attempts to improve the quality of cotton in Jiangsu met with failure, its cultivation was one of the successes of trade expansion.

Tea

China's tea trade expanded from the 1860s to the 1880s, and then declined rapidly. In Guangdong, by the 1920s, the tea export was one-

Table 6.1

Cotton Consumption and Prices in Jiangsu, 1872–1929

	Number of Spindles in China*	Consumption of Cotton in Jiangsu ('000 piculs)	Imports of Cotton		Exports of Cotton from Shanghai ('000 piculs)	Price of Cotton	
			From Abroad ('000 piculs)	From Chinese Ports ('000 piculs)		Imports (hk.tls./ picul)	Exports (hk.tls/ picul)
1872–6	—	—	—	2	458	n.a.	n.a.
1877–81	—	—	—	2	349	n.a.	n.a.
1882–6	—	—	—	1	254	9.63	11.03
1887–91	—	—	—	1	467	9.99	10.33
1892–6	135,440	n.a.	4	5	723	12.41	11.07
1897–1901	539,895	n.a.	114	7	483	13.55	14.05
1902–6	568,113	n.a.	51	41	598	16.16	17.34
1907–11	728,057	n.a.	77	49	558	18.85	20.94
1912–16	1,031,297	n.a.	232	315#	213	21.10	20.22
1917–21	1,468,142	961†	522	609	276	25.66	27.23
1922–6	3,645,226	4,518‡	1,504	1,135	194	33.58	33.90
1927–9	3,850,016	5,084	1,756	1,590	142	36.79	32.15

Notes: * Figures for middle year in each quintile.
 † Excluding foreign-owned factories, average of 1919–21 only.
 ‡ Average of 1924–5.
 # Average of four years only, data for 1914 not available.

Sources: Kang Chao (1977), pp. 301–2; Shanghaishi mianfangzhi gongye tongye gonghui choubeihui (1950), p. 16; MC, trade reports; T.R. Bannister (1933b), pp. 179 and 189.

sixth of what it had been in the late 1870s (see Table 6.2), and the reasons for the decline are well known. T.R. Bannister stated them succinctly as he summarized the views expressed in the Maritime Customs' reports:

There were (and are) no plantations such as were established in India and Japan. The tea shrub is grown in waste ground, on the edges of terraces, or in any place where it does not interfere with the main crops. To the small farmer, who was everywhere the primary producer of tea, the increased foreign demand during the sixties represented a windfall, an unexpected gain accruing from happenings beyond his control. There was nowhere any appreciation of it as a new market to be studied, or the slightest adaptation of method or product to meet it. The only reaction was a desire to seize the opportunity by picking and selling as much leaf as possible. The shrubs were often overplucked; there was little renewing; and what replanting took place was on the old haphazard lines and without any planned objectives as regards the foreign market. The same spirit animated the teamen who first purchased the tea leaves in the different districts. The central idea was quantity. The tea was improperly fired, hastily cured, inadequately packed, and rushed to the most convenient treaty port. Adulteration was attempted in many ways . . . In most cases the foreign merchants were perfectly cognizant of what they were buying, adulterated teas being known in the trade as 'lie teas'. But the point is that such tea was now competing in the market places of the world with tea grown in *plantations* in India and Japan. Such plantations were devoted to tea and tea only. The shrub was properly looked after, and every step in the process was studied and carried out with the fixed and definite object of turning out a product of a dependable standard, having the characteristics required by the ultimate consumer, the foreign tea drinker. In other words, a certain quality was deliberately sought after. Chinese tea was produced by millions of independent peasants, from odd shrubs planted in chance corners, and brought to market haphazard by thousands of independent dealers operating in different districts. The only method by which it was attempted to meet Indian and Japanese competition was to increase quantity and to lower price. For a time this was partly successful in enabling the Chinese tea trade to hold its own. But in the decade following the present, [the word 'present' referring to the 1870s] defeat became manifest. Had social and economic conditions in China made it possible to organize the production of tea in such a way as to care for quality, it is certain that this valuable source of profit would not have been lost to the country.[4]

Although the passage was directed not at Guangdong alone, but at all tea-growing districts in China, it would have applied to this province as well.

Indeed, China's tea had only been able to hold its own until the 1880s because British India developed its own variety late, having

Table 6.2

Exports of Tea and Sugar from Guangdong, 1872–1929 (annual averages) ('000 piculs)

	Tea Exported from		Sugar Exported from	
	Shantou	Guangzhou*	Shantou	Guangzhou
1872–6	3.0	96.6	1,064	233
1877–81	4.8	118.3	1,137	182
1882–6	8.3	114.8	1,474	217
1887–91	8.8	108.2	1,507	421
1892–6	7.1	78.7	1,155	313
1897–1901	6.6	51.6	1,476	395
1902–6	5.6	43.4	906	120
1907–11	4.5	34.9	846	98
1912–16	4.3	27.3	591	54
1917–21	3.0	18.2	512	53
1922–6	2.2†	22.5	636	23
1927–9	2.4	19.8	235	3

Notes: * Including exports from Jiulong.
† Green tea omitted for 1924 and 1925, approximately 400 piculs per annum.
Source: MC, trade reports.

concentrated to little avail on Chinese varieties in earlier decades.[5] Whether plantation farming was necessarily superior to the peasant farm is debatable, but efforts made in discovering a species, raising the capital that for years yielded little return, developing machinery that could be used in tea processing, and promoting the product in the home market to make it acceptable, were totally foreign to tea production and marketing in China. By the 1880s, Ceylon had entered the market, and together with India, soon overtook China in export volume.

None the less, China was herself a large tea consumer, and the question remains of whether losing the export market greatly affected tea growing. It would seem, in Guangdong at least, that it did. The comprehensive survey of agriculture conducted by Zhongshan University in the 1920s confirms that, in tea-growing districts, tea production had declined in the several decades before the survey. However, as Bannister noted, tea growing was only marginal to the farm economy, at least in Guangdong, and its loss caused little stir.[6]

Jiangsu was not a major tea producer, and was not seriously affected by changes in the tea trade.

Sugar

Like tea, Chinese sugar lost to foreign competition from the 1890s. Exports from Shantou, the port for the most important sugar-producing district in China, dropped from 1,507,000 piculs in 1887–91 to 235,000 piculs in 1927–9, and from Guangzhou and Jiulong, which exported for the Zhujiang delta, from 421,000 piculs to 3,000 piculs.[7] In contrast, sugar production in Java grew from just under 200,000 metric tons in 1875 to 380,000 metric tons in 1885, to 580,000 metric tons in 1895, and to just over 1,000,000 metric tons in 1905.[8] During the First World War, Chinese sugar exports recovered slightly, but thereafter again declined.

Guangdong sugar lost because its price was not competitive. As early as 1884, the Maritime Customs had noted that sugar imported into Hong Kong from Java or the Philippines was cheaper than that from Shantou.[9] A refinery opened in 1880 by Jardine, Matheson and Co. closed in 1886 because it was thought that refining local sugar would not be sufficiently competitive.[11] In the 1880s, however, Guangdong sugar was given a reprieve by the expansion of the north China market. Sichuan, which had formerly exported to north China, was gradually given over to opium cultivation, and as its sugar exports declined, Shantou merchants seized the opportunity to take over the market. None the less, the price of imported refined sugar continued to decline through the 1890s and the early 1900s.[11] The decline, from 5.71 Haikwan taels per picul in 1892–6 to 5.30 Haikwan taels per picul in 1907–11, was substantial, especially when it is remembered that this was a time of general inflation.[12] By 1902, the Maritime Customs reported:

The Hong Kong product is so much cleaner than the native article that it is rapidly gaining popularity . . . The price, too, is in favour of the imported article, as the average value of Swatow [Shantou] brown during the year was Hk.Tls. 3.45 per picul, and that of the Hong Kong variety was Hk.Tls. 3.30. Swatow white was quoted at Hk.Tls. 5.25, and Hong Kong white at Hk.Tls. 4.75, while Hong Kong refined sugar could be laid down here at the same figure as was asked for the local white sugar.[13]

The collapse of the export market for sugar was, by then, a foregone conclusion.[14]

It is tempting to think that, like tea, Chinese sugar lost to plantation production. However, like China, Java was land-short and densely populated, and the cost breakdowns available suggest that the rent and wage components in the overall cost of cane growing were not necessarily smaller than those in China.[15] Where the cost components differed substantially was in the relative proportion between cane growing and sugar making in the overall cost. In Java in 1899–1902, annual agricultural costs amounted to 36.4 per cent of the total cost required for the production of sugar. In Guangdong in about 1921, cane production amounted to 60 to 70 per cent of overall costs.[16] It seems that the disadvantage faced by Chinese sugar was in many ways related to the primitive method by which it was produced. The juice was extracted from the cane with stone grinders. It was boiled and reboiled with little control in several cauldrons over a primitive furnace. Impurities were removed by filtering the juice with cloth after the addition of oystershell powder.[17] Compared to this operation, in the words of two knowledgeable scholars on the international sugar trade:

The manufacture of sugar from sugar cane in Java has attained to great perfection . . . The ample investment of funds in the newest machinery, the activity of the sugar experiment stations, the adequate training of sugar chemists and factory chiefs — all these have contributed towards making the Java sugar industry a model one.[18]

The demise of the sugar industry in Guangdong should also be considered in the context of the rising price of rice and other food crops from the 1890s to the 1920s. The land on which cane was grown was good paddy land, and the labour that went into its cultivation could just as easily be employed to grow paddy. Paddy was, after all, grown as part of the three-year or four-year rotations that included cane. The costs and benefits of cane growing were, therefore, pegged to the costs and benefits of rice growing. It would have been profitable for the farmer to put his land to cane only if the profit derived from it was above that of paddy. In decades of rising prices for rice, but declining prices for cane, the farmer's incentive would have been to stop cane cultivation and to revert to rice. The loss of large areas to cane cultivation possibly held up the price of cane in places for short periods of time, further eroding its competitive position in the large urban markets. However, with rice as a crop to fall back on, the loss of the cane market did not lead to any sharp loss in farm income, even though it formed a noticeable loss in the export trade.[19]

Silk

It was silk, more than cotton, tea, sugar, or any other produce, that opened Guangdong and Jiangsu to world trade in the years from 1870

Table 6.3

Exports of White Silk from Jiangsu and Guangdong, 1872–1929
(annual averages) ('000 piculs)

	From Shanghai		From Suzhou	From Guangzhou	
	Raw and Re-reeled	Filatured		Raw and Re-reeled	Filatured
1872–6	48	—	—	16	—
1877–81	47	—	—	14	—
1882–6	37	—	—	15	—
1887–91	39	—	—	21	—
1892–6	43	2	—	17	9
1897–1901	36	10	—	16	32
1902–6	24	11	—	2	34
1907–11	24	16	—	2	37
1912–16	3*	23	14	3	35
1917–21	—	27	12	1	40
1922–6	1	32	12	1	49
1927–9	1	49	10	1	49

Notes: * Average of four years; data for 1915 not available.
Source: MC, trade reports.

to 1929. The history of the industry is well known and this discussion will, therefore, be brief.[20] Overall, exports increased from the 1870s to the 1920s. Moreover, income from silk was enhanced by the introduction of the steam filature, the product of which gradually exceeded the hand-reeled variety in export.[21] Guangdong adapted to the filature much more rapidly than did the lower Changjiang.[22] As filature silk was not recorded separately in the Maritime Customs' reports until 1895, it is not clear if Guangdong's rapid progress in the export trade had directly resulted from this innovation. Rather, the success of the filature appears to be part of the enterprising development that saw silk exports from Guangdong expand steadily through the 1880s, while exports from the lower Changjiang almost remained stagnant. Table 6.3 shows, however, that the lower Changjiang caught up in the 1910s. Between 1902 and 1916, the product of the filature rose from 31 per cent of Shanghai's silk exports to 88 per cent. In terms of value, none the less, into the 1920s, Guangdong's silk exports matched those of Shanghai.[23]

Historians have not found the performance of China's silk exports impressive, despite continuous expansion from the 1870s to the

1920s. Compared with silk exports from Japan, which rose from below 20,000 piculs per annum in the 1870s to over 100,000 piculs per annum before the First World War, and then to 500,000 piculs per annum in the late 1920s, China's performance appears to be more of a failure.[24] China had begun with a dominating position in the international silk market in the 1870s, and lost its pre-eminence to Japan, a relatively late starter in the trade. The reason for China's failure is not hard to find. Japanese producers had been much more ready to adopt scientific methods in silkworm rearing. Under government control and supervision, Japanese egg farmers were required to adopt the Pasteur method for selecting eggs that were free from pebrine. Chinese production, however, from breeding to cocoon marketing, was undertaken by unorganized small farmers using traditional methods, in which price speculation rather than quality was given priority. Foreign purchasers complained that the quality of Chinese silk was uneven, and in contrast to Japanese silk, was not improved over time.[25]

It should also be noted, none the less, that during the First World War and in the several years that followed, a short period that was highly favourable to silk producers in the Far East, Chinese producers also had to contend with rising silver prices, while Japanese producers, whose currency was not silver-based, would have maintained lower prices. Thereafter, Chinese producers had had to face the disruptions of civil wars. Where Chinese farmers might be held responsible for losing the market to their Japanese counterparts was in the slow start in the 1890s and early 1900s. They did not take sufficient advantage of the expansion of the silk market in the United States. Inflation and polical disruptions were, of course, quite beyond their control.

Still the point must be made that this supposed failure on the part of the Chinese silk industry may only be so described in a relative sense. Silk exports expanded steadily from the 1870s to the 1920s, and contemporaries noted local developments not with a sense of gloom but with excitement. As silk production in Guangdong and Jiangsu was concentrated in only a few localities, its growth in these decades brought considerable changes to their economy, which did not go unnoticed.

A description of Wuxi county in 1921, just before the boom which lasted until 1927,[26] states:

Twenty years ago, the farmers grew paddy, wheat, and beans. In recent years, because of the proliferation of the silk factories [that is, steam filatures], farmers see that silk and mulberry are more profitable than paddy and wheat. They grow mulberry and raise silkworms in addition to their other crops.

In the days before the railway was constructed, cocoon warehouses had not been established and there were few silk factories; not many households grew mulberry. The shortage of mulberry imposed limitations on the production of cocoons. In those days, because no cocoon warehouse was there to purchase cocoons, silk was reeled by hand, tied into bundles and sold at such counties as Wujin, Wu, and Jintan. In the late Qing, in Guangxu 31 [1905], the Shanghai-Nanjing Railway was constructed, and the Yuchang Silk Factory was established. From then on, more and more households grew mulberry and raised silkworms. In Xuantong 1 [1909] and 2 [1910], entrepreneurs saw that silk was profitable and established the Jinji, Yuankang and Zhenyi silk factories one after the other. Later on, more factories were added every year. Altogether, fifteen factories were set up, and because of the needs of these factories, 950 square *li*, amounting to 30 per cent of the area of the county, has become devoted to mulberry. There are now 30 cocoon houses in the county, producing 160,000 piculs of spring cocoons, 30,000 piculs of summer cocoons, and 10,000 piculs of autumn cocoons every year, totalling 200,000 piculs . . . Outside the city walls, mulberry and hemp are grown in a continuous stretch. Every family grows hemp and every household raises silkworms. At the cocoon harvest people surge like the tide to the cocoon warehouses to sell their cocoons. The old hand-reeling machines cannot be found any more.[27]

This passage is important as an account of the technological and commercial progress that brought about the development of mulberry farming in Wuxi. The importance attached to the railway, cocoon warehouses, and silk factories is well justified, even though Wuxi's position as a silk producer was not newly won within the twenty years before 1921, as the passage implies. As early as 1880, it was known to rival Suzhou as a silk producer, and its position of strength in the silk trade was noted sporadically in contemporary accounts from 1880 to 1900.[28] That the early success should count for so little in a contemporary account in 1921 emphasizes the rapidity of later developments. The passage also does not make sufficiently clear that the growth of the silk industry in Wuxi was accompanied by the development of mulberry farming as a specialized activity. The development was not confined to Wuxi county. Along the banks of the Grand Canal, where the soil was sandy, in a stretch that went from Wuxi to Wujin, these specialized mulberry farms sprang up. It was a development peculiar to this area.[29]

The growth of mulberry farming and silkworm rearing in Shunde county on the Zhujiang delta was no less striking. The change-over from paddy farming can be traced from the 1860s, before the introduction of the steam filature. It was the growth of international demand for silk that led to this development, and the steam filature was an enterprising growth from it. The filature was not readily accepted, but it is safe to assume that filature silk found an eager market long before 1895, in which year an export of 21,000 piculs was noted. By 1925, there were 135 steam filatures in Shunde, out of a total of 167 in all of Guangdong. Transport never posed a serious problem in this delta county: river boats served the villages and markets, and junks towed by steam launches connected the markets to Guangzhou. The centres of the cocoon trade were the towns of Yongqi and Guizhou.[30] According to Howard and Buswell, writing in 1925:

Here are found the largest cocoon markets and 80 per cent of the cocoon warehouses. To these towns most of the supplies of cocoons from all other districts converge and from here they are redistributed to the steam filatures. Only about one-quarter of the cocoons go elsewhere for marketing. Because of this highly profitable business Shuntak [Shunde] is the financial centre of Kwongtung [Guangdong]. A great amount of the business of Canton [Guangzhou] and other towns of the province depends upon this district and its operations in silk for financial backing. About 80 per cent of the Canton banks are financed by Shuntak capital. So we may well say that Shuntak is the bank town of Kwongtung and whatever affects the industry there will be reflected in the financial life of the province.[31]

There should be little wonder, therefore, that 70 per cent of the land area (not cultivated acreage) and 80 per cent of the population of Shunde were devoted to mulberry farming and the silk industry, according to the same authors. No other district in Guangdong was so exclusively given to these activities as Shunde.

Outside the Wuxi-Wujin area and Shunde, evidence is abundant that silkworm rearing and mulberry farming spread to others places between 1870 and 1929. Aside from references in the gazetteers, a comparison between the exhaustive study by the Imperial Maritime Customs in 1881 and the reports in the *Shina shobetsu zenshi* of 1920 show that silk production became more extensive in Jiangsu, even though not in Guangdong. Production in Jiangsu, none the less, remained concentrated in the south.[32] Attempts to introduce the industry to the transitional region or the north were for the most part unsuccessful.[33] In Guangdong, the gazetteers note numerous reasons for the failure of the silk industry to spread. The Dongguan gazetteer of 1927 suggests that because mulberry markets were not established,

Table 6.4

Imports of Rice and Paddy into Guangdong and Jiangsu as Recorded by Maritime Customs, 1872–1931 (annual averages) ('000 piculs)

	Zhujiang Delta			Shantou			Shanghai		
	Foreign	From Other Provinces	Total	Foreign	From Other Provinces	Total	Foreign	From Other Provinces	Total
1872–6	19	760	779	176	543	719	—	10	10
1877–81	—	1,637	1,637	144	442	586	4	62	66
1882–6	20	2,164	2,184	83	543	626	1	3	4
1887–91	4,690	2,278	6,968	89	646	735	1	57	58
1892–6	7,072	2,946	10,018	207	1,949	2,156	1	106	107
1897–1901	4,230	1,592	5,822	156	1,512	1,668	20	104	124
1902–6	3,470	3,635	7,105	239	2,468	2,707	25	75	100
1907–11	5,317	1,236	6,553	608	1,605	2,213	147	160	307
1912–16	5,308	647	5,955	202	1,514	1,716	1	141	142
1917–21	4,511	1,952	6,463	399	1,908	2,307	11	258	269
1922–6	9,522	918	10,440	1,651	813	2,464	1,824	414	2,238
1927–31	6,125	498	6,623	1,414	748	2,162	2,921	455	3,376

Source: MC, trade reports.

attempts by the county gentry to promote silkworm and mulberry thirty years earlier were not successful. There was always the danger that insufficient feed was available for the worms, it notes.[34] The Panyu gazetteer of 1931 places the limiting factor on the county not having cocoon markets, and hence although cocoons were produced for sale to Shunde, the silk was reeled locally.[35] Farther away, the Sihui gazetteer of 1935 notes that while silkworms were raised in many villages, eggs had to be purchased from nearby Xinhui county.[36] The Gaoyao gazetteer that covers events up to 1911 sees the continuation of hand reeling as the principal drawback, for as long as hand-reeled silk could not be sold readily on the export market, local farmers sold their cocoons to the steam filatures instead.[37] These arguments, it may be noticed, emphasized the absence of a commercial infrastructure that combined the mulberry farms, cocoon markets, and the villages, but did not notice that bank credit was an essential element in building the infrastructure that Shunde enjoyed.

Rice

It is, of course, well known that rice was by far the most extensively cultivated crop in Jiangsu and Guangdong. Because it was grown as a staple, it is not always sufficiently realized that it was also the most extensively traded farm produce. It was estimated in the 1930s that Shanghai alone consumed 8.1 million piculs of the cereal per annum.[38] At 1933 prices, the Shanghai population would have paid 71 million silver dollars for the product, three times the total receipts for white silk exported from Shanghai for that year. In Guangdong, an estimate of food consumption in rice equivalent for the total urban population of the entire province in 1931 placed it at 41.6 million piculs per annum.[39] At current prices, if only half this quantity of food was made up of rice, the total outlay for this cereal in Guangdong would have amounted to over 200 million dollars, which exceeded substantially the total foreign trade receipts for local produce exported from all Guangdong ports. Neither cotton nor silk could possibly have claimed as large a domestic market as rice. Tremors in the rice trade, therefore, had much wider effects on the rural economy than in that of any other rural produce.

Because the export of rice to foreign countries was banned at various times, and that to other provinces occasionally subject to local embargoes, export statistics for this cereal are highly unreliable.[40] None the less, it is fairly clear that, for years, Guangdong had been a net rice-importing province and Jiangsu a net rice-exporting one. In the early eighteenth century, when the Guangdong population was considerably smaller than what it was to become in the nineteenth century, the province imported 1 to 2 million piculs of rice annually from Guangxi. In later years in the century, Guangdong and Fujian imported a further 'several hundred thousand' piculs from Siam.[41] It is not clear when Guangxi imports gave way to imports from the Changjiang valley; but by the late nineteenth century, Guangxi had ceased to be a major grain supplier to Guangdong, its place having been taken over by the Changjiang provinces. As Table 6.4 shows, by the mid-1870s, the ports of the Zhujiang delta imported 779,000 piculs, and Shantou 719,000 piculs, per annum, most of which came from the Changjiang. The figures for these early years of the Maritime Customs' history in all likelihood understate overall imports into Guangdong. None the less, even if it is assumed that actual imports in the 1870s amounted to two or three times the amounts recorded, which would be close to what they became in the 1880s when the Maritime Customs had become more established, imported rice could have constituted only a small portion (say 5 per cent) of urban consumption in the province. Obviously, Guangdong's urban markets remained major outlets for rice locally produced within the province, even as rice imports increased.

In both the Zhujiang delta and Shantou, from the 1870s to the 1920s, rice imports increased rapidly. In the Zhujiang delta, they increased from 2 million piculs per annum to well over 6 million piculs, and in Shantou from 0.7 million piculs per annum to a peak of 2.7 million piculs in the early 1900s. Much of this amount was imported in times of, or in anticipation of, poor harvests. Part of it may also be accounted for by expanded consumption, the result of urban growth and changes in diet brought on by prosperity. Such factors aside, the import figures indicate underlying long-term trends that reflect the competitiveness of imported rice over locally produced rice, and among the imported portion, of Southeast Asian rice over the Changjiang product.[42] The competition is most marked in the Guangzhou import figures cited in Table 6.4, for they show that while total imports climbed rapidly to 10 million piculs per annum between 1892 and 1896, imports never again dropped below 5 million piculs per annum in the years to follow, substantially exceeding imports in the 1870s and 1880s, and that among imports, it was foreign rice that from the 1890s formed the greater portion. In Shantou, Changjiang

CASH CROPS AND TRADE

rice held its own until the 1920s, but thereafter it lost its predominance to Southeast Asian rice. Even in Shanghai, where foreign imports were quite insignificant until the 1920s, they reached well over 1 million piculs per annum during that decade.[43]

The success of imported rice cannot readily be explained. High population density in Guangdong is, in itself, a poor explanation, for it cannot account for the purchasing power that must have been essential in generating the imports. However, if the ability of the Guangdong rice-purchasing population to purchase may be assumed (as being the result of export expansion or the diversion of funds traditionally expended on local produce to imported varieties), the crucial question that should be asked is why local produce in Guangdong was less competitive than the imported product, and then why the Changjiang product was less competitive than the Southeast Asian variety. Even this question is highly complex. To answer it, account must be taken of the entire Asian rice market, of monetary conditions within China and in China's foreign trade, and of production factors in China's rice-producing areas.

As far as Guangdong rice is concerned, it can be safely argued that its price in Guangzhou reflected high prices at sources of supply and that these prices had not been substantially magnified by transport costs. Earlier figures are not available, but transport costs in the 1930s have been summarized in Table 6.5. They show that, in general, junk transport on the tributaries of the Zhujiang (Beijiang, Dongjiang, and Xijiang) was cheaper than steam transport from the Changjiang or from Southeast Asia, and cheaper still than the rail transport that was applicable, however, to only small portions of the delta area near Guangzhou. Much local rice, moreover, could be brought down the rivers by junk into Guangzhou. Changjiang rice was transported by steamer, and unloaded at Guangzhou, while Southeast Asian rice was taken by steamer to Hong Kong only, and transhipped from there to Guangzhou by trawlers. Read against this background, the price differentials that are apparent in Figures 6.1 and 6.2 indicate quite clearly the direction of trade: Guangzhou, Shantou, and the upper reaches of the Hanjiang River, were foci of trade that originated in markets on the rivers that led to these areas. In 1921, the average price of local rice in Guangzhou was 7.70 dollars per picul. As it would have taken 1.4 piculs of paddy to produce a picul of rice, this figure implies that paddy, with milling costs included, would have been worth on average 5.50 dollars. The margin left for insurance, wastage, storage,

Figure 6.1 Regional Rice Prices in Guangdong, 1921, in dollars per picul

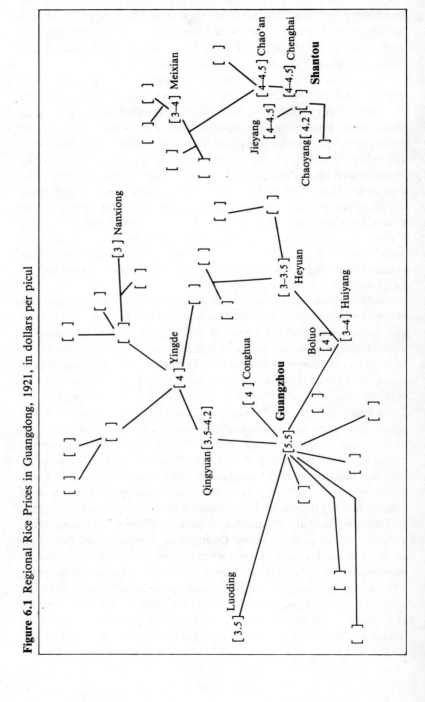

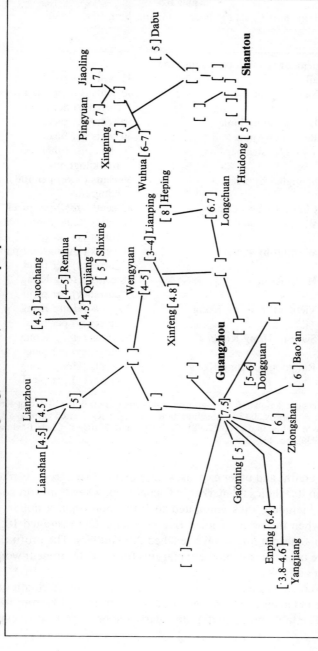

Figure 6.2 Regional Rice Prices in Guangdong, 1927–1928, in dollars per picul

Note: In Figures 6.1 and 6.2, each pair of brackets represents a county noted in Guoli Zhongshan daxue nongke xueyuan (1925, 1929). Figures in brackets are the local prices of paddy in dollars per *shi*. The straight lines indicate likely trade routes. The prices of paddy in Guangzhou are estimated from Zhang Shantu (1930).

Source: Guoli Zhongshan daxue nongke xueyuan (1925, 1929, 1933).

Table 6.5

Transport Costs for Rice to Guangzhou, Early 1930s

Journey	Cost
1. From delta area south of Guangzhou by rail	95 cents per picul
2. From Shaoguan on Beijiang by rail	80 cents (Guangzhou paper currency) per picul
3. From Dongjiang by junk	50 cents per picul
4. From Beijiang by junk	40 cents per picul
5. From Wuhu by steamer	70–80 cents (*fabi*) per 100 kilograms
6. From Shanghai by steamer	60 cents (*fabi*) per 100 kilograms
7. From Changsha by steamer	82 cents (*fabi*) per picul
8. From Wuzhou by junk	50 cents (Guangzhou paper currency) per picul
9. From Wuzhou by steamer	70 cents (Guangzhou paper currency) per picul
10. From Hong Kong	18 cents (Hong Kong currency) per picul
11. From Vietnam to Hong Kong	30 cents (Hong Kong currency) per picul
12. From Siam to Hong Kong	55 cents (Hong Kong currency) per picul
13. From Rangoon to Hong Kong	70 cents (Hong Kong currency) per picul

Note: Conversion: 1 dollar *fabi* = approx. 1.44 Guangzhou dollar; 1 Hong Kong dollar = approx. 1.35 Guangzhou dollar (1931); 1 Kg = 1.65 catties.
Sources: Chen Qihui (n.d.), pp. 26081–2, 26101, and 26103–5; Chen Bozhuang (1936), pp. 131–2.

handling, credit, and other expenses for a picul of rice from its place of origin to its wholesale market in Guangzhou, when transport costs had been included, thus amounted to little more than a dollar. In 1927–8, when the price of local rice in Guangzhou averaged 10.50 dollars, this margin might have reached 2.00 dollars. The profit that could have been derived on these margins for the entrepreneur would have been quite small.

Table 6.6 lists the prices of local rice and imported South-east Asian rice in Guangzhou, and the price of rice in Shanghai from 1912 to 1929. The table brings out quite clearly the price competitiveness of both South-east Asian and Changjiang rice over locally produced rice in Guangdong. Given the high price of locally produced rice at source, the question should be asked whether competition had very much effect on local production or pricing. The answer is not altogether clear. Rice production, certainly, depended on well established practices that were not readily altered. Moreover, because of the shortage of agricultural land in Guangdong, production was, in any case, not highly elastic. However, it should also be noted that local rice was considered to be of a higher quality than South-east Asian rice, and the South-east Asian variety probably did not take over the market of the local variety but only supplemented it. In some places, farmers who had not been in the habit of purchasing rice sold the rice that they themselves had grown, and consumed South-east Asian rice purchased from the markets. In other places, especially in the cities, it probably provided an alternative for subsidiary foodstuffs such as root crops, especially for the poorer population. No indication may be detected from the sources of any contraction in the market for locally produced rice.

The table also demonstrates the competitiveness of South-east Asian rice over Changjiang rice in the 1920s. To begin first with the 1910s, it may be recalled that South-east Asian rice dominated the Guangzhou market but was not imported into Shanghai or Shantou in substantial quantities (see Table 6.4). During these years, as Table 6.6 demonstrates, the price of rice in Shanghai remained lower than that of foreign rice imported into Guangzhou. In the 1920s, foreign rice was imported into Shanghai in substantial quantities: in 1922 (1.6 million piculs), 1923 (1.3 million piculs), 1926 (5.8 million piculs), and in 1927 (5.0 million piculs).[44] In these years, the price of rice quoted for Shanghai was close to, or above, that quoted for foreign rice in Guangzhou. In both the 1910s and the 1920s, even in those years in which the price of rice fell below that of foreign rice in Guangzhou, the difference was apparently insufficient to cover transport and handling to give Changjiang rice price competitiveness over South-east Asian rice. The large companies that imported foreign rice into Guangzhou were more efficient than the native merchants who imported Changjiang rice from Shanghai and other places. For instance, a merchant purchasing rice from Wuhu had himself to arrange for transport from Shanghai and the shipment took twenty days to reach Guangzhou, whereas South-east Asian rice could be delivered within a week.[45]

Table 6.6

Price of Rice and Rice Imports into the Zhujiang Delta, 1912–1929

	Price of Rice in Guangzhou		Price of Rice in Shanghai (dol./picul)
	Local Rice (dol./picul)	Foreign Rice (dol./picul)	
1912	6.30	6.40	5.30
1913	5.60	5.60	4.80
1914	5.60	4.90	4.30
1915	6.10	5.30	4.90
1916	6.10	5.70	4.80
1917	5.00	4.90	4.40
1918	6.30	5.60	4.40
1919	7.60	n.a.	4.60
1920	6.70	n.a.	6.40
1921	7.70	6.80	6.50
1922	8.60	7.70	7.50
1923	9.10	8.50	7.50
1924	9.50	9.60	6.90
1925	10.10	9.50	7.30
1926	10.50	10.00	10.50
1927	11.20	10.10	9.90
1928	10.60	9.80	7.50
1929	10.40	9.50	9.00

Note: The price of local rice in Guangzhou is the median of 13 varieties cited, and that of foreign rice, of 7 varieties. The price of rice in Shanghai is reproduced here as cited in the source, and except for conversion from dollars/*shi* to dollars/picul, is converted at 0.667 *shi* per picul. The monetary unit for Guangzhou prices is not specified in the source, but the prevalent currency was the *haoyin* (a subsidiary silver coin). In the 1910s, the Guangzhou dollar reckoned in this currency was close to par with the Shanghai silver dollar. In the 1920s the Guangzhou dollar in *haoyin* depreciated against the Shanghai dollar by approximately 20 per cent.

Sources: Zhang Shantu (1930), Shanghai shangye chuxu yinhang diaochabu (1931a); MC, trade reports.

To understand the implications of these market trends for rice, it is necessary to appreciate that trade for this cereal was conducted, by the late nineteenth century, in a unified market that spanned the whole of East Asia.[46] Guangzhou and Shantou, along with Japan, were major purchasers of rice, while the Changjiang and South-east Asia, especially

Rice Imports into the Zhujiang Delta		
From Abroad ('000 piculs)	From Other Provinces ('000 piculs)	Total ('000 piculs)
1,822	1,165	2,987
3,748	417	4,165
5,338	231	5,569
6,496	708	7,204
9,138	714	9,852
7,761	288	8,049
5,839	12	5,851
1,526	6,368	7,894
760	3,075	3,835
6,671	17	6,688
11,429	11	11,440
14,003	478	14,481
10,216	2,664	12,880
7,399	1,389	8,788
4,565	38	4,603
9,075	45	9,120
7,773	685	8,458
6,043	371	6,414

Vietnam and Thailand, were principal sellers. From the mid-1890s, the price of rice in Shanghai had been rising: firstly, because of the depreciation of the silver currency from that year; secondly, because of the alarm caused by the Sino-Japanese War and the vast shipments of rice to Japan; and thirdly, because of the depreciation of the copper coinage after 1907.[47] The price of rice remained at this high level throughout the 1910s, but further advances soon came. From 1919 to 1920, as the result of a sudden demand for South-east Asian rice from Japan, prices rose, and Guangzhou imported an unprecedented quantity from the Changjiang provinces.[48] In 1920 and 1921, alarm had developed over the North China famine and high prices became acceptable. Farmers reacted to the sudden price increase by withholding their supply from the market, thus contributing to further increases in the short term.[49] Political instability in the Changjiang provinces and in Guangdong, and embargoes placed on rice by exporting provinces must also have had their short term effects, but on the basis of the regression analysis conducted by Loren Brandt, it would seem that the price of rice on the international market and the gold price of silver were much more powerful determinants of the price of rice within China than the country's internal politics.[50]

Because China adhered to silver while her trading partners went on to the gold standard (British India, including Burma, in 1899, Thailand in 1902, although French Indo-China as late as 1930) it might be thought that any silver depreciation would have suppressed rice imports.[51] It should be noted, however, that any effect the depreciation of silver might have had on import volume was not noticeable. Increases in the price of imported rice, according to Table 6.6, were fully matched by increases in the price of local rice. It is not easy to explain this if we assume a relatively uncontrolled market within China. It is possible that, because of easing demand, China's suppliers could bring prices down more rapidly than silver depreciation could push them up; but perhaps a continued tradition of calculating in terms of copper in China's interior might also have made silver prices react more rapidly to silver depreciation than might otherwise have been the case.

1930 to 1937

Silk

In 1930 the best improved cocoons in Jiangsu sold for 70 dollars per picul. In 1932 the same quality cocoons sold for 60 dollars, and in 1934, 32 dollars. From 1929 to 1933 total exports of raw silk from China dropped from 190,000 piculs to 76,000 piculs.[52] The silk industry was the first victim of the world depression among China's budding enterprises. The economic calamity had come with little warning and its effects were disastrous.

Apparently, the silk farmers had not anticipated the collapse of the market. In 1931, when the price of silk began to drop, a glut had already built up from the previous year's sale, and the decline in price in the countryside was rapid. In both Wuxi and Shunde there was considerable hardship from 1931 to 1934.[53] In Wuxi, in 1931, numerous incidents of rice-looting were attributed to silk farmers who failed to sell their crops.[54] In Shunde, Chen Hansheng left a vivid account:

In this famous district, 70 per cent of the cultivated land is covered with mulberries. For both the mulberry and the rice lands, in Shun-teh [Shunde], cash rent is being paid, which in the course of the last thirty years has become a rent paid nearly always in advance. The amount of this rent is anywhere from

6 to 50 Yuan per mow [*mu*], usually from 20 to 25 Yuan. Within the last three years [1931–4], the average price of cocoons per catty has dropped from 2.00 to 0.30 Yuan; consequently, the price of mulberries per.picul has dropped from 5.00 to 0.60 Yuan, when 0.60 to 0.65 Yuan per picul has to be paid as a wage for leaf picking. Under such conditions, many mulberry peasants prefer not to pick the leaves. Now, seven crops of mulberries are expected in Shun-teh every year; when the leaves of one crop are left unpicked, those of the next naturally become tough and therefore cannot be sold. Hence, at least 30 per cent of the mulberry fields have been abandoned. The peasants own less than 10 per cent of all the mulberry fields; and many a tenant has to pay a rent even for the abandoned land. Moreover, according to the custom of Shun-teh, the tenant must pay the land tax for his landlord, which is later deducted from his rent payment. The Shun-teh tenants are now being pursued not only by the landlord, but also by the tax collector. The prices of silk and cocoons are so unremunerative that peasants throw the silkworms into ponds to feed the fish: men suffer hunger while fish are well nourished. The fish may be sold; but even so,.the tenants can hardly afford to eat rice-gruel twice a day; how can they pay the rent? The landlord would never cancel it, the best he would do is to grant a rent reduction. Such a reduction may be as high as 50 per cent; but for the tenant it can only mean a further indebtedness.[55]

In Wujiang, Jiangsu, Fei Xiaotong also noted the following:

When the silk industry was prosperous the production of raw silk could yield an average household about 300 dollars with a surplus (profit and wages) of 250 dollars. (The highest price of native silk exceeded 1 dollar per Liang and the total production for an average household is 280 Liang. The cost of production, excluding wages, is about 50 dollars.) . . . The villagers had then sufficient money to finance the various recreative and ceremonial activities which have been suspended for more than ten years.

The price of native silk has fallen. In 1935 the price was 1 dollar for 3 Liang. Without any decrease in the amount of production, an average household could then only obtain a profit of 45 dollars. In such conditions and with the traditional system of production, it is difficult to balance the domestic budget . . . A new industry has been introduced and . . . the villagers have also attempted to increase their income by expanding their trading activities. But in many cases they have sold their rice reserves in the winter and borrowed rice from the shop in the summer. In case of urgent need they have appealed to usurers. On the other side they have tried to cut down expenses which are not immediately necessary, such as those for recreative meetings and marriage.[56]

Chen's account goes on to describe the conversion of mulberry land into sugar-cane fields in Shunde, and other sources confirm that between 1934 and 1935 this transformation was taking place on a

Table 6.7

Exports and Prices of White Silk, Jiangsu and Guangdong, 1929–1937

	Jiangsu (piculs)	Guangdong (piculs)	Prices in	
			US Dollars per lb.	Dollars per picul
1929	68,110	53,936	4.96	1,782
1930	48,025	47,563	3.56	1,713
1931	29,650	40,399	2.61	1,612
1932	22,093	24,108	2.14	1,108
1933	28,901	26,606	1.53	964
1934	13,024	26,062	n.a.	625
1935	41,667	16,982	n.a.	635
1936	31,894	17,160	n.a.	809
1937	34,746	20,879	n.a.	857

Sources: MC, trade reports; Zhongguo jingi nianjian 1936, p. E.150, and Shanghai jiefang qianhou wujia ziliao huibian (1958), p. 237.

large scale in the Zhujiang delta. Fei briefly describes the 'new industry' that was shortly to be introduced into the village he studied: sheep raising. He gives no estimate of income derived from it, but it is unlikely that it could have replaced silk. As in the Zhujiang delta, in southern Jiangsu, much mulberry land was converted to other uses following the collapse of the silk market. In Wuxi the 250,000 mu of mulberry land in 1930 dwindled to 84,000 mu in 1932; in Jiangyin 124,000 mu was reduced to 54,000 mu; and in Wujin, one-quarter of the mulberry trees were cut in 1933 and the land on which they had been planted was converted into paddy fields.[57]

Table 6.7 shows that the decline in the price of silk persisted from 1929 to 1937. However, in Jiangsu, the market recovered somewhat from 1935 to 1937. The reason for the recovery may be traced to the political influence of the Xue family that dominated the silk-reeling co-operatives in Wuxi. Quality could conceivably also have been raised, as a result of more stringent direct control in a diminished market.[58]

Rice

The trend in rising prices for rice in the 1920s continued into 1930, as Table 6.8 shows. The effects of the world depression followed in the

Table 6.8

Prices and Imports of Foreign Rice into the Zhujiang Delta and Southern Jiangsu, 1928–1937

	Price of Silver (US cents/oz.)	Price of Foreign Rice in Guangzhou* (dollars/picul)	Price of Rice in Shanghai† (dollars/picul)	Foreign Rice Imports	
				Into Zhujiang Delta (mill. piculs)	Into Shanghai (mill. piculs)
1928	60.10	9.20	7.50	7.8	0.1
1929	52.00	10.50	9.10	6.0	0.5
1930	38.80	12.50	11.50	3.7	7.1
1931	31.50	10.60	8.70	4.1	0.8
1932	27.60	9.80	9.30	10.3	3.8
1933	34.80	10.90‡	6.30	12.7	0.9
1934	48.70	8.00	7.10	6.1	1.0
1935	65.40	7.60	8.30	5.7	9.7
1936	47.30	10.90	7.40	2.9	0.2
1937	45.80	n.a.	8.40	3.2	0.5

Note: Guangzhou prices entered here are quoted in paper currency (*haozhuan*). To compare Guangzhou and Shanghai prices, the silver dollar in Shanghai (0.72 Haikwan Tael) may be taken as equivalent to 1.2 to 1.3 times the Guangzhou dollar up to 1935. In 1936 and 1937, after the monetary reform, 1 dollar *fabi* was equivalent to 1.44 Guangzhou dollars.

* Median of 7 varieties of rice cited.

† 1932 entry from price in July, all others annual averages of monthly figures.

‡ Possible error, see text.

Sources: Dickens H. Leavens (1939), p. 303; *Guangdong jingji nianjian 1941*, pp. K72–3; Liu Zhonglian (1948), pp. 402–3; Shiyebu yinjia wujia taolun weiyanhui (1936), p. 53; Xu Daofu (1983), pp. 132 and 137; MC, trade reports (1928–35); Chen Qihui (n.d.), pp. 26022–3.

next year. The price of foreign rice began to decline from 1930 to 1931. In fact, in French Indo-China, price depression was felt as early as 1929, when Saigon No. 1 went from 7.00 piastres per picul in that year to 6.72 in 1930, but the downturn only set in firmly when it dropped to 4.01 piastres in 1931, 3.27 in 1932, 2.46 in 1933, and 1.97 in 1934. The price of foreign rice in Guangzhou from 1931 to 1934 followed this trend, except for the entry for 1933 in Table 6.8. This particular entry could have been biased by government reports for that year, 1933 being the year in which a tariff was imposed on imported rice, and it is contradicted by other sources.[59]

The immediate increase in imports of foreign rice into the Zhujiang delta as a result of the decline in price in 1932 is phenomenal. In that year 10.3 million piculs were imported, and in 1933 this rose to 12.7 million piculs. The tariff imposed in 1933 might have had some effect, for imports declined until, by 1936, another critical shortage developed that resulted in the partial removal of the tariff.[60]

Imports into Shanghai are complicated, and it is difficult to find a satisfactory explanation that might account for the continuous rise in the price of rice from 1928 to 1931. It was not the result of political turmoil (which came in January 1932), or natural disaster (the Changjiang flood that affected Jiangsu began as late as August 1931). It was not confined to the city (as we know from the Wujin reports quoted on Table 4.5), and was part of a general inflation that affected not only rice but other foodstuffs, manufactures, metals, fuels, building materials, and miscellaneous goods (as we know from the Shanghai wholesale price index). It is hard to see what else could have contributed more to the increase other than the sudden influx of silver into China that was started by the world depression (see Table 4.6). The general decline in the world silver price up to 1934 had brought about a depreciation of China's international currency, but within China itself the two-tiered monetary system that spanned village and city economies, and the large quantities of silver absorbed in the initial years of the depression created the anomalous situation of an inflation.

The price gap that resulted from the weakening of the rice market abroad and the initial inflation within China would have greatly stimulated foreign rice imports. Towards the end of 1931, prices dropped, firstly, because imports from South-east Asia became highly competitive, and secondly, because rural depression had begun to set in as a result of the collapse of export handicrafts. Moreover, silver movements reversed, for net exports of silver can be documented from

1933. By that year, there was also news that the Japanese government might subsidize the dumping of Japanese rice in China as a measure to relieve rural depression in Japan.[61] Imports of foreign rice into Shanghai were not abnormal for 1933 and 1934, but in 1932 and 1935, when the price in Shanghai rose only moderately, large quantities of foreign rice were imported. By 1932 reports began to appear that declining prices were hurting farmers in rice-exporting areas.[62]

From 1934, as the result of the United States Silver Purchase Act, large quantities of silver were exported from China and the rural depression deepened. In November 1935, China took measures to reform the currency. The shortage of credit curtailed needed efforts to revitalize the rural economy, and then the over-supply of money that this currency reform made possible brought on another inflationary trend that was to last into the 1940s. Towards 1937 the price of rice in terms of the new paper currency rose, just as prices for other commodities also rose.[63]

Again, Chen Hansheng left an insightful description of the misery that low prices caused in Guangdong:

In Chungshan [Zhongshan] it is estimated that only when the price of unhusked rice per picul is 6 Yuan or more can a rent of 10 Yuan per mou [*mu*] be paid. Up to recent years, when the rice mills of Shek-ki [Shiqi] collected rice from each new harvest, 7 Yuan per picul was paid. But the price dropped so rapidly that in the spring of 1934 even the best grade of unhusked rice was marketed for 4.20 Yuan per picul. Similar conditions exist in the southwestern part of the province . . .

With the decline in the price of rice, the prices of taro, potato, carrots, and peanuts have also gone down. From the North River [Beijiang] Valley great quantities of taro and peanuts are transported southward to various cities of the delta region; but recently the prices have fallen to a level which barely covers the transportation charges. Within the last five years, the price of unhusked rice in Pan-yu [Panyu] has been cut by 38 per cent; and during the same period the prices of peanuts, taro, and potato have been cut by 15 per cent, 25 per cent, and 50 per cent, respectively.

The prices of various products which in the peasant economy are of an auxiliary nature have met with equal if not more drastic reduction . . .[64]

In 1936 a general depression was setting in, affecting all prices, as Fei Xiaotong also noted in southern Jiangsu.[65] The downward trend in commodity prices was also noted by Zhang Liluan in Wujin, who reported that land prices were also declining. Apparently, the land tax was not reduced and landlords who were faced with tenants refusing to pay rent began to find it a serious burden. Tenants paying commuted rent were the hardest hit. They rioted and attacked rent-collecting offices in 1934, 1935, and 1936, primarily in Suzhou.[66]

Other Products

While the depression must have been felt intensely in most parts of Guangdong and Jiangsu, its effects in different areas varied, depending on the crops that were grown and how their trade and prices were affected. Some of these variations are brought out in Table 6.9, which traces the progress of wheat, flour, cotton, and sugar from 1929 to 1937.

The most striking feature in the table is the phenomenal increase in imports of wheat from 1931 to 1935, and the accompanying decline in the price of this commodity from 1930 to 1934. The international depression and availability of vast supplies from abroad would readily account for the trend, Australia being, by far, the principal supplier of wheat into Shanghai in 1932 and 1933.[67] Australia's position as supplier was taken over by the United States in 1934, and this change must be taken into account in any discussion of the Wheat Loan of 1931 and the Cotton and Wheat Loan in 1934 which contemporary writers and later historians correctly condemned as inexcusable encouragements for imports at a time when China's rural producers obviously needed protection.[68] The inflow of silver, the weakness of the export trade, and the reduction in overseas remittances that had also resulted from the international depression, brought about an alarming balance-of-payments problem. The natural disasters of the 1930s, on the other hand, created a need for the financially hard-pressed Nationalist government to provide relief: the 1931 Wheat Loan was a direct consequence of the floods of that year. It might have been thought, in the circumstances, that a loan in silver from domestic or foreign sources would have been a more rational solution, even on a short-term basis, than an export credit loan from a foreign government. The 1934 loan, therefore, justifiably met with a tremendous popular outcry, and the available credit to be extended was reduced in 1935 from 5 million US dollars to 2 million, the reduction being taken entirely out of the portion allotted for cotton purchase.[69] In combination with the loan, tariffs imposed in 1933 apparently had an effect in cutting off supplies from Australia. The slow upturn in the price of wheat and cotton in 1935 might also be the result of the recovery of US

Table 6.9
Imports and Prices of Cotton, Wheat, Flour, and Sugar, 1929–1937

	Cotton		Wheat		Flour			Sugar		
	Imports into Jiangsu ('000 piculs)	Price	Imports into Jiangsu ('000 piculs)	Price	Imports into Jiangsu ('000 piculs)	Imports into Guangdong ('000 piculs)	Price	Imports into Jiangsu ('000 piculs)	Imports into Guangdong ('000 piculs)	Price
1929	1,908	39.0	5,464	4.93	247	964	3.15	4,754	1,612	14.3
1930	2,720	39.1	2,691	5.64	226	852	3.43	2,453	1,828	13.2
1931	3,759	41.5	20,932	4.63	83	1,113	2.96	3,047	988	18.6
1932	3,335	35.7	12,781	4.23	2,721	1,082	2.77	2,109	598	22.2
1933	1,851	34.1	15,261	3.63	168	1,005	2.40	1,934	136	27.1
1934	1,819	33.4	7,413	3.53	407	435	2.24	1,703	85	19.1
1935	820	33.6	8,157	4.01	121	480	2.55	1,545	123	n.a.
1936	641	41.1	1,834	5.21	97	293	3.37	1,000	251	n.a.
1937	233	39.3	489	6.07	100	301	4.07	866	76	n.a.

Note: Prices for cotton and wheat given in dollars/picul; for flour, in dollars/bag of 49 lb.; for sugar, dollars/picul, as given for brown sugar no. 23. In all cases, prices are quoted in silver from 1929 to 1935, and in *fabi* from 1936 to 1937.
Sources: MC, trade reports, 'Kwangtung government sugar factories', p. 158; *Shanghai jiefang qianhou wujia ziliao huibian* (1958), pp. 213 and 229.

prices from 1934. Price increases in 1936 and 1937 would also have been related to the depreciation of the *fabi*, the paper currency that replaced silver in China, and the onset of the war with Japan.

Despite the international depression, the inflow of silver created an environment for an industrial boom in China in the early 1930s.[70] Investment in cotton spinning and flour milling increased and the demand so created is apparent from the figures in Table 6.9.[71] The price of flour declined between 1929 and 1934, recovering in 1935 to 1936 for the same reasons as the price of wheat did. That the increased production of flour did not stimulate higher prices for wheat is indicative of the small share that the mills consumed of China's wheat production.[72] Based on wholesale prices reported in Shanghai, Richard A. Kraus has calculated that, between 1930 and 1933, the price of cotton relative to rice increased by 66 per cent, and relative to wheat by 36 per cent.[73] The net result of such price changes was an expansion of the cotton acreage. In Jiangsu, the National Agricultural Research Bureau's statistics show that it increased from 11.4 million *shimu* in 1931 to over 12.0 million *shimu* in 1933 and 1934, and the Chinese Cotton Mill-owners' Association's surveys show that it increased from 7.0 million *shimu* to 9.0 million *shimu* between the same years.[74] As with the prices of rice and wheat, the price of cotton increased slightly from 1929 to 1931 and then declined to 1934. Unlike the cereals, import volumes declined after 1932, despite the Wheat and Cotton Loan of 1934.[75]

The cultivation of sugar-cane, primarily in Guangdong, was another area that might have been affected by changes in imports and prices, the figures for which are also given in Table 6.9. The trend is clear even though the reasons for it are not obvious: sugar imports into both Shanghai and Guangdong declined rapidly from 1929,[76] while the price of sugar increased from 1932. These trends might have been affected by the imposition of import duties in 1930, 1933, and 1934, which, according to one report, increased tenfold during those few years.[77] The attempts of the Guangdong government to establish several factories might also have helped, but even by the reports of the government, a not inconsiderable amount of locally produced sugar was used as raw material.[78] The more direct cause of these changes was probably export restrictions imposed in Dutch Indonesia, which considerably reduced Javanese exports.[79] Equally unclear is the extent to which the cultivation of sugar-cane might have increased in these years. In the Chaozhou area, some extension of the sugar acreage may be documented.[80] Elsewhere, except in areas in which the government sugar refineries directly promoted cultivation, for instance, in specially designated plantations, the records imply more of a general sense of hope for the revival of the trade rather than clear instances of the addition of cultivated land.

7

Income from Cash Cropping

As prices rose, as trade expanded, and as the market served to involve producers in competitive trading, it is a foregone conclusion that opportunities were available for farmers to benefit from cultivating cash crops. Whether they did depended on their operating costs, likely profits, and their ability to produce the capital that might be needed. These questions are also tied to the need to take risks in commercial operations and the likelihood of bankruptcy.[1] They relate to differential access to economic opportunities by different sectors of the social structure, and were justifiably of central concern to the researchers of the 1920s and 1930s. In the absence of direct evidence on income distribution, these are important questions that relate to the immediate well-being of the cultivators.

It should be made clear, however, that like every other topic that was studied in field research in the 1920s and 1930s, the source material for these subjects is anything but straightforward. In particular, farm income-and-expenses studies, of which a large number are available and that would, at first sight, appear to be highly relevant to the present concern, must be treated with great scepticism. In the field studies of the 1920s and 1930s, it was common practice to report all farm income and expenses in monetary terms and to deduce from these figures whether the farm operation was profitable.[2] The practice results from an obvious error in methodology. Much farm produce was not sold, and much labour was contributed by members of the farm family for which no monetary wages were paid. Fei Xiaotong criticized the practice most succinctly: 'Those goods ... do not enter into the market. Their money value is unknown because the price would be affected if they entered the market.'[3] On top of this criticism, it may be added that the assigning of monetary values to goods and services that had not been sold was subject to arbitrary manipulation. Whether the farm budget resulted in profit or loss depended on arbitrary values assigned to such items as wages, house rent (as distinct from rent paid for cultivated land), or fertilizers, and because the studies of the 1920s and 1930s hardly ever provide a basis for the values assigned, they must be treated as suspect.

The Evidence on Distribution

The available evidence shows that, in southern Jiangsu, when owner-cultivators and tenants are compared, owner-cultivators tended to be better equipped and to command a higher standard of living. The evidence comes first from Qiao Qiming's survey of Nantong and Kunshan in 1924 and is corroborated by that of the Shanghai Social Affairs Bureau of the Shanghai suburb in 1930, the principal statistical findings from which are reproduced here in Tables 7.1 and 7.2.[4] Kunshan was a predominantly rice-cultivating county in southern Jiangsu (see Table 3.1), while Nantong, located on the northern bank of the Changjiang, was rapidly developing into a major cotton-producing and manufacturing centre in the first two decades of the twentieth century.

In Kunshan and Nantong, Qiao found that the majority of farmers were tenants (Table 7.1-A), who tended to cultivate, on average, more land than the owner-cultivators. In Kunshan, their farms were larger by as much as 150 per cent (Table 7.1-B). Despite this difference, owner-cultivators seem to have enjoyed a higher standard of living. They were considerably older when they became household heads (Table 7.1-C), an indication either of longer lives or larger households, or of career patterns that culminated in the farming of primarily self-owned land. Owner-cultivators also had more adequate and better quality tools and farm animals (Table 7.1-D and E), and houses of greater value (Table 7.1-F). A higher proportion of them had children attending school (Table 7.1-G). Moreover, all owner-cultivators were married, and they married at an earlier age (Table 7.1-H). However, they had fewer children than tenants (Table 7.1-H). Early marriage probably indicates adequate means. That a higher proportion of owner-cultivators was married probably reflects no more than their age. That tenants should have more children is quite inexplicable.

Qiao's study was designed to explore the longitudinal changes in tenancy structure from the early years of the twentieth century to the 1920s. His methodology, which depended on comparisons of impressionistic statistics of earlier times supplied to him by his informants, is open to criticism.[5] However, this objection does not invalidate his findings regarding the impressions pertaining to the time of his survey. It also does not invalidate the impressionistic explanations given to him by his informants, some of which were quite insightful.

According to Qiao's informants, Kunshan had always had a high

Table 7.1

Owner-cultivators, Half-owners, and Tenants in Kunshan and Nantong,
Jiangsu, 1924

	Owners	Half-owners	Tenants
A. Distribution by farm households (per cent)			
Kunshan	8.3	14.1	77.6
Nantong	13.0	22.6	64.4
B. Size of holdings (mu)			
Kunshan	9.4	16.9	23.2
Nantong	10.0	11.0	11.8
C. Age at which head of farm acquired this position (years)			
Kunshan	49.5	36.8	26.8
Nantong	48.3	36.7	24.3
D. Proportion of households possessing 'adequate and good quality' tools (per cent)			
Kunshan	69.5	n/a	40.0
Nantong	65.3	n/a	56.8
E. Proportion of households possessing 'adequate and good quality' animals (per cent)			
Kunshan	69.1	n/a	43.6
Nantong	24.2	n/a	21.8
F. Value of house (dollars)			
Nantong	522	325	153
G. Proportion of households having children receiving or having received education at different levels (per cent)			
Kunshan			
Junior Primary	38.6	n.a.	7.7
Senior Primary	7.8	n.a.	1.6
Middle School	1.3	n.a.	0.1
Nantong			
Junior Primary	64.4	n.a.	19.0
Senior Primary	19.8	n.a.	4.8
Middle School	5.3	n.a.	0.3
H. Age at marriage (years), proportion married (per cent) and number of children per household (persons) in Nantong			
Age at marriage	20.4	20.5	22.1
Proportion married	100.0	92.1	69.7
Number of children	2.4	3.2	4.9

Source: Qiao Qiming (1926).

tenancy rate. However, after the Shanghai–Nanjing Railway was completed, commerce expanded, and many owner-cultivators rented out their land in order to enter business. Consequently the proportion of tenants increased. Moreover, in the decade before the survey, farm produce could be sold at a high price and much waste land was opened for cultivation by tenants and 'half-owners'. In Nantong, the high tenancy rate was attributed to high population and the concentration of holdings in the hands of large landlords. According to Qiao,' it was difficult for hard-working tenants to buy even a little land because there was little to sell.'[6] In the district of Liuqiao, an area that produced very good quality cotton, because cotton prices rose and profits were high, many landlords terminated their tenants' leases and themselves took up farming. Also, coastal reclamation undertaken by the Tonghai Coastal Cultivation Company and the factories that were set up in the county city provided outlets for the increase in population. Land prices were kept high, none the less, in both Kunshan and Nantong, because 'commercial companies' (gongsi — Qiao's term) were purchasing land in both counties. In Nantong, these were presumably the reclamation companies, but in Kunshan, they must have been the newly developing rent-collection offices, for other commercial developments were not common.[7]

Changes in crop prices brought considerable migration. The tenants of the reclamation companies in Nantong were largely settlers from outside. Elsewhere in Nantong, however, 95.9 per cent of the tenants reported that they were natives. In Kunshan, tenants in this category dropped to 86.8 per cent. Qiao did not discuss the conditions of newly reclaimed areas, but he showed that tenancy in Nantong and tenancy in Kunshan were quite different. In Kunshan, as in many parts of southern Jiangsu, many tenants paid rent to rent-collection offices which worked for landlords who lived away from the villages where their land was located. In Kunshan, these absentee landlords accounted for 65.9 per cent of all landlords. In Nantong, most landlords (84.2 per cent) lived in the villages where they owned land. Also, in Kunshan, landlords provided their tenants with nothing other than the land that was rented. However, in the poorer areas of Nantong, landlords provided the essential tools. Kunshan tenants, apparently, did not need as much capital as those in Nantong. On average, their capital varied from 220 to 560 dollars, while Nantong tenants had from 310 to 1,850 dollars, the difference being attributed by Qiao to the greater capital needed for labour and fertilizers in cotton production. Despite these differences, landlords in both Kunshan and Nantong inherited, rather than purchased, most of their land. In Kunshan, 85.2 per cent of all land held by landlords was inherited, compared to 86.5 per cent in Nantong.

According to Qiao, most tenants needed money loans. In Kunshan, they borrowed from their landlords but in Nantong they borrowed from unspecified 'rich people'. In Kunshan, interest stood at 25 per cent, and in Nantong at 20, presumably for a year. Qiao did not provide the figures, but he stated that in Kunshan tenants harvested higher yields from their land than owner-cultivators, while in Nantong, owner-cultivators had higher yields. He attributed the difference to the harder work that tenants put into their farms and to the large number of absentee landlords, implying that the land owners who were left to farm in Kunshan were the poorer ones who had less capital to invest in their farms. In Nantong, because it was common practice for land owners to remain farmers, they kept their holdings at manageable sizes and could invest more capital in them than the tenants could. Because Kunshan tenants, on the whole, enjoyed a lower standard of living than owner-cultivators even though they cultivated more land and reaped higher yields, it may be concluded that rent payment had a marked depressing effect on the standard of living.

The Shanghai Social Affairs Bureau's study in 1930 came to similar conclusions about the differences between owner-cultivators and tenants, and these are summarized in Table 7.2. However, because its sample does not reflect a representative mix of these statuses within the population, for this item of information we have to turn to a separate survey of village life conducted in 1931. This 1931 survey shows that in 13 out of the 15 districts covered in the 1930 survey, a total of 263,000 persons lived in 54,000 households in 2,500 villages. These were divided into 14,500 owner-cultivators, approximately the same number of half-owners, 8,600 tenants, and 16,500 'subsidiary farmers', presumably persons whose principal occupations lay outside farming but who farmed none the less to gain a subsidiary income. These households altogether cultivated 317,000 mu.[8]

The 1930 survey did not enumerate the 'subsidiary farmers' as a separate category, but, instead, listed the major occupations other than farming held by the surveyed households (Table 7.2-B). The list shows that more owner-cultivators were also engaged as handloom weavers, that a small number of owner-cultivators and half-owners were embroiderers and officials, but no tenants were. All four households engaged in teaching were also owner-cultivators. However,

Table 7.2
Owner-cultivators, Half-owners, and Tenants in the Shanghai Suburbs,
1930

	Owner-cultivators	Half-owners	Tenants
A. Number of households surveyed (non-random sample)			
	49	47	44
B. Number of households practising specified subsidiary occupations			
Weaving	22	15	10
Embroidering	3	2	—
Other handicrafts	15	22	29
Peddling	6	8	5
Teaching	4	—	—
Public office	7	4	—
C. Number of households comprising specified number of persons and age distribution of sampled populations (per cent)			
Under 3 persons	2	8	9
4–6	13	13	27
7–9	19	15	7
10–12	10	8	1
13–15	3	1	—
16–18	1	2	—
27	1	—	—
Below age 15	36.2	32.6	34.8
Age 15–60	58.3	61.2	58.1
Above age 60	5.5	6.2	7.1
D. Number of households producing a specified number of persons who had attended school			
None	2	11	25
Below 2	24	22	17
3–4	16	10	2
Over 5	7	4	—
E. Number of households operating specified sizes of farm*			
Below 5 mu	7	n.a.	26
5–10	7	n.a.	10
10–20	16	n.a.	6
20–30	11	n.a.	1
30–40	5	n.a.	1
Over 40	3	n.a.	—

Table 7.2 (continued)

	Owner-cultivators	Half-owners	Tenants
F. Number of households possessing specified types of subsidiary land			
Garden	36	32	16
Grove	8	3	—
Grass	2	2	—
Pond	4	4	—
Houseland	49	47	17
Land for unspecified uses	5	3	—
G. Number of households possessing different types of farm implements			
Hoes	49	47	44
4-pronged rakes	47	47	42
Manure buckets	40	40	28
Sickles	34	33	30
Chain pumps	22	13	6
Shovels	12	8	7
Threshers	11	13	3
Rakes	8	8	3
Ploughs	10	6	1
H. Number of households possessing spinning and weaving machines			
Spinning machines	20	20	14
Weaving machines	35	33	15
I. Number of households possessing farm animals			
Cows	15	11	3
Sheep	7	11	12
Pigs	23	16	3
Chicken	46	44	35
Ducks	14	10	12
Geese	1	—	—
J. Number of households making use of specific types of hired labourers			
Daily paid labourers	28	15	7
Labourers on monthly contracts	2	3	1
Labourers on annual contracts	6	—	—

Table 7.2   (continued)

	Owner-cultivators	Half-owners	Tenants
K. Number of households producing specified types of crops			
Paddy	29	25	19
Cotton	46	43	26
Beans	21	20	16
Wheat	45	41	30
Broad beans	18	17	15
Green vegetables	21	20	18
Mulberry	1	1	—
Others	7	6	—
L. Yields of major crops grown (catties per mu)			
Paddy	326	312	287
Cotton	67	64	56
Beans	106	106	113
Wheat	154	186	140
Broad beans	118	117	107
M. Number of households owing debts and total amounts owed (in dollars)			
No. of households	24	36	32
Amounts owed	24,980	15,130	4,910
N. Number of households owing specified amounts of debt (in dollars) and providing specified guarantee			
Below 100	3	5	19
100–200	8	12	6
200–400	4	11	7
400–1,500	7	8	—
2,000	3	1	—
5,000	2	—	—
By surety	1	8	25
By mortgage of land deeds	23	29	—

Note: * Figures for half-owners omitted because of ambiguity in report.

Source: Shanghaishi shehuiju (1930).

slightly more tenants were engaged in other handicrafts, including primarily such work as masonry and carpentry. The descriptive account in the report that accompanies the table also explains that some owner-cultivators owned businesses with considerable capital, such as rice stores, and even half-owners had sugar refineries and flour mills, but tenants, so far as their engagement in commerce was concerned, were engaged only in peddling. As the table should make clear, some households were engaged in more than one subsidiary occupation. A separate table in the report shows that proportionally more owner-cultivator and half-owner households were engaged in a single subsidiary occupation, and more tenant households held two of these occupations. Very few households of any category held more than two.

On the whole, owner-cultivators and half-owners tended to live in larger households than tenants (Table 7.2-C). In terms of age distribution, the three groups did not vary greatly (Table 7.2-C). Tenant households produced fewer persons who had attended school (Table 7.2-D). These features may partly be explained by owner-cultivators and half-owners being more wealthy, but also partly by the higher proportion of immigrants found among tenants noted in the report but not reproduced in numerical terms in Table 7.2. The report states that out of the 118 households surveyed, 22 had moved into the area from other counties, and all of them were tenants.

The high proportion of outsiders among tenants also explains some features of the land cultivated or possessed by them. Most tenant households operated farms that were below 5 *mu*: 26 out of 44 compared to 25 out of 47 half-owners and 7 out of 49 owner-cultivators (Table 7.2-E). The tenants were also the only group that did not all own houseplots, and a much smaller proportion of tenants owned gardens (Table 7.2-F). The large proportion of half-owners who operated small farms is hard to explain and the report does not suggest any explanation. It can be imagined, however, that in the Shanghai suburbs, many village males would have found work in the city, leaving their families in the villages. These families would have found it both necessary and acceptable to remain in the village because they owned the houses that they lived in. Moreover, as members of the village, they possessed the right to exploit village resources, including wasteland not privately claimed, that came to be used as gardens, groves, ponds, and so on. Because half the tenants were outsiders, a substantially higher proportion of them did not own house plots. It is not a coincidence that the report goes on to show that all the surveyed households but for 14 tenants owned tile-roofed houses; these 14 lived in thatch-roofed houses.

The owner-cultivators and half-owners were better equipped than the tenants. They had more farm implements (Table 7.2-G), more spinning and weaving machines (Table 7.2-H), and more farm animals (Table 7.2-I). Owner-cultivators hired more labourers than half-owners, and half-owners more than tenants (Table 7.2-J). There were few long-term labourers, partly because there were few large farmers (only 3 owner-cultivators cultivated more than 40 *mu*), and partly, as the report explains, because wages in Shanghai were much higher than agricultural wages and long-term labourers were hard to find.

The 1931 survey of agriculture in Shanghai cited earlier, makes it quite clear that in the Shanghai suburbs, market gardening had become quite important.[9] Nevertheless, the major portion of the cultivated acreage went to cotton, paddy, wheat, beans, and lentils, in this order. The pattern is generally reflected in the number of owner-cultivator and half-owner households that were involved in producing these crops (Table 7.2-K). Almost every household in these two categories grew cotton and wheat, and slightly more than half grew paddy and beans. A much lower proportion of tenant households grew cotton. It is not possible to tell from the report what the non-cotton-growing households were primarily engaged in. Presumably, they would have mixed grain cultivation (paddy or wheat) with vegetables and beans. The report does make clear, however, that tenants received lower returns for all crops but beans (Table 7.2-L).

Again, indebtedness was widely reported (Table 7.2-M). More tenant households reported indebtedness than owner-cultivators or half-owners, but the magnitude of the debts accumulated by them was very much smaller. None the less, most debts incurred by any household were quite small (Table 7.2-N). Only 12 owner-cultivators and 9 half-owners owed more than 400 dollars. Most tenant households in debt reported that their debts were guaranteed by middlemen who provided surety. Most owner-cultivators and half-owners secured their debts by mortgaging their land deeds. This perhaps explains why owner-cultivators and half-owners were able to raise much larger loans.

Land prices in the Shanghai suburb were extremely uneven. Prices quoted in the survey ranged from 1,200 dollars per *mu* to just under 100 dollars. Property that could demand top prices was probably rapidly being integrated into the urban fringe of Shanghai City. It is difficult to imagine any owners but those who possessed property priced towards this extreme being able to raise 2,000 to 5,000 dollars on the strength of their land. As mortgaging land was often sale in disguise, such figures suggest that the land had in fact been sold at high profit for urban development, even though the original holders might temporarily be residents on it on payment of interest in lieu of a rent. These were not poor peasants slipping into bankruptcy, but farmers who had succeeded in cashing in their holdings while the market was favourable.

The results of the two surveys show, therefore, that all things being equal, owner-cultivators stood at an advantage over tenants. The practice of managing sizeable estates of rented land by the employment of hired labourers seems to have been uncommon in southern Jiangsu, and such results would seem inevitable. However, the question of distribution is less straightforward than these surveys would suggest, as the next two sections will show.

Rural Indebtedness

Studies of the 1920s and 1930s on rural indebtedness all agreed that it was a feature of the widespread poverty found in the countryside. Most of these studies left the issue there: they discussed the institutions of loan-making, recorded interest rates, rural incomes and expenses, and reiterated the need for monetary and financial reforms.[10] The 1930 study conducted by the Shanghai Social Affairs Bureau went a step further, for it distinguished the number of persons owing debts from the total value of these debts, and found that although a substantial proportion of the poor, in this case the tenants, were in debt, they owed considerably less than the better-off, the owner-cultivators and the half-owners. Not all contemporary writers appreciated the importance of the finding, that is, that the very poor could hardly have contracted substantial loans.

None the less, whether or not writers of the 1920s and the 1930s personally appreciated the relationship between creditworthiness and the ability to borrow, the general tone of the contemporary argument stressed the effect of debts incurred by landholders, that is, primarily by owner-cultivators and half-owners. It was argued that these debts led to the loss of their land, so that in order to continue farming, they had to become tenants. Rising tenancy rates detected by surveys in the early 1930s were quoted as confirmation for the argument.

Enough has been said about the onset of the world depression to show that the hardship encountered in the 1930s was quite unprecedented. Tenancy rates might well have been rising in these years, but they would not have been indicative of a long-term trend. For the long-term trend, it is essential to stress the close connections between loans and commercial development. The evidence is not obvious, but the following may be noted.

Firstly, in 1933, 34 pawnshops were enumerated in Wuxi county, working with a total circulating capital of 1,210,000 dollars. These figures compared with 20 pawnshops in Changshu, working with a total circulating capital of 720,000 dollars, 17 in Songjiang with 510,000 dollars, and 11 in Rugao with 340,000 dollars.[11] Wuxi was, of course, the most commercially developed of the four, being the main silk-producing county in Jiangsu. Changshu, predominantly rice-growing and partly silk-producing, and Songjiang, rice and cotton-growing, would have followed in order of commercial development. Rugao was the least commercially developed. In Guangdong, the siting of pawnshops exhibits a similar pattern.[12] As is well known, pawnshops were important local credit institutions, and their distribution reflects local demand for loans and the willingness of business or landed interests to make them.

Secondly, as the Shanghai Social Affairs Bureau's 1930 study found, while owner-cultivators and half-owners mortgaged their land to raise loans, tenants depended on the surety of middlemen. On a provincial basis, a study by the Land Committee in Jiangsu in 1934 found that in the counties to the south of the province, loans were predominantly collateralized by land mortgages, but all three northern counties studied reported a high percentage of debtors (60 per cent in Dongtai, 72 in Xiao, 79 in Guanyun) whose debts were not secured. The regional distribution is significant: the loan that was not secured was probably a small one, and given the greater economic development in southern Jiangsu, these figures suggest that the southern Jiangsu land market was the more actively developed, that land value was higher than in northern Jiangsu, and that more land changed hands.[13]

Thirdly, account must also be taken of the credit contraction in the 1930s, following close upon economic expansion in the 1930s, due. partly to collapse in the export trade and partly to the outflow of silver. It affected financial institutions such as banks and pawnshops as much as individual farmers. One study notes that in 1934 alone, pawnshops in Jiangsu together lost a total of 3 million *yuan*, estimated at approximately 10 per cent of all loans and deposits made in the province. One reason for the loss was the high inter-institutional interest that was charged for loans. According to a committee set up in Jiangsu to make suggestions to improve the pawnshops, inter-institutional interest had risen to 13 or 14 per cent, up from 7 or 8 per cent, and the increase had cut seriously into pawnshop profits. The situation was aggravated by the depression, for products that were pawned were not redeemed, while, because trade was slack, the pawnshops could not easily resell them. In Yixing county, the depression hit the local banks as much as the farmers: five of the seven banks in the county city closed within five years (approximately 1930 to 1934.)[14]

All this is hardly definite, but it suggests that the growth of indebtedness in the countryside might have much to do with a regional pattern of development that takes account of variations in tenancy rates and the distribution of cash crops. Ironically, the extension of credit was a sign not of impoverishment but of growing opportunities.

Profit from Cash Crops

Ultimately, the question has to be asked if cash cropping was profitable, and the answer must depend on estimates of costs and benefits, however defective the statistics. As a defect in the statistics, reference has already been made to the unwarranted designation of monetary values to items that farmers did not pay for (such as family labour or a rent for the farm house). In compiling Tables 7.3 to 7.6, I have taken care not to include such items, with the exception of the rare nineteenth-century estimate given by Tao Xu quoted in Table 7.3. Nevertheless, it should be understood, as for practically all figures derived from the reports of the 1920s and 1930s, the tables represent, at best, informed guesses, and no attempt to interpret them should be regarded as straightforward.

As a start, Table 7.3 quotes two of the more detailed estimates available on cereal farming in Jiangsu. An estimate of profit from cereals (principally rice and wheat) is useful not only because from the 1870s up to the 1930s they remained the most widely grown crops in Jiangsu and Guangdong, but also because in many cash-cropping areas, paddy and wheat were reverted to when industrial crops failed to reap a good price. The estimate from Suzhou in the 1880s is taken from a well-known political tract written by Tao Xu, a local landlord.[15] He was obviously acquainted with the local situation, and because his tract was written to champion tax reduction, his figures must perhaps have been biased towards a low estimate for the farmer's standard of living. His report of 2.4 *shi* of paddy per *mu* in Suzhou was a low yield figure for the area. The price quoted for paddy, at 1,800 cash per *shi*,

Table 7.3

Two Estimates of Farm Budgets in Cereal-growing Areas in Southern Jiangsu, 1880s and 1930s

Income		Expenditure	
A. Near Suzhou, 1880s (size of farm: 10 mu)			
Beans, wheat, vegetables	9,000 cash	Labour (rice and wages)	20,700 cash
Paddy (24 *shi*)	43,200	Labour (meat, oil, etc.)	12,500
Straw, husk	8,800	Tools	800
		Fertilizer (beancakes)	5,000
Total	61,000		
		Total before rent and tax	39,000 cash
		Rent (commuted to cash)	21,600
		Tax (commuted to cash)	6,350
B. Wujiang, 1930s. (size of farm: 8.5 mu; household size: 4.1 persons (2.9 adult male equivalents))			
Rice (51.6 bushels, equivalent to 418 catties of paddy per *mu*)	2,592 catties	Consumption (20.3 bushels, at 7 bushels p.a./adult male equivalent)	1,020 catties
Other produce, in rice equivalent	503	Total before rent and tax	as above
		Rent (50 per cent of rice grown)	1,297

Sources: Tao Xu (n.d.), pp. 17b–20a; Fei Xiaotong (1949), pp. 79–81.

can be corroborated from other sources from the 1880s. Naturally, his figures do not imply that the entire produce of 24 *shi* was sold. Much of it, including the straw and husk, would have been consumed on the farm: the straw as fuel, and the husk possibly also as animal feed. Moreover, his figures do not represent the entire produce of the farm, for they exclude poultry rearing and handicrafts, both common farm activities in southern Jiangsu. On the side of expenses, it seems clear that Tao assumed minimum labour provided by the farm household, and that where a rent had to be paid, it was the landlord's duty, and not the tenant's, to pay the tax.

The Wujiang figures were cited by Fei Xiaotong as data gathered in his village study in that county. They were not published in his monograph report, but were cited by him in an essay that argued that, in broad terms, the Chinese owner-cultivator led a life 'free from hunger or cold' (*buji buhan*) that was 'moderately comfortable' (*xiaokang*).[16] Unlike Tao and his own contemporaries, Fei stated explicitly that farmers did not by any means sell all they grew. Like Tao, he ignored income from animal rearing and handicrafts. His estimates of 'other produce' and rent were close to Tao's: 19 per cent and 50 per cent of the rice income respectively, compared to 21 per cent of the rice income for 'beans, wheat, vegetables', and exactly 50 per cent for rent in Tao. The yield that he postulated, 418 catties of paddy per *mu*, none the less, should be considered high for southern Jiangsu.

Neither report can be considered sufficiently detailed to permit an analysis of overall farm income and expenses. Nevertheless, they show that within a wide range of yield estimates, in a normal year, it is reasonable to assume that the grain produce on a *mu* of farmland in southern Jiangsu was capable of supporting the grain consumption of the producers who worked on it, even if rent to the amount of half the grain produced had been paid. This is not to say that the farm population that subsisted on its grain production was not poor: after rent payment, it was left with its food consumption and little else. That would have been an extreme case, however, for handicraft *was* prevalent in southern Jiangsu and extra income could also have been derived from industrial crops and services.

Before income from other sources than grain production are considered, it would be useful first to consider how changes in the price of grain, rent, and tax might have affected the standard of living of rice farmers. Much depended on whether they were prepared to sell their grain produce and to shift their diets to substitutes that fetched lower prices on the market, if sold. In southern Jiangsu, it seems that even though grain was widely sold, a substantial quantity of rice produced was consumed on the farm. According to Fei, farm families sold little more than was required to produce the money income that was needed.[17] As the sweet potato seems to be less commonly grown in southern Jiangsu than in Guangdong, since South-east Asian rice was not imported in large quantities until the 1930s, and as rice seems to be more commonly consumed than wheat flour or sorghum, Fei's observation is quite credible. However, this must mean that the standard of living was not declining in this area. Moreover, because the paddy acreage did not see any substantial increase, it must also mean that despite the high price of rice, no more rice was reaching the market from southern Jiangsu in the late 1920s than in the 1870s. Changes to the rice farmer's income, in addition to changes introduced through his participation in the cultivation of industrial crops and in handicrafts, depended to a large extent on whether he paid very much rent, and if his rent was commuted to money.

It is important to note that the amount of land rented in southern Jiangsu was unevenly distributed: perhaps 90 per cent of all cultivated land near Suzhou was rented while reports varied from 20 to 80 per cent for Wuxi. In Chapter 4, it has already been argued that the commuted rent was concentrated in the Suzhou surroundings in the late nineteenth century, and spread only in the twentieth century to areas where landlords were more efficiently organized for rent collection, and that it rose more rapidly than the price of rice. When the price of rice rose, therefore, initial benefits were reaped by owner-cultivators and part-owners. The tenant who paid his rent in grain had little spare grain to sell, and his benefit from the price change would have been quite limited. It is difficult to tell if he would not have welcomed converting to money rent at this stage. If he succeeded in commuting his rent to money, he might have enjoyed an initial increase in his net income. However, the landlords' rent-collection offices would probably soon have caught up with him. It is important to note that outside Suzhou and the immediately neighbouring counties, the majority of tenants did not pay their rent to these agencies. For most of them, rent continued to be paid in grain. They would have made slight gains from higher prices for the grain that they could spare for the market. One suspects that they also gained from opportunities for extra services and supplementary crops that might have been created by widening prosperity.

Although direct observations are scanty, the increase in the price of rice would also have affected extensive areas in Guangdong that exported to the cities, market towns, and areas enriched by industrial crops and remittances from the cities and from abroad. As rent commutation was far less common in Guangdong than in southern Jiangsu, it should be expected that farm benefits from rising prices were more direct. None the less, because Guangdong imported substantial quantities of rice from outside the province, this would only have been true of rice-surplus counties in the Zhujiang delta.

Unlike rice, industrial crops were extended over a substantially larger acreage between the 1870s and the 1920s. It must follow from this that many places that produced industrial crops did so by changing their traditional cropping patterns. Where land had to be reclaimed and fishponds had to be dug, to do so might have involved considerable capital investment. Existing sources hardly provide material to examine the ramifications that follow from such complications. In the following paragraphs, farm operations in areas producing silk, sugar, and cotton are cited merely as examples that illustrate likely changes to the standard of living.

Table 7.4 reproduces estimates of costs and profit from the Nanhai county gazetteer published in 1910 and from Howard and Buswell's survey report in the Guangdong silk district published in 1925. In both sources, the estimates are given separately for mulberry growing and silkworm rearing, and both sources acknowledge that the two activities were frequently conducted by the same farm families. In fact, the gazetteer advocates combining the two on the same farm:

[The operational cost on a *mu* of mulberry land] amounts to approximately 40 dollars exclusive of labour. This is why of the farmers who grow mulberry, none does not also raise silkworms. For silkworm waste [*cansha*] can save him the cost of the bran [used as fertilizer].[18]

The statement is interesting not only as a description of the operations of the farm, but also as an indication of the high profit expected in the silk district. In 1910, as in the entire period from 1870 to 1929, a tael exchanged for approximately 1.39 dollars. The mulberry leaves produced on a *mu* of land that was totally devoted to the crop would, by the gazetteer compiler's estimate, have yielded 16.7 dollars after rent and fertilizer, enough to purchase 3 *shi* of rice in Guangzhou at the time. This was by no means a poor yield in the Zhujiang delta. However, as noted in an earlier chapter, only 60 per cent (50 according to the Nanhai gazetteer) of the farmland could be devoted to mulberry in this area that specialized in mulberry and silk, the remaining portion

Table 7.4

Estimates of Profits from Mulberry Growing and Silkworm Rearing in
Guangdong, *c.*1910 and 1923

Nanhai c.1910

(a) From mulberry growing

Yield of mulberry per *mu*	3,400	catties
Price of mulberry for above (at 1.2 taels per 100 catties)	40.8	taels
Rent (for 1 *mu*, including portion left for fishpond)	20	dollars
Fertilizers: bran (6 dollars/100 catties)	15	dollars
urine (25 cents/2 buckets)	5	dollars
Wages	unspecified	

(b) From silkworm rearing (undertaken by family of five)

Cost of eggs (2 sheets at 5 taels/sheet)	3	dollars
Mulberry consumed	4,500	catties
Cocoons produced	16,000	items
Price for above	0.42–0.6	taels/rack
Size of rack	unspecified	

Shunde 1923

(a) From mulberry growing

Yield of mulberry per *mu*	23	*tan*
Price for above (at 3.50 dollars/*tan*)	80.50	dollars
Rent of land	25.00	dollars
Labour for cultivation	10.00	dollars
Fertilizer	20.00	dollars
Cost of picking leaves	10.00	dollars
Profit per *mu*	15.50	dollars

(b) From silkworm rearing (per crop)

Cost of 2 egg sheets, at 2.50 dollars/sheet	5.00	dollars
Cost of leaves, 48 *tan* at 3.50 dollars	168.00	dollars
Charcoal, etc.	10.00	dollars
Labour	supplied by farm family	
100 catties of cocoons from 2 sheets of eggs, at 3 dollars/100 catties	300.00	dollars
Profit per crop	117.00	dollars
Number of crops per year	7	
Total profits	819.00	dollars

Sources: Xuxiu Nanhai xianzhi (1910), pp. 4/32b–41lb; C.W. Howard and K.P. Buswell (1925), pp. 59 and 94–5.

being transformed into fishponds. This distribution would have somewhat lowered farm profit and the estimate must be taken further.

Variation in farm costs due to fish farming is not discussed in the gazetteer, which continues its description to prove that silkworm rearing was profitable. Unfortunately, even for this part of the description, it quotes the price of cocoon in terms of the 'rack' without making clear how much each 'rack' should weigh. The analysis of likely profit from fish farming and silkworm rearing must consequently be taken from Howard and Buswell's report. Nevertheless, before doing so, we should find a comparison of the figures from the two sources instructive.

Briefly, the Nanhai gazetteer gives a more optimistic estimate of mulberry yield (34 piculs per *mu*) than Howard and Buswell (23 piculs per *mu*). Between 1910 and 1923, however, prices had risen. A picul of leaves sold for 1.2 taels (1.7 dollars) in 1910, but for 3.5 dollars in 1923. The rent had also risen, but only from 20 to 25 dollars. Fertilizer costs, meanwhile, had remained stable for each unit area. Howard and Buswell's report assumes that a substantial amount of labour was provided by the farm family, but it notes expenses made towards hired labour. Excluding labour provided by the farm family, therefore, the balance from the sale price of leaves from a *mu* of land devoted entirely to mulberry in 1923 amounted to 15.50 dollars, enough to purchase 1.7 piculs of rice in Guangzhou. By Howard and Buswell's estimates in 1923, mulberry growing was not really more profitable than paddy farming when it was conducted as an exclusive activity.[19]

If we continue with Howard and Buswell's figures, it should be quite apparent that profit derived from mulberry growing was quite overshadowed by that from silkworm rearing. Howard and Buswell's estimate is quoted on the basis of the amount of cocoons that might be harvested from 2 eggsheets. According to the Nanhai gazetteer, this was the amount that might be reared by a family of five. Had leaves been purchased to feed the worms, the family would have needed an outlay of 183 dollars (cost of eggsheets, leaves, charcoal, and sundries) in recurrent expenses to produce cocoons that would sell for 300 dollars, leaving a profit of 117 dollars (equivalent to 12 piculs of rice in Guangzhou). In arriving at these figures, Howard and Buswell apparently did not take into account wastage of silkworms due to disease, estimated at as much as 30 per cent of the crop in an earlier portion of their report. When this is taken into account, the profit from a crop of silkworms drops to as low as 27 dollars. That, however, is the profit from one crop, and in the Zhujiang delta, as many as seven crops could be harvested each year. The annual earnings of the family could, therefore, reach 819 dollars, which would have been no mean profit for a Guangdong family of five, but it could decline to only 189 dollars.

Few farm families would have had farmed enough land to produce mulberry that could feed seven crops of worms from 2 egg sheets for each crop. None the less, the economy of combining mulberry growing with silkworm raising should not be missed. Howard and Buswell's figures show that 2 *mu* of land must be devoted to mulberry to produce almost as much leaf as might be needed for each crop. Because mulberry growing had to be combined with fish farming, for every 10 *mu* of farmland only 6 *mu* could be planted with mulberry, and 4 *mu* had to be converted into fishponds. In a later section of their report, Howard and Buswell state that profit from fish taken from 4 *mu* of fishponds would amount to 120 dollars per year. On the basis of these figures, the household of five that farmed 10 *mu* of rented land in the silk district could reap as much as 1,032 dollars per year as profit (without allowing for cocoon wastage) or as little as 402 dollars (when 30 per cent cocoon wastage has been included). According to Howard and Buswell, a family of eight would have spent 436 dollars on food, 105 on clothes, and 60 on rent (presumably for the house and the fishponds only, rent for mulberry land having been already considered).[20] Working from an income that included only gains from cocoon and fish (apparently overlooking savings from mulberry supplied by the farm), amounting to 939 dollars (forgetting also cocoon wastage), they argued that when the balance had been spent on repairs to the mud house and replacement or repair of equipment, little would have been left for the education of the farmer's children.[21] The balance after food, clothes, and rent would be, according to Howard and Buswell's estimate, 338 dollars, which would be equivalent to 38 piculs of rice in Guangzhou, or a year's savings in rice for a family of eight. Howard and Buswell, however, concluded their study on a note suggesting that the silk farmer's life was far from easy. A wide leeway must, therefore, be allowed for losses due to silkworm disease.

Considerable capital was needed to start a mulberry farm and to raise silkworms, even though the sum was not prohibitive. For growing mulberry, it included the costs of digging the ponds, preparing the embankments, and the initial seedlings. Howard and Buswell did not include an estimate for the land preparation, but a report published in 1922 notes that it cost 2 to 3 dollars per *mu* to employ labourers to dredge mud from the bottom of the pond each year.[22] As these ponds were only several feet deep, the cost of excavating 4 *mu* of ponds could not go beyond 10 to 20 dollars. In comparison, the cost of mulberry seedlings was minimal, at less than 1 dollar for each *mu* cultivated. In the silk district, the farmer would also have needed to pay his rent (in cash) in advance. For 10 *mu*, this would amount to approximately 250 dollars.[23] Equipment (80 baskets, 160 spinning racks, knives, charcoal stoves), according to Howard and Buswell, amounted to only 140 dollars.[24] Thus, an initial outlay was needed, amounting to between 400 and 500 dollars for an operation of 10 *mu*.

High profit in mulberry and silk attracted immigrants to Shunde. This is why Glenn T. Trewartha noted a different pattern of settlement in the mulberry area:

Unique and distinctive in its land-use system, the specialized mulberry area of the Canton Delta is equally so in its settlement forms. Nowhere else in Kwangtung Province do most of the farm houses stand alone and isolated outside of villages. Here the disseminated pattern of rural settlement predominates in the midst of what is otherwise a region of rural villages. The isolated farm houses of the silk regions most commonly are of mud plaster mixed with straw which covers a wall made of mulberry stems woven into a wattle over cross pieces of bamboo. Grass thatch covers the high-gabled steep-sloping roofs. Village houses, especially those in larger settlements, more commonly have walls of brick and tile roofs.[25]

These houses were meant to be temporary structures, for the migrant living apart from the village was not given the right to build his house by the villagers.[26]

The Shunde farmers, of course, borrowed. According to Chen Hansheng, 70 per cent of the farm households in the silk district were in debt. However, he suggests that until the early 1930s, many borrowed from loan associations formed among themselves, and that these loans became hard to raise after the depression set in in the early 1930s.[27]

In southern Jiangsu, mulberry yield per *mu* amounted to no more than 1,000 to 2,000 catties, and no more than three crops of cocoons were harvested each year. The profit from a *mu* of land for the silk farmer there may, therefore, be expected to be lower than for his counterpart in the Zhujiang delta. None the less, he did not set aside a portion of his land for fish-ponds, and consequently his initial capital could be smaller. Fei Xiaotong estimates from his village study that the average silkworm-rearing household might be left with a surplus of 250 dollars for 'profit and wages', as noted. Because silkworm

Table 7.5

Estimates of Profits from Sugar-cane and Sugar in Heyuan and Jieyang
Counties, Guangdong, 1921

Heyuan	
Cost of capital and labour per *mu**	16 dollars
Cane yield per *mu*	4,800 catties
Sugar refined from above	400 catties
Price of sugar (at 7 dollars/picul)	28 dollars
Profit per *mu*	12 dollars
Fertilizers: Pressed beans 110 catties	6 dollars
pigs' dung	unknown
Wages for long-term labourer	3.3 dollars
Rent and labour for sugar-cane press and	
syrup boiler (for 4,800 catties)	4.80 dollars
Jieyang	
Yield per *mu*	3,000–4,000 canes
Sugar refined from above	500, 600–800, or
	900 catties
Price of yellow sugar (9 dollars/picul)	45–81 dollars
Fertilizers: ash	unknown
pressed beans 200–300 catties	11–16 dollars
Wages for growing cane	unspecified
Rent for sugar-cane press and syrup boiler	
(for 800 catties of sugar)	11–12 dollars
Wages for sugar pressing and boiling	5.30 dollars
Estimated profits (excluding rent for farmland,	
seedlings, food for workmen, at 800 catties of	
sugar produced per *mu*)	41.70 dollars

Note: * Food for workmen excluded.
Source: Guoli Zhongshan daxue nongke xueyuan (1925), pp. 108–11.

rearing made use of surplus labour on the farm, this must represent also an increase in farm income.[28]

The profit that might be derived from the cultivation of sugar-cane and the production of sugar is estimated in Table 7.5.[29] Before any attempt is made to compare this estimate with the profit from silkworm rearing or mulberry farming, however, it should be noted that in the 1920s, the period covered in Table 7.4, the silk industry in Guangdong was approaching the peak of its performance, while in 1921, the year to which Table 7.5 relates, the sugar industry had long passed its prime. Yet in Heyuan county, on the Dongjiang in Guangdong, the farm family could reap a profit of 12 dollars per *mu* if it combined sugar-cane growing with sugar making. In 1921, paddy sold for 3.00 to 3.50 dollars per picul in Heyuan, and the yield of rice reached 400 to 500 catties per *mu* even on medium-quality paddy land. It may be expected, therefore, that sugar-cane was grown in this county only on lower-quality farmland. In Jieyang county, near Shantou, the estimates in the table suggest that where sugar-cane growing was combined with sugar making, the produce of a *mu* fetched 41.70 dollars. Paddy was sold at Jieyang at 4.00 to 4.50 dollars per picul, and receipts from sugar would thus substantially exceed likely receipts from rice. None the less, even in Jieyang, if the land was rented, the profit after rent would only have been moderate: approximately 30 dollars per *mu*. Such profits were far below what could be gained from silkworm rearing in the silk district.

The discrepancies between the Heyuan and Jieyang figures require comments. The major source of the discrepancies, it may be seen, arises from differences in the estimate of the amount of sugar that might be produced from a fixed weight of cane. The discrepancies are understandable and may be related to the different types of land being put under the crop. Sugar-cane required well-watered land, and could thrive well on paddy land provided the drainage was well maintained. It would seem from the figures in Table 7.5 that despite the contracting market, cane continued to be grown on high-quality agricultural land in Jieyang, while it was restricted primarily to poor-quality land in Heyuan. The Jieyang cane, being of a higher standard, also fetched a better price. The contracting market might also have affected the price of sugar-cane pressing, for the sugar-cane presses were probably installed at substantial cost when the market for sugar remained strong, and the rent for their use would have lowered as sugar making became less extensive. The Heyuan figures, therefore, represent the remnants of a once prosperous industry that had lingered despite low returns.[30]

Figures for the capital costs of cane growing and sugar making are not available in the sources. However, no alteration to the farm needed to be made for cane growing, the initial cost required was restricted to the purchase of new shoots, estimated in a 1927 source at 4 dollars per *mu*. While paddy farming was very labour-intensive, sugar-cane did not require much looking after. But it required considerably more fertilizer than paddy, and this cost must be allowed for in the initial outlay even though it should count as an operational cost rather than capital investment. The capital needed in sugar making was invested in the stone sugar-cane press: two sizeable stone rollers that had to be turned by a buffalo. In addition, a shed had to be built and fitted with a boiler for making sugar. The establishment was estimated in 1927 to cost as much as 1,000 dollars. Obviously, this was beyond the means of most cane farmers. One might suppose that the need for this piece of equipment provided an opportunity for the wealthy to monopolize the trade. However, the frequent reference to a rent for its use by cane growers suggests that, on the contrary, the cane growers themselves pressed the cane that they grew.[31]

The low investment needed for sugar-cane growing contrasts sharply with the high investment needed for silkworm rearing, but both the sugar-cane grower and the silkworm rearer acted as independent farmers who responded directly to the market. In this respect, they were more similar to the owner-cultivator rice farmer, or to the tenant rice farmer who paid his rent in cash, than to the tenant rice farmer who paid a crop rent. The owner-cultivator rice farmer or the tenant who paid his rent in cash would have sold his produce directly; the tenant rice farmer who paid his rent in kind, and did not engage himself in cash crops or handicraft, had little to sell, and his produce entered the market through the rent he paid.

Tables 7.6 and 7.7 capture the costs and benefits of cotton growing and contrasts them with those of paddy farming. In general, they show that the income that could be earned from cotton was not higher than that earned from the same acreage of good paddy land. In Table 7.6, can be seen that in 1926, the autumn crop of cotton in Taicang, a major cotton-producing county in southern Jiangsu, amounted to 60 catties per *mu* (a low estimate), and it fetched only 9 dollars. The paddy produced on one *mu* would have fetched 26 dollars. When costs are taken into consideration, the crop of paddy yielded an extra 11.50 dollars beyond what cotton might have yielded. Table 7.7 shows that Chuansha county, also in southern Jiangsu, where the report available lists the household distribution of yields and prices, the produce of one *mu* would have been sold at the median price of 14 dollars, whether it was devoted to cotton or to paddy (1 picul of cotton sold for 14 dollars, and 3.5 piculs of paddy sold for 4 dollars each).

In making this comparison between cotton and paddy farming, a few essential features of cotton growing should be noted. Firstly, cotton could be interplanted with other crops such as bean, corn, or melon, that might fetch extra income, but paddy could not. Secondly,

Table 7.6
Profits of Cotton and Paddy Compared, Southern Jiangsu, Late 1920s:
Taicang County, 1926

Income (dollars)			Expenditure (dollars)
A. *Spring wheat, autumn cotton, per* mu			
Wheat (1 *shi* plus)	8	Towards growing wheat	3.0
Cotton (60 catties)	9	Towards growing cotton:	
		Labour	5.0
		Fertilizer	2.0
		Tools	0.5
		Seeds	0.5
		Tax	0.6
Total income	17	Total expenses	11.6
B. *Spring wheat, autumn paddy, per* mu			
Wheat (1 *shi* plus)	8	Towards growing wheat	3.0
Paddy (2 *shi*)	26	Towards growing paddy:	
		Fertilizer	7.5
		Water	3.0
		Labour	2.0
		Tools	0.5
		Seeds	0.5
		Tax	0.6
Total income	34	Total expenses	17.1

Source: Zhou Tingdong (1927).

as with mulberry and sugar-cane, the cotton crop could support economic activities that might employ idle farm labour. The spinning machine was widely found in cotton-growing areas, for home spinning did not give way completely to imported yarn, as noted in an earlier chapter. Thirdly, cotton was grown in districts that were not well suited to paddy, even though paddy was grown on cotton land as part of the crop cycle. Cotton was grown particularly on newly reclaimed saline soil located towards the eastern and south-eastern portions of Jiangsu, in the counties of Yancheng, Funing, Dongtai, Chuansha, Nanhui, Fengxian, Tongzhou (Nantong), Chongming, and Qidong. Some of this land was reserved as salt farms in the Qing dynasty, and was reclaimed in the Republican era by reclamation companies with

Table 7.7
Profits of Cotton and Paddy Compared, Southern Jiangsu, Late 1920s:
Chuansha County, 1928

Number of Households Surveyed	Yield per mu (catties)	Prices Received per Picul (dollars)
A. Cotton Yields and Prices		
1	110	
6	100	
1	90	
1	60	
1		16.0
2		15.0
1		14.5
15		14.0
1		13.0
B. Paddy Yields and Prices		
3	400	
1	375	
5	350	
4	250	
1		4.2
9		4.0
8		3.5

Source: Huang Yanpei (1936).

government approval.[32] Fourthly, in some places, especially on land reclaimed by the companies, cotton was required as a portion of rent. Even when the fixed crop rent was commuted to money in the 1920s, commutation and handling costs would have made the money rent higher than the crop rent, and tenants might have preferred to continue to pay in cotton.[33] The stipulation of paying rent in cotton might, therefore, be an added reason for cultivating the crop.

The cultivation of cotton on newly reclaimed land poses a special problem for an assessment of changes in the standard of living brought about by the introduction of industrial crops. In the earlier years of the nineteenth century, the centre of cotton growing in Jiangsu included the surroundings of Shanghai. By the early twentieth century, cotton was no longer restricted to this area. The opening of the saline land implies a shift in the cotton-growing area and also considerable migration into hitherto poorly inhabited regions. Our records are totally silent on the economic well-being of the migrants before they settled in these parts. Moreover, opportunities in these regions varied. In Tongzhou, which became one of China's major industrial centres, the settlers might have derived some added income from occupations in the cotton mills. In Yancheng, Qidong, and Haimen, there were few such opportunities. None the less, in most of these parts, cotton farmers were subjected to powerful landlords who were efficient in rent collection, whether or not they rented directly from the reclamation companies.

The decisive factor that shaped the landlord's power in these areas is that land reclamation required substantial capital and political influence. The reclamation companies budgeted for hundreds of thousands of dollars (the Tonghai Company in Nantong, for instance, claimed a capital of 600,000 dollars, although it is not clear if all this was paid up). The companies were responsible for providing the basic infrastructure (the dykes, bridges, drainage), and they signed contracts with their tenants that required a down payment, fixed crop rent, and annual service (that was possibly paid for in money). Many of these companies, such as the Tonghai Company, had a vested interest in the cotton trade. The Tonghai, for instance, was owned by Zhang Jian, the industrialist who was responsible for developing Nantong into a major cotton-milling centre. The companies maintained the right to expel the tenants if rent was not paid, and adopted a patronizing policy that included prizes for high yields, the provision of schools, and penalties for the breach of regulations. Moreover, the companies were more organized for the purpose of enforcing these regulations than were the tenants, being first-generation settlers, for opposing them. The question of whether these tenants were better off than before their settlement in these areas is unanswerable, but that, with lineage and village connections yet to be built up, they were less powerful than tenants in long-reclaimed areas may be expected.[34]

Available documentation does not permit the following to be stated as more than a tentative hypothesis: that is, that there seem to be close connections between investment, high yields, commercialization, and the development of high rates of tenancy. The connections are probably not fortuitous. Those areas in which tenancy rates were historically high, for instance, southern Jiangsu and the Zhujiang delta, were also historically high-yielding and commercialized. The development of high rates of tenancy in areas controlled by the reclamation companies was the outcome of a process that had been repeated many times in Chinese rural history since the early Ming. High yields and the possibility of selling the crops attracted migration into a newly reclaimed area, and the migrants had to submit to tenancy terms laid down by the incumbents. Moreover, this history was played out not only in these newly reclaimed areas, but also in long-settled areas such as the silk district in Shunde. Incumbents who mortgaged and then sold their land did not do so just because they were bankrupt: they must also have been attracted by rising land prices. Of 540 native bankers in Guangzhou in 1932, 281 were of Shunde origin.[35] How many entered the banking business without ever having had to mortgage or sell their highly priced land?

The close connection between high tenancy rates and commercial development makes it nonsensical to argue that owner-cultivators were better placed to take advantage of commercial development. Pared down to essentials, it was not tenancy that determined the farmer's standard of living, but commercial and productive conditions. Despite the high rent he had to pay, the tenant silk farmer in Shunde enjoyed a higher standard of living than the owner-cultivator of northern Jiangsu. To blame the Chinese farmer's low standard of living on tenancy arrangements and to ignore the lack of an infrastructure for commercial development is to put the cart before the horse.

8

Landlords and Tenants

WE come finally to the question of landlord-tenant relationships that was in the 1920s and 1930s and still is regarded as crucial in any discussion on the distribution of income in rural China. To pursue such a discussion, it is necessary to face squarely a number of problems in the Chinese land data. They include the problem of how the substantial estates held in institutional names in both Jiangsu and Guangdong are to be understood, how permanent tenancy, which in effect gave the permanent tenant the right to sub-lease, might transform the status of the tenant, how access might be gained to land other than through ownership or tenancy, and the implications of the geographic distribution of tenant farming. None of these issues is well understood at the time of writing, and they are discussed only too often without any reference to the rural political structure. It is easy to assume that, because the tenant had to pay a rent, he was the weaker party in a land-holding relationship. But was he, and why should his weakness *vis-à-vis* the landlord be taken for granted? This is the question this chapter tries to answer.

Statistical Cross-sections

Table 8.1 reproduces statistics gathered by J.L. Buck that provide a cross-sectional view of the distribution of owner-cultivators, part-owners, and tenants in Jiangsu and Guangdong. The terms are defined in relation to the ownership of the land being farmed by the cultivator. The owner-cultivator was taken by Buck to be someone who owned practically all the land he farmed, the part-owner someone who owned a portion of what he farmed, and the tenant someone who owned none or almost none of it, the land he farmed being rented. These were broad categories into which the farming population was divided by social investigators in the 1920s and 1930s.[1]

These terms are extremely misleading. An owner-cultivator, for instance, could as easily have been a farmer, who with the help of a large family cultivated a sizable estate, as a lone cultivator who eked out a hand-to-mouth living from one or two small plots. The tenant, on the other hand, could be the hard-oppressed cultivator of a tiny farm or an enterprising man who farmed a substantial area with the help of hired labourers.[2] The vagueness of the category known as the 'part-owner' is also immediately obvious from the table. It includes those cultivators in Gaoyao county who owned as little as 13 per cent of their farms as well as the ones in Maoming who owned 74 per cent. The high proportion of households in this category is therefore not surprising, and it obscures the overall picture. For this reason, the proportion of land rented is presented in Table 8.1 to give an indication of the degree of disparity in land ownership in each locality.[3] These figures on tenancy status, in themselves, therefore, do not indicate income distribution.

The table does not give much more than a very crude impression of the distribution of households by tenancy statuses and the amount of land owned or used by each household within these categories. Moreover, especially for a regional study, Buck's data are not likely to be unbiased. In each locality he surveyed, his interviewers drew on no more than about 100 farm households and it is unclear how they or the villages they resided in were selected. The small local sample is inevitable in a survey on a national scale, such as Buck's survey was. However, when the survey data are used for local studies, they necessarily oversimplify. With reference to Table 8.1, for instance, the data for Jiangdu reflect the conditions only of the irrigated portion of the county, and tenancy was more concentrated there than in the non-irrigated areas.[4] The report for Zhongshan, the only report we have in Buck for the whole of the Zhujiang delta, comes from a single village where all 100 households surveyed did not own the farmsteads they lived in. This description would fit the conditions of tenants on the reclaimed land (*shatian*) of the delta, but it was not generally typical of all parts of the region. The reports for Yancheng county, in fact, illustrate these variations quite clearly. In the first locality surveyed, which reference to Table 3.1 will show was the only one of the four that was largely devoted to cotton farming, 52 per cent of all farmland was probably rented out. In contrast, in the other three localities, two of which (noted as Yancheng (2) and (4)) we know from Table 3.1 were largely put to grain, only 17 to 18 per cent of all cultivated land was rented out. The small sample in each locality surveyed, and the haphazard choice of sample subjects, open Buck to the charge that his data favoured the better-off farm households, a criticism that is not unjustified.[5]

Despite the shortcomings, the statistics included in Table 8.1

Table 8.1

Land Tenure in Jiangsu and Guangdong, c.1930

	Status Distribution (per cent)			Land Owned (mu)		Land Rented (mu)		Total Land Rented (per cent)
	Owner-cultivator	Part-owner	Tenant	By Owner-cultivator	By Part-owner	By Part-owner	By Tenant	
	(1)	(2)	(3)	(4)	(5)	(6)	(7)	(8)
Jiangsu								
Southern:								
Jiangning	72.2	16.7	11.1	28.0	9.6	8.1	12.2	11
Changsu	2.0	40.6	57.4	2.8	3.7	6.0	5.9	79
Kunshan	18.1	47.0	34.9	21.7	7.2	18.1	9.8	62
Yixing	52.0	29.0	19.0	41.6	16.9	13.7	33.2	28
Wuxi (1)	47.5	44.3	8.2	9.1	7.5	4.7	7.0	26
Wuxi (2)	—	32.1	67.9	—	4.1	4.7	7.0	83
Wujin (1)	47.7	49.6	2.7	17.6	9.8	6.2	8.3	20
Wujin (2)	15.0	46.0	39.0	21.5	16.4	12.2	17.4	53
Wujin (3)	48.0	35.0	17.0	18.6	10.3	10.9	14.2	33
Transitional:								
Funing	29.3	17.4	53.3	19.9	13.5	18.9	39.4	75
Huaiyin	48.0	40.2	11.8	36.3	13.2	11.1	22.3	24
Yancheng (1)	42.0	20.0	38.0	44.4	37.0	22.8	62.3	52
Yancheng (2)	75.0	18.0	7.0	21.2	17.3	15.0	21.5	18
Yancheng (3)	59.0	36.0	5.0	46.4	32.2	18.1	34.7	17
Yancheng (4)	83.3	6.3	10.4	21.2	11.2	8.0	30.4	17

	Status Distribution (per cent)			Land Owned (mu)		Land Rented (mu)		Total Land Rented (per cent)
	Owner-cultivator (per cent) (1)	Part-owner (per cent) (2)	Tenant (3)	By Owner-cultivator (4)	By Part-owner (5)	By Part-owner (6)	By Tenant (7)	(8)
Jiangdu (1)	43.9	29.9	26.2	24.9	11.6	10.3	14.5	32
Jiangdu (2)	87.1	7.5	5.4	13.5	8.8	6.2	18.1	10
Taixian	70.7	23.2	6.1	18.6	9.8	9.4	20.5	18
Dongtai	45.6	26.1	28.3	147.6	34.5	27.7	33.0	18
Northern:								
Guanyun	68.7	7.1	24.2	54.5	28.2	16.3	108.1	41
Guangdong								
Zhujiang delta:								
Zhongshan	—	—	100.0	—	—	—	24.1	100
Xijiang:								
Gaoyao	—	16.0	84.0	—	2.1	14.0	21.7	98
Beijiang:								
Qujiang	13.9	18.8	67.3	26.2	10.1	16.0	15.8	71
Hanjiang:								
Chao'an	39.0	47.0	14.0	6.7	6.5	7.8	9.4	47
Jieyang	48.0	52.0	—	7.3	6.4	2.8	—	17
North and east:								
Maoming	12.0	64.0	24.0	21.2	12.7	4.4	12.4	35
Nanxiong	23.0	76.0	1.0	23.1	12.9	4.7	2.8	19

Note: Column 8 = ((2)(6) + (3)(7))/((1)(4) + (2)((5) + (6)) + (3)(7))
Source: J.L. Buck (1937b), pp. 57–60.

indicate a very general impression of regional variations. Two features may be noted. Firstly, that the proportion of tenant households as well as that of rented land was highest in the Zhujiang delta and parts of southern and transitional Jiangsu, and that these proportions declined to the north and east of southern Jiangsu and beyond the Zhujiang delta in Guangdong. This description agrees with impressions given by other surveys.[6] Secondly, the amount of land cultivated by owner-cultivators and tenant farmers varied quite systematically from south to north in Jiangsu and in different parts of Guangdong. In southern Jiangsu, with the exception of the reports from Changshu county, all the owner-cultivators on average cultivated more land than the tenants. In transitional Jiangsu, approximately half of the reports indicate that tenant farmers farmed more land than the owner-cultivators, and in the single example from northern Jiangsu, the tenants farmed twice as much land as owner-cultivators or part-owners. In Guangdong, the reports from the Hanjiang delta indicate larger farms cultivated by tenants; elsewhere, owner-cultivators cultivated larger farms.

The shortcomings of the tenancy categories were recognized by contemporaries, and one of the consequences was the adoption of income categories in rural surveys. These categories, that divided farmers into 'rich', 'middle', and 'poor' peasants, are no more precise: the surveyors that used these terms hardly ever explained clearly how these statuses were defined, and what controls were employed so that the 'rich' or the 'poor' in one village might be fairly equated with households reported as being in the same categories in the next village.[7] None the less, Table 8.2, making use of surveys that categorized rural households in terms of income statuses, takes further the regional variations noted in Table 8.1.

Table 8.2 reproduces statistics on income status, tenancy status, and land holding in four counties in Jiangsu and one in Guangdong. Of the Jiangsu counties, Peixian is in northern Jiangsu, Yancheng and Qidong are in the transitional region (Qidong being to the south of Yancheng), and Changshu is in southern Jiangsu. The statistics are derived from surveys conducted by the Rural Rehabilitation Commission in Jiangsu in 1933 and by Chen Hansheng in Guangdong in 1936. The Guangdong county, Panyu, is located in the Zhujiang delta. In four of these five counties, the group described as the 'poor peasants' formed the majority, the exception being Yancheng, where there were approximately as many 'middle peasants' as 'poor peasants'. However, the distributions by tenancy statuses varied. In the northern counties, Peixian and Yancheng, the majority of households interviewed was made up of owner-cultivators, but in the south, it was tenants. In terms of the interrelationship of income and tenancy statuses, in Peixian, of the 130 owner-cultivators, 95 were 'poor' (73.1 per cent), compared to 27 out of 41 tenants being classified in the same category (65.9 per cent). In Yancheng, 44 out of 100 owner-cultivators (44 per cent) were classified 'poor', in contrast to 9 out of 22 tenants (40.9 per cent). In both counties, therefore, owner-cultivators stood a marginally higher chance than the tenants of being classed as 'poor'. The pattern was reversed in the southern counties in Jiangsu. In Qidong, 179 out of 251 tenants (71.3 per cent) were classified as 'poor', in contrast to 19 out of 71 owner-cultivators (26.7 per cent); and in Changshu, 79 out of 109 tenants (72.5 per cent) were classified in this category in contrast to 1 out of 5 (20 per cent) owner-cultivators. In the south, therefore, tenants stood a very much better chance of being classed as 'poor' than owner-cultivators. Panyu was similar to the southern counties of Jiangsu in this respect. In this county, 57 out of 249 owner-cultivators (22.9 per cent) were 'rich' in contrast to 50 out of 591 tenants (8.5 per cent). In other words, almost 1 out of every 5 owner-cultivators was so classified, but fewer than 1 out of every 10 tenants was. The variation from north to south seems to be quite systematic.[8]

A major difference between the 'rich' and the 'poor' in all five counties lay in the amount of land farmed, irrespective of whether it was owned or rented. In Peixian, the 'rich' peasant farmed 81 *mu*, in contrast to the 'middle' peasant's 26 *mu*, and the 'poor' peasant's 4 *mu*. Expressed in terms of land distribution, the top 7.6 per cent of the households farmed 39.4 per cent of the total cultivated acreage (averaging 5.2 per cent for each percentage point of households), the next 25.0 per cent of households farmed 42.3 per cent (averaging 1.7 per cent), and the poorest, 67.4 per cent of households, farmed 18.0 per cent (averaging 0.3 per cent). It may be seen from Table 8.2 that uneven distribution of land farmed characterized all five counties.[9]

In terms of the percentage of cultivated land rented, however, some variations may be detected. In Peixian, the 'rich' peasants rented 52.7 per cent of the land that they farmed, the 'middle' peasants almost the same proportion (53.8 per cent), but the 'poor' peasants only 33.2 per cent. In Yancheng, the 'rich' peasants rented very little land (17.6 per cent), while the 'middle' and 'poor' peasants rented respectively 42.1 and 38.2 per cent. In the two southern counties in Jiangsu, the 'rich' peasants of Qidong rented relatively little land (35.8 per cent), and those of Changshu none at all. In contrast, the 'middle' and 'poor' peasants in both counties rented relatively much more (75.6 and 89.6

Table 8.2
Distribution of Households and Cultivated Land by Income Statuses in Various Localities of Jiangsu and Guangdong, 1930s

Income Status	Tenancy Status			Total Number of Households	Percentage of All Cultivated Land Used	Land Rented as Percentage of Land Used	Average Size of Farm (mu)
	Owner-cultivator	Part-owner	Tenant				
Peixian, Jiangsu							
Rich	7	3	4	14(7.6)	39.4(5.2)*	52.7	81
Middle	28	8	10	46(25.0)	42.3(1.7)	53.8	26
Poor†	95	2	27	124(67.4)	18.0(0.3)	33.2	4
Total	130	13	41	184	99.7	49.6	16
Yancheng, Jiangsu							
Rich	17	7	1	25(17.4)	53.8(3.1)	17.6	80
Middle	39	9	12	60(41.7)	36.2(0.9)	42.1	22
Poor	44	6	9	59(41.0)	9.7(0.2)	38.2	6
Total	100	22	22	144	99.7	28.4	26
Qidong, Jiangsu							
Rich	20	1	5	26(7.5)	34.7(4.6)	35.8	62
Middle	32	14	67	113(32.6)	40.8(1.3)	75.6	17
Poor	19	10	179	208(59.9)	23.4(0.4)	89.6	5
Total	71	25	251	347	98.9	64.2	13

Income Status	Tenancy Status			Total Number of Households	Percentage of All Cultivated Land Used	Land Rented as Percentage of Land Used	Average Size of Farm (mu)
	Owner-cultivator	Part-owner	Tenant				
Changshu, Jiangsu							
Rich	3	—	—	3(2.1)	6.4(3.0)	—	27
Middle	1	8	30	39(27.5)	49.5(1.8)	91.0	16
Poor‡	1	20	79	100(70.4)	40.8(0.6)	86.0	5
Total	5	28	109	142	96.7	81.6	9
Panyu, Guangdong							
Rich	57	—	50	107(12.7)	33.9(2.7)	59.2	26
Middle	75	—	118	193(23.0)	28.1(1.2)	70.3	12
Poor	117	—	423	540(64.3)	37.9(0.6)	82.8	6
Total	249	—	591	840	99.9	71.3	10

Notes: * The values in parentheses are the percentages of the total cultivated land used by each percentage point of the total households classed in this category.

† Excluding 48 households whose income depended almost entirely on wages.

‡ Excluding 1 household whose income depended almost entirely on wages.

Source: Nongcun fuxing weiyuanhui (1934), pp. 43–4 and 51–2; Chen Han-seng (1936), p. 124.

per cent respectively in Qidong, 91.0 and 86.0 in Changshu). In Panyu, like Peixian, the 'rich' peasants rented more than half their land (59.2 per cent); however, unlike Peixian but like Qidong and Changshu, the 'middle' and 'poor' peasants also rented a relatively large proportion of the land they farmed (70.3 and 82.8 per cent). When the high proportions of rented land farmed by the 'rich' peasants of Peixian and Panyu are considered, it must be concluded that renting land could be a strategy for obtaining a higher income. None the less, it would also seem from the statistics that at least in southern China, the 'middle' and 'poor' peasants could not increase the acreage farmed even by renting.

The distribution of farmland by use, as indicated in Tables 8.1 and 8.2, therefore, was quite uneven; but, of course, its distribution by ownership must have been even more so. Figures concerning landlords and landless peasants have not been included in Table 8.2, and when they are taken into account, they accentuate the importance of having access to land, through ownership or renting. In Peixian, the Rural Rehabilitation Commission recorded only two landlord households who possessed 110 *mu*, and 47 households who farmed little land. In Yancheng, the single landlord household reported owning 33 *mu*, and 12 households farmed little land. In Qidong and Changshu, two landlord households were reported in each county, owning respectively 165 and 90 *mu*. In Qidong, 11 households were reported who farmed little land, and in Changshu, 9 households were similarly reported. In Panyu, all the 'rich' farmers surveyed also farmed. None, therefore, qualified as a landlord as such. The survey enumerated 83 agricultural labourers, who had little land to farm.[10]

The number of landlords is probably understated in the surveys. Landholding is always a difficult subject to define in formal surveys, and one wonders if the surveys of the 1920s and 1930s could have been more successful than government attempts to register land in these years or earlier. Sporadic references show that in some places large landlord holdings amounted to a great deal more than Table 8.2 would suggest. In the counties of Yizheng, Jiangyin, and Wujiang, in the transitional region and in southern Jiangsu, Malone and Taylor reported that two households possessed over 1,000 *mu* each, and two more between 500 and 1,000 *mu*. The four households together possessed over 7,000 out of 23,500 *mu* surveyed, in a sample of 1,300 households. It is also well known that in both northern Jiangsu and in the Zhujiang delta, there were landlords who owned huge estates. In one report, a landlord in Xiao county (northern Jiangsu) was stated as owning

20,000 *mu*, while the Jiluo Convent and its subsidiaries in Suqian (northern Jiangsu) owned 200,000 *mu*. In Dongguan (Guangdong), the Minglun *tang* owned enough land to derive an annual income of over 1,000,000 dollars from rent in the 1920's, and two ancestral trusts received annual incomes varying between 500,000 and 800,000 dollars, primarily from their landholdings.[11]

So far, survey data have been employed to give an indication of the regional distribution of rented land. Enough has been said, on the basis of these statistics, to underline the importance of access to farmland, through ownership or rental arrangements, as a source of increased farm income. However, do the statistics really say very much about landlord-tenant relationships? The answer is that they do not; in particular, they say very little about how landlords were in any position to extract rent from their tenants, or to control the land that they owned. These are crucial subjects that must be further explored.

The Landlord's Ability to Increase Rent

In a paper on the Jiangsu rural economy published some years ago, I argued that farm rent was increased not by the imposition of a new rate as such, but by altering the mode of rent payment.[12] Rent that was charged as a proportion of the harvest, for instance, was converted to a fixed measure of the crop, and in the Suzhou suburbs, after 1870, the fixed crop rent was commuted to cash at a rate purportedly equal to, but in reality higher than, the market price of grain. I suggested that commutation was possible in Suzhou because the landlords collected their rent through professional rent-collection offices, but I did not offer a more general explanation. On reflection, it would seem that I could have added that the circuitous manner by which rent was raised arose from a desire to adhere to an established standard that landlords could not alter at will. Documents on rent collection published since that article demonstrate that tenants resisted what they considered to be unjust rent as a matter of right. These documents would tend to support such a hypothesis.[13]

The capability of the landlord to increase rent, which was closely tied to his capability to collect it, is an important aspect of the landlord-tenant relationship which was only too often taken for granted in the surveys of the 1920s and 1930s.[14] At heart is the political structure of rural society. In the complex social structure of rural China, where residential and lineage ties cut across social classes, the relative strengths of landlord and tenant varied.[15] Suggestions that rent might be substantially increased during the development of cash crops must take into account the issue of power for rent collection, loaded in the landlord's favour in some places, in the tenant's in others. The statistics on tenancy collected in the surveys of the 1920s and 1930s are quite useless in the analysis of such issues. This section attempts to probe them through case studies.[16]

The New Territories of Hong Kong: Varieties of Land Rights

The New Territories of Hong Kong provides some of the very few cases where the question of land rights has been studied as part of the political process of rural society. These studies are valuable, therefore, as a starting point for any discussion on landlord-tenant relationships. Until 1899, the New Territories formed part of Xin'an (later Bao'an) county, and the conditions of traditional village society found in this area should be applicable to other places in the Zhujiang delta.[17]

Land rights in the nineteenth century and in the early twentieth were of three sorts. Firstly, members of the village held customary rights over common land. These rights differed from outright ownership in that they were derived from membership of the village community. They were inheritable until the villager departed from the village and settled elsewhere, but they were not subject to sale. Villagers had clear conceptions of such rights, which included the right of building on undeveloped land near existing village houses, the right to open undeveloped land for cultivation, the right to gather firewood and grass from nearby hillsides, to graze their cattle there, and to channel water from the streams into their fields. Being a land owner or a tenant had little to do with the exercising of such rights. Being a member of the village had much to do with it.[18]

Common land rights were distinct from rights over land that was privately owned, by individuals or corporate groups such as lineages. Private land ownership might be established by various means, most commonly by registration at the *yamen*, by bringing common land into cultivation and by contract. By law, in the Qing as in the Republican era, cultivated land had to be registered for the purpose of tax, but much of it was not, and consequently whether or not a tax was paid by the cultivator was a poor criterion of ownership. Moreover, like other places south of the Changjiang, multiple ownership was common in the New Territories. That a tenant might be said to 'own' the 'top-soil' even though a rent was paid, and that a landlord owned merely the 'bottom-soil', considerably complicates the question of ownership.

Documents from the New Territories show that deeds of perpetual tenancy were initially granted over extensive tracts of uncultivated land. As this land was brought under cultivation, two consequences followed. In the first place, in time, as more land was cultivated, the per-unit acreage rent demanded declined. In the second place, because the rights of reclamation were inheritable, and because inherited property was divided among descendants or sold under condition that members of the lineage were given the right of first refusal, in a matter of generations, the 'bottom-soil' landlords would have been faced, not by an individual tenant but by an entire settled lineage. The development of land ownership at this stage might take many forms. Some land might be held under a lineage trust. Or, the original tenant lineage might accept other surname groups into the settlement, some of whom might buy or rent 'top-soil' land from individual members of the lineage or the lineage trust itself. Or, members of the village might also sell, mortgage, or rent individual plots of land among themselves, and occasionally also to members of other villages. Some plots would be sold with the provision that a 'bottom-soil' rent should be paid to the original 'bottom-soil' landlord. Other plots might be sold without such a provision. Despite these changes, villagers might still accept th'at the land on which they farmed was 'rented' from 'bottom-soil' owners.

The ownership of the 'bottom-soil' of extensive tracts of land was, therefore, quite distinct from common land rights claimed over the immediate vicinity by a village, or private ownership established by reclamation or contract. In the New Territories, such rights can best be described as overlordship, and it was exercised over largely uncultivated but potentially fertile land. There was little legal basis for such rights, but a half dozen or so powerful lineages claimed it over vast territories beyond their own settlements. Within these territories, they claimed not only the right of imposing a rent on developers, but also the right of opening markets for trade, and charging fees for various policing duties, which included the provision of water from the main rivers. The territorial boundaries within which each lineage exercised its overlordship were known to villagers, and were defended by alliances and open warfare. Rent was collected by teams of lineage members and their servants, and stories of excessive demands have been preserved in legends. However, at times, the tenants opposed them. In two documented incidents in the early nineteenth century, clashes between rent collectors and tenants resulted in proceedings at the county magistracy. By the late nineteenth century, it seems, the overlord's power had waned for village alliances consisting of tenant villages had succeeded in imposing some control.

The three forms of land rights overlapped. A stretch of land might fall within the territorial control of an overlord lineage and be leased perpetually to a tenant lineage. Portions of it might come to be cultivated and in this way pass into private ownership, while the remainder might remain the common land of the entire village consisting of the lineage. Under these circumstances, such terms as landlords and tenants tend to be ambiguous, and neither term sufficiently describes the plight of the truly landless, that is, people who were not members of any village and had no right to open waste land for cultivation.[19]

The problem of access to land is also complicated by lineage arrangements. Where land was considered to be owned by a lineage trust, it follows that a large number of cultivators would be reported as tenants. Chen Hansheng, studying tenancy in Guangdong in the 1930s, saw the theoretical complications created by the possibility that some of these 'tenants' would be in the position of deriving benefits directly from the rent that they paid, but dismissed it outright arguing that embezzlement by the few who controlled lineage funds would have drained away the balance left after paying taxes, temple expenses, the cost of repair on lineage properties, and education expenses for members of the lineage. Ongoing research in the New Territories of Hong Kong suggests that he had dismissed the problem rather too readily. These expenses were important for village life: the 'temple expenses', for instance, could easily account for the villagers' communal life, with its very rich implications. In some places, as Chen also noted, through lineage holdings, members of the lineage had access to land for farming, for lineage land was sometimes rented exclusively to lineage members. A peasant who owned no land but who was a member of a well-endowed lineage would, therefore, be in a very different economic position from one who similarly owned no land but who did not have the support of a lineage trust. Both would have been very different from the outsider who owned no land and had no access to any.[20]

Research in the New Territories, therefore, suggests that the question of landlord-tenant relationships has to be examined in two dimensions. Landlords and tenants who belonged to the same or neighbouring villages, who rented in small plots, were bound by relationships that differed markedly from those that were established between overlord lineages and their tenant villages.[21] To appreciate their relationships, one must understand village and territorial politics, for the ability to enforce rent payment depended not only on ownership but also on power. The simple classification of a village population into landlord, owner-cultivator and tenant, as one so frequently encounters in the surveys of the 1920s and 1930s, does not take into account the distribution of power and leaves unanswered such vital questions as whether rent was successfully collected, or whether landlords were entitled to, or did control, the land they were said to have owned.

Wuxi: Cash Crops, Disorganized Landlords, and Permanent Tenure

According to a survey of twenty villages in Wuxi county, southern Jiangsu, conducted by the National Research Institute of Social Sciences of the Academia Sinica in 1929, 5.7 per cent of the total number of households in these villages consisted of landlords, 5.6 'rich peasants', 19.8 'middle peasants', and 68.9 'poor peasants'. They owned respectively 47.3, 17.7, 20.8, and 14.2 per cent of the total cultivated acreage.[22] According to another survey, by He Menglei, which compared the tenancy arrangements of Wuxi with those of Changshu and Suzhou, 50 per cent of all cultivated land in Wuxi was left under contracts of permanent tenure, compared to 80 per cent in Changshu and 90 per cent in Suzhou. In local parlance, land placed under permanent tenure was spoken of as the 'top-soil' and the 'bottom-soil'. According to He, both 'top-soil' and 'bottom-soil' might be independently bought and sold.[23]

According to He, the landlords of Wuxi were poorly organized compared to those of Changshu and Suzhou. Cash rent was much less common in Wuxi, the fixed crop rent was more common, and as late as the 1930s, 10 per cent of the tenants in this county shared their harvests with the landlords. Unlike Changshu and Suzhou, where professional rent collection offices had developed, 62 per cent of Wuxi tenants still delivered their rent to their landlords' houses. Possibly because professionalism in rent collection was less well developed, rent was lower in Wuxi, being 0.85 *shi* of unhusked rice and 0.2 *shi* of wheat each year. However, He did not specify if this rent was paid by permanent tenants or those on fixed-term contracts, or if indeed, it applied to both categories. His description implies that the major difference between the two consisted only in the down payment (*yazu*) required of tenants without permanent tenure, amounting to between 10 and 40 dollars per *mu* (which at the time of He's report would have been equivalent to 1 to 4 *shi* of husked rice on the wholesale market, or between the yields of one to two rice harvests on a *mu* of land.) Tenants with permanent tenure would have paid a purchase price for the ownership of the 'top-soil'. This down payment could be increased in the course of tenancy.[24]

Rising income that could be derived from cash crops, especially from mulberry and wheat, came into conflict with the system of multiple tenancy. The value of 'bottom-soil' rights naturally declined as rent could not be raised, and attempts were made by 'bottom-soil' owners to sell their rights or by 'top-soil' owners to purchase them. According to another source, those few rent collection bureaus that operated in Wuxi resorted to litigation in 1930 in an attempt to intervene in the sale of the 'top-soil' by their tenants. It is not clear if these attempts were successful.[25]

Nevertheless, outsider-cultivators — cultivators who were not members of villages where their fields were located — did not benefit from these permanent tenancy contracts. The Jiangsu Farmers' Bank in 1931 surveyed the Fourth District in Wuxi and noted that 754 thatched houses (compared to 18,918 tiled houses) were all occupied by outsiders. It explained that this was because landlords gave these outsider tenants short leases for the land that they cultivated, and as a result, they had little reason to invest in permanent homes. The survey offered no information on the rent they were charged, but it would be consistent with rising land prices for it to be increased as leases were renewed.[26]

More information may be had on Li She, a small town in another portion of the county, that was the subject of a study in 1932.[27] The town was dominated by the Xue lineage. Numerically, members of the lineage constituted two-thirds of the town households, and 61 out of 68 landlords enumerated (one of which was a temple trust). The other people in the town were mostly farmers, farming totally 30,000 *mu*. The study did not specify whether they rented their land from the land-owning Xues, but most must have. At the time of the survey, the Xues together owned 10,000 *mu*, a figure that suggests that their holdings stretched far beyond the town. This was already a substantial decline from their earlier holdings in the nineteenth century before the Taiping Rebellion, which amounted to 40,000 *mu*. It is not clear if they owned all this land outright, or only the 'top-' or more likely the 'bottom-' soil.

The Xues were a historically rich and powerful lineage.[28] In their heyday, they owned seven pawnshops locally, and six and a half in other places. They also owned more than forty grain boats that purchased grain at other places in southern Jiangsu and sold it in Suzhou, Changshu, or even in Zhejiang Province. The lineage had suffered from the Taiping Rebellion and changes in the rice market. None the less, in early Republican years two members of the lineage still owned over 2,000 *mu* each and in addition collected considerable interest from usury. Such individual holdings continued to decline, so that by the time of the study the largest individual landlord owned only 900 *mu*. However, as a lineage, the Xues continued to wield political influence. Members of the lineage made up the entire township committee, all nine members of the local Guomindang Party, all four office-bearers of the local Chamber of Commerce, half of the twenty-man strong Chamber of Commerce guards (in effect the town police), and three out of the five men on the committee of the local Farmers' Association, of which a Xue was also chairman. The Xues continued to maintain a lineage estate of 1,350 *mu* and collected 1,000 *shi* of wheat each year in rent. For poor members of the lineage, male or female, the estate provided 2 *shi* of rice for each one who was over sixteen years of age, and 1.2 *shi* for each one under sixteen. It also provided 7 dollars for the weddings of male members, 10 dollars for a funeral, 4 dollars for a child's primary school fees, 6 for secondary school fees, and 10 for university fees. Another lineage estate owned 400 *mu*, and received 300 *shi* of rice per year. It provided monthly income in cash as well as rice for widows and orphans, but such provisions were not restricted to members of the Xue lineage. The lineage also ran a school, endowed with 220 *mu* of poor farmland, that yielded 100 *shi* of rice in rent each year.

The Xues were probably in a position to enforce higher rent had they wanted to, but their charges were only marginally higher than the general trends described in He Menglei's study. Three-quarters of the farmland in Li She were given to paddy, and a quarter was planted with mulberry. In good years, 2 *shi* of rice (milled) and 0.6 to 1.2 *shi* of wheat could be harvested from a *mu* of paddy land, while 20 piculs of mulberry leaves could be gathered from a *mu* of mulberry land. Rent on paddy land was charged at 0.8 *shi* of rice (milled) and 0.2 *shi* of wheat, with remissions allowed for poor harvests. On mulberry land, a money rent of 8 to 10 dollars was charged per *mu*. Rent in cash or in kind was delivered by the tenants to the landlords. Rent in arrears was not commuted, but paid in full in years of good harvest. However, no interest was charged for this delay. Down payments (*yazu*) were required when land was rented. On paddy land, they ranged from 10 to 30 dollars, and if they were not paid, an annual interest of 0.2 *shi* of rice would be added to the rent. On mulberry land, they ranged from 20 to 40 dollars and must be paid. Having made the down payment, the tenant was given permanent tenure, which he could transfer at a fee known as 'potash-fertilizer money'. He could also sublet and charge a rent. The landlord was entitled to demand additional down payments when desired. On occasion, tenants worked for the landlords, but they were paid normal wages due to short term labourers, at 30 to 40 cents for each shift, meals being provided by the employers.

Few villages would have been as powerful as Li She, but Rongxiang, a market town within the Fourth District, might be comparable.[29] The home town of the family of powerful industrialists of the Rong surname,[30] it was surveyed in 1941 by the South Manchurian Railway's Shanghai Bureau together with three small villages in its vicinity, Xiaodingxiang, Zhengxiang, and Yangmuqiao. Like the Xues of Li She, the Rongs had a lineage estate (holdings unknown) that paid for the feast at the annual grave worship, and provided 1 to 2 piculs of grain each year for elderly members of the lineage, widows, and orphans, as well as school fees and other subsidies such as wedding and funeral grants for most lineage members. The survey did not note large holdings belonging to individual lineage members, but this could be the result of dislocation due to war, the Sino-Japanese War having broken out by the time of the survey. It is quite unlikely, for instance, that Rong Desheng, who succeeded to the family's industrial fortune, had only 50 to 60 *mu* to his name, or that the head of the lineage, who owned ten houses and two fishponds, had only 30 *mu*.[31]

In this survey, we know much more about the villages in the vicinity of Rongxiang than we do of the villages of Li She that were inhabited by villagers who did not have the Xue surname. Xiaodingxiang was a village of fourteen households in 1941 occupying 23 tiled and two thatched houses. Five households of the Rong surname, five of the Ding surname, and one of the Zheng surname, owned tiled houses. A single household of the Wu surname and one of the Qian surname did not own any house, but lived in tiled houses, while a household of the Peng surname owned the two thatched houses. Wu, Qian, and Peng must have been outsiders who settled in the village, even though their status as such was not noted in the survey report. None of the three owned any agricultural land. Wu was described as a mulberry farmer who also worked as a cook. He rented 0.5 *mu* of mulberry land from a Shanghai merchant by verbal contract in 1925. Qian was described as a farmer who also worked as a labourer. He rented 3 *mu* of paddy land from a Rong of Rongxiang by verbal contract, also in 1925. Apparently he farmed no mulberry land, but the possibility must not be ruled out that he did plant some mulberry trees by his house. Peng rented 2.5 *mu* of paddy land, 0.5 *mu* of mulberry land, and 0.2 *mu* of garden (for vegetable farming) from another Rong of Rongxiang, also by verbal contract, in 1937. Wu and Qian were among the very small minority (four out of 14 households) who did not report that they also worked as short term farm labourers in the village.

Apart from the three outsiders, only two households, both of the Rong surname, rented any land.[32] None of the other nine households did. One of these already possessed 1.5 *mu* of paddy land, but rented another 1.5 *mu* from a Yuan family of Wuxi county city some 'fifty years earlier', and another 0.5 *mu* of mulberry land from the village temple from 1920. In village parlance, 'fifty years' was probably synonymous with any fairly lengthy period of time, and suggests that he held the land practically in perpetuity. The other villager, who already had 1.23 *mu* of paddy land and 0.07 *mu* of mulberry land of his own, rented 1.23 *mu* by verbal contract in 1934 from a Rong of the village of Dongpangtou, on which the survey report provided no information. He also owned 0.1 *mu* of grave land as well as his own house. No native villager at Xiaodingxiang, therefore, was a tenant who was dependent on a landlord. It was practically an owner-cultivator village.

Zhengxiang and Yangmuqiao, likewise, were occupied predominantly by owner-cultivators. Only six of the 44 households rented any land, and three of these had surnames that were uncommon in the village, owned no houses, and were for these two reasons probably outsiders. One of them rented 0.7 *mu* of mulberry land from a man of the Rong surname, described as a hawker, in Shanghai. Another rented 4.5 *mu* from a coppersmith, also from Shanghai, whose name was listed among the village households but who owned an exceptionally small house in the village. The third rented 5 *mu* of paddy land from a fellow villager, and 0.5 *mu* of mulberry land from the Rong family ancestral hall of Rongxiang. The other three who rented land were apparently native villagers who rented it from owners who resided elsewhere and who had no apparent connection with Zhengxiang. In Yangmuqiao, the ten households that owned the tiled houses they lived in possessed paddy as well as mulberry land. Of the eleven households that did not own houses, seven rented farmland, again in small plots, mostly from landlords who lived outside the village. These included four land-owners of Rongxiang (only two of them were of the Rong surname) who rented out respectively 3.9, 3.2, 1.0, and 0.6 *mu*; the Foundlings Home in Wuxi county city that rented out 2 *mu*; and seven landowners who lived in Shanghai who rented out eight plots of land ranging from 0.5 to 4.0 *mu*. In both Zhengxiang and Yangmuqiao, all but five of the native villagers (four in the former and one in the latter) did not have some mulberry land.

These studies on Li She and the villages near Rongxiang support the distinction between native villagers and outsider-residents observed in the New Territories of Hong Kong. The cultivators who needed most to rent were the outsiders, for native villagers had access to uncultivated land. The distinction was probably more aggravated in the context of the silk industry, for the wasteland in or near the village that was used for growing mulberry would have been counted as the common land of the village to which native villagers had the right of exploitation. It is conceivable that outsiders were subject to the pressure of rent increase to a more serious extent than native villagers, many of whom would have been protected by long-established, permanent-tenure contracts.[33]

One last feature on tax collection completes this brief description of landlord-tenant relationship in Wuxi. In the areas discussed, all of which were located in the eastern section of the county, land tax was customarily collected by the *yitu* method, whereby villagers took turns to collect tax so that government functionaries might be kept away from the village. It was not always successfully managed, but its common use stresses the independence of the villagers in such matters and the urge to limit opportunities whereby government functionaries might overcharge them. It also illustrates the perception of the villagers of their weakness *vis-à-vis* the functionaries. In a later section, it will be seen that in areas where the landlords could exert their influence on the local government, the emphasis was quite different.[34]

Northern Jiangsu: Low Rates of Tenancy and Powerful Landlords

Studies available on northern Jiangsu are less detailed than the ones on Wuxi. They give the impression that in this region tenancy rates were low but landlords were oppressive and this apparent anomaly provides further insights into landord-tenant relationships.

The low tenancy rates have been referred to in Table 8.2 in relation to aggregate statistics reported by the Jiangsu Rural Rehabilitation Commission.[35] Descriptions of the landlords invariably refer to their fortified villages. According to Wu Shoupeng, whose observations became the standard view of the north Jiangsu village:

The unit of people's livelihood in northern Jiangsu is the 'earthwall' (*tuweizi*), also know as the *zhai* (fort), *ji* (market), or *zhuang* (estate). These compounds are surrounded by earth walls that stretch 3 to 5 *li* in perimeter (but some are made of brick or stone) — [*sic*], and on all four corners are erected gun towers. Inside the earthwalls, there is always a tall and larger tiled-roof building in the centre, which has an additional gun tower; this should be the palace of the master of the compound. All around, tens or hundreds of farmers farmed the master's land. He owns 100 to 200 *qing* [1 *qing* = 100 *mu*] and perhaps more . . . Outside the earth walls are scattered some small villages. They are inhabited by the tenants, farming the master's land.[36]

The earthwalls served a paramilitary purpose from at least the mid-nineteenth century. During the Taiping Rebellion, earthwall communities were recognized by the county magistrate for local defence against the rebels and from then on their independence from county government control was well known. Banditry continued to be rampant into the twentieth century. According to Wu, these walled villages were well armed: he listed seven villages that possessed among them in total 98 guns. In Shuyang county, he was told that farmers went to their fields with guns on their backs because bandits might come to rob them of their draught animals. In Xiao county, he was told that at harvest time, while some men went to harvest the wheat, a party must be left near the walled compound to keep watch, for otherwise bandits would rob them of the harvested grain. The masters of these villages often took the law into their own hands. They fought the bandits and executed without trial the ones they captured. With the same authority they tortured the tenants who did not pay their rent.[37]

Again, it must be pointed out that in these reports from the 1920s and 1930s, words such as 'landlord' and 'tenant' were not precisely used. Given the low overall tenancy rates, many of these walled communities and the villages near them must have consisted primarily of owner-cultivators. Wu Shoupeng himself noted that in each county, there were no more than several households that owned more than 100 to 200 *qing*. This is also quite obvious when we examine descriptions of individual villages. In the six villages collectively known as Chang'ancun, an area of 3,160 *mu* was farmed by 214 households, of which only 300 *mu* was rented from outside landlords, and 875 was rented from owners living within the villages, much of which could well have been part of the 944 *mu* owned by the 11 landlord households. It is possible also to detect the interplay of power relationships in the tenancy arrangements, for five of the six villages were dominated by 'big surnames' (*daxing*). In these villages, households of the same surname formed a majority of the population, owned practically all the land and dominated the politics.[38] In contrast, in Balitun, a village of 127 households 50 *li* from Chang'ancun, 1,600 *mu* was cultivated, of which 911 was rented from landlords who did not live in the village, 4 *mu* from a landlord in the village, and 28 *mu* from common holdings in the village.[39] Of the six villages in Peixian in which the Rural Rehabilitation Commission interviewed in 1930, only two rented substantial amounts of land. One of these, a village of 42 households owning altogether 110 *mu*, rented 792 *mu* from landlords of the Tai surname of another village, said to be one of four large landowning lineages in the village. The Tais were described as landlords who lived in large houses within walled compounds, in control of a sizable defence corps. Their tenants farmed under contracts that could at any time be withdrawn. The landlords provided half the seeds, but the tenants paid all other production expenses, presumably with the exception of taxes. At harvest, the landlords sent their agent (or agents) to assess the yield, and on the basis of the assessment the landlords claimed half the harvest. Besides, the tenants were obliged to work for the landlords without wages, except for meals.[40]

The evidence is patchy, but it illustrates the varied nature of landlord-tenant relationships. The village that rented only a quarter of its cultivated acreage from outside landlords must have posed a very different problem in rent collection from the one that rented seven times the land it owned. The resident landlord who rented out only 4 *mu* must also have been in a different position of strength from the lineage in the neighbouring village whose members together rented out 792 *mu*. Unfortunately, existing documents do not permit a more detailed exploration of these relationships in these parts of Jiangsu.

Suzhou and Vicinity: Professional Rent Collection

The employment of professionals to collect rent in Suzhou was not a novel development of the late nineteenth century. From the early years of the century, the practice of employing prompters to assist in rent collection was quite widespread, and county magistrates had always lent their support to rent collection and tolerated 'prompting'. Moreover, whether or not prompters were employed, landlords made use of standard estate-management practices, such as the keeping of rent accounts, or the offer of incentives, in the form of rent remissions, to tenants who paid rent before an announced deadline.[41]

The innovation in rent collection in the late nineteenth century in Suzhou lay in the provision of a rent-dunning office (*zhuizuju*) by the prefectural government to assist landlords in rent collection. With the support of this agency, the landlords' rent-collection offices were able to collect rent more effectively and were able to increase the rent.[42]

The institutionalization of government aid for rent dunning was started at the time of the Taiping Rebellion. The Taipings destroyed many *yamen* in southern Jiangsu and with them their tax collection records. Moreover, in their early idealism, the rebels redistributed the cultivated land, only to find that as a result they were quite unable to collect the tax. Thereupon, semi-official institutions were founded in numerous counties whereby, under the support of the Taiping government, landlords and locally recruited officials collaborated to collect rent. These offices were not always successful. In Wujiang the rent-and-tax collectors were slow to hand over the tax and the institution collapsed when they were arrested by Taiping officials and punished. In Wuxi, the *zongcangting* (chief granary office), as the instituion was called, was destroyed by the tenants almost as soon as it was established in 1861. In Suzhou, similar offices were apparently in operation until the city was retaken by Qing government forces in 1862 when a central rent-collection office was set up. The office did not survive for many years, but some co-ordinated effort for rent dunning among landlords remained. The decided change came in 1886, for a government rent-dunning office was established in that year that lasted into the twentieth century.[43]

The establishment of such central rent-collection agencies extended to nearby counties in the twentieth century, but not earlier. In the 1920s, the landlords of Kunshan county formed a Landlords' Association (*tianye gonghui*) and petitioned the county government to set up a rent-collection office. The office was to be manned by the local police, whose salaries the landlords were willing to pay. It is not clear if this office was successfully set up, but with or without it, the Kunshan accounting offices (*zhangfang*), as the landlords' private offices were called in this area, employed prompters to collect rent from late-payers, and if necessary asked the magistrate for warrants to have them arrested. Qiao Qiming, who described this arrangement in 1926, visited the detention centre for tenants who owed their rent, and saw ten men and five women detained there. The largest amount owed was no more than 30 dollars. Some of the women were arrested in place of their husbands, who had gone into hiding.[44]

In Wujiang, Fei Xiaotong reported that a similar institution existed. The landlords had a union that regulated the rate at which rent was charged each year. Rent-collection offices, acting through their own staffs, collected the required amounts from the tenants. Their agents were 'entrusted with police powers by the district government', and they were 'semi-political bodies'. As a result, according to Fei, 'the tenants do not know and do not care who is their landlord, and know only to which bureau they belong'.[45] Besides, in the 1930s, a 'rent-dunning committee' (*zhuizu weiyuanhui*) was formed for a similar purpose in Wuxi, and a 'rent-dunning office' (*zhuizuju*) in 1933 in Changshu by the county government, which arrested three to four hundred tenants whose rents were in arrears.[46]

Nowhere else in Jiangsu was rent collection carried out with as much professionalism as in Suzhou and its neighbouring counties, and two reasons may account for its development. Firstly, Suzhou landlords were politically powerful. Through their family connections in high officialdom, they exerted influence far beyond the county *yamen*.[47] Unlike the Wuxi landlords, who for most of the period up to the 1930s maintained a tax-collection method that kept the *yamen* functionaries out of their villages, these Suzhou landlords were sufficiently exertive to be able to employ them in their rent collection. The rent-dunning office in Suzhou, moreover, began at a time when the larger landlords had made a successful concerted effort to pressure the imperial government for tax remission. The agency demonstrated its usefulness in those days, but was not copied in other counties until the 1920s.

Secondly, the employment of professionals with the connivance of the county *yamen*, which was the gist of the rent-collection strategy in Suzhou, was adopted primarily in counties in which permanent tenure was common.[48] It should be recalled that in these same areas, commercial crops for export were being developed from the late nineteenth century to the early twentieth century. The development brought new sources of income for cultivators, but the landlords, saddled with permanent tenure, could not readily evict or raise rent. The demand for rent commutation to cash according to a rate issued unilaterally by the landlords circumvented the restrictions of the permanent contracts. None the less, an increase in rent, under whatever pretence, was hardly likely to go unnoticed by the tenants. It cannot be a coincidence, therefore, that strong-handed measures for rent collection were introduced at approximately this time.[49] The need to adopt such measures was probably greater than ever in the early 1930s, for faced with collapsing prices for their farm produce, tenants were refusing to pay the high commuted rent arrived at in more prosperous days. What in Suzhou evolved in the 1860s as a calculated strategy was adopted in Wuxi in the 1930s as a panic measure.

Signs of Professionalism in Guangdong

Guangdong landlords did not organize any rent-dunning office as such, but the larger property trusts, for example lineage estates, had their own collectors. Isolated instances of rent-collecting agencies may be noted nevertheless. The Xiangshan gazetteer notes, for instance, that in 1895 the Fushan *tang*, a charity organization, in the township of Xiagong, collected rent on property that was 'donated' to it, but returned 70 per cent of the rent received, less maintenance charges, to its benefactors. In such an arrangement, the charity acted as a virtual rent-collecting agency.[50] In 1932, members of the Liu lineage of Hengtou *xiang* in Xinhui county established a company to take over the development of what its establishment deed referred to as 'wasteland' but which included a substantial amount of property held by individual sub-lineage trusts. The company's capital consisted of 4,000 shares of five dollars each, sold to members of the lineage, who were not allowed to resell to people outside the lineage. The lineage properties were entrusted to the company for a term of thirty years, during which time rent was paid to the sub-lineage trusts at a steadily increasing rate. The document available on the company does not discuss the relationship between the company itself and prospective tenants. However, it would be most unlikely that the arrangement did not imply a more centralized rent-collection administration than management under individual sub-lineage trusts.[51]

Centralized land management and rent collection were also instituted by the Tanjiang Association, set up with the support of overseas members of the lineage by the Yuan surname from Tanjiang *xiang*, also in Xinhui county, in 1919. The association was formed to rebuild the village after it was destroyed in inter-village warfare in the 1910s, and conducted its affairs in the village with considerable authority. Members of the lineage, for instance, were not allowed to withhold their property from the management of the association. They were obliged to pay a considerable fee to the management, which hired the local police, and gradually repaid the loans raised in the rebuilding of the *xiang*. The organization of the association was unique, but the professionalism that was introduced is unmistakable.[52]

Newly Reclaimed Land

It would seem from their landholding records that the landlords of Suzhou acquired their holdings parcel by parcel in small plots. An estate acquired in this manner was necessarily scattered and difficult to manage. The landlord lineages of the New Territories of Hong Kong, on the other hand, maintained territorial claims over large tracts of land, even though within these tracts, holdings were parcelled out to a large number of permanent tenants. In order to exert control, they maintained themselves as territorial powers.[53] The ability of landlords to collect rent had much to do with the concentration of their holdings and the efficiency of the rent collection organizations they relied on. In cost-effectiveness terms, the more concentrated the holdings, the more effective the rent-collection organization could be per unit cost. However, in so far as rent collection depended also on the show of manpower on the spot, the larger the holdings, the more worthwhile it was for landlords to set up a sizeable rent-collection body. Under these considerations, the environment most conducive to the building up of effective rent-collection bodies was provided by land reclamation. In a newly reclaimed area, it was possible for a landlord, through exercising political influence at the county *yamen*, to claim a sizable tract of potentially cultivable land which he could sublet to tenants. The overlordship of the great land-owning lineages in the New Territories was the product of such a process of development.

In both Jiangsu and Guangdong, the reclamation of wasteland was a perpetual source of political lobbying in the late nineteenth and early twentieth centuries as it was in earlier times. In southern Jiangsu and the Zhujiang delta, vast tracts of potentially cultivable land were formed by sediments deposited by the rivers. In the transitional region in Jiangsu, in addition to newly formed land of this sort, the coastal lowland that in the Qing was maintained as salt pans by government regulation was opened for cultivation in the last years of the dynasty. There, 'reclamation companies' claimed substantial tracts which they leased to tenants on fixed-term contracts, the tenants being responsible also for providing the labour for reclamation. A substantial portion of this newly gained acreage was put to cotton, which was exported to nearby Tongzhou and Shanghai. It is difficult to estimate the total acreage available from reclamation. In most counties in southern and transitional Jiangsu newly reclaimed land constituted from 5 to over 10 per cent of the total cultivated acreage. In Guangdong newly reclaimed land was estimated in the 1930s to be over 4,500,000 *mu*, of which 4,000,000 *mu* was located in the Zhujiang delta.[54]

The availability of extensive unregistered potentially cultivable land complicates the analysis of landlord-tenant relationships. The process of reclamation brings into motion the act of settlement: the demarcation of territories rented on permanent terms, the founding of lineages and villages settled within these territories by the cultivators, the inclusion of outsiders into the villages, and the growth of the villages and their exertion of independence. The process is well documented in the history of the New Territories, but the surveys of the 1920s and 1930s spanned too brief a period to portray the process in its entirety. The inevitable conflicts tended to be interpreted outside the context of the reclamation process. The interpretation biases the issue, for the crux of the relationship between landlord and tenant rested not on the payment or non-payment of rent, but on the exertion of authority over territories not yet reclaimed.

The conflict of interest between landlord and tenant in the reclamation process is well brought out in the founding of Qidong county in 1928. Qidong was before this time the 'outer sands' (*waisha*) of the fore-shore of Chongming Island, and 'bottom-soil' rights were owned by residents of the areas that had been reclaimed earlier, that is, of the 'inner sands' (*neisha*).[55] In petitioning to detach Qidong from Chongming, the 'outer sands' residents claimed that the area was too far from the county city for it to be properly policed or to benefit from social amenities provided by the county city. In retort, the *neisha* representatives referred to *waisha* residents as their tenants, the *neisha* owners claiming that they had begun to pay a tax on land being farmed by *waisha* owners even before the land was formed. In other words, the dispute concerned a tract that was partially registered but potentially capable of much expansion. Within this context, the establishment of a county *yamen* in the *waisha* would have given the *waisha* owners an edge over the *neisha* owners in the exertion of claims. In return for paying land tax, they, rather than the residents of the 'inner sands' would have established ownership to the land. Understandably, the issue was vehemently disputed. Lobbying continued for 17 years before the county was finally established.[56]

A study of tenancy in Qidong and adjacent Haimen in 1934

illustrates how misleading tenancy studies can be if the changing power relationship between incumbent landlords and later-settled tenants are not taken into account:

Fifty year ago, all land was held in the hands of large landlords. Large landlords were unable to do their own farming, and so invited tenants to rent [the land from them]. As a result, most land, by far, was occupied by tenants.

Thirty years ago, because the times were unstable, the large landlords declined. So, former tenants took the opportunity to bounce [into the positions of] owner-cultivators or half-owners, and former owner-cultivators also took the opportunity to buy land, and bounced [into the positions of] semi-landlords. As a result, the number of owner-cultivators increased and that of tenants declined.

Ten years ago, because grain prices rose and harvests were good, much land was taken over. Former owner-cultivators took over more land and became semi-landlords, but unfortunate ones degenerated into tenants or half-owners. At the same time, outsiders moved in and swelled the ranks of tenants. Consequently, the number of tenants gradually increased, and that of owner-cultivators declined.[57]

Significantly, the replacement of landlords of the *neisha* by those of the *waisha* is interpreted here as a process of upward mobility. In this respect, although it is far from clear that the *waisha* landlords necessarily began as tenants (for some could, presumably, have settled as merchants in the market towns), there is a ring of truth in the broad description given. It is only biased by the omission of the cause of the supposed decline of the *neisha* owners, which was the loss of their claim to unregistered land. That, in turn, was due to their loss of political control over the *yamen*. The conflict arose as a struggle for political power: rent was not at all the issue.

A similar split between established powers working through the county city and developers in an area where land was being reclaimed may be detected in the Chuansha riot of 1910. Chuansha county (south Jiangsu) consisted mainly of land which local families had been active in reclaiming. In the last two decades of the Qing dynasty, a group that had prospered through commercial activities in Shanghai were involved in supporting reclamation and managing the charity institutions that directly owned some of the reclaimed land. The same group also won in the local elections that were instituted in these years. One of the reforms carried out by this small group of *nouveaux riches* was to take rent collection on land owned by the public school in Chuansha city out of the hands of the functionaries of the county *yamen*. The

reformers also instituted new regulations in the payment of rent by the
tenants, notably by demanding that rent should be paid in advance of
cultivation. Unfortunately for them, the rising inflation immediately
before 1911 had come to be associated with the reforms of these years,
in Chuansha as in other counties. A riot broke out in 1911 in which
rioters attacked the symbols of the reforms, for instance, the new
school and the homes of elected local councillors. Unlike other
counties, however, in Chuansha the functionaries sided with the
rioters in the incident, inciting them to attack the charity institutions
in the city. A rift thus existed, so it would seem, not only between the
land developers and the functionaries, that is, earlier established
territorial interests, but also between them and their tenants.[58]

Yet another incident occurred on the shores of Lake Tai near
Suzhou and Wujiang in 1935. The attempt to reclaim the foreshore
there was said to have been prompted by drought in 1934, and six
reclamation companies laid claim to 20,000 *mu*. Labour was to be
provided by their tenants, who were to receive one-third of the
reclaimed land in lieu of wages for working on the embankment.
Conflict started immediately between them and incumbent settlers.
The incumbents argued that they had always had immediate access to
the lake, from which they drew water for irrigation and in which they
fished. They also argued that building the embankment for the
reclamation project would increase the likelihood of flooding. Left
out of the argument was that by claiming the foreshore, the companies
were in effect blocking the incumbents' future right to extend their
cultivated acreage. They were prepared to resort to violence to
demolish the portions of the embankment that had already been built,
and as objections were raised also at the *yamen*, the issue was reported
in the newspapers. Violence was averted only by the involvement of
the provincial government. The incumbents were given permission to
demolish the embankment, as immigrant farmers worked frantically
to plant rice seedlings, hoping thereby to blur the distinction between
the current and former reclamations. When that effort failed, they
asked for two months' reprieve so that they might harvest the first crop
— a standard delaying tactic. The request was refused and the
embankment was demolished.[59]

In Guangdong, considerable dispute developed over the *shatian*
(sandy land) in Shunde, Xiangshan, and Dongguan on the Zhujiang
delta. The details of the dispute over one portion of the *shatian*
between Shunde and Xiangshan, and another portion between different
parties in Dongguan and Panyu, need not be entered into here. Suffice

it to note that, on the one hand, the parties involved were powerful lineages in the counties, that the dispute required the support of county magistrates, especially over the issue of county boundaries that defined the jurisdiction the magistrates might have had in awarding the newly formed sand banks to natives of their own counties, and that, on the other hand, policing continued to be provided by the lineages that succeeded in staking their claims. The history of the *shatian*, therefore, fully demonstrates the two prongs of territorial influence needed in claiming the right of overlordship: influence at the county *yamen* in matters of legal jurisdiction, and power at the location of one's holdings in enforcing control. The disputed territories were extensive. The Wanqingsha of Dongguan was registered as 67,000 *mu* in the last years of the Qing dynasty, and the Donghai sandbanks were many times larger. The Minglun *tang* of Dongguan, which was the county school, was suspected in 1887 to be little more than a front for the leading families of the county that owned land in the *shatian*, and the Yongqi and Guizhou Alliance (*Yong-Gui gongyue*) formed in 1804, as well as the Donghai Sands Protection Bureau (*Donghai hushaju*) formed in 1854, later renamed the Donghai Sands Protection Alliance (*Donghai husha gongyue*) in 1872, were agencies that offered armed protection on the payment of a fee. Settlements that were not parties to these alliances organized their own defence.[60]

Tenancy in the sandbanks is a dubious term. In the 1880s, the Minglun *tang* itself was a tenant of the Guangya School in Guangzhou that was given legal ownership of the bulk of the area by the Governor-General of Guangdong and Guangxi. The Minglun *tang* managed the area under contract, agreeing to pay a flat rate of two taels per *mu* to the school as rent. It became the sole registered owner of the sands only in 1903, when the then Governor-General terminated the former arrangement, succumbing to lobbying from Dongguan. The Minglun *tang* in its turn subleased its holdings to tenants, who rented 'sometimes as much as several thousands or tens of thousands of *mu*', according to Chen Hansheng.[61] These tenants were the *de facto* territorial overlords in the *shatian*. They were not the cultivators, but holders of permanent rights who subleased to sub-tenants who might even then sublease. The cultivator, was, in this way, several removes from the registered owner.

Chen Hansheng reported that under this system of multiple tenancy, the cultivators paid up to 71 per cent of their harvests as rent and other charges. In addition to the rent proper, a fee had to be paid for policing, and subsidies had to be paid to rent collectors. Chen argued that the cultivators were poor: in the *shatian*, 60 to 70 *mu* was required to feed a tenant household, but this requirement must be balanced against the 70 to 80 *mu* that he reported was available for a household of three working men and women. It is also possible to detect indications of a profit where the land was put to sugar-cane, for unlike paddy farming, wherever sugar-cane was cultivated, farm labourers were hired. Chen also gave the impression that lineages settled on the *shatian* tended to keep their estates undivided, because the need for physical protection was an overriding concern. As members of the lineages rented land from the lineage trusts, much wealth was probably kept within the lineages. Again, it should only be expected that tenants who were outside the settled lineages stood at a disadvantage, especially when tenancy contracts were short-term and rent was increased as the leases were renewed.[62]

General Observations

On the basis of the studies summarized above, it would seem that tenancy in Jiangsu and Guangdong was extremely varied. So varied, indeed, that a simple statistical division of the population into 'landlords' and 'tenants' is not highly meaningful. Permanent tenancy, the authority of the village or the lineage, and the fact that much land holding was scattered, worked against the effectiveness of the landlords' rent-collection organizations. Professionalism in rent collection, the concentration of holdings, and territorial rights over large stretches of cultivated or potentially cultivable land, on the other hand, worked in their favour. In some areas in which an export economy developed, such as parts of Wuxi, the authority of the landlord was curtailed by permanent tenancy, but in others, where newly reclaimed land was readily available, as in much of the Zhujiang delta, landlords could be much more powerful. It is not possible, therefore, to conclude if the authority of the landlords was strengthened or weakened by the development of the export economy. All that may be said is that in time, landlords in these areas tended to want to introduce more authority into rent collection, but their success was not by any means universal.

Who Were the Destitute?

The above discussion emphasizes the importance of access to land as a distinction of wealth, regardless of whether the land available for

farming was rented or owned. It follows from this that the smaller the amount of land that was farmed by a household, the poorer it was likely to be if it depended on crop cultivation for its income. This argument is consistent with the ratios of farm size to farm income that
* has been demonstrated in Philip C.C. Huang's North China study. Huang shows that (a) the larger the farm, the larger the farm household it supported; (b) the larger the farm, the less labour intensively the land was worked; and (c) because the yield per unit-area in small farms did not differ significantly from that in large farms, the larger the farm, the greater the per-capita output from cultivation. Huang concludes, therefore, that small farms tended to be overworked, to the extent that returns for labour fell below the going wage. After a process of 'involution', these small farms provided barely enough for the subsistence of their operators, and driven by necessity, members of these households hired themselves out, contracted loans and worked more intensively on handicrafts.[63]

These observations are, in general, well supported by the survey statistics of the 1920s and 1930s in Jiangsu and Guangdong. Statistics gathered by J.L. Buck on Jiangsu and Guangdong are presented in Table 8.3, and it can be seen that whether or not a farm household could produce enough for subsistence from its crop cultivation was strongly affected by the great inequity in land distribution.[64] Using the average yields arrived at in Tables 3.2 and 3.4, I have noted in bold Table 8.3, for each group of statistics, those size groups that reported household and farm sizes implying per-capita yields close to, or below, the subsistence requirement of 400 catties of milled grain per year. In the last column I have also included the percentage of farms that produced at, or less than, subsistence level. In Changshu county, for instance, bold type for all entries relating to the second size group (averaging 3.4 *mu* per farm) indicates that farms that fell within this group barely produced enough for subsistence. It can be seen that in this size group, a household included, on average, 2.9 persons, that a single able-bodied adult workman, or women and children who could perform as much work, would have cultivated 8.6 *mu*, and that 39 per cent of farm income came, not from cultivation, but from subsidiary occupations. The last column notes that this size group included 39 per cent of all farm households in this county. [65]

When the table is read downwards line by line, it can be seen that in most counties surveyed, a substratum of small farms hovered on the border of subsistence in all of Jiangsu and Guangdong. On the whole, the size of farms that minimally surpassed subsistence tended to be smaller in size but returned higher yields per unit area, for instance, in southern Jiangsu and the Zhujiang delta (see Guangzhou). None the less, whatever their yield per unit area, a single labourer tended to cultivate three to four times as much land on the largest farms as on the smallest farms, and on those farms that were food deficient, farmers tended to derive a larger proportion of their income from subsidiary occupations. Most of these conclusions are duplicated in the results of other surveys.[66]

In his Kaixiangong study, Fei Xiaotong discussed what happened to this low-income fringe in rural society. In this village, Fei noted that population pressure exercised a noticeable effect on reproduction: those households having little land being reluctant to have more than one child. Yet, although households holding more land raised more children, large families could be sustained for no more than a few generations. As land was divided among sons in the inheritance process, new households that were formed gradually came under increasing population pressure. The result, Fei argued, was a fine balance between household size and farm size, which accounted for the lack of a market for hired labour. He found no more than 17 hired labourers in this village of 360 households, for 'the chance of labour in the *chia* [household] proving insufficient is considerably reduced by the population pressure and the ideology of kinship'. This description implies that downward pressure within the social hierarchy continuously displaced the lowest stratum from the village.[67]

This observation is well brought out in the following biographical sketch, a rare account among the patchy documentation on the life of the very poor villagers:

Han Lin was the son of Han Tai. His native village was in the southeast *xiang* of Tongshan. His family was poor. He rented 2 *mu* of poor quality land, and hired himself out to Madam Liu of the same village and the monks of Yunlong Mountain in order to [find the food] to serve Tai. Tai himself cooked and drew water, until he was over eighty years of age, fell ill and could do no more work. Lin, then, returned home to serve him, and had no income for food. He worked as a short-term labourer, and there was not enough food for father and son. Lin Zhiqi, a neighbour, heard about his plight, and assisted him every year. Otherwise, he [Han Lin] borrowed frequently from Madam Liu and the monks. [He received] approximately two *xing* of food each day. This was made into ten steamed buns. Tai had a good appetite and could eat six; Lin made gruel of the remaining four which he himself sipped. He often went hungry, and his face became swollen. Zhiqi said to his family, 'Han Lin is a filial son; tell him to think about coming here and [I] shall continue to supply him with grain.' However, Lin did not go to him for a long time. Zhiqi

Table 8.3

Farm Size, Household Size, Yield per Unit of Labour, and Non-farm Income in Jiangsu and Guangdong, c.1930

	Household Size						Crop mu/Man Equivalent						Percentage Income Non-farm						Percentage at or Below Subsistence[†]
	(1)	(2)	(3)	(4)	(5)	(6)	(1)	(2)	(3)	(4)	(5)	(6)	(1)	(2)	(3)	(4)	(5)	(6)[*]	
Jiangning	—	**4.2**	**7.0**	8.0	9.1	10.7			n.a.		n.a.				n.a.				63
Changshu	—	**2.9**	4.4	4.5	7.5	—		**8.6**	14.2	17.9	17.3	—		**39**	32	30	28		39
Kunshan	3.1	4.3	4.8	6.9	8.1	—	9.8	16.8	19.7	21.7	25.4	—	19	7	2		2		—
Yixing		4.4	5.1	6.6	6.9	9.9			n.a.						n.a.				—
Wuxi (1)		**3.8**	4.8	7.4	—	—			n.a.	n.a.					n.a.				28
Wuxi (2)		**3.2**	**4.4**	5.7	5.8	8.1		**2.8**	**3.7**	5.9	6.7	7.3		**50**	**43**	38	28	44	49
Wujin (1)		4.6	5.8	7.8	—	—			n.a.						n.a.				—
Wujin (2)		4.6	5.0	6.4	8.4	19.0		8.5	15.1	16.3	20.8	24.7		23	12	10	16	12	—
Wujin (3)		**4.9**	5.3	7.4	8.6	10.6		**5.4**	13.2	15.0	18.7	23.8			1				19
Funing			**5.2**	6.1	8.5	17.0			**14.8**	27.8	35.5	50.9			41	12	9	5	51
Huaiyin		**5.3**	5.9	8.7	8.5	11.4		**10.1**	15.8	17.4	25.9	30.4		**24**	15	8	3		23
Yancheng (1)		4.1	4.6	5.2	—	—		13.4	14.7	20.8				1	3	9			—
Yancheng (2)[‡]		**4.6**	4.9	4.8	5.9	7.6		**6.0**	12.0	16.3	16.6	16.6		**23**	10	4	5	7	23
Yancheng (3)		4.8	5.8	6.2	6.8	9.8		13.2	16.3	20.0	24.6	26.0		13	1	1	1		—
Yancheng (4)[#]		**4.1**	4.8	5.8	5.5	7.5		**7.2**	11.1	13.0	16.6	17.1		**29**	19	3			28

	Household Size						Crop mu/Man Equivalent						Percentage Income Non-farm						Percentage at or Below Subsistence†
	(1)	(2)	(3)	(4)	(5)	(6)	(1)	(2)	(3)	(4)	(5)	(6)	(1)	(2)	(3)	(4)	(5)	(6)*	
Jiangdu (1)	—	5.0	5.6	—	6.3	—	—	—	n.a.	—	n.a.	—	—	—	n.a.	—	—	—	—
Jiangdu (2)	3.3	**5.1**	6.6	7.1	9.6	—	**4.7**	**4.2**	5.2	6.5	9.3	—	**13**	**14**	18	1	9	—	38
Taixian	—	4.3	6.1	6.8	12.4	—	—	9.6	14.2	18.1	18.9	—	—	10	8	10	—	—	—
Dongtai	—	6.2	8.5	12.6	—	—	—	—	n.a.	—	—	—	—	—	n.a.	—	—	—	—
Guanyun	—	**5.5**	6.6	8.3	8.7	14.9	—	**11.1**	21.2	33.0	38.9	46.9	—	**37**	10	0	2	4	23
Zhongshan	—	5.4	5.5	5.5	5.4	6.1	—	6.4	13.7	22.3	36.9	41.0	—	10	2	1	—	—	—
Gaoyao	—	3.3	4.6	5.6	6.1	7.3	—	11.4	15.3	18.2	23.3	27.7	—	8	5	4	—	7	—
Qujiang	—	3.8	4.8	8.0	8.0	15.5	—	5.1	8.8	11.4	12.7	15.6	—	11	6	5	13	8	—
Chao'an	—	**5.4**	6.3	8.2	10.9	—	—	**4.4**	8.8	9.6	12.5	—	—	**24**	16	12	15	—	30
Jieyang	**4.0**	5.2	7.1	9.4	11.5	—	**2.1**	**3.4**	4.1	5.1	6.5	—	**10**	**14**	17	20	17	—	35
Maoming	—	**4.6**	7.0	8.2	11.4	12.5	—	**7.5**	9.0	11.9	14.0	15.5	—	**18**	23	18	32	17	17
Nanxiong	—	3.6	4.6	6.6	8.3	9.3	—	7.0	12.0	13.0	15.5	19.9	—	14	2	—	9	—	—

Notes: Crop *mu* equals the number of *mu* of crops raised in one year; in a double-cropping area, a crop *mu* may be equivalent to 2 *mu* or more of cultivated area. Entries in bold imply standards below subsistence.

 * For details of size groups see supplementary tables below.

 † The percentage below subsistence is derived from the percentage of farms in each size group given in the supplementary tables below.

 ‡ Excluding 6 per cent of farms of household size 9.3 and 18.9 crop *mu*/man equivalent.

 # Excluding 11 per cent of farms of household size 6.4 and 9.2, and respectively 19.4 and 20.5 crop *mu*/man equivalent.

Table 8.3   (continued)
Supplementary Tables

	(1)	(2)	(3)	(4)	(5)	(6)
Average size of farm (in mu*) in each size group*						
Jiangning	—	7.2	13.7	22.6	33.0	79.3
Changshu	—	3.4	8.1	12.9	20.0	—
Kunshan	5.7	15.1	23.8	33.4	49.2	—
Yixing	—	8.5	17.4	29.5	40.5	79.8
Wuxi (1)	—	2.9	8.8	19.5	—	—
Wuxi (2)	—	2.3	4.6	7.7	10.3	16.9
Wujin (1)	—	7.5	16.0	31.9	—	—
Wujin (1)	—	7.7	16.9	28.8	48.3	123.5
Wujin (3)	—	4.4	12.9	23.0	32.7	57.1
Funing	—	—	9.8	33.9	73.1	177.9
Huaiyin	—	9.8	19.9	38.4	53.1	107.3
Yancheng (1)	—	21.0	41.0	81.5	—	—
Yancheng (2)	—	5.9	13.7	23.0	33.4	46.6
Yancheng (3)	—	15.1	28.7	47.9	65.9	112.5
Yancheng (4)	—	6.7	14.0	22.8	32.6	43.1
Jiangdu (1)	—	10.6	21.0	—	48.0	—
Jiangdu (2)	4.6	7.7	12.0	17.4	30.9	—
Tai *xian*	—	7.8	16.3	25.9	51.9	—
Dongtai	—	32.4	73.2	241.5	—	—
Guanyun	—	11.2	37.8	93.6	132.5	242.7
Zhongshan	—	7.3	14.7	29.8	43.5	67.1
Gaoyao	—	9.0	15.6	25.1	35.0	47.4
Qujiang	—	5.7	13.4	24.3	34.0	60.4
Chao'an	—	4.7	9.9	15.1	26.5	—
Jieyang	2.9	5.4	8.1	11.2	15.3	—
Maoming	—	6.4	11.9	18.9	29.1	53.7
Nanxiong	—	7.3	15.3	21.3	30.3	47.7

summoned him and asked him. [Lin] answered, 'Can I always depend on other people for food?' Zhiqi asked him, 'How much food do you eat each year?' He answered, 'Over seven *shi*.' 'And how much [can you] harvest from your fields?' He answered, 'About one *shi*.' [Zhiqi] asked, 'So what do you do to make up for the shortage?' He answered, 'Since my father ceased to be able to cook, I have had to stay near him and depend on short-term labour, and for that I am not always paid in cash. I have received much great benevolence from you, Sir, and others and not repaid your kindness. Because of that, when I want to come over here, I see your door and feel ashamed. It has been like

Table 8.3 (continued)
Supplementary Tables

	(1)	(2)	(3)	(4)	(5)	(6)
Percentage of farms in each size group						
Jiangning	—	24	39	12	11	14
Changshu	—	39	42	15	4	—
Kunshan	17	18	35	18	12	—
Yixing	—	15	31	15	14	25
Wuxi (1)	—	28	43	29	—	—
Wuxi (2)	—	9	40	22	15	14
Wujin (1)	—	32	47	21	—	—
Wujin (2)	—	27	40	20	10	3
Wujin (3)	—	19	44	21	7	9
Funing	—	—	51	25	23	1
Huaiyin	—	23	38	23	11	5
Yancheng (1)	—	19	39	42	—	—
Yancheng (2)	—	23	30	19	11	11
Yancheng (3)	—	18	30	27	11	14
Yancheng (4)	—	28	31	18	6	6
Jiangdu (1)	—	34	52	0	14	—
Jiangdu (2)	4	34	37	8	17	—
Taixian	—	25	48	19	8	—
Dongtai	—	41	37	22	—	—
Guangyun	—	23	45	8	17	7
Zhongshan	—	28	30	20	13	9
Gaoyao	—	21	45	15	7	12
Qujiang	—	16	44	28	6	6
Chao'an	—	30	43	20	7	—
Jieyang	4	31	34	25	6	—
Maoming	—	17	41	27	11	4
Nanxiong	—	18	43	23	10	6

Source: J.L. Buck (1937b), pp. 289–90, 291, 298, 300, and 311.

this for fifteen years. Now my father is very old and weak, and depends on me for his living.' Upon hearing this, Zhiqi collected over a hundred thousand cash and bought [him] 20 *mu* of farmland so that he could reap 30 *shi* a year and marry a wife to serve Tai.[68]

The account is remarkable for the plausibility of the statistics: 1.5 *shi* (approximately 200 catties per *mu*) reflects the low yield of northern Jiangsu and 7 *shi* (approximately 1,000 catties) the subsistence needs of two men. However, it is the conclusion of the story that stands out.

With 20 *mu* the villager could marry, for 30 *shi* would support not only himself, his father, and his wife, but there would also be grain left over for offspring.[69]

The process whereby the poor were displaced from rural society is succinctly summarized by Philip C.C. Huang:

> The result [of overabundance of surplus labour] was that the completely proletarianized male agricultural workers tended to remain unmarried 'bare sticks' (*guanggun*) and become the last generation of their families.[70]

Huang's description is also consistent with the continuous process of downward mobility discussed by Edwin E. Moise. By taking into account sex-ratio imbalance and the disruptive effects of famine, Moise argues that 'in every generation a group of poor men amounting to between 10 and 15 per cent of the men in their generation failed to reproduce themselves because of their poverty'.[71]

The destitute in the village were the people who had access to little or no land. They were people who were or were being dislodged from their own villages.[72] It has to be noted, however, that the displacement of the poor from the village was a continuous process within the community, but working for wages on somebody else's farm did not imply it. Fei Xiaotong's observations from Kaixiangong, again, are significant. He reported that even those long-term labourers who had absolutely no land could save up and eventually acquire some small holdings. He stated categorically:' I did not meet anyone who had been landless all his life.'[73] His statement means that, for some people, at least, landlessness was only a stage in the course of their lives. This observation is supported by a survey in Jintan and Liyang (southern Jiangsu) in which 364 farm labourers were interviewed, of whom 92 per cent were men and 47 per cent were aged between 25 and 35, and 83.5 per cent had been employed for less than two years at the time of the interview.[74] The figures suggest that full-time wage labour, for many, was a short-term occupation rather than a vocation.

This discussion demonstrates again that the emphasis on the supposed landlord-tenant distinction that occupied so much of the survey literature of the 1920s and 1930s altogether missed the salient features of income-distribution mechanisms in the countryside. A distinction must be made between access to land by right of village, or lineage, affiliation, and access to land by right of ownership or tenancy. When this distinction is made, it should be seen that the destitute in the village were not tenants as such, but the outsiders, or villagers displaced from their own villages. These were people who not only owned no land, but did not have access to any. In other words, the tenant who had the right to settle in a village must be treated very differently from the tenant who did not have such right in any village. This is not to say that landlords necessarily could not enforce their will on the land that they owned, but that in the webs of power relationships in the countryside, few of them could ride roughshod over their tenants on the strength of land ownership alone.

9

Conclusion: World Trade and the Rural Economy

The Depression of the 1930s

This book began with the problem of how trade expansion affected the farm economy, particularly, how it affected the farmers' standard of living. In answer, it has argued that from the 1870s to the 1920s, the rural economy in Jiangsu and Guangdong, especially in areas that produced export crops, saw considerable prosperity. It has also argued that this prosperity must have translated into a higher standard of living for the majority of farmers and owner-cultivators, as well as tenants. It does not deny that historically the standard of living of these farmers had been low, or that this low standard was due, at least in part, to great disparity in the control of resources. Nevertheless, it has argued that this disparity is not readily explicable in terms of class oppression. Instead, it has stressed continuous prosperity for both landlords and tenants until the 1930s, and the arrest of this trend when the effects of the world depression came to be felt in China. The effects were fourfold: firstly, the silk market collapsed; secondly, prices dropped considerably; thirdly, massive imports of rice into China brought prices down further in the lower Changjiang; fourthly, the outflow of silver from 1934 dried up rural credit. The imposition of import controls from approximately this time, and currency reforms from 1935, were designed to alleviate the situation — even though their effects may be doubted — but these attempts were soon overtaken by events. The outbreak of war with Japan rapidly changed the political and economic fundamentals in China. China's wartime economy is an important study that should be a sequel to this one, but that is another book.

The Chinese depression is well documented, and it accounts for the strong pessimism expressed by social observers of the Chinese scene regarding the detrimental effects of China's involvement in foreign trade. Not that the exploitation of the tenant farmer was a new argument in the 1930s, for a strong current in Chinese social research in the 1920s had depicted class differentiation in the countryside as a major cause of rural poverty. The difficulties that faced the farmer, owner-cultivator, or tenant, because of land shortage, the vagaries of the weather, technological backwardness, and usury, were well known. However, in the 1920s, they were not related by many writers to the growth of foreign trade. The argument that China had fallen into a semi-colonial status in her dealings with foreign countries, most obvious in the imposition of extraterritoriality and tariff control by foreign powers on China, and popularized by the surge in nationalist feelings that expressed itself in vociferous movements demanding the boycott of foreign-made goods, was voiced only by a minority involved in the study of the rural economy. When the depression of the 1930s had set in, however, it was the order of the day to relate all aspects of rural poverty to the contraction of trade. The collapse of the export market, the inroads made by foreign goods into China, the imports of South-east Asian rice, and the outflow of silver, became ready-made explanations for the plight of the rural economy. Moreover, past events were seen as having led up to all this calamity. Where the tone of late Qing publications on the encouragement of rural industries was hopeful, the reports of the 1930s were certain that the new wealth had been a lop-sided blessing, weighed down as it was by income disparity and widespread bankruptcy.

Whether the depression of the 1930s was a necessary outcome of the contradictions within world capitalism is not an issue that can be entered into here. The argument advanced in this book is a simpler one, that is, that the depression had come upon the heels of a long period of prosperity, and that its impact must be understood in relation to the earlier success of world trade in raising farm income in China. Not being able to measure the volume of China's internal trade, we cannot measure the impact of world trade on China even in crude terms. However, given the breakdown of the political order after the Qing, and given the sluggishness with which technological changes were brought about, it is hard to see another source of change in the early twentieth century that would have brought an impact on the rural economy as quickly and as effectively as an expansion of the market provided by international trade. Of course, the involvement in international trade posed a dilemma. The likelihood of economic gains through trade was matched by the likelihood of cyclical depressions. It is as much an error to downplay the one as it is to downplay the other.

Export Growth and Social Change

The areas that benefited immediately from the growth of trade were those that could produce for export beyond the province. In Jiangsu, because cotton came to be more widely grown, these areas were more extensive than in Guangdong, whose chief export from the 1870s to the 1930s continued to be silk. Whether prosperity could be siphoned from these export-oriented areas into other parts of the two provinces which produced little for export, however, depended on the possibilities of trade between the two kinds of economies. An important linkage would have been the rice trade, which remained strong in Jiangsu until the 1930s, but which came under heavy competition in Guangdong from imported rice from South-east Asia, even though locally produced rice continued to claim a substantial portion of the urban markets within the province. If depression had not set in earlier in Guangdong, it was because relief was provided by the export of labour, for considerable income was generated by remittances from the cities and from abroad. That the overseas Chinese included some of China's most successful merchants and industrialists is well known, but one searches in vain for indications of rural technological or commercial innovations introduced by them that had more than very local effects, with the important exception of the initial foundation of the steam filature in Shunde. Left to the stimulus of the export trade alone, much of Guangdong would have seen little development.

The surveys of the 1920s and 1930s found an increase in the proportion of tenants within this period. They attributed the trend to a higher proportion of owner-cultivators or part-owners falling into debt and being forced to sell their holdings as a result. The trend of events was probably much more complicated. First, opportunities for development often led to the exploitation of land that had not previously been cultivated. Among land that may be described in these terms, distinction must be made between land that was located within the territorial confines of a village, over which villagers could by custom claim the right of reclamation, and the vast tracts of coastal land, made up of swamps and mudbanks, either largely unregistered or formerly defined by law as salt fields. Because new settlers were not automatically granted villager status, it was the incumbent villager, owner-cultivator, or tenant, who stood at an advantage in the exploitation of village wasteland. The distinction between newcomer and incumbent blurred on the mudbanks, for these areas were largely uninhabited before the end of the nineteenth century and they were being reclaimed in the first few decades of the twentieth century by the employment of the labour of new settlers under the direction, control, and financial interest of groups that could exert influence in local government offices. The tenants on the resulting reclamations were poor not only because they were tenants, but also because they were first generation settlers.

Tenancy in well-settled áreas varied considerably from these conditions. In general, it may be said that cash crops were developed in areas that had been historically highly tenanted, but the concept of tenancy in the Chinese countryside was very broad, and could be used to include the farmer who was status-bound to service his lords at lineage ceremonies, as well as the perpetual surface-rights holder whose landlord might be none other than an ancestral trust of which he was also a member. As should be expected, once customary rights are taken into consideration, the term 'tenant' used in a legal sense tells us little about the respective bargaining positions of rent-paying and rent-collecting parties. The increase in tenancy that researchers in the 1920s and 1930s discovered might have taken place under very different circumstances. Holders of surface rights might have sold these rights and themselves rented land, as the researchers recognized. However, wasteland could be brought into cultivation and rented out by incumbent villagers to new settlers. Or, holders of surface rights might have rented out their land for fixed terms, either to other villagers or to new settlers. Or, holders of the soil in its entirety (that is, of both surface and bottom rights) might have sold the bottom rights at a time when land value had risen and retained perpetual surface rights.

The researchers of the 1920s and 1930s did not by any means consider these different possibilities, ignoring, in particular, the complications that would have been introduced by migration. With little appreciation for the political structure of village society, scant interest to relate the bland statistics they gathered to varied practices in the villages, it was not for the researchers of the 1920s and 1930s to unravel the progress of tenancy in the Chinese countryside.

The increase in tenancy that could be attributed to the late nineteenth and early twentieth centuries in long-settled regions was, in any case, quite marginal. When it is taken into consideration that these studies were concentrated primarily in the 1930s, the case for long-term increase in tenancy is further weakened. Most owner-cultivators remained owner-cultivators for most of this period, and most tenants remained tenants. But for migration into the export-oriented areas, the major change that came about must have been the strengthening of some groups of landlords in some parts of southern Jiangsu through the growth of rent-collection offices. In part, this growth could have been a response to rising crop values: it was only worth the landlords' while to increase the cost of rent collection when there was more to collect. In part, it was due to changes in local politics after the Taiping Rebellion, for local groups that had long been powerful could, with the recognition of the need for local organization of defence, openly collude with the *yamen* in rent collection. In the Republican era, local power grew further, and with it the influence of the rent-collection offices.

The growth of local power is one of several developments that must be taken into consideration with the growth of export in order to understand changes in the rural economy. Other factors that should be considered include the devastation by local warfare in the Republican era, the growth of industries within China, and the growth of cities. Local warfare, like bad weather, does not seem to have had more than short-term effects on the development of the export-oriented areas. The growth of industry and the growth of cities expanded the market for rural produce, and had very much the same effect as the growth of international trade. Inflation, which resulted from the lack of central control of the authorities that set up the modern mints, itself a sign of the break up of centralized government, produced long-term effects of a very different nature.

The inflation that resulted from currency depreciation from the mid-1890s has to be assessed against a background of currency and price stability just as the depression of the 1930s must be assessed .against that of several decades of steady growth and rising prices. The depreciation of the currency was quite unexpected; not for centuries had any government the ability to depreciate its currency on the scale that the late Qing government did towards the last years of the dynasty. Coming as it did at a time of government financial stringency, the sudden depreciation upset long-established standards in commodity prices and rent, as well as in tax. The disturbance that was brought about is evident in the outbreak of violence in both Jiangsu and Guangdong that was directed primarily at symbols of the late Qing government reforms. Riots, which were directed at newly established police stations, local consultative assemblies, schools, and even flour-mills, were most concentrated in the years from 1905 to 1907. However, during the 1910s, high prices had become accepted by the town and city populations. No doubt, this change had come about partly because increased business opportunities were now quite obvious, and partly because the political climate had changed when the Qing government collapsed. Undisciplined soldiers might extort, bandits might ravage, but the governments as such were not in a position to dictate to the towns and the major cities. The trend continued until the depression set in, and particularly in southern Jiangsu, another wave of protest broke out, this time directed primarily at rent and tax collection.

Again, Fei Xiaotong recorded a very perceptive account of the disruption that was brought to rent collection in the village that he studied in the silk district of Jiangsu:

By the old people, rent payment is regarded as a moral duty . . . Recently the situation has been changing. The economic depression in the rural district has made rent a heavy burden on the peasant, and the income derived from the rent much more vulnerable for the landlord . . . Peasants unable to pay rent now feel justified in neglecting to do so, and those who are able to pay will wait and see if they are compelled to do so. On the side of the landlords, strong measures must be taken to maintain their privileges, and their available capital tends to be no longer in agricultural land. The result is an intensification of conflict between tenants and landlords, and a financial crisis in rural economy. The district jail has been repeatedly crowded with the default cases. Organized action of the peasants in refusing rent payment has provoked serious conflict with the landlords who are backed by government force. In this part of China, a peasant revolt took place in 1935 and led to the death of many peasants in villages near Soochow [Suzhou]. The value of land has depreciated rapidly, and the whole financial organization of the village is at stake.[1]

The depression of the 1930s, like the inflation of the late Qing, had created a situation in which both landlords and tenants felt that they had been unjustly treated. In essence, a sudden change to a long established relationship may be detected.

In a sense, it may be said that the changes that can be documented from 1870 to 1937 were external to the operation of the farm. The evidence is admittedly meagre, but there are hardly any signs that farm operations had changed from traditional patterns. Most large landowners parcelled out their land to tenants. Not a single case can be documented in Guangdong or southern Jiangsu of a change-over from leasing to farming a larger estate with the use of hired labour. Nor is there any indication at all that rural inhabitants in southern Jiangsu and Guangdong had shaken off their traditional village bonds to swell the ranks of an urban protletariat. The 'north Jiangsu vagabonds' who wandered into southern Jiangsu cities in the winter and in times of famine were not recruitment targets for the factories of Shanghai or Nantong. And the women workers in the steam filatures of Shunde were not in any sense expelled from the village.[2] This is not to say that village society did not change. Many signs indicate that late Qing or Republican rural society underwent fundamental changes, but those changes did not make any inroad into the mode of farm operation.

An important example of this argument is Philip C.C. Huang's linkage of the 'commercialization of production relations' to the change-over from share cropping to fixed rent in north China, and the suspension of customary ceremonials between rural employers and labourers.[3] In Jiangsu, I find the development of rent-collection offices in the more commercialized parts of the south supports the argument, but elsewhere, I think personal bonds and non-wage arrangements in work relationships persisted.

It must first be pointed out that an argument concerning personal relationships in work is singularly difficult to test with historical data. The argument calls for descriptions of relationships as participants felt them, and neither tenants nor labourers left written descriptions of their experiences. I am suspicious, in particular, of descriptions of economic relationships that do not take account of the participants' positions in the lineage or the village. The point is, where a tenant was a native of another village, where by custom natives of a village were mostly tenants of particular households in another village, the relationship between landlord and tenant had historically been highly depersonalized. The reverse would hold if the tenant had rented from a member of his own lineage, sub-lineage, or village.

As an earlier chapter in this book has argued, the crucial change in rent collection, chiefly in Jiangsu, was the development of professional rent collection offices and the collection of rent in cash, according to a commuted rate of the fixed crop rent. The rent-collection offices acted on behalf of a large number of landlords, including small ones, and presented a unified front to the district administration. As professionals, their concern was rent collection, and hence the comment that was often made about them was that they were not personally known to the tenants. In this area, therefore, as cash rent became more prevalent, one might also have noticed depersonalized relationships between landlords and tenants.

In Guangdong, the payment of rent in cash also became more prevalent in the more commercialized areas. Chen Hansheng noted, in particular, that 'in most of the villages on the Pearl River Delta and the

Han River Delta, agricultural wages are paid in cash; but in many villages of the southwestern part of the province [that is, Guangdong], the day labourers as well as some of the year labourers are paid by a certain amount of grain, entirely without cash'.[4] Our records leave few signs of changes in personal relationships between landlord and tenant, but we should be reminded that many Guangdong tenants rented from institutional landlords which included ancestral trusts with which the tenants might be personally related. It is doubtful if lineage and village relationships broke down to the extent that they might be noticeable, and hence, for many tenants, quite unlikely that the progression from payment of rent in kind to payment in cash would have also meant a loss in personal connections.

In the non-commercial parts of Jiangsu, we have several descriptions of some of the larger landlords, chiefly in the north. They were well armed, they lived in fortified villages, were always on the alert for bandits, offered protection to their tenants, and recruited them into their paramilitary forces. It is hard to see how a depersonalized relationship could have been meaningful in these areas. Instead, indications are that non-wage relationships persisted, of which a study of Xiao county in 1935 provides some enlightening descriptions.

The study drew its information from a survey of nine villages, consisting of a total of 483 households, farming 10,300 *mu*. Most of these households, 366 in all, were described as 'poor peasants and hired labourers', 63 were 'middle peasants', 39 were 'rich peasants', and 13 were 'landlords'. The 'poor peasants and hired labourers' owned a total of 2,470 *mu*.[5]

The study describes the three forms of production relationship that were current in the county. They were: (a) 'helping' (*bangshou*), being service provided by farmers who farmed 10 *mu* (owned or rented) in return for the use of draft animals for farming; (b) 'tool sharing' (*geji*), being the sharing of draft animals for ploughing, raking, and sowing; and (c) 'grain-wage' (*gongliang*), being a quantity of grain loaned by 'rich peasants' to 'poor peasants' in spring to be repaid by labour service in the busy seasons. The study describes 'helping' as a form of long-term labour. It was negotiated through an intermediary. The 'helper' and his 'employer' (that is, the owner of the draught animals) each provided the seeds and fertilizer for his own land. However, while the 'helper' worked for the 'employer', he was given his food, but was not paid for the work. The kind of work required of him varied. Some 'helpers' were required only to do such farmwork as ploughing, weeding, and harvesting. Others were required to work also in the household. Out of the 366 households of 'poor peasants and hired labourers', 26 were 'helpers'.

'Tool sharing' arose because draught animals had to be used in a work team. Most households had only a single animal, an ox, or a donkey. However, two to three animals were required to make up the team. Under 'tool sharing' arrangements, the animals were brought together when they were needed for work, but they continued to be fed each by its owner. Essential tools, such as carts, sowers, ploughs, or rakes were provided by the owner of the ox, because he was the one who had more land. Teamwork extended to manual work that did not require animal labour, such as sowing or putting in the fertilizer. Work was reckoned in terms of the land individually owned (so the tool-sharing farmer who had less land would have had more labour to spare which he could probably hire out). Food was provided by members of the team. Altogether 84 households (status unspecified) participated in tool-sharing teams.

Only 33 households in the survey were found to owe 'grain-wage'. The employer reckoned the value of grain loaned at its price in spring. No interest was charged. It was then set against a nominal wage that was recorded for work done. Work for the 'employer' who had supplied 'grain-wage' must be given priority over the debtor's own work or service owed to other people.

According to this study, many 'rich peasants' employed two to three long-term labourers and a large number of short-term labourers. 'Middle peasants' hired long-term and short-term labourers as well as 'helpers'. Small farmers often banded together to 'share tools'. Farmers who had no animals served as 'helpers'. It is significant that in all this description, no labour service was paid in money. Money wage was paid, the report continued to explain, to 'transient' (*liudong*) service provided by outsiders from Shandong Province who were hired for the day from the market. Unlike these 'transient' labourers, farmers who owed 'grain-wage' were under long-term arrangements with their 'employers' so that their service at every busy season might be counted upon.

I conclude, therefore, that the rise of the non-personalized relationship between landlord and tenant was the result of a very peculiar development. It suggests that professionalism in rent collection, associated with commercialization, might have been related to it, but it should not be thought that this development was occurring in many places.

   Could the export sectors of the rural economy have recovered
quickly from the depression of the mid-1930s ? This could have been
a meaningful question had the events of the early 1930s not been
followed by war with Japan in the late 1930s and early 1940s, and then
by runaway inflation in the 1940s fuelled by an almost ceaseless
supply of paper money. As it was, the image of a rural economy gone
to ruins was imprinted in China's political ideology. The view that
trade is a sign of resource drain rather than of economic vitality took
decades to wear out, and it is only in recent years that it is finally
giving way.

Appendix. Statistics on Crop Yields in Jiangsu and Guangdong

THE method by which estimates for Table 3.2 have been arrived at are described on pp. 46–8 in the text. It is the object of this appendix to compare the figures entered in this table with reports and estimates in other sources. The comparison is presented in Tables A.1, A.2, and A.3.

To facilitate comparison, the following steps have been taken to standardize units of measurement quoted in the different studies.

To Convert Paddy Capacity Measures to a Weight Measure

The basis for converting a *shi* of paddy into catties is Chuan and Kraus's estimate of 132.2 pounds for a *shi* of 103.55 litres (Chuan and Kraus (1975), pp. 92–3). Allowance has had to be made for a larger *dou* used in Suzhou City which was 10.50 litres (average of four reports in H.B. Morse (1888–9), p. 91) and a yet larger one at Xuzhou which was 11.97 litres (Jiangsusheng nongmin yinhang (1931), p. 365). Reference to Shanghai shangye chuxu yinhang diaochabu (1931), pp. 94–5, shows that the 10.50 litre *dou* was close to those used for measuring grain in most of southern Jiangsu with the exception of

Table A.1

Paddy Yield Estimates for Jiangsu (catties/*mu*)

	Buck	Dongnan Daxue	Others	Faure 1	Faure 2
Jiangning	251	—	268[1]	370	250
Suzhou	378	307	440[2]	320–420	375
	—	—	402[3]	—	—
Songjiang	—	249	371[4]	300–450	325
Changzhou	366	429	443[3]	400–450	375
	273	—	—	—	—
Zhenjiang	—	—	268[5]	300–400	300
Huai'an	238	—	—	250	250
Yangzhou	347	—	259–300[6]	370	300
Xuzhou	—	—	92[7]	250	80
Haimen	—	—	72[8]	300–450	80
Taicang	—	194	72[8]	300–450	250
Haizhou	—	—	—	250	80
Tongzhou	—	223	—	270–300	220

Sources: See Table A.3.

Table A.2
Wheat Yield Estimates for Jiangsu (catties/*mu*)

	Buck	Dongnan Daxue	Others	Faure 1	Faure 2
Jiangning	76	—	68[1]	80	80
Suzhou	119	90	90[3]	80	80
Songjiang	—	—	146[4]	—	80
Changzhou	71	130	102[3]	100–150	100–150
Zhenjiang	—	—	108[5]	120	100–120
Huai'an	111	—	—	90	90
Yangzhou	149	—	114–128[6]	120	120
Xuzhou	—	—	95[7]	90	90
Haimen	—	—	96[8]	—	90
Taicang	—	—	96[8]	—	80
Haizhou	66	—	—	80	80
Tongzhou	—	128	—	90	90

Sources: See Table A.3.

Shanghai and its surroundings, which used a *dou* that was larger by just over 10 per cent. The discrepancy with the Shanghai *dou*, however, may be ignored as the reports for this area in the table are quoted in weight and not capacity. For the purpose of conversion, therefore, a *shi* of paddy is taken here to be 100.6 catties in all of Jiangsu with the exception of Xuzhou, and a *shi* in Xuzhou to be 114.6 catties. A further exception is made in the case of Wu Zhihua's report (dated 1935) on Jiangdu, for the rate of conversion is specifically noted, ranging from 120 to 140 catties for the *shi*, at 14.4 *liang* per catty. In Guangdong, the Guoli Zhongshan Daxue reports give no indication of the weight of a *shi* of paddy. However, H.B. Morse(1888–9), p. 92, gives 11.98 and 12.60 litres for the *dou* in Shantou. Moreover, although on the same page, the *dou* of *rice* (that is, husked rice) in Guangzhou and Xinhui is noted as measuring 6.25 catties, on p. 94, his informant reports, 'in some cases grain-selling guilds use a tou [*dou*] of 10 or 13 and even 14 catties'. According to Chuan and Kraus's estimate, the *shi* of grain in Shantou amounts to 115 to 121 catties, falling well within the range of reports for the grain-selling guilds.These values are also corroborated by a reference in the *Guangdong jingji nianjian* (*1940*), p. K55, to a conversion ratio of 1 *shi* to 120 catties of grain, and various measures of the *dou* recorded on a 1777 tablet in the Dawang Temple in Yuen Long Market in the New Territories of Hong Kong that imply that the local market *dou* was 5 per cent larger than the granary *dou* which was 13.6 per cent larger than the official *dou*, possibly used for tax collection(see Ke Dawei and others (1986), p. 41). As Chuan and Kraus's estimate is based on an official *dou* promulgated by the imperial bureaucracy, it may be expected that it would have been close to the tax-collection *dou*. In that case, these figures

Table A.3

Paddy Yield Estimates for Guangdong (catties/*mu*)

	Buck	Zhongshan Daxue	Others	Faure 2
Guangzhou		268–288	100–400[9]	250–400
Shaozhou	170	248–420		230–350
Huizhou		340–480		250–400
Chaozhou	278	520–547		250–450
Zhaoqing		240–438		200–400
Gaozhou	143	275		150–450
Leizhou		475		150–450
Qiongzhou		180		150
Lianzhou		225–425		230–350
Nanxiong		300–540		230–350
Jiaying		380–510		150–450
Luoding		100–450		100–300
Yangjiang		120–480		

Sources: Buck: J.L. Buck (1930, 1937b); Dongnan daxue: Dongnan daxue nongke (1923), Feng Hefa (1933), pp. 527–29; Zhongshan daxue: Guoli Zhongshan daxue nongke xueyuan (1925, 1929, 1933); others:
1. Zhang Xinyi, Tao Huanfen, Zhuang Jiceng (1934), pp. 139–40.
2. Fei Hsiao-tung (1939), p. 201, Fei Xiaotong (1946), p. 5.
3. He Menglei (n.d.), p. 32995.
4. Shanghai shi shehuiju (n.d.), pp. 23 and 29–30.
5. Zhang Hanlin (1930), pp. 13–14.
6. Wu Zhihua (1935), p. 34944.
7. Wu Shoupeng (1930), p. 348.
8. Shen Shike (1934), p. 30889.
9. Patrick Hase (1981), p. 196.
Faure 1: David Faure (1978).
Faure 2: Table 3.2 on p.

imply that the market measure for the *shi* would have amounted to 123.5 litres, and hence the equivalent of 118 catties of grain. It seems, therefore, that 120 catties per *shi* of grain is a well supported estimate for Guangdong.

To Convert Quintals into Catties

J.L. Buck's reports are given in terms of quintals per hectare. At standard rates of conversion (1 catty = 0.6 kg. and 1 *mu* = 614.4 sq.m) 1 quintal per hectare works out to be 10.24 catties per *mu*. This estimate ignores the very wide variations of the local catty and the local *mu* reported by Buck (J.L. Buck (1937), p. 473). Buck's figures imply that one quintal per hectare might, in southern Jiangsu, range from 10.0 catties per *mu* to as much as 15.4 catties per *mu*, and in Guangdong, from 7.7 catties per *mu* to 17.7 catties per *mu*.

To Convert Rice to Paddy

Most reports on yields are quoted in terms of paddy, that is, unhusked rice. For the few reports that quote yields in terms of husked rice, the equivalent in paddy is calculated on the assumption that the loss to milling amounts to 50 per cent by volume and 30 per cent by weight. The loss of 50 per cent by volume in the milling process is well known. The loss by weight is worked out from Chuan and Kraus's conclusion that an imperial *shi* of milled rice weighed 185 pounds (Chuan and Kraus (1975), p. 98). As the imperial *shi* weighs 132.2 pounds, the loss of 30 per cent by weight in milling is implied (185/(132.2 x 2)). This figure differs somewhat from their sources quoted on p. 93: 'The rule of thumb estimate is that the milling process from paddy to cleaned rice reduces volume by 50 per cent and reduces weight by some 15 to 20 per cent, although the commonly accepted figure for oriental rice is 35 per cent to 40 per cent. At present in Japan the respective reductions in volume and weight from paddy to brown rice are 45 per cent and 20 per cent respectively, while in the United States some 34 per cent of the weight is milled away in the process from paddy to cleaned'. However, as their study makes very clear, the loss due to milling can vary substantially, depending on how finely the rice is to be milled.

To Convert a Shishi/Shimu to Shi/Mu

The *shishi* and the *shimu* are standardized measures designed in the Republican period to replace the traditional *shi* and *mu*. As 1 *shishi* is equivalent to 100 litres and 1 *shimu* 0.067 hectare (1 hectare = 15 *shimu*), 1 *shishi* per *shimu* is equivalent to 0.878 *shi* per *mu* (the *shi* measuring 105 litres and the *mu* 614.4 sq. ml.) 1 *shishi* per *shimu* of paddy is, therefore, equivalent to 88.3 catties per *mu*, and 1 *shishi* per *shimu* of wheat 112.4 catties per *mu*.

To Convert Bushel/Acre to Shi/Mu

Conversion of the US bushel to the official *shi* (103.55 litres) is given in Chuan and Kraus (1975), p. 211, n. 54. This demonstrates that the official *shi* amounts to 2.94 US bushels. The acre is taken to be 6 *mu* (which differs from the earlier quoted coversion of 1 *mu* to 614.4 sq. m. by about 10 per cent).

To Convert a Shi of Wheat to Catties

Zhang Yifan (1984), pp. 13–14, and Shehui jingji diaochasuo (1935), p. 4, quote standards accepted by the Shanghai Supplementary Food Commodities Market that categorize wheat in five grades ranging from 133 catties per *shi* to 141 catties per *shi*. Values are quoted in *dan* (picul) in Zhang and in *shi* in Shehui jingji diaochasuo, but are identical. Moreover, Zhang states that measurement is made by the *haihu*, by which measure 1 *shi* is equivalent to 118.3 litres. If it is assumed that the Suzhou *shi* for wheat remains 105.0 litres, the standards of the Shanghai Supplementary Food Commodities Market imply that the *shi* of wheat in southern Jiangsu weighs 118 to 125 catties. These values may be compared to Wu Shoupeng (1930), p. 348, which reports that 1 *shi* of wheat in Xuzhou amounted to 150 catties. As according to Lin and Chen (1967), p. 99, the Xuzhou *dou* measured 1.13 the standard *dou*, the weight of 1 litre of wheat as calculated from Wu's report (1.28 catties) differs from the Shanghai Supplementary Food Commodities Market's figures (1.12 to 1.19 catties) by approximately 10 per cent. At 105 litres to the *shi*, and a weight per litre averaged from the Xuzhou and the Shanghai Supplementary Food Commodities Market figures, a *shi* of wheat would weigh approximately 128 catties. This value is applied to Table A.2, with the exception of Wu Shoupeng's report, for which conversion at 150 catties per *shi* is adopted.

The Size of the Mu

The variation of the *mu* is well established by Chen Hansheng and others (1929) and Ho Ping-ti (1959). Measurements provided by J.L. Buck (1937b), p. 473, show that in Jiangsu the *mu* varied substantially from 0.0598 hectare to 0.07434 hectare (the average of 13 counties being 0.06835 hectare), and that in Guangdong, it varied from 0.06143 hectare to 0.08214 hectare (the average of seven counties being 0.07641 hectare). The variations certainly affect the accuracy of the yield figures reported and should be taken into account in any interpretation. Yet for two reasons no attempt has been made to correct for them in Table A.1, A.2, and A.3. The first reason is sheer necessity: variations in the *mu* are quite unsystematic and the data needed for correction simply do not exist. Secondly, variations in the *mu* probably affect total acreage figures in much the same way they do the yield figures and the biases would be cancelled out when per capita yields are calculated. In other words, the locality that uses a larger *mu* would, when reporting acreages in the same unit, report fewer *mu*, and hence what appears as a higher yield would be balanced by an under-reported acreage. Ultimately, it has to be admitted that the yield reports from the surveys of the 1920s and 1930s represent commonly accepted values rather than precise measurements.

The Bu in Haimen and Qidong

The *bu* was a local unit used in Haimen and Qidong in Jiangsu. According to *Dongfang zazhi*, August 1927 (vol. 24, no. 16), p. 22, 1,000 *bu* was equivalent to 4.16 *mu*.

Reference to the tables here will show that in arriving at the figures of Table 3.2, I have amended considerably some earlier estimates (given in Faure (1978)). In the case of Songjiang, I have revised the yield estimate downwards to take account of the very low yields reported in Shen Shike (1934) for nearby

Taicang. I am also discounting the report submitted by E.L. Oxenham to the North China Branch of the Royal Asiatic Society in 1889 (Morse (1889–90)). In revising the estimates, I have also been influenced by Hu Huanyong (1958).

Regarding Guangdong paddy estimates, I have also taken into consideration, in addition to the limits discussed in relation to Guangzhou, the county paddy production and cultivated acreage statistics published by the Guangdong Bureau of Agriculture and Forestry in 1938 (in Chen Qihui (n.d.), pp. 25781–6). With the exception of one instance (Nan'ao) that provides the absurd average yield of 24.35 piculs per *mu*, no country average calculated from these figures exceeds 2.65 piculs per *mu* per harvest, most instances ranging from 2.00 to 2.50 piculs. Because the average figures have been subject to manipulation, I have not included them in Table A.3, but they show that 2.00 to 2.50 piculs per *mu* per harvest was considered a credible average yield by contemporaries.

Notes

Notes to Chapter 1

1. I use the term not to underrate the difficulties that any attempt to improve rural livelihood must face, but to stress the vague feeling, shared by the 1930s 'optimists', that improvement under the existing social and political regimes was possible. Other than an outright rejection of the fatalism of the 'pessimists', the 'optimists' held few common positions. For lack of an overriding common argument, Myers (1970), pp. 13–24, refers to them as 'eclectic'.

2. Representative of the pessimistic view in the 1930s are Zhou Gucheng (1931), Feng Hefa (1933, 1935) and Chen Han-seng (1933, 1936). In addition, quite a few rural reformers in the 1930s, for example, see Liang Shuming (1937) and Jin Lunhai (1937), accepted the pessimists' arguments. The most solid presentation of the optimistic view is J.L. Buck (1930, 1937). Qiao Qiming (1926) confirmed the deterioration of the position of tenants, but his 1946 book came much closer to Buck. Gu Mei (1935) did not address the problem of likely changes in the standard of living, but his argument also came close to Buck's. For a discussion of these different historical points of view on the Chinese rural economy, see Ramon Myers (1970), pp. 13–24, Philip C.C. Huang (1975) and (1985), pp. 3–32, and Susan Mann Jones (1981).

3. Li Wenzhi (1957), Zhang Youyi (1957).

4. This argument is also presented in Li Shiyue (1958) and is widely circulated.

5. I am aware of the odd exception such as George Jamieson (1888–9), but even that is made up of crude impressions gathered from unidentified informants, and valuable as it is as an early source, it is not a survey report.

6. David Faure (1979), pp. 72–3.

7. Alfred Kai-ming Chiu (1933) describes the major surveys conducted in the Republic up to the time of his study. A useful assortment of these surveys is provided in Feng Hefa (1933, 1935). G. William Skinner (1973) is also a very useful guide to titles not included in Chiu or Feng.

8. Albert Feuerwerker (1980), p. 6.

9. Ralph Thaxton (1983), p. 2.

10. See Alvin Y. So (1986). For examples of poorly documented and untenable arguments in this book, see his discussion on the rise of the bourgeoisie on pp. 114–16, the chapter on proletarianization, and the summary of his argument on pp. 155–6.

11. Buck also argued, for instance, that high rates of tenancy were not found all over China, that from 1885 to 1911 the prices of agricultural commodities had risen more sharply than manufactured articles, and that farmers would have found it profitable to farm more intensively. Buck summarized his statistics on this question in his (1937a), p. 458–61.

12. A vast literature is available on commercial developments in the Changjiang and the Zhujiang delta before the mid-nineteenth century. See, for instance, Evelyn Rawski (1972), Li Longqian (1982), Huang Qichen (1984).

13. The cotton industry has in recent years been studied by Ramon Myers (1965), Albert Feuerwerker (1970), and Richard A. Kraus (1980) and the silk industry by Lillian M. Li (1981), Lynda S. Bell (1985a), and Robert Y. Eng (1986a).

14. Joseph Esherick (1972), one of the strongest statements continuing from the pessimistic stance, rests its case on the impact that the depression of the 1930s made on the rural economy. I do not dispute the effects of the 1930s depression, as this book and my 1985 article make clear, but I think the stress on the 1930s underestimates the benefits Chinese farmers might have derived from trade in the six decades that intervened between the end of the Taiping Rebellion and the 1930s.

15. Rubie S. Watson (1985), pp. 55–82, Edgar Wickberg (1981a and b), Philip C.C. Huang (1985), and David Faure (1986) are recent studies that recognize different types of landlord and tenant.

16. Muramatsu Yūji (1970) was the pioneer in recognizing the southern Jiangsu landlords as a type. Jing Su and Lo Lun (1959) drew attention to the persistence of the 'managerial landlords' of northern China, and the subject has been elaborated by Philip C.C. Huang (1985). See also the work on the 'one-field two-lords' type of tenancy by Fu Yiling (1961) and Niida Noburo (1960), vol. 2, pp. 164–215.

17. See Ramon Myers (1970) and Philip C.C. Huang (1985). Huang's argument (see pp. 162–3) is not that small farms were less willing to adopt cash crops, but that they had to opt for a 'less well-balanced cropping pattern' and so incur greater risks. Myers (p. 201) sees the adoption of cash crops as a reflection of the willingness to make the additional labour and capital investment needed but does not examine the question of whether small farms were disadvantageously placed to do so.

18. For an enthusiastic espousal of these views in the context of Chinese economic history, see Alvin Y. So (1986).

19. The term 'moral economy of the peasant', when first used in E.P. Thompson (1971), referred to popularly held beliefs concerning the responsibility of the state to keep food prices low. The applicability of the concept in this sense to China is borne out in R. Bin Wong (1982), as pointed out in Paul R. Greenough (1982). As used more recently in James C. Scott (1976), it refers to a supposed risk-avoidance strategy that was practised by farmers prior to large-scale commercialization. This vague concept has given rise to different arguments in the China field. That Scott exaggerates the security provided by the village and the uniformity of a 'moral' ideal is pointed out in James M. Polachek (1983), and the criticism in a broader context is elaborated in Samuel L. Popkin (1979). That poor farmers were not adverse to taking risks is documented in Philip C.C. Huang (1985), pp. 161–5. Huang, however, seems to accept an implication from Scott that increasing commercialization weakened interpersonal bonds in the village.

20. See, for instance, the leading proponent of this developmental view, Theodore W. Schultz (1964).

21. See the impressive presentation of historical material in Lloyd G. Reynolds (1985) and the discussion of the 'trickle-down' theory in H.W. Arndt (1983). Marxist scholars do not accept the shift in emphasis. The argument in Arghiri Emmanuel (1972), for instance, is that the absolute standard of living in Third World countries is kept low by 'unequal exchange'.

22. Ramon Myers (1970) and Philip C.C. Huang (1985).

23. Chen Han-seng (1939), Jing Su and Luo Lun (1959), Ramon Myers (1970), Philip C.C. Huang (1985).

24. Ramon Myers (1970).

25. Philip C.C.Huang (1985).

26. The prefecture (*fu*) and sub-prefecture (*zhou*) were administrative divisions in the Qing dynasty that comprised a number of counties (*xian*). In the Republican era, other local divisions were introduced. For the sake of simplicity and consistency, Qing administrative divisions within the province are used as reference points throughout this book.

27. For an introduction to the geography of Jiangsu, see G.B. Cressey (1934), Rhoads Murphey (1953), and Wang Weiping (1956). Data on the climate are taken from J.L. Buck (1937b), pp. 3 and 7.

28. This is not to say that the canal was easily navigable or always serviceable. See 'The ruin of the Grand Canal' in NCH, 25.7.1908 and p. 221, note 4, below.

29. Li Changfu (1936), pp. 319–20, 330, 353; Wang Peitang (1938), pp. 131–2. The Long-Hai Railway joined Gansu Province to Jiangsu. The section in Jiangsu went from Tongshan to Haizhou.

30. The *lixiahe* area takes its name from the Lihe, an abbreviation of the Liyunhe (inner canal) and the Xiahe (the lower river). The Liyunhe is the section of the Grand Canal located

in this part of Jiangsu, and the Xiahe is the popular name for the Chuanchanghe that runs parallel to it to its east, and the two smaller rivers that join the Chuanchang to the Liyunhe. See Li Changfu (1936), p. 31.

31. J.L. Buck (1937b), pp. 3 and 7.

32. Qing and Republican Guangdong included also the areas that in the Qing had come under Lianzhou Prefecture and Qinzhou Sub-prefecture, which, since 1965, have become a part of Guangxi province. These areas are not included within the scope of this book. For an introduction to the geography of Guangdong, see Liang Jen-ts'ai (1956) and Chen Zhengxiang (1978).

33. J.L. Buck (1937b), pp. 4 and 7.

34. G.B. Cressey (1934), pp. 48, 359.

35. Huang Zhenyi (1936).

36. Maurice Freedman (1966), pp. 68–96, John Watt (1972), James Polachek (1975).

37. A useful guide for a chronicle of warfare in Jiangsu and Guangdong in the Republican era is Gao Yinzu (1957).

38. Reports on military campaigns, piracy, and banditry in the newspapers are too many to list in full here. See *NCH*, 7.6.1919, pp. 625–6 and 12.1.1924, p. 45, for two useful summaries on Guangdong. Jiangsu also suffered from similar disorder. See *NCH*, 16.11.1920, p. 156; 9.7.1921, p. 96; 5.12.1925, p. 428; 12.12.1925, p. 476; and 29.4.1930, p. 171.

39. Morton Fried (1952), p. 351, in effect, also advances this argument.

40. N.C. Shen (1936).

41. Kong Xiangxi (1935), a report by the then Finance Minister (H.H. Kung) notes that seven counties in Jiangsu had completed land registration. Registration in Guangdong is reported in Guangdong sheng zhengfu mishuchu bianyishi, (1940).

42. A useful background study is Lloyd E. Eastman (1974), pp. 181–243. See also Zhongyang dangbu guomin jingji jihua weiyuanhui (1937), *xia*, Chapters 3 and 9 for a summary of accomplishments claimed by the Nationalist Government.

43. The impact of transocean steamships on Jiangsu and Guangdong was apparent from the 1870s. For further up the Changjiang River, William T. Rowe (1984) argues convincingly that at Hankou, up to the 1890s, the impetus for trade increase came from domestic rather than foreign trade. A preliminary case for the impact of the railway on rural economic development is made in He Hanwei (1979) and Ernest P. Liang (1982).

44. This does not alter the fact that it is difficult on the basis of traditional historical sources to assess the amount of increase in any cash crop. Loren Brandt (1987), for instance, takes Philip C. C. Huang (1985) to task for not acknowledging the impetus of the railway on cotton cultivation in northern China whereas Huang sees the change as a more gradual process dating back to the sixteenth century (see Philip C. C. Huang (1985), pp. 111–14 and 125–37).

45. Loren Brandt (1985) provides the clearest documentation for this view to date.

Notes to Chapter 2

1. F.E. Hyde (1973) is a very useful introduction to the subject of trade expansion in the Far East in the late nineteenth century. He Hanwei (1979) and Ernest P. Liang (1982) discuss the impact of the railway on agriculture in North China. The impact of motor roads on the Chinese economy is an unstudied subject. Useful background may be found in Zhongyang dangbu guomin jingi jihua weiyuanhui (1937), *xia,* Chapter 3, pp. 26–34, Zhou Yishi (1957), pp. 94–188, and perceptive newspaper discussions of which *NCH* 12.5.1905, p. 310; 11.1.1919, p. 79, 10.5.1919, p. 355; 18.12.1920, p. 789; and 23.5.1925, p. 319 are examples.

2. F.E. Hyde (1973), pp. 22–6.

3. I examined various editions of this book at the British Library. For a useful discussion, see Timothy Brook (1981a), (1981b), and (1982).

4. The following are vivid descriptions of the canal: 'Those who live near Shanghai, with many steam transportation facilities, cannot appreciate the difficulties of transportation in this part of the country. The grain boats were towed by tugs from Chinkiang [Zhenjiang] to Tsingkiangpu [Qingjiangpu], 120 miles; from there they must pass three locks, and some seventy miles without steam tugs. The average time of the boats from Chinkiang to Suchien [Suqian] was probably more than twenty days.' (*NCH* 10.6.1911, p. 681, report from Suqian county in northern Jiangsu.) 'Last summer, as usual, it [that is, the Grand Canal] was so full that launches could not use it for several months. Last winter it was frozen tight for fifty days. And now finally it is so low that traffic has been seriously delayed for a month or two, and there is no prospect for improvement till the June rains come. Today the launches run 100 *li* above Yangchow [Yangzhou]. And above this there are hundreds of large goods-boats lying like logs in the mud. Even mat stuffs cannot get through. All passengers have to be transferred several times, each time they are duly "squeezed" [extorted] and, moreover, have to accept what accommodation they can get. It is the only traffic road for six or eight million people. Sea junks serve the eastern district. The Tientsin-Pukow [Tianjin-Pukou] Railway [serves] the Anhui section. But these people are tied down to this ancient irrigation ditch.' (*NCH*, 21.4.1917, pp. 119–20.)

5. The route from Foshan to Beijing is given in Xiao Yizhang (n.d.), 1/4b–5b. For a later account of the route from Guangdong into Hunan and Jiangxi, see Sun Tangyue (1937).

6. *NCH*, 1.7.1876, p. 9; 22.7.1876, p. 76; 5.8.1876, p. 124; Canton Advertising and Commission Agency (1932), pp. 59 and 124; Peng Chuheng (1937), tables between pp. 444 and 445; and Mizuno Kokichi (1907), pp. 614–15.

7. MC, 1892–1911, pp. 395, 437, 456; Kwang-ching Liu (1962), p. 437.

8. *Zhongguo nianjian 1924*, p. 904; of the figures quoted, the Shanghai-Hangzhou-Ningbo line carried 169,000 tons of vegetable products and 22,000 tons of animal products, and the Shanghai–Nanjing line 880,000 tons of the former and 57,000 tons of the latter.

9. A succinct summary of China's railway development may be found in Ralph William Huenemann (1984), pp. 37–97.

10. The following, none the less, gives some indication of the impact of the railways:

'The following comparative table, which gives the charges for transporting 30 tons of groundnuts from Pukow to Shanghai by rail and by steamer, speaks for itself:

'By railway
Train freight — about 330 bags = 497.40 piculs	$42.00
Likin, at 6 cents per bag	19.80
Lighterage, coolie hire, and sundry	21.52
Total	$83.32

'By steamer
Freight — net weight 497.40 piculs at Tls. 0.16	
per picul = 79.58 at 0.70 = $113.68 less 5%	$108.00
Duty — 497.40 piculs at Hk. Tls. 0.15	
per picul = Hk. Tls. 74.61 at 153	114.15
Shipping hong charges, at 1 cent per bag	3.30
Total	$225.45'

Source: MC, Nanjing 1923, pp. 2–3.

11. MC, Suzhou 1896, pp. 290–1, Guangzhou 1898, pp. 459–60, Jiulong 1898, p. 535, Nanjing 1892–1901, pp. 430-1.

12. 'Travelling facilities have greatly improved during the last five years. Then the journey up the North River took fourteen days or more, according to the water and the wind available. Now it can be done in two days. First came the railway to Samshui [Sanshui], which made it possible to join one's boat, three or four days after it had left Canton. Next came the advent of the steam launch to the lower and middle reaches of the river, and when

the Canton-Hankow [Guangzhou-Hankou] Railway reached the North River it was possible by taking train and launch to reach Yingtak [Yingde] in one day. For the last stage to Shiuchow [Shaozhou] the water was seldom deep enough for any length of time for a steam launch, but last year a small draught stern-wheeler began to ply between Yingtak and Shiuchow giving us a service every second day. Between Yingtak and the railway head competition is so keen that passengers are being carried forty miles for ten cents. This rivalry came to a head a few days ago, when the crews of two opposing launches engaged in a free fight. That night only one launch made the trip to Yingtak.' (*NCH* 20.5.1911, pp. 484–5)

13. MC, Shantou 1879, pp. 206–7.

14. Rhoads Murphey (1970), pp. 44–5.

15. MC, Zhenjiang 1882–91, p. 314, *Zhongguo nianjian 1924*, p. 922.

16. *NCH* 18.1.1872, p. 33. See also *NCH* 8.2.1872.

17. MC, Shanghai 1882–91, p. 323.

18. T.R. Bannister (1933a), pp. 78–9, 93.

19. B.T. Chang (1929) p. 598: 'Credit plays no part in cocoon collection, the farmers always insisting upon cash payment. In many parts of the interior even notes issued by Shanghai banks of very good standing are rejected, because the farmers are unfamiliar with the form of currency. So during the cocoon collecting season large shipments of silver coins are moved from Shanghai to the interior by cocoon collecting firms. The sudden withdrawal of large sums of dollars and subsidiary coins from Shanghai often causes a rise in the dollar exchange rate.'

20. 'The number and tonnage of steamers trading at this port depend mainly on the state of the rice market. The tendency in recent years has been towards fewer steamers, but increased tonnage. Formerly, also, it was usual for enormous shipments of rice to be made within a few days, especially in those years when, at New Year time, all *likin* was exempted. This has not occurred, however, for some years. Conditions of trade seem to have altered, and for this improved telegraphic facilities are no doubt partly responsible. Instead of sending off promiscuous shipments, which often entailed losses, merchants now keep more in touch with the markets and arrange their shipments accordingly. The spectacle of thirty of more steamers loading rice in Wuhu simultaneously will probably never be seen again.' (MC, Wuhu 1902–11, p. 380.)

21. Yeh-chien Wang (1973), pp. 79–83.

22. For a summary of the late Qing debasement, see Yang Duanliu (1962), and David Faure (1978), pp. 428–38.

23. Wang Yejian (1981), Wei Jianyou (1955), pp. 192–213.

24. This is because Hong Kong, as a colony, counted as a foreign country, but Shanghai was part of China.

25. The most detailed discussion on the statistics of the Maritime Customs is still Li Taichu (1964). See pp. 233–7 for a discussion of the change in reporting.

26. Harold C. Hinton (1956), pp. 94–6.

27. Kang Chao (1977), pp. 102–5.

28. Lillian M. Li (1981), pp. 108–12, summarizes development in Jiangsu. On the rise of Wuxi as a major silk-producing area, compare MC, 1917, p. 62, with Yong An's report in 1927, quoted in Zhang Youyi (1957), vol.2, pp. 223–4. Jiao Longhua, writing in 1934, put the development even later, within the Republican era. Jiao is quoted in Zhang Youyi (1957), vol. 2, p. 100. See also David Faure (1978), p. 371, for further documentation.

29. The clearest statement on Shanghai's wheat supplies before the 1930s is given in the reply of the Shanghai Chinese General Chamber of Commerce to enquiries from the Ministry of Agriculture and Commerce, reported in *NCH* on 16.3.1918, pp. 624–5. The statement reads, 'Shanghai is not a wheat-producing district; all the wheat required is imported. About 3,000,000 *shih* [*shi*] of wheat is imported every year from Chihli, Shantung, Szechuan, Hupeh, Honan, Hunan, Anhui and Chekiang, and about 2,500,000 *shih* from other places in our own province, Kiangsu'. For further corroboration, see the discussion of the Rong family's operations on pp. 100–102 above, and the development of

flour milling in Nantong in *Ershi nianlai zhi Nantong* (1938), vol. 2, pp. 13–17. Contemporaries in the 1930s gave the impression that local purchase expanded in that decade. See 'Flour industry in Kiangsu', p. 41, and Shehui jingji diaochasuo (1935b), pp. 15–26. For an account of the establishment of flour milling in China, see Zhu Guanghua (1985).

30. Peng Chengwan, Yin Ruli (1920), Huang Zhenyi (1936) are useful studies on Hainan.

31. On the mulberry dykes and fishponds, see Zhong Gongfu (1958), Glenn T. Trewartha (1939), Foshan diqu geming weiyuanhui Zhujiang sanjiaozhou nongyezhi bianxiezu (1976), vol. 4, pp. 57–61, and Lillian M. Li (1981) pp. 149–53. On this subject, I am also grateful to Winston Hsieh for showing me a chapter from his forthcoming book on Shunde.

32. Figures for fruit and tobacco exports from Shantou are calculated from MC, *Foreign Trade of China* (1924). I have included for the calculation of fruit exports only figures listed under 'orange, fresh', 'fruits, dried and preserved, not otherwise classified', and 'fruits, fresh, not otherwise classified'. Rural exports from Guangdong are examined in David Faure (1980b), using material from MC annual reports for 1883, 1904, and 1924. On tobacco, see 'Tobacco production in Kwangtung', and on trade with Hong Kong, Ho Ping-yin (1935).

33. Dwight H. Perkins (1969), pp. 293–5, is the source of the urban population figures. MC, Shantou (1902–11), p. 130, puts the emigration from Shantou alone in 1902 at 100,000, and that in 1911 at 125,000. MC, Qiongzhou (1902–11), p. 248, reports that the total emigration to Singapore and Bangkok, presumably from Hainan Island alone, for the 10 years up to 1911, was 250,000. MC, Jiangmen (1902–11) does not quote a figure for the size of the emigration from the port, but notes (p. 190), 'In some villages in this district, out of a clan numbering, say, 500, nearly one-half have gone abroad, leaving no one at home but old folks, children and a few farmers.'

34. Zou Yiren (1980), pp. 114–16 shows that in 1935, for instance, out of a total population of 3.2 million in Shanghai, only 1.9 million claimed Jiangsu origin.

35. Jean Chesneaux (1968), pp. 64–70.

36. *Chaozhou zhi* (1946), p. *hukou zhi* 18a, records that of a population of 190,000 enumerated in Shantou in 1936, 160,000 people had settled there from counties within Chaozhou prefecture. Of a population of 850,000 enumerated in the Hong Kong census of 1931, 660,000 people were born in Hong Kong or on the Zhujiang Delta. ('Report of the Census for the Colony of Hong Kong 1931', p. 129.) The county origins of the population in Guangzhou in the 1920s or 1930s are not known.

37. Chen Zhengxiang (1978), p. 68, Lin Jinzhi (1980), p. 199.

38. Examples may be found in Hu Linge, Zhu Banxing, Xu Sheng (1939), pp. 97–8; and Huang Wei, Xia Lingen (1984), pp. 310–28. Jean Chesneaux (1968), p. 112, reports that an interview subject recalled that 'only those workers who had some means and the prospect of a comparatively steady job could be sure of being able to maintain wives and children left behind in the village, or could at least hope to make a substantial contribution toward their livelihood'. It is very likely that the emigrants from Guangdong were in a much better position to remit funds home than the emigrants from the villages of Jiangsu who worked in Shanghai. The following observation from MC, Jiangmen (1902–11), p. 190 is quite revealing: '... in the United States, a laundryman could earn at least Mexican $40 a month, whereas here he would certainly not get more than Mexican $9.'

39. Chen Ta (1939), pp. 87–99, 114–17. The sample consists of 100 families in an unnamed community near Shantou from which emigration had continued since 1823, and 100 families from a 'non–emigrant' community.

40. MC, Jiangmen (1902–11), p. 190; MC, Shantou (1902–11), p. 131; Li Taichu (1964), pp. 281–3; Xie Xueying (1935), pp. 41–2; *Guangdong jingji nianjian 1940*, pp. S119–41; Lin Jinzhi (1980).

41. See Lillian M. Li (1981), pp. 23–4, Lillian M. Li (1982), and Xu and Wei (1983).

42. C.W. Howard and K.P. Buswell (1925), pp. 76 and 97.

43. Kang Chao (1977), pp. 25–6; Yan Zhongping (1963), pp. 309–12; Randall Stross (1982), pp. 189–91; Zhang Kai (1984), pp. 54–6, and Wang Shuhuai (1984).

44. Edward Shim (1925), p. 81.

45. For mechanical spinning, see Ramon Myers (1965); the steam filature, Wang Jingyu (1962), Marjorie Topley (1975), and Janice E. Stockard (1985); and for the mechanical pump, brief references in Nongcun fuxing weiyuanhui (1934), pp. 86, Fei Hsiao-tung (1939), pp. 161–2, and Randall Stross (1982), pp. 221–5.

46. Shannon R. Brown (1981) has pointed out the requirement for the new technology to be accepted by the guilds of merchants and producers. This requirement seems to have varied from trade to trade. In both silk-reeling and hand-weaving industries, early opposition was quickly overcome.

47. Fei Hsiao-tung (1939), pp. 170–1.

48. Fei Hsiao-tung (1939), p. 173.

49. Zhang Kai (1984), Min Zongdian and Wang Da (1985), Wang Da (1987).

50. Wu Ruilin (1937), p. 270.

51. Feng Rui and Ping-hang Yung (1931), p. 176.

52. Fei Hsiao-tung (1939), p. 173.

53. Chen Han-seng (1933), p. 10.

Notes to Chapter 3

1. An example of this line of reasoning is Guangdong liangshi diaojie weiyuanhui (1935). A similar argument also appears in the *Guangdong jingji nianjian, 1940*.

2. It must be realized that these figures are compiled from crude approximations given by local informants. See Zhang Xinyi (1932), pp. 4–6, for a description of the procedure by which the provincial figures quoted in Table 3.1 are calculated, and see Dwight H. Perkins (1969), pp. 241–4, for a discussion of NARB (National Agricultural Research Bureau) figures, of which these were a part. The Guangdong figures quoted here agree broadly with the reports of the Guangdong Agricultural and Forestry Department in the 1930s, reproduced in Chen Qihui (n.d.), pp. 25769–90, 25805–17.

3. Opium was also grown in parts of northern Jiangsu in the late nineteenth century, but the crop was suppressed in the early 1900s. See *NCH* 16.7.1886, 6.8.1901, 12.12.1908; *SP* 14.5.Tongzhi 13, 25.6.Guangxu 8.

4. No precise report on the Jiangsu mulberry acreage before the 1930s is available. The figure quoted here is Luo Sibing's estimate based on the quantity of silk produced in the province. See his (1935), p. 71. The Jiangsu cotton acreage is quoted in Zhongguo mianye tongjihui (1935), pp. 138–9. In the early years of the twentieth century 500,000 *mu* might also have been given to opium poppies. See production estimate made by the International Opium Commission in 1909 quoted in Zhang Youyi (1957), vol. 3, pp. 47–8; the Guangdong mulberry acreage is given in C.W. Howard and K.P. Buswell (1925), table between pp. 36 and 37; and the Guangdong tobacco and sugar-cane acreages are reported in *Zhongguo jingji nianjian 1934*, pp. F132 and F127 respectively. For the overall cultivated acreages, see Table 3.3 below.

5. C.W. Howard and K.P. Buswell (1925), pp. 48–9, Luo Sibing (1935), pp. 69–71; and Fei Hsiao-tung (1939), p. 157, especially map IV.

6. Lillian M. Li (1981), pp. 150–3.

7. Chen Han-seng (1936), p. 129.

8. David Faure (1978), pp. 367–70; Guoli Guangdong daxue nongke xueyuan (1925), pp. 13, 34, and 50; 'A study of the sugar industry in China', (1927), pp. 879–80.

9. 'Balitun nongcun jingji diaocha baogao' (1932), p. 12; 'Chang'ancun nongcun jingji diaocha baogao' (1932), p. 23.

10. *Guangdong jingji nianjian 1940*, p. K33.

11. Guoli Zhongshan daxue nongke xueyuan (1925), pp. 7, 25; (1929), pp. 59, 119, 297; (1933) pp. 5, 9.

12. See note 11 (1929), p 331.

13. See note 11 (1933), pp. 95–6.

14. The report of the National Reconstruction Committee is Guomin jingji jianshe yundong weiyuanhui, Guangdong fenhui (1937), the sweet potatoes statistics may be found on pp. 20–4. The Guangdong Bureau of Agriculture and Forestry statistics may be found in Chen Qihui (n.d.), pp. 25781–6.

15. I have used the following series of production figures for paddy: (a) Guomin jingji jianshe yundong weiyuanhui, Guangdong fenhui (1937), pp. 12–19; (b) Chen Qihui (n.d.), pp. 25712–17, quoting the Guangdong Bureau of Agriculture and Forestry; (c) *Guangdong jingji nianjian 1940*, pp. K17–34; (d) Chen Qihui (n.d.), pp. 25769–80, again quoting the Guangdong Bureau of Agriculture and Forestry; and (e) *Guangdong jingji nianjian 1940*, pp. G29–37, quoting figures reported by the Guangdong Bureau of Agriculture and Forestry for 1938. Series (a), (b), and (c) are practically identical, and quite obviously compiled from (d). The first three series are quoted in terms of cultivated acreages, and the last in crop acreages, which, except for a few instances, work out to be exactly double the cultivated acreage. Series (e) seems to be independent of the other four. My surmise is that all these series were compiled in the first place by the Guangdong Bureau of Agriculture and Forestry, possibly from reports gathered in two different years.

16. Gu Yanwu (seventeenth century), p. 10/18a–b; Chen Hengli (1958), pp. 26–34, Bao Shizhen (*c.* 1850), ch. 26, p. 4a; Tao Xu (1920 ed.), p. 19a; and Wu Hui (1985), pp. 169–70, 176–7 provide estimates before the twentieth century. Dongnan daxue (1923), pp. 405–13 and Feng Hefa (1933), pp. 527–29, report Dongnan daxue survey results. J.L. Buck (1937), p. 210; Fei Xiaotong (1946), p. 5; and He Menglei (1934), p. 32997, provide the twentieth-century survey figures. Some confusion arises from the fact that some of the earlier sources, for example the *Bunongshu* and Bao, quite clearly quote the yield figures for rice (that is, *husked* rice), and not grain (*unhusked* rice). However, it seems quite impossible for yield to have been generally as high as 3 *shi* of rice per *mu* (450 catties of rice, or the equivalent of 600 catties of grain) in Ming and Qing southern Jiangsu as they claimed, because, before the Second World War, experimental farms did not manage to do better. (In Zhejiang Province in the 1930s, experimental farms could reap as much as 600 catties of grain per *mu* on land growing a single early crop a year, and 400 to 500 catties on land growing a single late crop. However, on farms that experimented with double-cropping 400 catties could be harvested for each of the two harvests in the year. See Wang Chengyin (1946), p. 196.) The figures quoted by J.L. Buck for the Suzhou area, respectively 25.49 and 48.23 quintals per hectare (261 and 494 catties per *mu*), were 'most frequent yields', and were both more than 10 per cent below what his informants considered 'average yields'. In arguing against what he considered exaggerated claims by Buck, Fei Xiaotong was emphatic that 40 bushels per acre (463 catties per *mu*) was possible on what he considered 'ordinary fields' (*putong de tian*). He Menglei reported 2 *shi* per *mu* of husked rice, which would have been equivalent to 402 catties of grain per *mu*.

17. Patrick Hase (1981), p. 196.

18. *Dongguan xianzhi* (1927), pp 15/14b–15a.

19. For a comparison of yields in various sources, see Appendix.

20. J.L. Buck's figures are quoted from *Statistical Monthly* (1932), and his procedure is discussed in his (1937b), p. 29, from which page this quotation is also taken. Subsequent tables show that the figures quoted here in places vary quite substantially from values obtained by his survey. See Tables 2, 3, and 8 on pp. 30 and 37.

21. Kong Xiangxi (1935) shows that determined efforts by the government in the 1930s could add substantially to the tax acreage. In Jiangsu, these additions were much greater in the north than in the south. Shuyang added 1.7 million *mu* to its original 1.4 million *mu* of registered farmland, and Xiao *xian* 1.1 million *mu* to its 1.3 million *mu*, while Yixing added only 42,000 *mu* to an original 1.3 million *mu* and Jiangyin 28,000 *mu* to 1.2 million *mu*.

Significantly, the acreage registered in 1935, which resulted from central government pressure to revamp land registration records, came close to the *Statistical Monthly* figures quoted by J.L. Buck in six of the seven counties noted by Kong:

	Statistical Monthly (1932)	Kong Xiangxi (1935)
Shuyang	3,375,000	3,145,561 *mu*
Xiao *xian*	2,258,000	2,453,665
Jiangdu	2,139,000	2,326,889
Liyang	1,392,000	1,426,177
Yixing	1,160,000	1,296,533
Zhenjiang	754,000	1,102,087
Jiangyin	1,243,000	1,242,141

The figures suggest that the *Statistical Monthly* reports were acreages known to county government officials, even though they were not quoted in tax reports to the central government. They also suggest that the discrepancy between the locally known acreages (and hence, in all likelihood, taxes) and the officially registered acreages were smaller in southern Jiangsu than in the north. The difference between an officially registered acreage and a locally known acreage would be a result of the employment of local people in tax collection over whose efforts the county government had very little direct control. On this question, see also David Faure (1976).

For Guangdong, comparison with other sources (Chen Qihui (n.d.), table between pp. 25700 and pp. 25701, pp. 25705–11; *Guangdong jingji nianjian 1940*, pp. B18–25, B27–34, G10–16; Guangdong liangshi diaojie weiyuanhui (1935), pp. 18–21) shows that the *Statistical Monthly* figures were Guangdong provincial government statistics quoted in the 1930s. They differ from a series quoted in the *Guangdong jingji nianjian 1940*, pp. G4–10 and Chen Qihui (n.d.), pp. 25738–43, which give a provincial total of 75,337,000 *shimu*, that is, 82,117,000 *mu*. The *Guangdong jingji nianjian* describes this as a figure produced by the provincial government's statistical bureau (*tongjishi*) in 1940, on the basis of 50,000 : 1 military maps, while Chen Qihui quotes his source as the *Guangdong dizheng jikan*, vol. 1, no. 1. It seems, therefore, that this was a later revision. Again, the earlier figure seems to be a tax-registered acreage, for it is described as information released by the Financial Bureau (*caizheng ting*) in the *Guangdong jingji nianjian 1940*, p. G10. Chen Qihui (n.d.), p. 25698 also recognizes it as such.

22. Ho Ping-ti (1967), pp. 67–86.

23. See Ta-chung Liu and Kung-chia Yeh (1965), pp. 171–81 and Dwight H. Perkins (1969), pp. 192–216.

24. Li Wenzhi (1957), p. 9, Ta-chung Liu and Kung-chia Yeh (1965), p. 178, Shiyebu guoji maoyiju (1933), pp. 12–16, Zhang Xinyi (1932), p. 13, and Hu Huanyong (1958). Liu and Yeh's figure for Jiangsu does not include municipalities, that is Shanghai and Nanjing. The figures quoted in Table 3.3, taken from Zhu Kezhen (1926), pp. 98–100, include them.

25. Li Wenzhi (1957), p. 9, Zhang Xinyi (1932), p. 13, Ta-chung Liu and Kung-chia Yeh (1965), p. 178, Hu Huanyong and Zhang Shanyu (1984), p. 207. Table 3.3 excludes those Guangdong counties that were transferred to Guangxi province after 1949, with a total population amounting to 1,136,000 in 1928–31. Comparison with Chen Qihui (n.d.), pp. 25607–11, also shows that the *Guangdong jingji nianjian 1940* figures exclude the population of Guangzhou and Shantou. Adjustments have been made in Table 3.3 by adding them to the populations of Guangzhou and Chaozhou.

26. The list is introduced by the following preamble: 'The following list of cities with generally accepted population estimates is the result of postcard questionnaires sent to missionaries in every mission station in China. Estimates received in this way were carefully compared with estimates previously published in Customs' reports, guidebooks, geographies and atlases, city population lists of large business houses, Mission Board reports, Police

Commissioners' reports, etc. and a number of changes were made'. (Milton Stauffer (1922), p. lxxxviii.) The list is made up of 358 cities from all over China, the smallest inhabited by 25,000 people. It includes 33 cities in Jiangsu and 31 in Guangdong. For a summary of Jiangsu figures from this source, see Zhu Kezhen (1926), p. 108, and for a comparison with other sources, see Liu Shiji (1978), pp. 36–7.

27. Gilbert Rozman (1973), pp. 218 and 239, estimates that from the mid-ninteenth century to 1953, the urban population of Jiangsu rose from 7 per cent to 29.1 per cent of the total provincial population, and that of Guangdong from 7 to 12.2 per cent. The figures given in Table 3.3 here make allowance for 12.2 per cent urban in Jiangsu and 11.7 per cent in Guangdong. The discrepancy is due partly to the exaggerated estimates of individual city populations in the Protestant Missions' report, and partly to a smaller total provincial population base quoted here for Jiangsu. Rozman refers to the pre-Taiping provincial population. Table 3.3 here quotes the post-Taiping estimate.

28. J.L. Buck (1937b), pp. 233, 238, 242–3, with two exceptions, gives 1–7 per cent as the portion of paddy left for seeds, 4–13 per cent as that of wheat, and 2–4 per cent as that of sorghum. Kenneth R. Walker (1984), p. 288, puts the proportion of grain set aside for seeds in 1953–7 in Jiangsu at 5.49 per cent, and in Guangdong at 5.05 per cent. On the milling factor for rice, see Chuan Han-sheng and Richard A. Kraus (1975), pp. 92–8, and for wheat, Zhang Yifan (1948), pp. 13–14, quoting the regulations of the Shanghai Supplementary Food Commodities Market. Note that these standards applied to the milling of rice and wheat for city consumption. A lower factor could have been applied to rural consumption if by force or circumstances the population was prepared to eat coarser grain or flour.

29. Dwight H. Perkins (1969), pp. 14–15 and 297–307, concludes that 200 kilograms (333 catties) of unmilled grain 'represents something like a minimum level of subsistence' (p. 14) while 350 kilograms (583 catties) represents the upper range of average per capita grain output in China. Kenneth R. Walker (1984), p. 3, puts a 'good self-sufficiency level' at 275 kilograms (458 catties) per head. Guangdongsheng liangshi diaojie weiyuanhui (1935), p. 25, quoting C.C. Chang, *China's Food Problem, Report for the Biennial Conference of the Institute of Pacific Relations* (publication details unknown) estimates that village males required 501 catties of *rice* per year, village women 438 catties, urban males 391 catties, and urban women 340 catties. Philip C.C. Huang (1975), p. 134, notes: 'Perhaps the simplest indicator [of subsistence] is that used by the Japanese researchers who studied Shajing — food consumption of 300 catties of grain per adult per year, which also corresponds roughly with current grain rations in China'. The reason for a rather wide range of estimates is that the concept of subsistence is not very precise. On this point, see Colin Clark and Magaret Haswell (1966), p. 49.

30. It must be noted that the low per-capita estimates in northern Jiangsu have been achieved by accepting very low paddy and wheat yields, and in the transitional areas, only in those circumstances where it is assumed that rice is not grown. In Jiaying and Gaozhou, the high population density may also be partly the result of underestimating the urban population.

31. Allowing for, say, a 20 per cent exaggeration in the yield figures, we may revise the proportion that must be kept for food crops to 60 per cent, in full awareness that supplementary food crops have not been taken into account in the estimate.

32. I find quite unacceptable Lynda S. Bell (1985b), p. 25: 'Even if all the land in Wuxi devoted to mulberries were converted back to grain cultivation . . . the amount of additional grain that could have been produced with prevailing techniques would still have fallen short by 35 per cent of what Wuxi peasants normally consumed'. I cannot understand why she and others have found it objectionable that farmers should be 'locked into' a mode of production whereby they obtained enough to eat.

33. The Jiangsu reports come from *Shiyebu guoji maoyiju (1933)*, pp. 36–7 and 77–8. They should be read in conjunction with tables on pp. 22–4 and 64–7, which give the percentages of local grain sold in each county. Practically all the counties noted as inadequate in grain are also noted as consumers of all the grain locally produced. The

Guangdong reports are taken from Guoli Zhongshan daxue nongke xueyuan (1925, 1929, and 1933).

34. L.L. Chang (1932), p. 457: 'On the average about 60 to 70 per cent of the total quantity of polished white rice marketed is sold in the months of December to April when the price in silver currency is more than three per cent below the yearly average. If this is compared with the highest price, which occurs in September, it is more than ten per cent lower. See also Cao Liying (1937) and Chuan Han-sheng and Richard A. Kraus (1975), pp. 19–23.

35. The 1876 drought covered an extensive area in north China: He Hanwei (n.d.) gives a detailed account of it. For the 1897–9 famine, see primarily accounts in the newspapers, for example, NCH 7.5.1897, p. 816, 25.6.1897, p. 1137, 22.10.1897, p. 740, 10.12.1897, p. 1036, 24.12.1897, p. 1129, 23.1.1898, p. 105, 18.4.1898, p. 660, 9.5.1898, p. 795, 31.10.1898, p. 814, 28.11.1898, p. 1003, 30.1.1899, pp. 170–1, and the 1906–7 flood, 20.7.1906, pp. 132–3, 3.8.1906, pp. 254–5, 5.10.1906, pp. 11–12, 21.6.1907, p. 694, 19.4.1907, p. 141. The 1911 flood, according to Zhongyang qixiangju kexue yanjiuyuan (1981), p. 226, covered primarily Shandong Province, but see NCH 6.1.1911, p. 15, 3.3.1911, p. 499, 17.3.1911, pp. 624–5, 23.9.1911, pp. 751–2, and the 'Famine Fete Supplement', 25.5.1912, which gives a map of the affected area on p. 6. A map of the 1921 flood may be found in MC, Nanjing 1911–21, p. 374, but see the very interesting dispute concerning the famine in NCH, 6.8.1921, pp. 417–9. The 1931 flood is a well-documented subject. A contemporary assessment of damage is given in Jinling daxue nongke xueyuan nongye jingjixi (1932). For the overflow of the Huanghe (Yellow) River in 1935, Yang Ruxiong (1937) is an eyewitness account.

36. Aside from newspaper accounts, for instance, NCH 2.6.1877, p. 544, 9.6.1877, p. 567, 11.7.1884, p. 37, 13.8.1902, p. 320, 24.8.1906 p. 400, 15.5.1909, p. 363, 11.7.1914, p. 115, 21.8.1915, p. 527, 21.4.1917, p. 116, 16.6.1917, p. 622, details of floods in Guangdong may be found in Xuxiu sangyuanwei zhi (n.d.), pp. 15/35a–40b, and Chen Qihui (n.d.), pp. 25899–913.

Notes to Chapter 4

1. Eduard Kann (1927), pp. 177–98, 413–35, 511–21, and 532–51; Peng Xinwei (1958), pp. 600–17; Yang Duanliu (1962), pp. 283–308.

2. For rent payment, see the reports on tenancy conveniently summarized in Zhongguo jingji nianjian (1934, 1936, 1937), and for wages, Chen Zhengmo (1934). Note also C.K. Yang (1959), p. 38,Fei Hsiao-tung (1939), p. 173, and the observation of an elderly village woman paying the doctor with an egg in Wuxi in Weng Zushan (1937), p. 80.

3. Thomas Rawski (forthcoming) makes the important observation that for the monetary reform of 1934–5 to have made the impact it did, banknotes must have been extensively used at the time and that this implies considerable expansion of notes in the decades leading up to the 1930s. None the less, this does not alter the fact that notes were designated in both copper and silver and that they were subjected to fluctuation that arose from changes in the copper/silver exchange.

4. Frank H.H. King (1965), pp. 25–90, gives a general view of currencies circulated at the end of the nineteenth century. The widespread circulation of debased coins and paper notes makes the twentieth-century situation much more complex. For an impression of monetary confusion, noted in particular in northern Jiangsu, see Wu Shoupeng (1930), pp. 350–1 and Nongcun fuxing weiyuanhui (1934), pp. 68–9. A summary of the regional distribution of China's various metallic currencies may be found in Tokyō chigaku kyōkai (1917), pp. 313–20.

5. Zhongguo renmin yinhang Shanghai shi fenhang (1960), pp. 593–5, 603–5.

6. K. Bloch (1935), p. 621, B.T. Chang (1929), pp. 598–9.

7. The Rong family's remittance business between Wuxi and Shanghai in 1896,

described in Shanghai shehui kexueyuan jingji yanjiusuo (1980), pp. 5–6, and their subsequent engagement in the cocoon business, illustrate the commercial opportunities that arose from currency handling. For informative treatment of the operations of native banking, see Ma Yinchu (1929) and Andrea Lee McElderry (1976).

8. Both the *Shenbao* and the *North China Daily News* carried daily financial reports.

9. For background, see Herbert M. Bratter (1932), Shiyebu yinjia wujia taolun weiyuanhui (1936), and Dickens H. Leavens (1939), pp. 86–107, and 195–223.

10. The same cause also led to the illegal private production of small cash, in effect counterfeits, that contained less copper than government-minted cash. In local markets, money-changers and merchants made allowance for these small cash but restricted their circulation. As these small cash were handmade, the volume was probably limited. See F.E. Taylor (1896–7), Frank H.H. King (1965), pp. 51–65.

11. Eduard Kann (1927), p. 433: 'The depreciation, which had taken place between the years 1906 and 1911, was due to overproduction, and not to adulteration of the metal content. But shortly after the inauguration of the republican regime, and especially after the ending of the World War in 1918, the production of copper coin became so prolific and the metal content so variable that, within five years, the situation had become desperate'. The sharp break at approximately 1906 in the linkage between the international price of silver and the copper coinage is also apparent in the correlations of the *annual* figures that are used to produce Table 4.1. The correlation of the annual prices of silver (summed up in column 1) and annual averages of the quantity of cash exchangeable per silver dollar in Ningbo (summed up in column 4) between 1870 and 1906 is 0.93. The correlations of the prices of silver on the other measures of the copper exchange ratio from 1907 to 1931 (columns 5 to 8) are insignificant. These correlations are: with cash per silver dollar in Wujin, 0.19; with cash per 10-cent silver coin in Wujin, 0.19; with copper dollars per silver dollar in Ningbo, 0.48; with discount for subsidiary silver coins in Ningbo, 0.22.

12. Regression analysis of the *annual* prices of rice in Shanghai used in computing Table 4.2 on the annual prices of silver and the copper/silver exchange rates illustrates the changes discussed in this paragraph:

	Standardized Regression Coefficient	R^2
On Price of Silver, 1870–1906	−0.772	0.596
On Cash/dollar, Ningbo 1870–1906	−0.839	0.705
On Price of Silver, 1907–1934	−0.270	0.072
On Cash/dollar, Wujin 1907–1928	0.858	0.736

The weak relationship with the price of silver from 1907 to 1934 suggests that what mattered was the exchange rate between cash and silver rather than the gold price of silver. The negative value of the standardized regression for the Ningbo cash/dollar exchange rate in 1870 to 1906, and the change to a positive value may be explained by the pricing of rice in copper in local markets. In the earlier period, when the copper price of rice changed little from year to year, a higher cash-silver exchange meant a lower silver price for rice; in the later period, the copper price of rice was rising with the depreciation of the copper currency, and hence a higher cash/silver exchange rate applied as the price of rice rose.

13. Between 1895 and 1931, China imported net 832,718,000 Hk.Tls. worth of silver, of which over 324,672,000 Hk.Tls. was imported between 1928 and 1931 (Hsiao Liang-lin (1974), pp. 128–9). It can be argued that much of it was needed to meet the demand for currency that was generated by expansion in the economy, but it also created inflation.

14. *NCH*, 28 February 1896, p. 318.

15. *NCH*, 16 April 1908, p. 173.

16. *NCH*, 12 December 1909, p. 525.

17. *NCH*, 13 May 1910, p. 379. The foreign mill referred to was a flour mill that was finally burnt down in a riot in 1911. See *NCH*, 5 August 1911, p. 338.

18. *NCH*, 14 September 1912, p. 769.

19. *NCH*, 7 January 1913, pp. 13–14.

20. *NCH*, 3 January 1914, p. 50.

21. *NCH*, 28 November 1914, p. 697.

22. *NCH*, 30 October 1915, p. 319.

23. *NCH*, 31 October 1925, p. 195.

24. *NCH*, 8 December 1928, p. 391.

25. The Zhenjiang figures are import prices, and the Guangzhou figures averaged from what were probably wholesale prices. It is quite unclear, however, what the Shanghai prices were.

26. Reference to Table 6.1 will also show that import prices for raw cotton rose more rapidly than export prices between the 1880s and the 1920s. This is yet another example of the depreciation of silver protecting China's market.

27. Six market towns according to L.L. Chang (1932), p. 450, but four according to Zhang Liluan (1933), p. 3.

28. The correlation coefficient for all years for which reports are available for the price of rice in Shanghai (as summarized in Table 4.2) and the price of rice in Wujin (as summarized in Table 4.5) is 0.995.

29. The rise in the price of land is also documented in J.L. Buck (1937-2), pp. 168–9, and Ke Dawei and Lu Hongji (1980).

30. The standardized regression coefficient of annual prices of land on the annual prices of rice in Wujin is 0.858, and the variance explained (R^2) is 0.736.

31. World production of silk had increased from 26.5 to 61.4 metric tons between 1916 and 1929, and rayon from 14.2 to 198.9 metric tons. See Quanguo jingji weiyuanhui (1936), p. 8.

32. *Zhongguo jingji nianjian 1936*, pp. E151–1 and 'China's silk trade during 1935' (1936), p. 339.

33. See Dickens H. Leavens (1939), pp. 293–312, for the effects of the Silver Purchase Act on China in 1934–5. The discussion has recently been set in a broader perspective in Thomas Rawski (forthcoming) and Brandt and Sargent (1987). Rawski notes that while silver was drained from China by the Silver Purchase Act the volume of money in circulation was actually increasing, owing to increased bank deposits and notes. He argues that it fits the impression that can be documented from urban wages, railway haulage, and industrial production indices that the effects of the depression might have been less marked in China than in the United States, but acknowledges its severity in export-oriented rural areas. Brandt and Sargent accept this argument, but do not point out the reality of the rural depression.

34. Consider the following from Fei Hsiao-tung (1939), p. 185: 'The practical difficulty of ejecting a tenant is to find a substitute. Absentee landlords do not cultivate the land themselves. Outsiders from the villages will not be welcomed into the community if they come at the expense of old members. Villagers are not willing to cut the throat of their own members who for any good reason cannot pay their rent. In these circumstances it is in the interest of the landlord to tolerate the default in the hope of getting rent in the future. This situation does not really challenge the status of the landlord, since there are positive sanctions to enforce payment of rent whenever this [?] is possible'. Rent collection must certainly be closely tied to village membership, as Chapter 8 below will explain.

35. J.L. Buck (1937b), p. 61.

36. For a more detailed discussion, see David Faure (1978), pp. 392–404.

37. I am indebted to Phil Yang and Kathryn Bernhardt for making me consider evidence for commuted rent in Jiangsu before the mid-nineteenth century. Examples may be found in Kobayashi Kazumi (1967) and Liu Yongcheng (1980).

38. The standardized regression coefficient of annual commuted rates for rent collection in Suzhou on the annual average price of rice in Shanghai is 0.925 for the period 1870 to 1906 and 0.889 for the period 1908 to 1931.

39. For a discussion of the magnitude of the commutation rate relative to the price of rice in Suzhou, see David Faure (1978), pp. 394–6. For ease of comparison, the rent commutation rates as given in Muramatsu (1970), p. 726 and the year-end price of rice in Shanghai, as given in Shanghai shangye chuxu yinhang diaochabu (1931a), pp. 92–3, are listed below.

	Rent	Price of Rice
1912	4.473 (100)	6.67 (100)
1913	4.248 (95)	7.02 (105)
1914	4.454 (100)	6.59 (99)
1915	4.656 (104)	6.63 (94)
1916	4.445 (99)	6.28 (91)
1917	4.434 (99)	6.09 (91)
1918	4.468 (100)	6.35 (95)
1922	6.624 (148)	11.01 (165)
1923	7.024 (157)	10.38 (156)
1927	9.654 (216)	10.34 (155)
1928	8.421 (188)	11.59 (173)

The rent commutation rate is given in dollars per *shi* of rice and the price of rice in dollars per *shi*. The Suzhou *shi* was 0.88 of the Shanghai *shi*, and a Shanghai *shi* of rice weighed approximately 1.5 piculs.

40. Qiao Qiming (1926), p. 91; *Zhongguo jingji nianjian 1934*, pp. G40–1; *Zhongguo jingji nianjian 1936*, p. G123; Fei Hsiao-tung (1939), p. 189; He Menglei (n.d.), pp. 33154–5.

41. Chen Han-seng (1936), pp. 54–6.

42. Yu Lin (1932), p. 403.

43. See Shanghaishi shehuiju (1930), pp. 103–6. However, in nearby Songjiang, according to *Zhongguo jingji nianjian 1936*, p. G128, a fixed money rent was paid on cotton land, and a commuted rent on paddy land.

44. Zhang Huiqun (n.d.), pp. 31839–40.

45. Chen Han-seng (1936), pp. 54–5.

46. Zhan Ran (1934), p. 24, Shen Shike (1934), pp. 30942–51.

47. Reports on the *yazu* are among the most confusing in the studies conducted in the 1920s and 1930s. Chen Hansheng (Chen Han-seng (1936) pp. 46–7) seems to have counted as rent deposits all customary dues required at the time the tenancy contract was entered into, including the feast for the landlord. Other writers stress the relation of the *yazu* to security of tenure (He Menglei (n.d.), pp. 33161–3), and reduction in rent (Chen Zhengmo (1936), p. 20). I do not think there is any indication that the *yazu* became any more or less prevalent in the 1920s and 1930s than in earlier years. See also Chapter 8, note 24.

48. For examples of the sale of the crop before harvest, see Wang Nanping (1936), p. 618, Zhao Zongxu (1936), pp. 46043–5, and Zhang Youyi (1957), vol. 2, pp. 528–30.

49. David Faure (1978), pp. 390–400, and Robert Ash (1976), pp. 34–9 sum up the documentation on Jiangsu. For Guangdong, see *Zhongguo jingji nianjian 1934*, p. G34, and Guoli Zhongshan daxue nongke xueyuan (1925, 1929, 1933).

50. One reason for the difference is probably that the rent due to most public institutions was frozen at rates that were current at the time the landholdings were established. See, for instance, examples in *Xuxiu Jiangdu xianzhi* (1926), pp. 8 *shang*/30a–33a, and *Qingyuan xianzhi* (1937), pp. 15/53a–54a. Another reason is that these institutional holdings were often covers for claims exerted by local groups in land reclamation. See Chen Han-seng (1936), pp. 29–31 and 45–49, and *Jiangyin xian xuzhi* (1920), p. 6/4b.

51. Zhang Huiqun (n.d.), pp. 31823–36.

52. Chen Han-seng (1936), pp. 62–3.

53. Guoli Zhongshan daxue nongke xueyuan (1925, 1926, 1927), reports on Nanhai, Deqing, Gaoyao, Sihui, Yangchun, Enping, and Yangshan.

54. C.W. Howard and K.P. Buswell (1925), p. 47.

55. Guoli Zhongshan daxue nongke xueyuan (1929), p. 135.

56. Stanley F. Wright (1935) p.11: 'In April 1932 the Inspector General of Customs Revenue Dollar Account was opened in the Central Bank of China for the receipt of revenue remittances made in National Dollars and from the 10th March 1933 the Haikwan tael, which had been the Customs currency of account for 90 years, was abolished, and a new Standard Dollar, weighing 26.6971 grammes and composed of 88 percent silver and 12 percent copper, was introduced. From the latter date the rate of conversion between Shanghai taels and standard dollars was fixed at *Sh.Tls.* 71.5 = *Standard* $100, and duties formerly payable in Haikwan taels were converted into standard dollars at the rate of *Hk.Tls.* 100 = $155.80'.

57. Chen Han-seng (1936), p. 66.

58. Figures for the median price of rice quoted in this paragraph are taken from Zhang Shantu (1930) and *Guangdong jingji nianjian 1940*, p.K73, and for silk export from the latter, pp. G87–8.

59. Shen Shike (1934), pp. 30931–3.

60. Compare Robert Ash (1976), p. 39, which comes to a similar conclusion.

61. Xu Hongkui (1934), pp. 46423–4.

62. In land registration in Wuxi in the 1930s, it was found that many claims to holdings were based on mortgage deeds, many of which were made decades before. See Yuan Yinhuai (1935), pp. 18040–1.

63. Rong An (1927), p. 112.

64. Feng Hefa (1935), p. 25, Liu Chengzhang (n.d.), pp. 47588–9.

65. Chen Han-seng (1936), pp. 93–4, Fan Yijun (1983), p. 145.

66. Chen Han-seng (1936), p. 93.

67. Chen Han-seng (1936), pp. 94–5.

68. Luo Gengmo (1934), pp. 792–6, quoting statistics published by Jiangsu Farmers' Bank; Wang Yuquan, 'Zhongguo nongcun hezuo yundong', *Zhongguo jingji* (1935), vol. 3, no. 6, quoted in Zhang Youyi (1957), vol. 3, p. 191, and Huang Hao, 'Nongcun xin jinrong zhidu', *Jingji pinglun* (1935), vol. 2, no. 6, pp. 1–2, quoted in Zhang Youyi (1957), vol. 3, p. 196.

69. For a selection of reports on commercial bankruptcy in these years, see *Gedi jinrong zhi jinkuang* (1934), Liu Chengzhang (n.d.), pp. 47527–37, Xie Xueying (1935), pp. 86–7.

70. I refer to the substantial literature concerning the *lougui* in Qing dynasty records that stemmed from the perceived different social statuses of the *xiangshen* (rural gentry) and the *xuli* (underlings in the county government offices), and the absence of the literature in the Republic. The change had probably arisen from the absorption of local politics into the county government's administration in the late Qing reforms and the decline of the county magistrate's influence in the Republic. For some of these changes, see Philip Kuhn (1975).

71. For background on the grain tax and the land tax, see Yeh-chien Wang (1973).

72. David Faure (1978), p. 438, n. 123.

73. Zhongyang daxue jingji ziliaoshi (1935), pp. 101–2.

74. *Chuansha xianzhi* (1936), p. 8/25b.

75. Zhongyang daxue jingji ziliaoshi (1935).

76. *Gaoyao xianzhi* (1947), pp. 308–9.

77. For a more detailed discussion, see note 39.

78. J.L. Buck (1937a), pp. 345–7 comes to a similar conclusion.

79. The indices for prices received and priced paid by farmers quoted in this paragraph are weighted. The weights used in calculating the index of cereal prices received by farmers take into account five cereals as well as broadbeans and soya beans, and the index of prices paid by farmers for farm produce, processed foodstuffs, items of clothing, fuel, and such sundries as soap, nails, and umbrellas. For details, see Raeburn and Ko (1937a), pp. 255–7.

Notes to Chapter 5

1. For background on rural marketing, see C.K. Yang (1944), G. William Skinner (1964–5) and Gilbert Rozman (1973) and (1982). The operation of rural markets is, however, a largely unstudied subject.

2. Jiang Luo (1935), p. 293.

3. A recent attempt to examine the question of the openness of local trade is Susan Mann (1987). The chapter on rural marketing in the Republican era (pp. 171–99) argues that the proliferation of brokers made it extremely competitive.

4. Fei Hsiao-tung (1939), p. 260: 'Rice is produced partly for selling and partly for consumption. The amount of reserve does not necessarily fluctuate according to the price. Each household will try to reserve enough rice for a year's consumption. A high market price of rice will not induce the producer to sell his reserves, because the future price level is uncertain. But a low price will force people to sell more rice to the market; this is because the amount of money income needed by each household is more or less known at the time of harvest when the tenants are required to pay their rent in terms of money.'

5. Philip C.C. Huang (1985), pp. 162–3.

6. Although Songjiang was a major cotton-producing area, the report makes clear that of the total value of crops marketed in this village, 96.4 per cent arose from the sale of rice. See Mantetsu Shanghai Jimusho Chōsashitsu (1941b), p. 174. I understand that Philip C.C. Huang has in the last few years been able to combine the reports on this particular area with interviews and field research, and I look forward to his forthcoming volume on the southern Jiangsu rural economy.

7. David Faure (1978), pp. 396–8.

8. Fei Hsiao-tung (1939), pp. 240–62.

9. David Faure (1978), p. 405.

10. G. William Skinner (1964–5), p.207.

11. Compare Gilbert Rozman (1973), pp. 113–14.

12. For cases, see *Rongshi pudie* (1929), p. 16/21a–22a, *Shunde-Longjiang xiangzhi* (1926), p. 51a–b; *Xiangshan xianzhi* (1920), biography of Li Shanghua on p. 11/28b; *Chaozhou zhi* (1946), pp. 62a–63b; *Enping xianzhi* (1934), p. 7/15a; and *Changzhao hezhigao* (1904), pp. 5/1b and 17/11a.

13. *Shunde xianzhi* (1929), pp. 20/11a–b.

12. *Panyu xian xuzhi* (1931), p. 22/11b.

15. Compare Gilbert Rozman (1973), pp. 151–2, 157–8.

16. *Funing xian xinzhi* (1934), p. 14/2b.

17. *Qingyuan xianzhi* (1937), pp. 14/17a–24b.

18. For some examples, see *Qingyuan xianzhi* (1937), pp. 3/46a–52a, 55b, 56b, and *Nanhai xian gongbao* (1928), no. 15, pp. 2–4.

19. David Faure (1982).

20. Qiao Qiming (1934).

21. John A. Brim (1974) and David Faure (1986), pp. 70–86, and 100–27.

22. Daniel Harrison Kulp (1925).

23. Compare C.K. Yang (1944), p. 15: 'The factor of walking distance and the minimum area necessary to support a market seem to have been recognized by the local community. For there is an unwritten law in Chowping that, no new market is allowed to be established within five li or 1.8 miles of another market already in existence. The same rule exists in counties surrounding Chowping. According to the local people, the purpose of this unwritten law is to eliminate unnecessary competition and to protect the interest of "market heads" whose chief function is to collect sales taxes for the government on a business basis'.The passage implies that economic control complemented political control, not that competition was not possible. See also pp. 23–4.

24. Records on local produce are too numerous to list in full. A lengthy listing of local

234   NOTES TO PAGES 98–102

products in southern Jiangsu may be found in *Jiangsu* No. 5 (1903), and those in Guangdong are discussed at length in the reports given in Guoli Zhongshan daxue nongke xueyuan (1925, 1929, 1933). These products were the subject of a substantial compilation by the Post Office in Jiaotongbu youzheng zongju (1937).

25. C.W. Howard and K.P. Buswell (1925), pp. 61–2, 78–9, and 105–11.
26. See examples quoted in David Faure (1978), p. 422 and (1985), p. 11.
27. A report from *NCH*, 7.5.1897, p. 816, from northern Jiangsu: 'The continued rain in March drowned much wheat in the low plains, and the people who had wheat or breadstuff began hoarding it. The elders of the market towns forebade selling grain in quantities greater than two pecks. And if anyone was seen packing grain on the donkeys, the people felt free to rob, and they would cut open the bags with scissors or what not and the man who was driving would be helpless: "My name is so and so. Tell the Magistrate I did it and I will tell him I was starving".' See also R. Bin Wong (1982).
28. Shehui jingji diaochasuo (1935a), pp. 1–6, 15–18.
29. Shehui jingji diaochasuo (n.d.), pp. 13–15.
30. Yang Jicheng (1936), p. 8.
31. Wuxi mishi diaocha (1936), vol. 3, no. 7, pp. 61–2.
32. The clearest discussion of the connection between the warehouse and the bank, albeit in reference to a market outside Jiangsu and Guangdong, is Ma Yinchu (1929), pp. 117–23 and 151–7.
33. Shehui jingji diaochasuo (1935a), pp. 10–11.
34. 'Wuxi mishi diaocha' (1936), vol. 3, no. 8, pp. 21–2, and Shehui jingji diaochasuo (n.d.), pp. 21–2. See also *NCH*, 15.3.1913, p. 803 quoted from the *China Times, Trade Report Supplement:* 'The staple produces of Wusieh [Wuxi] are silk cocoons and rice, which are largely exported. In spring and summer every year, the cocoon trade is in full swing, amounting to between $5,000,000 and $6,000,000 in value. The rice handled during the autumn and winter seasons is worth about the same amount. But the banks in Wusieh are capitalized too low to meet the financial requirements of the merchants at all times, so it often happens that bankers at Soochow now and then net profits which might have gone to the Wusieh banks.

'Wusieh has storehouses for cocoons and barns for rice and other cereals, owned by wealthy natives. But as the majority of these buildings were built on old methods without much attention being paid to safety against fire, the insurance premium paid is usually very high. Now that the town is passed many times a day by trains of the Shanghai-Nanking Railway, some impetus must be given to its enterprising people to reform these old ways and to introduce novelties in trade.'
35. Yang Jicheng (1936), pp. 31–4.
36. Nongcun fuxing weiyuanhui (1934), p. 85.
37. Shanghai shangye chuxu yinhang diaochabu (1931), pp. 35–40.
38. Chen Qihui (n.d.), p. 26152.
39. Shanghai shehui kexueyuan jingji yanjiusuo (1980), vol. 1, pp. 5–13, 50–1, and 95–103.
40. Shiyebu guoji maoyiju (1933), Chapter 8, p. 351, and Shehui jingji diaochasuo (1935b), pp. 1–3.
41. Yang Yinpu (1930), pp. 46–7, and 199–216.
42. C.W. Howard and K.P. Buswell (1925), p. 107.
43. See Note 42, p. 16: 'About 80 per cent of the Canton banks are financed by Shuntak capital . . . A great amount of business of Canton and other towns of the province depends upon this district [Shunde] and its operations in silk for financial backing'.
44. Luo Sibing (1935), p. 110, and compare also *NCH*, 3.10.1914, p. 49, quoting from a letter by the chairman of the Shanghai Silk Trade Committee to the Shanghai 'Taotai': 'It is estimated that 3,500 piculs of silk per month are turned out by the Shanghai filatures, so in the six months or the latter half of the Chinese year, 21,000 piculs can be made; at Tls. 900 per picul as capital required, the total amount needed will be Tls. 18,900,000'.

45. *NCH*, 10.6.1911, p. 674. Also 20.4.1912, p. 164, and 8.6.1912, p. 670.
46. Lillian M. Li (1981), pp. 192–3, and Okumura Tetsu (1978).

Notes to Chapter 6

1. W.W. Rostow (1978), pp. 663–9.
2. This statement takes the side of Kang Chao (1977) and goes against Richard Arnold Kraus (1968) and Albert Feuerwerker (1970). All three authors arrived at the conclusions by the same methodology but made use of different estimates. Essentially, in the absence of direct numerical reports on the output of hand-spun yarn and hand-woven cloth, all three sought to deduce what these figures might be from estimates of raw cotton available for hand spinning and yarn available (including machine-spun yarn, both home-manufactured and imported) for hand-weaving. The relevant figures from their estimates are presented below:

	Feuerwerker (1871–80)	Kraus (1870)	Feuerwerker (1901–10)
Cotton available (mill. piculs)	7.1	10.7	6.3
Hand-spun yarn (mill. piculs)	4.9	8.9	2.4
Hand-woven cloth (mill. sq. yds.)	1,612	3,170	1,850
Yarn consumed by hand-woven cloth (mill. piculs)	4.8	8.9	5.5

	Chao (1905–9)	Kraus (1925–7)	Chao (1924–7)
Cotton available (mill. piculs)	10.4	14.1	14.9
Hand-spun yarn (mill. piculs)	3.9	4.4	2.9
Hand-woven cloth (mill. sq. yds.)	2,600*	3,630	845
Yarn consumed by hand-woven cloth (mill. piculs)	7.4	10.2	7.6

Note: * Corrected with reference to B. Reynolds (1977).

For additional sources on the continued use of hand-spun yarn, see 'Guangzhou tubuye diaocha' (1937), Fan Yijun (1982), and Xia Lingen (1984).

The problem with all these estimates is that the quantity of cotton available, taken as the quantity grown in China plus imports or minus exports, is basically guesswork. Feuerwerker's figure for 1871–80 is supposed to be a maximum estimate; Kraus' for 1870 is the minimum he thinks possible. What does this variation mean? In terms of production figures supplied by Feuerwerker, each 1.0 million piculs of cotton produced work for 1.1 million man-years of hand spinning and 0.37 million man-years of hand weaving. He has estimated the loss in work between 1871–80 and 1901–10 of the magnitude of 2.43 million man-years. This loss would, therefore, be made up for if the cotton available in 1871–80 has been overestimated by 2 million piculs. For two reasons, I think this is more than likely. Firstly, the only reliable estimates in the above table are Kraus' figures for 1925–7 and Chao's for 1924–7, both based on reports from the 1920s. Given the expansion of cotton acreage that we know from descriptive sources, I find it quite incredible that the amount of cotton available for all uses increased by a mere 32 per cent (by Kraus's estimate) between 1870 and the late 1920s. Moreover, it should be noted that although Kraus is meticulous in formulating his estimates for 1918–37, his study on earlier estimates, limited by the lack of information, is highly speculative. Ultimately, the 1870 figure for cotton available is calculated on the assumption that China's population in 1870 (itself a questionable figure) consumed per capita 8.1 sq. yd. of cotton cloth, a figure that he took from estimates made in the 1930s (see Kraus (1968), p. 159). One would have thought that per capita consumption of cloth would have varied with the price of yarn, and per-capita consumption in 1870 must have been considerably lower than in the 1930s. Kraus's estimate of cotton available in 1870 should, therefore, be revised substantially downwards. Secondly, for the same reason that per capita consumption of cloth would have varied over time, consumption of cotton for padding, by all accounts the major use of cotton other than for spinning, would have varied. In this respect, it is important to note how the introduction of machine spinning would have affected cotton prices: as demand for cotton increased, its price rose, hence the increase in acreage. Over time, one should expect, therefore, contraction in per-capita consumption of cotton for padding. As all the above estimates allow for 2.0 to 2.5 million piculs of cotton for padding in any one year, any revision that permits an increase in consumption for padding towards 1870 and a decrease towards the 1920s would substantially increase the amount of cotton that was available for spinning towards the later period. I am quite prepared to accept Feuerwerker's scenario that there was a substantial reduction in cotton available for hand-spinning when machine mills were first introduced into China, that is, in the period 1895–1911, but given the estimates here for the 1920s, I find it hard to accept that the loss in jobs was not made up for by the extra yarn that came to be available for hand spinning. It should also be noted that the income that might have been earned from weaving was substantially higher than that from spinning. Of the three studies noted here, Chao is the only one to have made this point.

Documentation that supports this interpretation may, in fact, be found in the studies of Tang Wenqi (1985) and Lin Gang (1985) on the connection between hand-woven cloth in rural Nantong and machine spinning that was an important industry in the county city. They suggest that the cheaper yarn provided the impetus for considerable expansion in hand weaving from 1904 to 1925, after which period it lost to foreign competition in the north eastern provinces, which were large native-cloth consumers. In a slightly different version of his 1985 article published in Sichuansheng Zhongguo jingjishi xuehui (1986), Tang Wenqi dates the decline from 1922, but the additional evidence he presents makes it amply clear that the decline set in in 1927–28.

Reference should also be made to Xu Xinwu (1988) which argues for considerable contraction of hand-spun cloth from the mid-nineteenth century to the 1930s. Xu's figures imply that one-third of all cotton cloth consumed in China in 1913 was imported, and that 45 per cent in 1936 was machine-manufactured, in addition to 12 per cent imports. These estimates seem quite excessive. I suspect the tables in this paper are compiled from independent statistical series that have not been adjusted for internal biases.

3. According to Shanghai shangye chuxu yinhang diaochabu (1931b), p. 18, in the late 1920s, each year, Shanghai absorbed 300,000 piculs of cotton from Nantong, 700,000 from its immediate surroundings, and 150,000 from Taicang and Changshu. This should amount to more than half the output of cotton in Jiangsu.

4. T.R. Bannister (1933a), pp. 123–4.

5. William H. Ukers (1935), vol. 1, pp. 147–52 and 179, and vol. 2, p. 235.

6. See Guoli Zhongshan daxue nongke xueyuan (1925), pp. 246–7, 254–5, and 316–17.

7. For a comprehensive discussion of the sugar industry and trade at Shantou, see Fan Yijun (1983).

8. H.C. Prinsen Geerligs and R.J. Prinsen Geerligs (1912), p. 121.

9. MC, Shantou 1884, p. 313.

10. MC, Shantou 1880, p. 245; 1887, p. 253.

11. MC, Shantou 1882–91, pp. 526–7, 1892–1901 pp. 154–5.

12. Prices quoted by T.R. Bannister (1933b), p. 179, for imported refined sugar are as follows:

	Hk.Tls./picul
1882–6	5.47
1887–91	8.91
1892–6	5.71
1897–1901	5.87
1902–6	5.35
1907–11	5.30
1912–16	6.50
1917–21	9.38
1922–6	9.61
1927–31	7.61

13. MC, Shantou 1902, p. 583.

14. Guoli Guangdong daxue nongke xueyuan (1925), pp. 7–8, on the production of sugar in Panyu county: 'Ten years ago, that is, in the early years of Xuantong [sic], the amount of sugar produced was three to four times the amount in recent years. At the time much white sugar was produced ... In recent years, the amount of white sugar produced has dropped to almost zero. As for the reasons, firstly, banditry has been rife after the revolution, and without peace, people dare not set up sugar sheds for processing cane; secondly, imported sugar is of good quality and cheap, while local sugar is poor, and, thirdly, sugar sheds have closed and cannot offer capital on mortgage for cane-growers. By the 5th year of the Republic [1916], there was no sugar industry to speak of here [Panyu county]. After the First World War, the price of sugar rose daily, and some cane farmers resumed their former trade. However, the sugar that was produced was only made into pressed brown sugar [*piantang*]'.

15. H.C. Prinsen Geerligs and R.J. Prinsen Geerligs (1912), p. 124. Figures quoted on p. 130 also show that, in addition to wages to native workers and rent, plantations had to pay substantially for the wages of their European staff, cultural expenses, and for the building of roads and bridges.

16. H.C. Prinsen Geerligs and R.J. Prinsen Geerligs (1912), p. 138 quotes the following expenses for the production of 1 picul (=136 lbs.) of sugar in Java (figures in florin, 1 florin = 1s.8d.):

'Employees	0.50
Transport of cane	0.60
Wages	0.14
Packing	0.16
Maintenance	0.32
Commission	0.27
Agriculture	2.00
Fuel	0.07
Sundries	0.07
Transport of sugar	0.31
Diverse expenses	0.17
New machinery	0.59
Interest	0.30
Total	5.50'

Cost breakdowns for 25 locations in Panyu, Zengcheng, Dongguan, and Zhongshan in Guangdong in about 1921 are given in Guoli Guangdong daxue nongke xueyuan (1925). An

English translation of most of this important report may be found in 'A study of the sugar industry in China' (1927).

17. 'A study of the sugar industry in China' (1927), pp. 964–6.

18. H.C. Prinsen Geerligs and R.J. Prinsen Geerligs (1912), p. 131.

19. MC, Shantou 1878, p. 246.

20. For recent studies on the subject, see Lillian M. Li (1981), Robert Eng (1986a), and Xu, Shen, and Tang (1986).

21. 'The finest quality of China silks is known as Steam Filatures. These are reeled on most modern lines, and in these there is much more uniformity of size than in either of the two classes mentioned above [that is, Tsatlee and Re-reels] . . . This kind of silk finds great favour in the British market, and, in spite of its expensiveness, it is largely used in the manufacture of silk fabrics.' Ratan C. Rawley (1919), p. 245.

22. Lillian M. Li (1981), pp. 24–30 and 72–81, Cheng Yaoming (1985).

23. This discussion has not taken account of domestic consumption of silk, which Lillian M. Li (1981), pp. 100–3, thinks was quite stable but Xu, Shen, and Tang (1986), p. 47, estimates to have doubled between 1871 and 1913.

24. I have taken these figures from Lillian M. Li (1981), pp. 86–88.

25. NCH, 3.5.1873, p. 387, 10.5.1915 pp. 388–9, 24.8.1918, pp. 478–9, 9.4.1921, p. 54.

26. On the expansion of silk in Wuxi in the 1920s, see Zhang Diken (1985).

27. Zhang Youyi (1957), vol. 2, p. 151, quoting Lu Guanying, 'Jiangsu Wuxi xian ershi nianlai zhi siyeguan' in Nongshang gongbao 1921.

28. Shenbao, 14.5.Guangxu 6, quoted in Li Wenzhi (1957), p. 427, MC (1917), and Yan Xuexi (1986).

29. As late as 1929, a report on the cocoon crops in Jiangsu and Zhejiang noted that sericulture in these two provinces was pursued by farmers 'as a sideline' (B.T. Chang (1929), p. 589).

30. Cheng Yaoming (1985), Robert Y. Eng (1986), pp. 99–10, and 117–18.

31. C.W. Howard and K.P. Buswell (1925), p. 16.

32. MC (1917) and Tōa Dōbunkai (1920).

33. David Faure (1978), p. 370, and Chen Ciyu (1983).

34. Dongguan xianzhi (1927), p. 13/3b.

35. Panyu xian xuzhi (1931), p. 12/35b.

36. Guangxu Sihui xianzhi (1925), p. 1/93b.

37. Gaoyao xianzhi (1938), p. 11/2a.

38. Shehui jingji diaochasuo (1935c), p. 49.

39 Guangdong liangshi diaojie weiyuanhui (1935), p. 6, quoting C.C. Chang, China's Food Problem (1934).

40. Cai Zhixiang (1981) discusses embargoes in Hunan Province in the 1920s and 1930s and their results on the rice trade, which affected the whole of the lower Changjiang.

41. Sarasin Viraphol (1977), pp. 81 and 90.

42. Jiang Luo (1935), p. 293; and MC, Shantou 1902, p. 583: 'The import of Bangkok rice, which came to 1,059,954 piculs, was quite unprecedented. Early in the year it became evident that, owing to the want of rain, the spring crops must be ruined, and that large quantities of rice must be brought in to supply the deficiency. Rice from the Yangtze [Changjiang] valley, which is the most popular here, was at that time quoted at $4.70 to $5.10 per picul, while Bangkok rice could be laid down here at $3.60 to $4. With a difference of over a dollar in its favour, the foreign grain was able to command a fair share of the business.'

43. MC, Wuhu 1897, pp. 184–5: 'Large quantities of rice from Saigon and further supplies from Kwangsi [Guangxi], where the opening of Wuchow [Wuzhou] and Samshui [Sanshui] is said to have facilitated the down-river traffic in rice, flooded the Canton market to such an extent that prevailing rates there fell at times to a point actually lower than the prices ruling here. The uncertainties of the Canton market and the narrow margin of profit left on the exported article after the payment of all charges induced traders in the interior to

seek for other outlets, and, as a consequence, considerable quantities of rice which might otherwise have come to the port were sent by native boats from Ning-kuo-fu [Ningguo *fu*] to Chehkiang [Zhejiang] and from Lu-chou-fu [Luzhou *fu*] to Kiangsi [Jiangxi], in both of which provinces, fortunately for the Anhui traders, a demand for rice had sprung up.'

44. Chen Bozhuang (1936), p. 107, notes that some of this import was related to military requisition.

45. Chen Qihui (n.d.), p. 26040.

46. Chen Baozhuang (1936), A.J.H. Latham and Larry Neal (1983), and Loren Brandt (1985).

47. See Chapter 4, for the depreciation, and MC, Wuhu 1898, pp. 191–2, *NCH*, 28.3.1898, p. 542, 18.6.1902, p.1211, 27.7.1906, p. 206, 14.9.1906, p.635.

48. Hong Kong Government (1920), pp. 1–3; *NCH*, 15.2.1919, p. 390, 8.3.1919, pp.605, 607–8, 22.5.1919, pp. 456–60, 16.8.1919, p.410, 27.9.1919, p.816, 15.5.1920, p.373, 12.6.1920, p.663, 24.7.1920, p.230.

49. This observation appears in a statement made by the Guild of Rice Hongs in Shanghai, quoted in *NCH*, 25.6.1921, p. 882. This relates to the problem of hoarding which was widely discussed in contemporary sources, which could have made a difference in the short term, but not in the long term.

50. Loren Brandt (1985).

51. W.F. Spalding (1920).

52. Zhang Youyi (1957), vol. 3, pp. 607, 623.

53. Following upon the boom from 1921 to 1927, the number of silk filatures in Wuxi doubled from 1928 to 1931 (Gao Jingyue [1983], p. 103) as bank credit expanded considerably (Gu Jirui (1985), pp. 110–11). This is as one would expect, given the inflow of silver in these years.

54. Li Heng (1932), p. 425, quoting the *Xibao*.

55. Chen Han-seng (1936), p. 66.

56. Fei Hsiao-tung (1939), pp. 202–3.

57. *NCH*, 12.1.1932, p. 45, on Wuxi: 'Out of 48 filatures, only 5 are running. The farmers have a double load to carry as well as the shopkeepers, since in spite of having a 70 per cent crop they cannot sell to the hongs, because the latter have no money'. See also Zhang Youyi (1957), vol. 3, p. 626.

58. Okumura Tetsu (1978), Robert Y. Eng (1986a), pp. 161–2.

59. Chen Bozhuang (1936), p. 123. For comparison, see Cheng Siok-hwa (1968), p. 73, and James C. Ingram (1964), pp. 102–26, for prices in Burma and Vietnam.

60. Chen Qihui (n.d.), pp. 26185–93.

61. Zhang Youyi (1957), vol. 3, p. 415.

62. Zhang Youyi (1957), vol. 3, pp. 617–19.

63. Dickens H. Leavens (1939), pp. 257–326, Zhang Youyi (1957), vol. 3, pp. 679–80, Chen Qihui (n.d.), p. 26196.

64. Chen Han-seng (1936), pp. 85–6.

65. Fei Hsiao-tung (1939), pp. 189–91.

66. Zhang Liluan (1933), pp. 174–5, Qian Junrui (1935), pp. 43–4, Xu Dixin (1935), p. 53, Zhang Youyi (1957), vol. 3, pp. 1020–2.

67. The countries of origin of wheat imported into Shanghai are apparent from the following table from Shehui jingji diaochasuo (1935b), p. 17. Figures are expressed in thousands of quintals (1 quintal = 1.65 piculs):

	U.S.A.	Australia	Canada	Argentina	Others	Total
1932	1,187	3,796	1,523	—	76	6,582
1933	109	6,796	787	885	—	8,577
1934	2,848	267	85	805	76	4,081

68. Zhang Youyi (1957), vol. 3, pp. 438–44.

69. For a different explanation, see Chen Ciyu's comments appended to Wang Shuhuai (1984).

70. John K. Chang (1969), p. 79, gives an annual index for the production of consumer goods in China of the following order: 1929, 80.9; 1930, 85.3; 1931, 91.7; 1932, 93.7; 1933, 100.0; 1934, 98.1; 1935, 93.5; 1936, 99.6; and 1937, 68.6. The index is based entirely on the production of cotton yarn and cloth for these years, but his discussion of the progress experienced in other industries on pp. 39–54 gives the same impression. However, there was little increase in the number of flour mills in the Shanghai area in these years according to Yan Zhongping (1963), pp. 162–4. .

71. Richard A. Kraus (1980), p. 57, gives the following figures for the number of spindles in place at year end : 1929, 3,767,000; 1930, 4,061,000; 1931, 4,408,000; 1932, 4,597,000; 1933, 4,734,000; 1934, 4,835,000; 1935, 5,025,000; 1936, 5,103,000.

72. 'There are many reasons why modern mills are obliged to use imported wheat instead of Chinese grain. In the first place, Chinese wheat is mostly inferior in quality, and not suitable for making high-grade flour. Secondly, the difficulty and high cost of transportation in the northern districts of the Yangtse [Changjiang] create great reluctance among millers along the Nanking-Shanghai Railway to buy wheat from that part of the country, thus giving an opportunity for foreign exporters to sell on the Chinese market. Moreover, the fact that Northerners consume more wheat than rice makes it impossible for them to dispose of any considerable quantity of grain for milling. In fact, what the mills collect is only the little left over after sufficient wheat has been set aside by farmers for their own food. Lastly, the large number of old-style mills in rural districts must have taken quite a large proportion of the available wheat supply from their modern rivals'. ('Flour industry in Kiangsu', (1933), p. 42)

73. Richard A. Kraus (1980), p. 48.

74. Xu Daofu (1983), pp. 204 and 209, and Richard A. Kraus (1980), pp. 13–37 for a discussion of the accuracy of these figures.

75. I have no good explanation for the trend. Some attempts were made in these years by the government to control the cotton industry, which, however, did not lead to significant changes. Perhaps export was indeed kept out because the local produce was competitive.

76. Notwithstanding considerable smuggling, estimated at 2.3 million piculs per annum in 1930 and 1931, 2.1 in 1932, 1.2 in 1933, and 1.5 in 1934. See Fukudai Kōshi (1940), p. 118.

77. 'Kwangtung government sugar factories', 1928, p. 158.

78. Six sugar factories were planned but only three were built: two started production in December 1934 and one in January 1935. Because of difficulties in securing supplies, the factories operated only for three months in 1935, producing 149,000 piculs of fine and 522,000 piculs of crude sugar. Considerable corruption was suspected in connection with the factories. Feng Rui, Director of Agriculture and Forestry in Guangdong Province, responsible for the factories, was made the scapegoat for the charges and executed in 1936. See 'Kwangtung government sugar factories' and *Guangdong tangye yu Feng Rui*.

79. H.C. Prinsen Geerligs and R.J. Prinsen Geerligs (1938), pp. 76–84.

80. Xie Xueying (1935), pp. 124–7; Chen Han-seng (1936), p. 69; and Chen Ta (1939), p. 33.

Notes to Chapter 7

1. In recent years, 'risk avoidance' has been introduced as a central theme in the discussion of China's traditional rural economy. James C. Scott (1976) was probably the stimulus for the argument, and Philip C.C. Huang (1985) is a crucial application. One should be careful, of course, not to assume that subsistence agriculture did not involve risks.

2. Such studies are too numerous to list in full. For an example, see Yan Xinzhe (1935).

Contrast this with J.L. Buck (1937a), pp. 437–72, for a very different approach. Instead of reducing income and expenses to single figures, Buck asked his respondents to assess changes in living conditions in qualitative terms. His report provides considerably more information on nutrition, clothing material, housing, and furniture than most other surveys.
3. Fei Hsiao-tung (1939), p. 136.
4. It should be noted that Qiao's survey of Nantong and Kunshan was not an enumeration of actual observations but, like many surveys of the Republican period, a collection of informed opinions from local people. In this case, the opinions of 217 local people were incorporated to draw up the tables. The report does not make clear how they were integrated, but presumably the values entered into the tables were averages obtained from these reports. The Shanghai Social Affairs Bureau's survey, in contrast, was an enumeration of a predetermined sample from 15 districts on the outskirts of Shanghai, consisting of 49 owner-cultivator households, 47 half-owner households and 44 tenant households. The reports may be found in Qiao Qiming (1926) and Shanghaishi shehuiju (1930). See also Alfred Kaiming Chiu (1933), pp. 171–3, for a discussion of Qiao's survey.
5. David Faure (1979), pp. 72–3.
6. Qiao Qiming (1926), p. 81.
7. Qiao Qiming (1926), pp. 100–2.
8. Shanghaishi shehuiju (n.d.), pp. 14–17.
9. Shanghaishi shehuiju (n.d.), pp. 4–14.
10. For example, Xu Hongkui (1934), Zhao Zongxu (1936), Liu Chengzheng (n.d.).
11. Chen Han-seng (1933), p. 21.
12. Ou Jiluan (n.d.), pp. 137–40.
13. Zhao Zongxu (1936), pp. 45990–1.
14. Zhao Zhongxu (1936), pp. 46080–3, and Xu Hongkui (1934), p. 46421.
15. Suzuki Tomoo (1967).
16. .Limin buji buhan di xiaokang shuiping, in Fei Xiaotong (1949), pp. 79–81.
17. Fei Hsiao-tung (1939), p. 260.
18. Xuxiu Nanhai xianzhi (1910), p. 4/33b.
19. It must be noted, however, that we are here comparing farm income with consumer prices in the city, and that the price given is for milled rice. Before milling, 1.7 piculs of rice would be equivalent to 2.4 piculs of grain.
20. C.W. Howard and K.P. Buswell (1925), p. 113.
21. C.W. Howard and K.P. Buswell (1925), pp. 112–15.
22. Guangdongsheng canye diaocha baogaoshu (1922), p. 21.
23. C.W. Howard and K.P. Buswell (1925), p. 59.
24. C.W. Howard and K.P. Buswell (1925), p. 90.
25. Glenn T. Trewartha (1939), pp. 9–10.
26. Pan Yiyun (1937), gives the same description as Trewartha.
27. Chen Han-seng (1936), pp. 89, 91.
28. These figures should be compared to Lynda S. Bell (1985a), pp. 122–4. Referring to her data in her (1985b), p. 23, she writes: 'Slightly higher cash income per mu did accrue to the peasant farming family for their sericulture effort, but the amount of labour-time expended . . . undercut any real gains in profitability'. As Bell's figures are quoted from prices in 1933, when, compared to 1929, the price of silk had dropped by 46 per cent and that of rice by only 31 per cent, her conclusion is not surprising, but is certainly not applicable to the years before the 1930s.
29. Cost estimates for the production of sugar are also available from Guoli Guangdong daxue nongke xueyuan (1925), but as the price of sugar in rural areas has not been included in this source, I have compiled Table 7.4 from reports given in Guoli Zhongshan daxue nongke xueyuan (1925).
30. As early as 1907, the Maritime Customs report on Jiulong had pointed out that sugar-cane growing was barely profitable. See MC, Jiulong 1907, p. 520. I am grateful to Ho Hon-wai for this reference.

242 NOTES TO PAGES 159–168

31. Guoli Guangdong daxue nongke xueyuan (1925), p. 29, notes that in Panyu county, where it cost sugar-cane press owners 2.80 dollars to refine a picul of sugar, farmers who did not own the press were charged 3.50 to 4.00 dollars for each picul refined.

32. Sun Jiashan (1984), Wang Shuhuai (1985).

33. Alternatively, we may note that the evidence suggests that it was only the Dayoujin and the Tonghai companies that allowed commutation, on the understanding that the cotton was sold to the Dasheng Spinning Mill. As all three companies were controlled by Zhang Jian, the difference that was introduced was probably no more than a matter of where the tenant should transport his cotton crop, for Zhang's various operations would still have been able to maintain control over the price. See Zhang Huiqun (n.d.), pp. 31839–40.

34. Zhang Huiqun (n.d.), *Ershi nianlai zhi Nantong* (1938), Yao Enrong and Zou Yingxi (1983), Wang Shuhuai (1985), pp. 222–3, Kathy Le Mons Walker (1986), pp. 357–483.

35. See Ou Jiluan and Huang Yinpu (1932), pp. 237–58.

Notes to Chapter 8

1. J.L. Buck (1937), p. 476, defines the 'operator' as 'the farmer who manages the farm and who usually participates in the manual labour', the 'owner' as the 'operator who works his own land', the 'part-owner' as an 'operator who works his own and rented land', and the 'tenant' as an 'operator who works rented land only'. Moreover, he provides two series of statistics for 'part-owners' and 'tenants' (1937b, p. 59), one series counting as part-owners those farmers who owned their 'farmsteads' (translated as *nongshe*, that is, 'farm houses') but rented all their land, and the other series counting these as tenants. The part-owners in Table 8.1 are those recorded in the latter series. Other than Buck, most contemporary writers used these terms without stating their definitions.

2. Fei Xiaotong (1946), pp. 12–18, Jing Su and Luo Lun (1959), and Philip C.C. Huang (1985), pp. 69–71.

3. It has been assumed, in order to make the necessary calculation for this, that the surveys by Buck covered both the local farming populations and the acreage farmed reasonably completely.

4. Wu Zhihua (n.d.), pp. 34695–741.

5. Philip C.C. Huang (1975), Joseph W. Esherick (1981), Randall Stross (1985), Linda Gail Arrigo (1986). It should be noted, however, that this criticism applies mainly to Buck's farm data. His survey also included local informants' impressions of county-level conditions and information gathered from local government sources.

6. For other reports on tenancy distribution in Jiangsu, see Robert Ash (1976), pp. 11–22, and David Faure (1978), pp. 452–9. For reports on Guangdong, see 'Kwangtung agricultural statistics' (1928), Guoli Zhongshan daxue nongke xueyuan (1925, 1929, 1933) and Chen Han-seng (1936).

7. That the terms were later defined in the 1950 Land Reform Law is not the point. The few definitions that we have of the terms illustrate fully the confusion that surrounds them. Compare Chen Han-seng (1936), p. 8, and Philip C.C. Huang (1985), pp. 69–70. For an example, Chen Hansheng's definition of 'poor peasants', that is, 'all peasant families whose number of cultivated mow [*mu*] falls below that of the middle peasants, and whose members besides living on the fruits of their own cultivation, have to rely upon a wage income or some income of an auxiliary nature, belong to the poor peasants in general', would have embraced a substantial number of silk farmers, who were by no means poor by Guangdong standards. Chen probably saw this anomaly, for he added, on p. 123, the provision that income from auxiliary sources should be

negligible. In the face of subjective biases in the use of these terms, it must be concluded that the statistics reflect not an objective income distribution, but only a subjective impression of it.

8. A word of caution is needed in reading these statistics, for they apparently do not include all households surveyed. Nongcun fuxing weiyuanhui (1934), pp. 11–12, lists 172 'poor peasants' enumerated in Pei, and 101 in Changshu. The single household in Changshu not included into the tabulations that form the basis of Table 8.2 is not likely to alter the pattern discernible here, but the 48 households excluded fom Pei would increase the distortion in land distribution. Other figures quoted on these two pages in the report are identical to the ones listed on Table 8.2.

9. It should be noted that in southern Jiangsu, the pattern of larger farms being managed by owner-cultivators is not by any means without exception. See Qiao Qiming (1926), p. 83.

10. Nongcun fuxing weiyuanhui (1934), pp. 11–12, and compare Joseph W. Esherick (1981) pp. 390–4.

11. C.B. Malone and G.B. Taylor (1924) pp. 17–18, Wu Shoupeng (1930), pp. 342–4, *Zhongguo jingji nianjian 1934*, p. G241, Chen Quan (1933), p. 297.

12. David Faure (1978), pp. 392–404.

13. I refer in particular to Zhongguo renmin daxue qingshi yanjiusuo, and others (1979) and Zhongguo diyi lishi danganguan, and others (1982).

14. An exception to note is Fei Hsiao-tung (1939).

15. Some of the best descriptions of these relationships may be found in Peng Pai (1926). See especially pp. 41–3, 71, and 135–6.

16. The quotation from Malinowsky's *Coral Gardens and Their Magic* on Fei Hsiao-tung (1939), p. 174, is worth reproducing in full here: 'We could lay down at once the rule that any attempt to study land tenure merely from the legal point of view must lead to unsatisfactory results. Land tenure cannot be defined or described without an exhaustive knowledge of the economic life of the natives . . . You must know first how man used his soil, how he weaves round it his traditional legends, his beliefs and mystical values, how he fights for it and defends it; then and then only will you be able to grasp the system of legal and customary rights which define the relationship between man and soil'. Failure to take account of the political situation in the village has led Robert Ash (1976), p. 40, to arrive at the erroneus assertion that 'security of tenure was notably lacking' in Jiangsu.

17. For background, see John Kamm (1977), James Hayes (1977), Edgar Wickberg (1981), Rubie S. Watson (1985), pp. 55–82 and Michael J.E. Palmer (1987). Documentation in some detail for this section may also be found in David Faure (1986).

18. David Faure (1986), pp. 78, 30–44, and 166–70.

19. The surveys of the 1920s and 1930s did not pay any attention to the status of farmers within the context of their villages. However, in the community studies, especially those by Fei Xiaotong and C.K. Yang, village rules and customs that controlled settlement and the right of exploiting unclaimed resources were given some recognition. In Kaixiangong, outsiders made up one-third of the number that were engaged in peripheral occupations in the village. In Nanching, outsiders had fewer rights in the village than those villagers who were considered incumbents. Fei Hsiao-tung (1939), pp. 141 and 175–6, C.K. Yang (1966), p. 11.

20. I am not aware of any in-depth study on the financial relationships between members of the lineage and their ancestral trusts. Jiang Luo (1935), p. 290, suggests that in Huaxian, Guangdong, down payments were waived when a member of the lineage rented from the lineage trust of which he was a member. Rubie S. Watson (1985), p. 69, drawing on research in the New Territories of Hong Kong, reported that lineage members did enjoy advantages in renting land from their own lineage trusts, even though they did not quite agree on what these advantages were.

21. For another description of overlordship, see 'Puning xian nongmin fankang dizhu shimoji' (1927).

22. Quoted in Chen Han-seng (1933), p. 4.

23. He Menglei (n.d.), pp. 33039–46, and for a brief introduction in English, see Evelyn Sakakida Rawski (1972), pp. 19–24.

24. The figures in this paragraph are quoted from He Menglei (n.d.), pp. 33054–60, 33121–34, 33151, and 33161–3. He's description of the *yazu* is confusing. The top-soil owner, who would by law as well as custom be regarded as a tenant of the bottom-soil owner, would also have paid a purchase price for the top-soil (see He, pp. 33081–3). He made clear that this price was not the *yazu* (pp. 33083–6), the purpose of which was to serve as a rental deposit. But on p. 33162, he argued that *yazu* none the less provided a guarantee for the tenant and that it was 'close to the purchase of the top-soil'. I think these descriptions show that whether or not land was held under permanent tenancy, tenants enjoyed some security of tenure. The distinction between permanent tenure and other forms of tenure where a fixed term was not specified was not clear cut.

25. *Zhongguo jingji nianjian 1934*, p. G80; Wong Yin-seng, and others (1939), p. 26.

26. Gu Zhuo, and others (1931), pp. 25–6.

27. Yu Lin (1932).

28. This was the lineage of the late Qing official Xue Fucheng, whose son Xue Nanming and grandson Xue Shouxuan became the leading silk manufacturers in Wuxi. See Wang Jingyu (1957), pp. 944–5 and 1023.

29. Mantetsu Shanhai jimusho chōsabu (1941a) is the principal source for these few paragraphs on Rongxiang. Gu Zhuo (1931) adds useful supplementary information. Note in particular that according to Gu Zhuo (1931), p. 50, Rongxiang was primarily a mulberry growing and silkworm raising village: it devoted 956 of its 1,336 *mu* of cultivated land to mulberry, 300 to fishponds, and only 80 to paddy.

30. On the Rong family, see pp.100–2.

31. The obvious alternative explanation is that the villagers were reluctant to divulge specifics related to land holdings to the investigators. I think this is highly likely given the political overtones of the research at the time.

32. Gu Zhuo, and others (1931), p. 54, records that 94 per cent of Rongxiang households were owner-cultivators and 6 per cent were tenants.

33. Compare He Menglei (n.d.), pp. 33072–3: 'Most farmers had no land and many wanted land to farm; and especially because many immigrant farmers moved in, a shortage of farmland developed. As a result, most farmers looking for land [to farm] were prepared to pay a substantial price to chisel out farming rights from tenants who had directly rented land from the landlords'.

34. See Yuan Yinhuai (1935), pp. 17481–3 and David Faure (1976).

35. Compare also Jiangsusheng nongmin yinhang (1931), p. 372.

36. Wu Shoupeng (1930), pp. 330–1.

37. Wu Shoupeng (1930), pp. 331–4, Elizabeth Perry (1985), pp. 88–94.

38. Chang'ancun nongcun jingji diaocha baogao (1932).

39. Balitun nongcun jingji diaocha baogao (1932).

40. Nongcun fuxing weiyuanhui (1934), pp. 70 and 93.

41. A very useful document that illustrates the involvement of the magistrate in rent collection in Jiangsu before the Taiping Rebellion is Li Chengru (1827).

42. The term 'rent-dunning office' is Kathryn Bernhardt's. See her (1987) and (n.d.). For rent increase in Suzhou, see Chapter 4.

43. Long Shengyun (1958), Wu Yannan (1958), Kojima Yoshio (1964), Dong Caishi (1981), pp. 122–38, Li Shuyuan (1984), Kathryn Bernhardt (1987).

44. Qiao Qiming (1926), pp. 100–2 and 108–9.

45. Fei Hsiao-tung (1939), pp. 188–9, *Zhongguo jingji nianjian 1934*, p. G170; according to the latter source, in 1912 the landlords' union (*tianye gonghui*) recruited

disbanded *yamen* functionaries as rent-prompters, while in previous years, they would have had to petition the magistrate who 'prompted' their tenants on their behalf.

46. Yamen functionaries had for a long time been involved in rent collection in Changshu (Nongcun fuxing weiyuanhui (1934), p. 83), and the commutation rate for crop rent had always been determined by the magistrate (He Menglei (n.d.), pp. 33154–5). In both 1932 and 1933, several hundred tenants were reported to have been jailed for not paying rent (*Zhongguo jingji nianjian 1934*, pp. G174–5 and *Zhongguo jingji nianjian 1936*, p. G124).

47. Frank A. Lojewski (1980) argued that landlords who entrusted rent collection to the rent-collection offices were not people of substance. This argument is not incompatible with the observation here. Some degree of patronage provided by powerful landlords for smaller ones may have to be allowed for, but such details must await further research on local records.

48. Permanent tenure in Suzhou is documented in detail in Hayashi Megumi (1953), pp. 93–174.

49. According to Frank A. Lojewski (1980), pp. 53–4, the rent-collection offices did evict tenants.

50. According to the *Xiangshan xianzhi* (1923), pp. 4/19b–20a, the Foshan *tang* was entrusted with 568 *mu* by six benefactors, including two women. That the land donated could not be sold by descendants might be an extra attraction. The charity hall started a branch in a market within the county in 1903, and this was entrusted with 870 *mu*. In addition, another charity institution, the Changsheng *shoushe* (a burial association), managed 590 *mu* for its benefactors under a similar arrangement. Also noted in the *Xiangshan xianzhi* (1923), pp. 4/16b–17b, the Chongyi *ci* (temple in veneration of the righteous), which housed 704 ancestral tablets deposited there by lineage trusts in the county when it was rebuilt in 1875, might also have had such an arrangement, for the gazetteer notes that although the *ci* was a 'communal hall' (*gongci*) for all the surnames involved, the property (*chan*) held remained 'private property' that belonged to each surname. The *ci* held 6,800 *mu* of newly reclaimed land.

51. *Liu Moufeng Wei zhengju zongbu* (n.d.), in my possession.

52. *Xinhui Tanjiazu xingzu jizhihui guizhang* [n.d.], in my possession.

53. David Faure (1986).

54. The Jiangsu figures are derived from Zhu Fucheng (n.d.), pp. 35953–6 and J.L. Buck (1937b), pp. 23–4. Zhu's statistics are quoted from estimates made by the Jiangsu provincial government in 1931, and are the lower of two sets of figures provided. The Guangdong figures are quoted from Lin Shidan (n.d.), p. 1979. Lin reports that this was the 'actually measured' (*shice*) acreage. Chen Han-seng (1933), p. 22 reports that the acreage measured for tax was 2,098,200 *mu*.

55. As late as 1934, the land on which surface rights held in Qidong was known as 'land demarcated from Chongming' (*chonghua tian*). See Nongcun fuxing weiyuanhui (1934), p. 41.

56. Chen Hong (1931), see especially the arguments on pp. 46, 88, 104, and 140.

57. Shen Shike (1934), pp. 30858–9.

58. The Chuansha riot is discussed in Chūso Ichiko (1971). For the new holders of power, see *Chuansha xianzhi* (1936), pp. 3/12b, 13a, 6/25b, 33b–34a, 35b, 16/17a, 18a–b, and 23/13a. Another view of the riot may be found in Roxann Prazniak (1986).

59. Zhang Qianjiu (1935).

60. Imahori Seiji (1956), Sasaki Masaya (1959), *Donghai shiliusha jishi* (1912), and Robert Y. Eng (1986) provide the basic documentation on this case. More material is provided in Huang Yonghao (1987). For another case, see Chen Deyun (1935), p. 19, which records the dissolution of the *shatian* office in Waihai *xiang* in Xinhui county, the holdings of which were reverted to its members.

61. Chen Han-seng (1936), p. 47.

62. Chen Han-seng (1936), pp. 30–1, 48, 63.

63. Philip C.C. Huang (1985) draws largely from data gathered by Japanese researchers in the early 1940s for these conclusions. The term 'involution' is borrowed from Clifford Geertz (1963) to refer to input of labour and capital into the farm despite diminishing returns.

64. This table divides the farms of each locality noted into six groups by size. For the average size of the farms and the percentage of farms in each size group, see the supplemetary tables. The percentage of farms at or below subsistence level is the sum of the percentages in the supplementary table corresponding to items in bold type in the principal table.

65. The surveyors from the Rural Rehabilitation Commission who visited Changshu were shocked by the rural poverty they confronted. They noted in their diary: 'On both banks [of the river] are paddy fields. Here groups of men and women farmers are treadling the water pump without stopping. The men are largely naked, and the women do not wear any upper garment, except for a patterned cloth wrapped round the chest'. (Nongcun fuxing weiyuanhui (1934), p. 80). They continued: 'We interviewed over 30 families for five full hours. Only 18 families farmed. Of the others, some made a living rowing boats. Others made a living outside the village. Some did odd jobs' (p. 81). On another day, they wrote: 'There are 25 farm households here. About one-fifth owned the land they farmed and hired labourers. Four families of owner-operators could maintain their livelihood. The others are all tenants, leading very hard lives' (p. 82). Researchers from the South Manchurian Railway interviewed a village in this county in 1939. Of 55 households in the village, most reported fishing or working on boats as their supplementary occupations. Aside from 17 households that did not farm, one operated a farm of 15 mu, two between 10 and 15, sixteen between 5 and 10, and 19 less than 5. Interestingly, few hired themselves out for farm work. Those that did were owners of buffaloes (6 in all) or water-drawing machines (10 in all owned by 9 households) who contracted out their service for designated acreages. Thirty households contracted in such service on their land. For instance, a typical family consisting of four persons (a 34 year-old man, a 30 year-old woman, and two 9 and 3 year-old daughters), owned 2.95 mu, rented in another 5.00 mu, rented out 0.6 mu, and contracted service for 5.5 mu. The households that supported themselves on such meagre acreages were poor, obviously, by any standard. (Mantetsu Shanhai Jimusho Chōsashitsu (1939), Tables 1 and 7.)

66. C.B. Malone and G.B. Taylor (1924), p. 18, Zhao Chengxin (1929), pp. 939–40, 'Jiangning xian Huacheng xiang' (1934), pp. 701–2, Mantetsu Shanhai Jimusho Chōsashitsu (1940b), pp. 93 and 97, and (1941a), pp 156–8, and Mantetsu Shanhai Jimusho Chōsabu (1941a), Tables 2 and 13.

67. Fei Hsiao-tung (1939), pp. 33, 170–1, 180, and 196; the quote is taken from p. 180.

68. Deng Jiaqi (1901), xia, pp. 63a–b.

69. That the poor raised fewer children is also recognized in Edwin E. Moise (1977). But note the complication introduced by adoption and uxorilocal marriages discussed in Wolf and Huang (1980).

70. Philip C.C. Huang (1985), p. 201.

71. Edwin E. Moise (1977), p. 8.

72. Failure to recognize the continuous displacement of villagers from village life has given rise to a false sense of security in village membership that has been given a lot of attention in the recent discussion on the 'moral economy of the peasant'. James C. Scott, whose study of Vietnamese society published in 1976 gave much publicity to this view, warns against exaggerating the economic protection that the village could give its members in these terms: 'It is all too easy, and a serious mistake, to romanticize these social arrangements that distinguish much of peasant society. They are not radically egalitarian. Rather, they imply only that all are entitled to a living [sic] out of the resources within the village, and that living is attained often at the cost of a loss

of status and autonomy. They work, moreover, in large measure through the abrasive force of gossip and envy and the knowledge that the abandoned poor are likely to be a real and present danger to better-off villagers. These modest but critical redistributive mechanisms nonetheless do provide a minimal subsistence insurance for villagers. Polanyi claims on the basis of historical and anthropological evidence that such practices were nearly universal in traditional society and served to mark it off from the modern market economy' (p. 5 in his 1976 book). Note that even here the stress is repeatedly placed on the protection of the *villager* and Scott ignores the fate of outsiders.

73. Fei Hsiao-tung (1939), pp. 179–80.
74. Chen Wusheng (1931), pp. 511–12.

Notes to Chapter 9

1. Fei Hsiao-tung (1939), pp. 189–91.
2. For this reason, I find Alvin So's discussion (in his 1986 book) of the women silk filature workers of Shunde under a chapter bearing the title 'Proletarianization' unconvincing.
3. Philip C.C. Huang (1985), pp. 202–16 and 264–70.
4. Chen Han-seng (1936), p. 98.
5. Lu Zhushou (1935).

Bibliography

'A study of the sugar industry in China', *Chinese Economic Journal*, 1927, pp. 876–83 and 963–71.

Ahern, Emily Martin and Hill Gates (eds.), 1981, *The Anthropology of Taiwanese Society* (Stanford, Stanford University Press).

Amano Motonosuke 天野元之助, 1962, *Chūkoku nōgyōshi kenkyū* 中國農業史研究 (Studies of the History of Chinese Agriculture) (Tokyo, Nōgyō sōgō kenkyūjo).

Arndt, H.W., 1983, 'The "trickle-down" myth', *Economic Development and Cultural Change*, Vol. 32, No. 1, pp. 1–10.

Arrigo, Linda Gail, 1986, 'Land ownership concentration in China, the Buck survey revisited', *Modern China*, Vol. 12, No. 3, pp. 259–360.

Ash, Robert, 1976, *Land Tenure in Pre-revolutionary China: Kiangsu Province in the 1920s and 1930s* (London, School of Oriental and African Studies, Contemporary China Institute).

'Balitun nongcun jingji diaocha baogao' 八里屯農村經濟調查報告 1932, (A report of an investigation into the rural economy of Balitun), Jiangsu shengli Xuzhou minzhong jiaoyuguan 江蘇省立徐州民衆敎育館 1932, *Jiaoyu xinlun* 敎育新論, No. 12, reprinted in Feng Hefa (1935), pp. 4–12.

Bannister, T. R., 1933a, 'A history of the external trade of China, 1834–81', MC, 1922–31.

—— 1933b, 'Synopsis of the external trade of China, 1882–1931', MC, 1922–31.

Bao Shichen 包世臣, c.1850, *Qimin sishu* 齊民四術 (Four Strategies for Pacifying the Masses), in *Anwu sizhong* 安吳四種 (Four Titles in the Government of Jiangsu), n.d. (Taibei reprint, n.d.).

Bell, Lynda S., 1985a, 'Merchants, peasants, and the state: the organization and politics of Chinese silk production, Wuxi county, 1870–1937' (unpublished Ph.D. dissertation, University of California, Los Angeles).

—— 1985b, 'Explaining China's rural crisis: observations from Wuxi county in the early twentieth century', *Republican China*, Vol. 11, No. 1, pp. 15–31.

Bernhardt, Kathryn, n.d., 'Tenants against the state: rent resistance in the lower Yangzi region, 1864–1937', private circulation.

—— 1987, 'Elite and peasant during the Taiping occupation of the Jiangnan, 1860–1864', *Modern China*, Vol. 13, No. 4, pp. 379–410.

Bloch, K., 1935, 'On the copper currencies in China', *Nankai Social and Economic Quarterly*, Vol. 8, No. 3, pp. 617–32.

—— 1939, 'Chinese copper currency and the peasantry', in *Institute of Pacific Relations* (1939), pp. 113–18.

Brandt, Loren, 1985, 'Chinese agriculture and the international economy, 1870–1930s: a reassessment', *Explorations in Economic History*, Vol. 22, p. 168–93.

—— 1987, review of Philip C. C. Huang (1985), *Economic Development and Cultural Change*, Vol. 35, No. 3, pp. 670–82.

Brandt, Loren and Sargent, Thomas J., 1987, 'Interpreting new evidence about China and U.S. silver purchases', private circulation.

Bratter, Herbert M., 1932, *The Silver Market*, U.S. Department of Commerce, Bureau of Foreign and Domestic Commerce, Trade Promotion Series, No. 139 (Washington D.C., U.S. Government Printing Office).

Brim, John A., 1974, 'Village alliance temples in Hong Kong' in Arthur P. Wolf (ed.) 1974, *Religion and Ritual in Chinese Society* (Stanford, Stanford University Press), pp. 93–103.

Brook, Timothy, 1981a, 'Guides for vexed travellers: route books in the Ming and Qing', *Ch'ing-shih wen-t'i*, Vol. 4, No. 5, pp. 32–76.

—— 1981b, 'Guides for vexed travellers: a supplement', *Ch'ing-shih wen-t'i*, Vol. 4, No. 6, pp. 130–40.

—— 1982, 'Guides for vexed travellers — a second supplement', *Ch'ing-shih wen-t'i*, Vol. 4, No. 8, pp. 96–109.

Brown, Shannon R., 1981, 'Cakes and oil: technology transfer and Chinese soybean processing, 1860–1895', *Comparative Study in Society and History*, Vol. 23, pp. 449–63.

Buck, John Lossing, 1930, *Chinese Farm Economy* (Chicago, University of Chicago Press).

—— 1937a, *Land Utilization in China* (Nanjing, University of Nanjing).

—— 1937b, *Land Utilization in China, Statistics* (Nanjing, University of Nanjing).

—— 1937c, *Land Utilization in China, Maps* (Nanjing, University of Nanjing).

Cai Zhixiang 蔡志祥, 1981, 'Jindai Zhongguo nongye fazhan jiqi yingxiang — Hunan sheng ge'an yanjiu' 近代中國農業發展及其影響 —— 湖南省個案研究 (The Development of Agriculture in Modern China and its Impact — a Case Study of Hunan Province), (unpublished M. Phil. disseration, Hong Kong, Chinese University of Hong Kong).

Canton Advertising and Commission Agency, 1932, *Canton, Its Ports, Industries and Trade* (Canton).

Cao Liying 曹立瀛, 1937, *Shanghai mijia zhi jijie bianqian* 上海米價之季節變遷 (Seasonal Changes in the Price of Rice in Shanghai), n.p.

CEJ: Chinese Economic Journal.

Chang, B.T., 1929, 'The cotton crops of Chekiang and Kiangsu in 1929', *Chinese Economic Journal*, Vol. 5, No. 1, pp. 588–603.

Chang, John K., 1969, *Industrialization in Pre-Communist China* (Edinburgh, Edinburgh University Press).

Chang, L.L. (Zhang Liluan), 1932, 'Farm prices in Wuchin, Kiangsu, China', *Chinese Economic Journal*, Vol. 10, No. 6, pp. 449–512.

'Chang'ancun nongcun jingji diaocha baogao' 長安村農村經濟調查報告 (A report of an investigation into the rural economy of Chang'an Village), Jiangsu Shengli Xuzhou Minzhong Jiaoyuguan, *Jiaoyu xinlu*, in Feng Hefa (1935), pp. 13–23.

Changzhao hezhigao 常昭合志稿 (Combined Record of Changshu and Zhaowen), 1904.

Chao, Kang, 1977, *The Development of Cotton Textile Production in China* (Cambridge, Mass., Harvard University Press).

Chaozhou zhi 潮州志 (A Record of Chaozhou), 1946.

Chen Bozhuang 陳伯莊, 1936, 'Guangdong quemi qingxing yiji Xiangmi xiaoyue de xiwang' 廣東缺米情形以及湘米銷粵的希望 (The shortage of rice in Guangdong and the prospects of selling Hunanese rice to Guangdong), in Wu Zheng 吳正, *Huanzhong daomi chanxiao zhi diaocha* 皖中稻米產銷之調查 (An Investigation into the production and sale of rice in Anhui), n.p., pp. 100–36.

Chen Ciyu 陳慈玉, 1983, 'Shijiu shiji houban Jiangnan nongcun de cansi ye' 十九世紀後半江南農村的蠶絲業 (The silk industry in Jiangnan villages in the second half of the nineteenth century), *Shihuo* 食貨 Vol. 12, Nos. 10 and 11, pp. 45–63.

Chen Deyun 陳德芸, 1935, *Chen Xiaobai xiansheng nianpu* 陳少白先生年譜 (An Annual Record of Mr. Chen Xiaobai), n.p. (Taibei reprint, n.d.).

Chen Han-seng, 1933, *The Present Agrarian Problem of China* (Shanghai, China Institute of Pacific Relations).

—— 1936, *Landlord and Peasant in China, a Study of the Agrarian Crisis in South China* (New York, International Publishers).

—— 1939, *Industrial Capital and Chinese Peasants, a Study of Chinese Tobacco Cultivators* (Shanghai).

Chen Hansheng 陳翰笙 and others, 1929, '*Mu de chayi*', 畝的差異 *(Variations of the mu), Guoli Zhongyang yanjiuyuan shehui kexue yanjiusuo jikan* 國立中央研究院社會科學研究所集刊 (Shanghai).

Chen Hengli 陳恒力, 1958, *Bunongshu yanjiu* 補農書研究 (A Study of the *Supplement to the Book of Agriculture*).

Chen Hong 陳弘, 1931, *Qidong shezhi huidu* 啓東設治彙牘 (Correspondence Related to the Establishment of Qidong County), n.p.

Chen Qihui 陳啓輝, n.d. (written 1930s), *Guangdong tudi liyong yu liangshi chanxiao* 廣東土地利用與糧食產銷 (Land use and the Production and Distribution of Food in Guangdong), Vols. 50 and 51 in Xiao Zheng, 1977, Taibei.

—— 1938, *Guangdong sheng dizhengju diaocha shixi riji* 廣東省地政局調查實習日記 (A Diary Kept During Survey Exercise at the Guangdong Land Administration Office), vol. 200, in Xiao Zheng, 1977, Taibei.

Chen Quan 陳權, 1933, 'Guangdong shatian jianwenlu' 廣東沙田見聞錄 (A

record of observations on the 'sandy land' of Guangdong), Guangxi
shengli shifan zhuanke xuexiao 廣西省立師範專科學校 , *Shizhuan
xiaokan* 師專校刊 , Vol. 2, Nos. 2 and 3; rep. in Feng Hefa (1935),
pp. 297–300.

Chen Ta, 1939, *Emigrant Communities in South China, A Study of Overseas
Migration and Its Influence on Standards of Living and Social Change*
(Shanghai, Kelly and Walsh).

Chen Wusheng 陳午生, 1931, 'Jintan Liyang gunong shenghuo zhi diaocha'
金壇漂陽僱農生活之調查 (An investigation into the livelihood of hired
farm labourers in Jintan and Liyang), *Guoli zhongyang daxue nong-
xueyuan xunkan* 國立中央大學農學院旬刊 , Vol. 85, No. 10, December
1931, rep. in Feng Hefa (1933), pp. 502–12.

Chen Zhengmo 陳正謨 , 1934, 'Gesheng nonggong guyong xiguan zhi
diaocha yanjiu' 各省農工僱佣習慣之調查研究 (A study into hiring practices for farm labourers in all provinces), *Zhongshan wenhua jiaoyuguan
jikan* 中山文化教育館季刊 , Vol. 1, No. 1.

—— 1936, *Zhongguo gesheng de dizu* 中國各省的地租 (The Land Rent of All
Provinces in China), (Guangzhou, Shangwu yinshuguan).

Chen Zhengxiang 陳正祥, 1978, *Guangdong dizhi* 廣東地誌 (A Geography of
Guangdong), (Hong Kong, Tiandi tushu youxian gongsi).

Cheng Siok-hwa, 1968, *The Rice Industry of Burma, 1852–1940* (Singapore,
University of Malaya Press).

Cheng Yaoming 程燿明, 1985, 'Qingmo Shunde jiqi saosiye de chansheng,
fazhan jiqi yingxiang' 清末順德機器繅絲業的產生、發展及其影響 (The
birth, development, and effect of the mechanical silk-reeling industry in
Shunde at the end of the Qing), in Guangdong Lishi xuehui (1985),
pp. 237–78.

Chesneaux, Jean, 1968, *The Chinese Labour Movement 1919–1927* (Stanford, Stanford University Press).

China, Maritime Customs, annual, *Returns of Trade and Trade Reports*
(Shanghai).

—— 1882–1891, 1892–1901, 1902–1911, 1912–1921, 1922–1931, *Decennial
Reports* (Shanghai).

—— 1917, *Silk*, Special Series No. 3, rep. of 1881 report (Shanghai).

'China's Silk Trade During 1935', 1936, *Chinese Economic Journal*, Vol. 18,
No. 3, pp. 330–43.

Chiu, Alfred Kai-ming, 1933, 'Recent statistical surveys of the Chinese rural
economy, 1912–1932: a study of the sources of Chinese agricultural
statistics, their methods of collecting data and their findings about rural
economic conditions' (unpublished Ph.D. dissertation, Harvard
University).

Chuan Han-sheng and Kraus, Richard A., 1975, *Mid-Ch'ing rice Markets
and Trade, an Essay in Price History* (Cambridge, Mass., Harvard
University, East Asian Research Centre).

Chuansha xianzhi 川沙縣志 (A Record of Chuansha County), 1936.

Clark, Colin and Haswell, Margaret, 1966, *The Economics of Subsistence Agriculture* (London, Macmillan).

Cressey, G.B., 1934, *China's Geographic Foundations: A Survey of the Land and Its People* (New York and London, McGraw Hill).

—— 1955, *Land of the 500 Million* (New York, McGraw Hill).

CSWT Ch'ing-shih wen-t'i.

de Cecco, Marcello, 1974, *Money and Empire, the International Gold Standard, 1890–1914* (Oxford, Basil Blackwell).

Deng Jiaqi 鄧嘉緝, 1901, *Bianshanzhai wencun* 扁善齋文存 (A Collection of Essays from the Bianshan Study), n.p.

Dong Caishi 董蔡時 1981, *Taiping tianguo zai Suzhou* 太平天國在蘇州 (The Taiping Heavenly Kingdom in Suzhou), (Jiangsu, Renmin chubanshe).

Donghai shiliusha jishi 東海十六沙紀實 (A True Record of the 'Sixteen Sands of the Eastern Sea'), 1912 (Guangzhou).

Dongguan xianzhi 東莞縣志 (A Record of Dongguan County), 1927.

Dongnan daxue nongke 東南大學農科, 1923, *Jiangsu sheng nongye diaocha: Suchang daoshu* 江蘇省農業調查錄：蘇常道屬 (A Survey of Agriculture in Jiangsu Province: the Suzhou and Changzhou Circuits), (Shanghai).

Eastman, Lloyd E., 1974, *The Abortive Revolution, China under Nationalist Rule, 1927–1937* (Cambridge, Mass., Harvard University Press).

Eng, Robert Y., 1986, *Economic Imperialism in China, Silk Production and Export, 1861–1932* (Berkeley, University of California. Institute of East Asian Studies).

—— 1986, 'Institutional and secondary landlordism in the Pearl River delta, 1600–1949', *Modern China*, Vol. 12, No. 1, pp. 3–37.

Enping xianzhi 恩平縣志 (A Record of Enping County), 1934.

Ershi nianlai zhi Nantong 二十年來之南通 (Nantong in the Last Twenty Years) 1938 (Nantong, Jiangsu).

Esherick, J., 1972, 'Harvard on China: the apologetics of Imperialism', *Bulletin of Concerned Asian Scholars*, Vol. 4, No. 4, pp. 9–16.

—— 1981, 'Number games, a note on land distribution in pre-revolutionary China', *Modern China*, Vol. 7, No. 4, pp. 387–411.

Fairbank, John K. and Liu Kwang-ching, 1980, *The Cambridge History of China*, vol. 11, pt. 2 (Cambridge, Cambridge University Press).

Fan Yijun 范毅軍, 1982, 'Shantou maoyi yu Hanjiang liuyu shougongye de bianqian' 汕頭貿易與韓江流域手工業的變遷 (The trade of Shantou and changes in the handicraft industry in the Hanjiang basin), *Zhongyang yanjiuyuan jindaishi yanjiusuo jikan* 中央研究院近代史研究所集刊 Vol. 11, pp. 131–60.

—— 1983, 'Guangdong Hanmei liuyu de tangye jingji' 廣東韓梅流域的糖業經濟 (The sugar economy in the Hanjiang and Meijiang basins of Guangdong), *Zhongyang yanjiuyuan jindaishi yanjiusuo jikan*, Vol. 12, pp. 127–61.

Fang Xianting 方顯廷 (ed.), 1938, *Zhongguo jingji yanjiu* 中國經濟研究 (Studies in the Economy of China), (Changsha, Shangwu yinshuguan).

Faure, David, 1976, 'Land tax collection in Kiangsu Province in the late Ch'ing period', *Ch'ing-shi wen-t'i*, Vol. 3, No. 6, pp. 49–75.

—— 1977, 'Rural marketing in China's economic development', *Proceedings of the Seventh International Association of the Historians of Asia Conference, 22nd–26th August, 1977*, Bangkok.

—— 1978, 'The rural economy of Kiangsu Province, 1870–1911,' *Journal of the Institute of Chinese Studies of the Chinese University of Hong Kong*, Vol. 9, pp. 365–471.

—— 1979, 'Neglected historical sources on the late Ch'ing and the early Republican rural economy', *Ch'ing-shih wen-t'i*, Vol. 4, pp. 58–93.

—— 1980a, 'Landlords and farm management: comments on Ching Su and Lo Lun', *Ch'ing-tai Shan-tung ching-ying ti-chu ti she-hui hsing-chih* (Tsinan, 1959), translated into English by Endymion Wilkinson as *Landlord and Labour in Late Imperial China, Case Studies from Shandong* (Cambridge, Mass., 1978), *Journal of the Institute of Chinese Studies of the Chinese University of Hong Kong*, Vol. 11, pp. 303–13.

—— 1980b, 'World trade and rural development, Kwangtung Province, 1870–1937', paper presented at the Eighth Conference of the International Association of Historians of Asia, Kuala Lumpur.

—— 1982, 'Saikung, the making of the district and its experience during World War II', *Journal of the Hong Kong Branch of the Royal Asiatic Society*, Vol. 22, pp. 161–216.

—— 1984, 'Lineage, village and alliance: the territorial organization of mainland New Territories', *Proceedings of the Sixth International Symposium on Asian Studies, 1984* (Hong Kong, Asian Research Service).

—— 1985, 'The plight of the farmers, a study of the rural economy of Jiangsu and the Pearl River delta, 1870–1937', *Modern China*, Vol. 2, No. 1, pp. 3–37.

—— 1986, *The Structure of Chinese Rural Society: Lineage and Village in the Eastern New Territories, Hong Kong* (Hong Kong, Oxford University Press).

Fei Hsiao-tung, 1939, *Peasant Life in China, a Field Study of Country Life in the Yangtze Valley* (London, Routledge and Kegan Paul).

Fei Xiaotong 費孝通, 1946, *Neidi de nongcun* 內地的農村 (Inland Villages). (Shanghai, Shenghuo shudian, Hong Kong rep., n.d.).

—— 1949, *Xiangtu chongjian* 鄉土重建 (Rural Reconstruction), (Shanghai, Guanchashe).

Feng Hefa 馮和法 (ed.), 1933, *Zhongguo nongcun jingji ziliao* 中國農村經濟資料 (Source Materials on the Rural Economy of China), (Shanghai, Liming shudian).

—— 1934, 'Zhongguo nongchanwu de yuanshi shichang' 中國農產物的原始

市場 (The source markets for farm produce in China), *Zhongguo nongcun* 中國農村 Vol. 1, No. 3, rep. in Feng Hefa, (1935), pp. 907–21.

—— (ed.), 1935, *Zhongguo nongcun jingji ziliao xubian* 中國農村經濟資料續編 (Supplement to Source Materials on the Rural Economy of China), (Shanghai, Liming shudian).

Feng Rui, and Yung Ping-hang, 1931, 'A general descriptive survey of the Honan Island village community', *Lingnan Science Journal*, Vol. 10, Nos. 2 and 3, pp. 153–86.

Feuerwerker, Albert, 1970, 'Handicraft and manufactured cotton textiles in China, 1871–1910', *Journal of Economic History*, Vol. 30, No. 2, pp. 338–78.

—— 1980, 'Economic trends in the late Ch'ing empire, 1870–1911', in John K. Fairbank and Kwang-ching Liu (1980), pp. 1–69.

'Flour industry in Kiangsu', 1933, *Chinese Economic Journal*, Vol. 13, No. 1, pp. 32–48.

Foshan diqu geming weiyuanhui 'Zhujiang sanjiaozhou nongyezhi' bianxiezu 佛山地區革命委員會《珠江三角洲農業志》編寫組 1976, *Zhujiang sanjiaozhou nongyezhi* 珠江三角洲農業志 (A history of the agriculture of the Zhujiang Delta), n.p.

Freedman, Maurice, 1966, *Chinese Lineage and Society, Fukien and Kwangtung* (London, the Athlone Press).

Fried, Morton, 1952, 'Military status in Chinese society', *American Journal of Sociology*, Vol. 57, No. 4, pp. 347–57.

Fu Yiling 傅衣凌 1961, *Mingqing nongcun shehui jingji* 明清農村社會經濟 (Rural Society and Economy in the Ming and Qing), (Beijing, Sanlian).

Funing xian xinzhi 阜寧縣新志 (A New Record of Funing County), 1934.

Fukudai Kōshi 福太公司 (ed.), 1940, *Nanshi keizai sōsho* 南支經濟業書 (A Series on the Economy of South China), Vol. 3 (Taibei).

Ganbo'er 甘博爾 (W.K.H. Campbell), 1936, 'Kaocha Zhejiang hezuo shiye hou zhi yinxiang' 考察浙江合作事業後之印像 (Impressions from a Survey of Co-operative Enterprises in Zhejiang), in Fang Xianting (1938), pp. 497–509.

Gao Jingyue 高景岳, 1983, 'Wuxi saosi gongye de fazhan he qiye guanli de yanbian' 無錫繅絲工業的發展和企業管理的演變 (The development of the silk-reeling industry in Wuxi and the evolution of its management), *Zhongguo shehui jingjishi yanjiu* 中國社會經濟史研究 No. 1, pp. 102–10.

Gao Yinzu 高蔭祖, 1957, *Zhonghua minguo dashi ji* 中華民國大事記 (Major Events in the Chinese Republic), (Taibei).

Gaoyao xianzhi 高要縣志 (A Record of Gaoyao County), 1938.

'Gedi jinrong zhi jinkuang' 各地金融之近況 (Recent financial conditions in various places), 1934, *Nonghang yuekan* 農行月刊 Vol. 1, No. 1, pp. 30–31.

Geertz, Clifford, 1963, *Agricultural Involution, the Process of Ecological Change in Indonesia* (Berkeley, University of California Press).

Greenough, Paul R., 1982, 'Comments from a South Asian perspective', *Journal of Asian Studies*, Vol. 41, No. 4, pp. 789–97.

Groves, R.G., 1964, 'The origins of two market towns in the New Territories', in Marjorie Topley (ed.), *Aspects of Social Organization in the New Territories* (Hong Kong, Hong Kong Branch of the Royal Asiatic Society).

Gu Jirui 顧紀瑞, 1985, 'Wuxi zai ershi niandai xingcheng jingji zhongxin de yuanyin jiqi zhineng' 無錫在二十年代形成經濟中心的原因及其職能 (Reasons for the development of Wuxi into an economic centre in the 1920s and its functions [as an economic centre]), *Lishi dang'an* 歷史檔案 no. 4, pp. 107–12.

Gu Mei 古楳, 1935, *Zhongguo nongcun jingji wenti* 中國農村經濟問題 (Problems of the Chinese Rural Economy), (Shanghai).

Gu Yanwu 顧炎武, n.d. (17th century), *Rizhi lu* 日知錄 (A Record of Knowledge Acquired Day by Day), (Taibei rep., n.d.).

Gu Zhuo 顧卓, Zhu Wenchuan 朱雲泉, Wang Liangfeng 王亮豐, Lu Weimin 陸渭民 1931, *Wuxi xian nongcun jingji diaocha diyiji* 無錫縣農村經濟調查第一集 (An Investigation into the Rural Economy of Wuxi, Volume 1), n.p.

Guangdong jingji nianjian 1940, see Guangdong jingji nianjian bianzhuan weiyuanhui (1941).

Guangdong jingji nianjian bianzhuan weiyuanhui 廣東經濟年鑑編纂委員會 1941, *Ershijiu niandu Guangdong jingji nianjian* 二十九年度廣東經濟年鑑 (Guangdong Economic Yearbook for 1940), (Guangzhou, Guangdong sheng yinhang jingji yanjiushi).

Guangdong liangshi diaojie weiyuanhui 廣東糧食調節委員會 1935, *Guangdong liangshi wenti* 廣東糧食問題 (Problems of Food Supply in Guangdong), (Guangzhou).

Guangdong lishi xuehui 廣東歷史學會 (ed.), 1985, *Mingqing Guangdong shehui jingji xingtai yanjiu* 明清廣東社會形態研究 (Studies into the Features of Guangdong Society in the Ming and Qing), (Guangzhou, Guangdong renmin chubanshe).

Guangdong sheng canye diaocha baogaoshu 廣東省蠶業調查報告書 (A Report of an Investigation into the Silk Industry in Guangdong Province), 1922 (Guangdong, Guangdong sheng difang nonglin shixianchang).

Guangdong sheng minzhengting 廣東省民政廳, 1934, *Guangdong quansheng difang jiyao* 廣東全省地方紀要 (Local Conditions of the Entire Province of Guangdong), Guangzhou.

Guangdong sheng nongye kexueyuan, qinggongyebu ganzhe tangye kexue yanjiusuo 廣東省農業科學院, 輕工業部甘蔗糖業科學研究所, 1963, *Zhongguo ganzhe caipei* 中國甘蔗栽培 (The Cultivation of Sugar Cane in China), (Beijing).

Guangdong sheng yinhang jingji yanjiushi 廣東省銀行經濟研究室, 1938, *Guangdong zhi miye* 廣東之米業 (The Rice Industry in Guangdong), (Guangzhou).

Guangdong sheng zhengfu mishuchu bianyishi 廣東省政府秘書處編譯室 1940, *Guangdong dizheng* 廣東地政 (Land Administration in Guangdong), (n.p.).

Guangdong tangye yu Feng Rui 廣東糖業與馮銳 (The Sugar Industry in Guangdong and Feng Rui), *c.*1937 (Hong Kong).

'Guangzhou tubuye diaocha' 廣州土布業調查 (A survey of the native cloth industry of Guangzhou), 1937, *Guangdong sheng yinhang yuekan* 廣東省銀行月刊 Vol 3, pp. 147–53.

Guangxu Sihui xianzhi 光緒四會縣志 (A Record of Sihui County in the Guangxu Era), 1925.

Guoli Guangdong daxue nongke xueyuan, 1925, *Panyu, Zengcheng, Dongguan, Zhongshan tangye diaocha baogaoshu*, 番禺、增城、東莞、中山糖業調查報告 (A Report on an Investigation into the Sugar Industry in Panyu, Zengcheng, Dongguan, and Zhongshan), n.p.

Guoli Zhongshan daxue nongke xueyuan 國立中山大學農科學院, 1925, 1929, 1933, *Guangdong nongye gaikuang diaocha baogaoshu* 廣東農業概況調查報告書 (A Report of an Investigation into the Agriculture of Guangdong), (Guangzhou).

Guomin jingji jianshe yundong weiyuanhui Guangdong fenhui 國民經濟建設委員會廣東分會, compiled 1937, *Guangdong jiben gongye, teshu gongye, nongcun fuye diaocha baogaoshu* 廣東基本工業、特殊工業、農村副業調查報告書 (A Report of an Investigation into the Basic Industries, Special Industries, and Rural Side-Industries of Guangdong), (Guangzhou).

Hase, Patrick, 1981, 'Notes on rice farming in Sha Tin', *Journal of the Hong Kong Branch of the Royal Asiatic Society*, Vol. 21, pp. 196–206.

Hayashi Megumi 林惠海, 1953, *Chūshi Kōnan nōson shakai seido kenkyū (1)* 中支江南農村社會制度研究 (1), (A Study of Rural Society in Southern Jiangsu, Central China), (Tokyo, Yūhikaku).

Hayes, James, 1977, *The Hong Kong Region, 1850–1911, Institutions and Leadership in Town and Countryside* (Hamden, Conn., Archon Books).

He Changling 賀長齡, 1826 (ed.), *Huangchao jingshi wenbian* 皇朝經世文編 (Essays on Affairs of State in the Present Dynasty).

He Hanwei 何漢威, 1979, *Jinghan tielu chuji shilue* 京漢鐵路初期史略 (The Early History of the Beijing-Hankou Railway), (Hong Kong, Chinese University Press).

—— n.d., *Guangxu chunian (1876–1879) Huabei de da hanzai* 光緒初年 (1876–1879) 華北的大旱災 (The Great Drought of North China in the Early Years of Guangxu), (Hong Kong, Chinese University Press).

He Menglei 何夢雷, n.d. (written 1934), *Suzhou, Wuxi, Changshu sanxian zudian zhidu diaocha* 蘇州、無錫、常熟三縣租佃制度調查 (An Investigation into the Tenancy Systems of the Three Counties of Suzhou, Wuxi, and Changshu), Vol. 63 in Xiao Zheng, 1977 (Taibei).

Hinton, Harold C., 1956, *The Grain Tribute System of China (1845–1911)* (Cambridge, Mass., Harvard University Press).

Ho, Franklin, 1930, 'Index numbers of the quantities and prices of imports and exports and of the barter terms of trade in China, 1867–1928', *Chinese Economic Journal*, Vol 7, pp. 1013–41.

Ho Ping-ti, 1967, *Studies on the Population of China, 1368–1953* (Cambridge, Mass., Harvard University Press).

Ho Ping-yin, 1935, 'A survey of China's trade with Hong Kong', *Chinese Economic Journal*, Vol. 16, pp. 331–59.

Hong Kong Government, 1920, 'Preliminary report on the purchase and sale of rice by the Government of Hong Kong during the year 1919', *Sessional Papers of the Legislative Council 1919* (Hong Kong).

Howard, C.W., and Buswell, K.P. 1925, *A Survey of the Silk Industry of South China* (Guangzhou, Lingnan Agricultural College).

Hsiao Liang-lin, 1974, *China's Foreign Trade Statistics, 1864–1949* (Cambridge, Mass., Harvard University, East Asian Research Centre).

Hu Huanyong 胡煥庸, 1958, 'Jiangsu sheng de renkou midu yu nongye quyu' 江蘇省的人口密度與農業區域 (Population density and agricultural regions in Jiangsu), *Huadong shida dili jikan* 華東師大地理集刊, rep. in his 1983, *Lun Zhongguo renkou zhi fenbu* 論中國人口之分佈 (On the Distribution of Population in China), Shanghai.

Hu Huanyong and Zhang Shanyu, 1984, *Zhongguo Renkou Dili* 中國人口地理, Vol. 1 (Shanghai, Huadong Shifan daxue chubanshe).

Hu Linge 胡林閣, Zhu Bangxing 朱邦興, Xu Sheng 徐聲, 1939, *Shanghai chanye yu shanghai zhigong* 上海產業與上海職工 (Shanghai Enterprises and Shanghai Workers), (Hong Kong, Yuandong chubanshe).

Huang, Philip C.C., 1975, 'Analyzing the twentieth century Chinese countryside, revolutionaries versus Western scholarship', *Modern China*, pp. 132–60.

—— 1985, *The Peasant Economy and Social Change in North China* (Stanford, Stanford University Press).

Huang Qichen 黃啓臣, 1984, 'Mingqing Zhujiang sanjiaozhou shangye yu shangren ziben de fazhan' 明清珠江三角洲商業與商人資本的發展 (Trade and the development of merchant capital on the Zhujiang delta in the Ming and Qing), *Zhongguo shehui jingjishi yanjiu*, pp. 37–50.

Huang Wei 黃葦, Xia Lin'gen 夏林根 (compilers), 1984, *Jindai Shanghai diqu fangzhi jingji shiliao xuanji, (1840–1949)* 近代上海地區方志經濟史料選輯 (A Selection of Source Materials for Economic History from the Local Histories of the Shanghai Region in the Modern Period), (Shanghai, Shanghai renmin chubanshe).

Huang Xiaoxian 黃孝先, 1927, 'Haimen nongmin zhuangkuang diaocha' 海門農民狀況調查 (An Investigation into the conditions of the peasants of Haimen), *Dongfang zazhi* 東方雜志 Vol. 24, No. 16, pp. 21–31.

Huang Yanpei 黃炎培, 1936, 'Minguo shiqi nian zhi Chuansha nongmin', 民國十七年之川沙農民 (The peasants of Chuansha in the 17th year of the Republic), in *Chuansha xianzhi 1936*, pp. 5/13b–20a.

Huang Yonghao 黃永豪, compiler, 1987, *Xu Shu boshi suoji Guangdong zongzu qiju huilu* 許舒博士所輯廣東宗族契據彙錄 (A Collection of Land Deeds Related to Guangdong Lineages Compiled by Dr. James Hayes), Vol. 1 (Tokyo, Tōyōbunka kenkyūsho, Tokyo University).

Huang Zhenyi 黃振彝, 1936, *Zuijin Qiongya jingji zhi qushi* 最近瓊崖經濟之趨勢 (Recent trends in the economy of Hainan Island), Haikou.

Huenemann, Ralph William, 1984, *The Dragon and the Iron Horse, the Economics of Railroads in China, 1876–1937* (Cambridge, Mass., Harvard University, Council on East Asian Studies).

Hyde, Francis Edwin, 1973, *Far Eastern Trade, 1860–1914* (London, Adam and Charles Black).

Ihara Hirosuke 伊原弘介, 1967, 'Hanji giden ni okeru shin-matsu no kosaku seido' 范氏義田における清末の小作制度 (The tenancy system of the late Qing period in the charity estate of the Fan lineage), *Hiroshima daigaku bungaku kiyo* 廣島大學文學部紀要 Vol. 26, rep. in *Chūgoku kankei ronsetsu shiryo* 中國關係論說資料, Vol. 7c.

Ichiko Chūso 市古宙三, 1971, 'The gentry and the Chuan-sha riot of 1911', in Ichiko Chūso, 1971, *Kindai Chūgoku no seiji to shakai* 近代中國の政治と社會 (The Politics and Society of Modern China) (Tokyo, Tokyo University Press).

Imahori Seiji 今堀誠二, 1956, 'Shindai ni okeru nōson kikō kindaika ni tsuite — Kōtōshō Kōsanken Tōkai chihō ni okeru 'kyōdotai' no suiten katei' 清代における農村機構の近代化について — 廣東省香山縣東海地方における「共同體」の推轉過程 (A study of the modernisation of village organization in the Qing period — the evolution of the 'communal structure' of the Eastern Sea area of Xiangshan County in Guangdong Province), *Rekishigaku kenkyū* 歷史學研究 vol. 191, pp. 3–17, vol. 192, pp. 14–29.

'Index numbers of wholesale prices', 1937, *Chinese Economic Journal*, Vol. 20, p. 722.

Institute of Pacific Relations, Research Staff of the Secretariat (comp. and transl), 1939, *Agrarian China, Selected Source Materials from Chinese Authors* (London, George Allen and Unwin).

Ingram, James C., 1964, 'Thailand's rice trade and the allocation of resources', in C.D. Cowan (ed.), 1964, *The Economic Development of South-east Asia, Studies in Economic History and Political Economy* (London, George Allen and Unwin), pp. 102–26.

Jamieson, George, 1888–9, 'Tenure of land in China and the condition of the rural population', *Journal of the North China Branch of the Royal Asiatic Society*, Vol. 23, pp. 59–118.

Jiang Luo 江犖, 'Guangdong Huaxian nongcun jingji gaikuang' 廣東花縣農村經濟概況 (The conditions of the rural economy in Hua County in Guangdong), *Zhongguo Nongcun*, Vol. 1, No. 4, rep. in Feng Hefa (1935), pp. 285–96.

Jiangyin xian xuzhi 江陰縣續志 (Supplement to the Records of Jiangyin County), 1920.

'Jiangning xian Huacheng xiang' 江寧縣化乘鄉 (Huacheng district in Jiangning county), 1934, Zhongyang nongcun shiyansuo 中央農村實驗所, *Nongqing baogao* 農情報告, vol. 2, no. 3, rep. in Feng Hefa (1933), pp. 698–705.

Jiangsu 江蘇 (Jiangsu), 1903–1904, monthly (Tokyo, Jiangsu Tongxianghui; Taibei reprint, 1968).

Jiangsu sheng nongmin yinhang 江蘇省農民銀行, 1931, 'Tongshan nongcun jingji diaocha' 銅山農村經濟調查 (An investigation into the rural economy of Tongshan), rep. in Feng Hefa (1933), pp. 362–88.

Jiaotongbu youzheng zongju 交通部郵政總局 1937, *Zhongguo tongyou difang wuchanzhi* 中國通郵地方物產誌 (A Record of the Produce of Places Served by the Post Office), Shanghai.

Jin Lunhai 金輪海, 1937, *Nongcun jianzao* 農村建造 (Rural Construction), (Shanghai).

Jing Su 景甦, Luo Lun 羅崙, 1959, *Qingdai Shandong jingying dizhu di shehui xingzhi* 清代山東經營地主底社會性質 (Shandong, Renmin chubanshe).

Jinling daxue nongke xueyuan nongye jingjixi 金陵大學農科學院農業經濟系 1932, 'Zhonghua minguo ershinian shuizai quyu zhi jingji diaocha' 中華民國二十年水災區域之經濟調查 (An investigation into the economy of the flooded area in the 20th year of the Republic), *Jinling xuebao* 金陵學報, Vol. 2, No. 1.

Jones, Susan Mann, 1981, 'Misunderstanding the Chinese economy — a review article', *Journal of Asian Studies*, Vol. 40, pp. 539–57.

Kamm, John, 1977, 'Two essays on the Ch'ing economy of Hsin-an, Kwangtung', *Journal of the Hong Kong Branch of the Royal Asiatic Society*, Vol. 17, pp. 55–84.

Kann, Eduard, 1927, *The Currencies of China* (Shanghai, Kelly and Walsh).

Kao Chi-yu, 1940, 'War and farm prices in China', *Economic Facts*, No. 14, pp. 107–16.

Ke Dawei 科大衛 (David Faure) and Lu Hongji 陸鴻基, 1980,'Xiangdongcun Dushi diqi jianjie' 向東村杜氏地契簡介 (A short description of the land deeds of the Du lineage of Xiangdong Village), *Journal of the Institute of Chinese Studies of the Chinese University of Hong Kong*, Vol. 11, pp. 141–62.

Ke Dawei, Lu Hongji, and Wu Lun Nixia 吳倫霓霞, 1986, *Xiánggang Beiming Huibian* 香港碑銘彙編 (A Collection of Historical Inscriptions in Hong Kong), (Hong Kong, Hong Kong Urban Council).

King, Frank H.H., 1965, *Money and Monetary Policy in China, 1845–1895* (Cambridge, Mass., Harvard University Press).

Ko Fuh-ting, 1937, 'Wholesale prices of important farm crops', *Economic Facts*, No. 5, p. 224.

Kobayashi Kazumi 小林一美 1967, 'Jūkyū ni okeru chūgoku nōmin tōsō no shodankei', 十九世紀における中國農民鬪爭の諸段階 (Stages of Chinese peasant struggles in the nineteenth century), Ōtsuku shigakukai 大塚史學會 (ed.), 1967, *Higashi ajia kindaishi no kenkyū* 東アじア近代史の研究 (Tokyo), pp. 160–302.

Kojima Yoshio 小島淑男, 1964, 'Shinmatsu no gōson tochi ni tsuite', 清末の鄉村統治について (A study of village government at the end of the Qing period), *Shicho* 史潮, Vol. 88, pp. 16–30.

—— 1967, 'Shingai kakumei zengo ni okeru Soshufu nōson shakai to nōmin tōsō' 辛亥革命前後における蘇州府農村社會と農民鬪爭 (Village society and peasant struggles in Suzhou Prefecture before and after the 1911 Revolution), in Tokyō Kyōiku Daigaku Tōyōshigaku Kenkyūshitsu and Ajiashi Kenkyūkai Chūgoku Kindaishi Kenkyūkai, 1967, pp. 297–363.

Kong Xiangxi 孔祥熙, 1935, *Zhengli difang caizheng jianyao baogao* 整理地方財政簡要報告 (A Concise Report on the Reorganisation of Local Finance), n.p.

Kraus, Richard A., 1980, *Cotton and Cotton Goods in China* (New York, Garland).

Kuhn, Philip A., 1970, *Rebellion and Its Enemies in Late Imperial China, Militarization and Social Structure, 1796–1864* (Cambridge, Mass., Harvard University Press).

—— 1975, 'Local self-government under the Republic: problems of control, autonomy, and mobilization', in Frederic Wakeman and Carolyn Grant (1975), pp. 257–98.

—— 1979, 'Local taxation and finance in Republican China', in Susan Mann Jones (ed.), 1979, *Select Papers from the Center for Far Eastern Studies, No. 3, 1978–79*, pp. 100–36.

Kulp, Daniel Harrison, 1925, *Country Life in South China* (New York, Columbia University, Teachers College, 1972 Taibei rep.).

'Kwangtung Government sugar factories', 1936, *Chinese Economic Journal*, Vol. 18, pp. 152–69.

'Kwangtung agricultural statistics', 1928, *Chinese Economic Journal*, pp. 328–33.

Lamb, Jefferson D.H., 1934, *The Development of the Agrarian Movement and Agrarian Legislation in China*, (Shanghai, Commercial Press, rep. 1980, New York, Garland Publishing Inc.).

Latham, A.J.H., 1981, *The Depression and the Developing World, 1914–1939* (London, Croom Helm).

—— 1978, *The International Economy and the Under-developed World 1865–1914* (London, Croom Helm).

—— and Neal, Larry, 1983, 'The international market in rice and wheat, 1868–1914', *Economic History Review*, Vol. 36, No. 2, pp. 260–80.

Leavens, Dickens H., 1939, *Silver Money* (Bloomington, Indiana, Principia Press).

Lei Yue Wai and Lei Hei Kit, 1926, 'Report on a steam filature in Kwangtung', *Lingnan Agricultural Review*, Vol. 3, No. 2, pp. 109–50.

Lewis, A.B. and Wang Lien, 1936a, 'Farm prices in Wuchin, Kiangsu', *Economic Facts*, No 2, pp. 73–91.

—— 1936b, 'Wholesale prices in different cities in China and in Hong Kong, 1930 to 1936', *Economic Facts*, No. 2, pp. 92–106.

Li Changfu 李長傅, 1936, *Fensheng dizhi: Jiangsu* 分省地誌：江蘇 (Provincial Geography: Jiangsu), (Shanghai).

Li Chengru 李程儒, 1827, *Jiangsu Shanyang shouzu quan'an* 江蘇山陽收租全案 (A Complete Record of the Tenancy Issue at Shanyang in Jiangsu), rep. in *Qingshi ziliao* 清史資料, Beijing, 1981, No. 2, pp. 1–32.

Li Fan 李範, 1934, *Wujinxian nongcun xinyong zhi zhuangkuang jiqi yu dichuan yidong zhi guanxi* 武進縣農村信用之狀況及其與地權異動之關係 (The Conditions of Rural Credit and Its Relationship to Changes in Land Rights in Wujin County), No. 88 in Xiao Zheng (1977).

Li Heng 李珩, 1932, 'Wuxi de qiangmi fengchao' 無錫的搶米風潮 (A wave of rice looting in Wuxi), *Xinchuangzao* 新創造 Vol. 2, Nos. 1 and 2, rep. in Feng Hefa (1933), pp. 422–28.

Li, Lillian M., 1981, *China's Silk Trade: Traditional Industry in the Modern World, 1842–1937* (Cambridge, Mass., Harvard University Council on East Asian Studies).

—— 1982, 'Silks by sea: trade, technology, and enterprise in China and Japan', Business History Review, Vol. 56, No. 2, pp. 192–217.

Li Longqian 李龍潛, 1982, 'Mingqing shiqi Guangdong xushi de leixing jiqi tedian' 明清時期廣東墟市的類型及其特點 (The types and special features of rural markets in Guangdong in the Ming and Qing), *Xuexu yanjiu* 學術研究.

Li Shiyue 李時岳, 1958, 'Qingmo nongcun jingji de bengkui yu nongmin yundong' 清末農村經濟的崩潰與農民運動 (The collapse of the rural economy and the peasant movement in the late Qing), *Shixue yuekan* 史學月刊, No. 6.

Li Shuyuan 李書源, 1984, 'Taiping tianguo "zuxiju" kaolue' 太平天國「租息局」考略 (A study of the "Rent Offices" of the Taiping Heavenly Kingdom), *Jindaishi yanjiu* 近代史研究, No. 5, pp. 122–36.

Li Taichu 李泰初 1964, 'Youguan Zhongguo jindai duiwai maoyi ruogan wenti zhi shangque' 有關中國近代對外貿易若干問題之商榷 (An examination of certain problems in China's foreign trade in the modern era), *Zhuhai xuebao* 珠海學報, pp. 174–287.

Li Wenzhi 李文治, 1957, *Zhongguo jindai nongyeshi ziliao* 中國近代農業史資料 (Source Materials on Modern China's Agriculture), Vol. 1 (Beijing).

Liang, Ernest P., 1982, *China: Railways and Agricultural Development, 1875–1935*, research paper no. 203 (Chicago, University of Chicago, Department of Geography).

Liang Jen-ts'ai, 1956, *Economic Geography of Kwangtung* (Beijing, transl. U.S. Government, CCM Information Corporation, n.d., n.p.).

Liang Shuming 梁漱溟, 1937, *Xiangcun jianshe lilun* 鄉村建設理論 (Theories for Rural Construction), (Zouping, Xiangcun shudian).

Lin Gang 林剛, 1985, 'Shilun Dasheng shachang de shichang jichu' 試論大生 紗廠的市場基礎 (A preliminary discussion of the market foundation of the Dasheng Spinning Mill), *Lishi yanjiu* 歷史研究, No. 4, pp. 180–92.

Lin Guangcheng 林光澂, Chen Jie 陳捷 n.d., *Zhongguo duliangheng* 中國度量 衡 (China's Measures of Length, Capacity, and Weight), (Taibei).

Lin Jinzhi 林金枝, 1980, 'Jindai huaqiao touzi guonei qiye de jige wenti' 近代 華僑投資國內企業的幾個問題 (Several problems related to modern overseas Chinese investment in China's enterprises), *Jindaishi yanjiu*, Vol. 3, No. 1, pp. 199–230.

Lin Shidan 林詩旦, n.d. (1930s), *Guangdong quansheng tianfu zhi yanjiu* 廣東 全省田賦之研究 (A Study into the Land Tax of the Entire Guangdong Province), No. 4 in Xiao Zheng, 1977, Taibei.

Liu Chengzhang 劉承章, n.d (*zu* dated 1934), *Tongshan xian xiangcun xinyong zhi zhuangkuang jiqi yu diquan yidong zhi guanxi* 銅山縣鄉村信用 之狀況及其與地權異動的關係 (Conditions of Rural Credit and Its Re- lationships to Changes in Land Rights in Tongshan County), Vol. 90 in Xiao Zheng, 1977, Taibei.

Liu Kwang-ching, 1962, *Anglo-American Steamship Rivalry in China, 1862–1874* (Cambridge, Mass., Harvard University Press).

Liu Maofeng wei zhengju zongbu 劉茂豐圍證據總部 (A Record of Documen- tary Evidence Related to the Liu Maofeng Dyke), n.d. (*c*.1932).

Liu Shiji 劉石吉, 1978, 'Mingqing shidai Jiangnan shizhen zhi shuliang fenxi' 明清時代江南市鎮之數量分析 (A quantitative analysis of market towns in southern Jiangsu in the Ming and Qing), *Si yu yan* 思與言, Vol. 16, No. 2, pp. 128–49.

Liu Yongcheng 劉永成, 1980, 'Qingdai qianji de nongye zudian guanxi', 清代 前期的農業租佃關係 (Agricultural tenancy relationships in the early Qing), *Qingshi luncong* 清史論業, No. 2, pp. 56–88.

Liu Zhonglian 劉仲廉, 1948, 'Minyuan lai woguo zhi liangshi wenti' 民元來我 國之糧食問題 (The food problem in our country since the first year of the Republic), in Yinhang xuehui 銀行學會 (ed.), 1948, *Minguo jingji shi* 民國經濟史 (An Economic History of the Republic), rep. in Zhou Kaiqing 周開慶 (ed.) 1967, *Jindai Zhongguo jingji congbian* 近代中國經濟 叢編 (Modern Chinese Economics Series), Vol. 5 (Taibei).

Lojewski, Frank A., 1979, 'Ting Jih-ch'ang in Kiangsu: traditional methods of surmounting dysfunction in local administration during the late Ch'ing,' *Zhongyang yanjiu yuan, Jindaishi yanjiusuo jikan*, Vol. 8, pp. 235–52.

—— 1980, 'The Soochow bursaries: rent management during the late Qing', *Ch'ing-shih wen-ti*, Vol. 4, No. 3, pp. 43–65.

Long Shengyun 龍盛運, 1958, 'Taiping tianguo houqi tudi zhidu de shishi wenti' 太平天國後期土地制度的實施問題 (Some problems related to the implementation of land policies in the later years of the Taiping Heavenly Kingdom), *Lishi yanjiu*, Vol. X., pp. 35–54.

Lu Zhushou 盧株守, 1934, 'Jiangsu Xiaoxian dongnan jiuge cunzhuang de nongye shengchan fangshi' 江蘇蕭縣東南九個村莊的農村生產方式 (Modes of production in nine villages in southeast Xiao County in Jiangsu), *Zhongguo nongcun*, Vol. 1, No. 5, rep. in Feng Hefa, 1935, pp. 691–97.

Luo Gengmo 駱耕漠, 1934, 'Xinyong hezuo shiye yu Zhongguo nongcun jinrong' 信用合作事業與中國農村金融, *Zhongguo nongcun yuekan* 中國農村月刊, Vol. 1, No. 2, rep. in Feng Hefa, 1935, pp. 785–803.

—— 1935, 'Zhongguo nongchan yunxiao di xin quxi' 中國農村運銷底新趨勢 (New trends in rural transport and distribution in China), *Zhongguo nongcun*, Vol. 1, No. 4, rep. in Feng Hefa (1935) pp. 921–39.

Luo Sibing 樂嗣炳, 1935, *Zhongguo cansi* 中國蠶絲 (Chinese Silk), (Shanghai).

Ma Baohua 馬寶華, n.d. (written 1930s), *Baoying xian zhi dianzu diaocha* 寶應縣之佃租調查 (An Investigation into Tenancy in Baoying County), Vol. 61, in Xiao Zheng, 1977.

Ma Yinchu 馬寅初, 1929, *Zhonghua Yinhang lun* 中華銀行論 (On China's Banks), (Shanghai, Shangwu yinshuguan).

Malone, C.B. and Taylor, G.B., 1924, 'The study of Chinese rural economy', translated in Feng Hefa, 1933.

Mann, Susan, 1987, *Local Merchants and the Chinese Bureaucracy, 1750–1950* (Stanford, Stanford University Press).

Mantetsu Shanhai Jimusho Chōsashitsu 滿鐵上海事務所調查室, 1939, *Kōsoshō Jōjukuken nōson jittai chōsa hōkokusho* 江蘇省常熟縣農村實態調查報告書 (A Report of an Investigation into Actual Conditions in the Villages of Wuxi County, Jiangsu Province), (Shanghai).

—— 1940a, *Shanhai Tokubetsushi katei-ku nōson jittai chōsa hōkokusho* 海特別市嘉定區農村實態調查報告書 (A Report of an Investigation into Actual Conditions in the Villages of Jiading District in the Special Metropolis of Shanghai), (Shanghai).

—— 1940b, *Kōsoshō Taishoken nōson jittai chōsa hōkokusho* 江蘇省太倉縣農村實態調查報告書 (A Report of an Investigation into Actual Conditions in the Villages of Taicang County in Jiangsu Province), (Shanghai).

—— 1941, *Kōsoshō Shōkōken nōson jittai chōsa hōkokusho* 江蘇省松江縣農村實態調查報告書 (A Report of an Investigation into Actual Conditions in the Villages of Songjiang County in Jiangsu Province), (Shanghai).

Mantetsu Shanhai Jimusho Chōsabu 滿鐵上海事務所調查部 1941a, *Kōsoshō Mushaku-ken nōson jittai chōsa hōkokusho* 江蘇省無錫縣農村實態調查報告書 (A Report of an Investigation into Actual Conditions in the Villages of Wuxi County in Jiangsu Province), (Shanghai).

—— 1941b, *Kōsoshō Nantsūken nōson jittai chōsa hōkokusho* 江蘇省南通縣農村實態調查報告書 (A Report of an Investigation into Actual Conditions in the Villages of Nantong County in Jiangsu Province), (Shanghai).

Marks, Robert B., 1978, *Rural Social Change in Haifeng County on the Eve of the Haifeng Peasant Movement, 1870–1920* (Cambridge, Mass., Fairbank Centre for East Asian Research).

MC, see China, Maritime Customs.

McElderry, Andrea Lee, 1976, *Shanghai Old-Style Banks (Ch'ien-chuang), 1800–1935* (Ann Arbor, University of Michigan, Center for Chinese Studies).

Min Zongdian 閔宗殿 and Wang Da 王達, 1985, 'Wanqing shiqi woguo nongye de xinbianhua' 晚清時期我國農業的新變化 (New agricultural changes in our country in the late Qing period), *Zhongguo shehui jingjishi yanjiu*, No. 4, pp. 64–72.

Mizuno Kokichi 水野幸吉, 1907, *Kanko* 漢口 (Hankou), (Tokyo).

Moise, Edwin E., 1977, 'Downward social mobility in pre-revolutionary China', *Modern China*, Vol. 3, No. 1, pp. 3–31.

Morse, H.B., 1889–90, 'Currency and measures in China', *Journal of the North China Branch of the Royal Asiatic Society*, Vol. 24, pp. 46–135.

Muramatsu Yūji 村松祐次, 1970, *Kindai Kōnan no sosan — Chūgoku chishū seido no kenkyū* 近代江南の租棧—中國地主制度の研究 (The Rent-Collection Offices of Modern Jiangnan — a study of the Landlord System of China), (Tokyo).

Murphey, Rhoads, 1953, *Shanghai, Key to Modern China* (Cambridge, Mass., Harvard University Press).

—— 1970, *The Treaty Ports and China's Modernization: What Went Wrong?* (Ann Arbor, Michigan Papers in Chinese Studies).

Myers, Ramon H., 1965, 'Cotton textile handicraft and the development of the cotton textile industry in modern China', *Economic History Review*, Vol. 18, No. 3, pp. 614–32.

—— 1970, *The Chinese Peasant Economy, Agricultural Development in Hopei and Shantung, 1890–1949* (Cambridge, Mass., Harvard University Press).

NCH: *North-China Herald and Supreme Court and Consular Gazette* (weekly edition of the *North-China Daily News*), (Shanghai).

Nanhai xian gongbao 南海縣公報, 1928 (Guangzhou, Nanhaixian jiaoyuju).

Negishi Benji 根岸勉治, 1940, *Minami Shina nōgyo keizai ron* 南支那農業經濟論 (On the Rural Economy of South China), (Taibei).

Niida Noburo 仁井田陞, 1960, *Chūgoku hoseshi kenkyū* 中國法制史研究 (Studies of Chinese Legal History), (Tokyo, Tokyo University Press).

Nongcun fuxing weiyuanhui 農村復興委員會, 1934, *Jiangsu sheng nongcun diaocha* 江蘇省農村調查 (Investigations into the Villages of Jiangsu Province), (Shanghai).

Okumura Tetsu 奧村哲, 1978, *Kyōkōka Kōsetsu sanshigyō no saihen* 恐慌下江

浙鼉絲業の再編 (The re-organization of the silk industry in Jiangsu and Zhejiang under the Depression), *Tōyōshi kenkyū* 東洋史研究 Vol. 37, No. 2, pp. 80–116.

Ou Jiluan 區季鸞, Huang Yinpu 黃蔭普, 1932, *Guangzhou zhi yinye* 廣州之銀業 (The Native Banks in Guangzhou), Guangzhou.

Oyama, Masaaki 小山正明, 1960, '*Shinmatsu Chūgoku ni okeru gaikoku menseihin no ryūnyū*' 清末中國における外國綿製品の流入 (The inflow of foreign cotton manufactures into China at the end of the Qing dynasty), *Kindai Chūgoku kenkyū* 近代中國研究, no. 4.

Palmer, Michael J.E., 1987, 'The surface-subsoil form of divided ownership in late Imperial China: some examples from the New Territories of Hong Kong', *Modern Asian Studies*, Vol. 21, pp. 1–119.

Pan Yiyun 潘翼雲, 1937, *Guangdong Shunde cannong de shenghuo* 廣東順德蠶農的生活 (The Life of the Silk-Farmer in Shunde, Guangdong), in Yu Qingtang, 1937, pp. 119–24.

Peng Chengwan 彭程萬, Yin Ruli 殷汝驪, 1920, *Diaocha Qiongya shiye baogaoshu* 調查瓊崖實業報告書 (Report of an Investigation into the Enterprises of Hainan Island), Haikou.

Peng Chuheng 彭楚珩, 1937, *Yuehan tielu beilan* 粵漢鐵路備覽 (Handbook for the Guangzhou-Hankou Railway), n.p.

Peng Pai 彭湃, 1926, 'Haifeng nongmin yundong' 海豐農民運動 (The peasant movement in Haifeng), reproduced in *Diyici guonei geming zhanzheng shiqi de nongmin yundong*, 1953, 第一次國內革命戰爭時期的農民運動 (The Peasant Movement During the First Revolutionary Wars in China), (Beijing, Renmin chubanshe, pp. 40–170).

Peng Xinwei 彭信威, 1958, *Zhongguo huobishi* 中國貨幣史 (A Monetary History of China), (Shanghai, Shanghai renmin chubanshe).

Perkins, Dwight H., 1969, *Agricultural Development in China, 1368–1968* (Edinburgh, Edinburgh University Press).

Polachek, James M., 1975, 'Gentry hegemony: Soochow in the T'ung-chih restoration', in Frederic Wakeman and Carolyn Grant (eds.) (1975), pp. 211–56.

—— 1983, 'The moral economy of the Kiangsi Soviet (1928–1934)', *Journal of Asian Studies*, Vol. 42, No. 4, pp. 805–29.

Popkin, Samuel L., 1979, *The Rational Peasant, the Political Economy of Rural Society in Vietnam* (Berkeley, University of California Press).

Potter, Jack M., 1968, *Capitalism and the Chinese Peasant, Social and Economic Change in a Hong Kong Village* (Berkeley, University of California Press).

Prazniak, Roxann, 1986, 'Weavers and sorceresses of Chuansha, the social origins of political activism among rural Chinese women', *Modern China*, Vol 12, No. 2, pp. 202–29.

Prinsen Geerligs, H.C. and Prinsen Geerligs R.J., 1912, *The World's Cane Sugar Industry, Past and Present* (Manchester, Rodger).

—— 1938, *Cane Sugar Production, 1912–1937* (London, Rodger).

'Puning xian nongmin fankang dizhu shimoji' 普寧縣農民反抗地主始末記 (An account of the peasants' rebellion against the landlords in Puning County from beginning to end), 1927, originally published as 'Guang-dong sheng nongmin xiehui Chaomei Hailufeng banshichu baogao' 廣東省農民協會潮梅海陸豐辦事處報告 (Report from the Chao-Mei and Hai-Lufeng Office of the Guangdong Peasants' Association), in *Guangdong nongmin yundong jingguo gaikuang* 廣東農民運動經過概況 (A General Account of the Guangdong Peasants' Movement), 1927, reproduced in *Diyici guonei zhanzheng shiqi de nongmin yundong*, Beijing, 1953, pp. 158–70.

Qian Jiaju 千家駒, 1936, *Zhongguo nongcun jingji lunwenji* 中國農村經濟論文集 (Essays on the Chinese Rural Economy), (Shanghai, Zhonghua shudian).

Qian Junrui 錢俊瑞, 1935, 'Muqian kongfang xia Zhongguo nongmin de shenghuo' 目前恐慌下中國農民的生活 (The Chinese peasant's livelihood under the present depression), *Dongfang zazhi*, Vol. 32, No. 1, pp. nong 35–44.

Qiao Qiming 喬啓明, 1926, 'Jiangsu Kunshan, Nantong, Anhui Suxian, nongdian zhidu zhi bijiao yiji gailiang nongdian wenti zhi jianyi' 江蘇昆山、南通、安徽宿縣農佃制度之比較以及改良農佃問題之建議(A comparison of the farm tenancy systems in Kunshan and Nantong in Jiangsu and Su county in Anhui, and suggestions for the problem of improving farm tenancy conditions), *Jinling daxue nonglin congkan* 金陵大學農林叢刊, Vol. 30, reproduced in Feng Hefa, 1933, pp. 80–117.

—— 1934, *Jiangning xian Shunhua zhen xiangcun shehui zhi yanjiu* 江寧縣淳化鎮鄉村社會之研究 (A Study of Rural Society in Shunhua *Zhen* in Jiangning County), (Nanjing, Jinling daxue).

—— 1946, *Zhongguo nongcun shehui jingjixue* 中國農村社會經濟學 (The Economy of Chinese Rural Society), (Shenghai, Shangwu yinshuguan).

Qiao Qiming and Jiang Jie 蔣傑, 1937, *Zhongguo renkou yu liangshi wenti* 中國人口與糧食問題 (China's Population and the Food Problem), (Shanghai, Zhonghua shuju).

Qingyuan xianzhi 清遠縣志 (A Record of Qingyuan County), 1937, rep. 1973, Hong Kong.

Quan Hansheng全漢昇 and He Hanwei,1978,'Qingji de shangban tielu' 清季的商辦鐵路 (Commercial railways in the Qing), *Journal of the Institute of Chinese Studies of the Chinese University of Hong Kong*, Vol. 9, pp. 119–172.

Quanguo jingji weiyuanhui 全國經濟委員會, 1936, *Renzaosi gongye baogao-shu, quanguo jingji weiyuanhui jingji zhuankan diliuzhong* 人造絲工業報告書，全國經濟委員會經濟專刊第六種, (A Report on the Artificial Silk Industry, Economics Monograph No. 6 of the National Economic Committee), n.p.

Raeburn, John R., and Hu Kwoh-hwa, 1937, 'The flexibility of prices in China', *Economic Facts*, No. 7, pp. 394–405.

Raeburn, John R., Hu Kwoh-hwa, and Ko Fuh-ting, 1937, 'Crop prices', *Economic Facts*, No. 7, pp. 312–75.

Raeburn, John R., and Ko Fuh-ting, 1937a, 'Prices paid and received by farmers in Wuchin, Kiangsu', *Economic Facts*, No. 6, pp. 250–61.

—— 1937b 'Crop prices', *Economic Facts*, No. 6, pp. 262–72. ·

Rawley, Ratan C., 1919, *Economics of the Silk Industry, a Study in Industrial Organization* (London, P.S. King).

Rawski, Evelyn Sakakida, 1972, *Agricultural Change and the Peasant Economy of South China* (Cambridge, Mass., Harvard University Press).

Rawski, Thomas, forthcoming, *Economic Growth in Prewar China*.

Remer, C.F., 1933, *Foreign Investment in China* (New York, H. Firtig, Taibei rep. 1968).

Reynolds, Bruce, 1978, review of Kang Chao (1977), *Journal of Asian Studies*, Vol. 37, No. 3, pp. 507–10.

Reynolds, Lloyd G., 1985, *Economic Growth in the Third World, 1850–1980* (New Haven, Yale University Press).

Rong An 容盦, 1927, 'Gedi nongmin zhuangkuang diaocha-Wuxi' 各地農民狀況調查——無錫 (Investigations into the Conditions of the Peasantry in Various Locations — Wuxi), *Dongfang zazhi*, Vol. 24, No. 16, pp. 109–13.

Rongshi pudie 容氏譜牒 (The Genealogy of the Rong Surname), 1929 (Guangzhou).

Rostow, W.W., 1978, *The World Economy, History and Prospect* (Austin, University of Texas Press).

Rowe, William T., 1984, *Hankow, Commerce and Society in a Chinese City, 1796–1889* (Stanford, Stanford University Press).

Rozman, Gilbert, 1973, *Urban Networks in Ch'ing China and Tokugawa Japan* (Princeton, Princeton University Press).

—— 1982, *Population and Marketing Settlements in Ch'ing China* (Cambridge, Cambridge University Press).

Sasaki Masaya 佐佐木正哉, 1959, 'Juntoku ken kyōshin to Tōkai jūrokusa' 順德縣鄉紳と東海十六沙 (The Gentry of Shunde and the Sixteen Sands of the Eastern Seas), *Kindai Chūgoku kenkyū*, Vol. 3, pp. 161–232.

Schultz, Theodore, 1964, *Transforming Traditional Agriculture* (New Haven, Yale University Press).

Scott, James C., 1976 *The Moral Economy of the Peasant, Rebellion and Subsistence in Southeast Asia* (New Haven, Yale University Press).

Shanghai jiefang qianhou wujia ziliao huibian, see: Zhongguo kexueyuan Shanghai jingji yanjiu suo, Shanghai shehui kexueyuan jingji yanjiusuo, 1958.

Shanghai shangye chuxu yinhang diaochabu 上海商業儲蓄銀行調查部, 1931a,

Shangbin diaocha congkan, diyibian: mi, Shanghai zhi mi ji miye 商品調
查叢刊第一編：米，上海之米及米業 (Commodites Investigation Series,
No. 1: Rice; Rice and the Rice Industry in Shanghai), (Shanghai).
—— 1931b, *Shangbin diaocha congkan, dierbian: Shanghai zhi mianhua yu
mianye* 商品調查叢刊第二編：上海之棉花與棉業 (Commodities Investig-
ation Series, No. 2: Cotton and the Cotton Industry in Shanghai),
(Shanghai).
Shanghai shehui kexueyuan jingji yanjiusuo 上海社會科學院經濟研究所 ,
1980, *Rongjia qiye shiliao* 榮家企業史料 (Source Materials on the Rong
Family's Enterprises), (Shanghai, Shanghai renmin chubanshe).
Shanghaishi mianfangzhi gongye tongye gonghui choubeihui, 上海市綿紡織
工業同業會籌備會, 1950, *Zhongguo mianfang tongji shiliao* 中國棉紡統計
史料 (Statistical Source Materials on Cotton Spinning in China),
(Shanghai).
Shanghaishi shehuiju 上海市社會局 , 1930, 'Shanghaishi baisishi hu nongjia
diaocha' 上海市百四十戶農家調查 (An investigation into 140 households
in Shanghai City), *Shehui yuekan* 社會月刊 Vol. 2, No. 2, rep. in Feng
Hefa, 1933, pp. 241–329.
—— n.d (*zu* dated 1933), *Shanghai zhi nongye* 上海之農業 (The Agriculture
of Shanghai), (Shanghai).
Shanghai xian xuzhi 上海縣續志 (Supplement to the Record of Shanghai
County), 1918.
Shehui jingji diaochasuo 社會經濟調查所 , n.d. (*c.*1930), *Zhenjiang mishi
diaocha* 鎮江米市調查 (An Investigation into the Rice Market of
Zhenjiang), (Shanghai).
—— 1935a, *Nanjing liangshi diaocha* 南京糧食調查 (An Investigation into
Food Supply in Nanjing), (Shanghai).
—— 1935b, *Shanghai maifen shichang diaocha* 上海麥粉市場調查 (An Investigation into the Wheat Flour Market in Shanghai), (*Liangshi diaocha
congkan, diwuhao* 糧食調查叢刊，第五號 (Food Investigation Series, No.
5)), (Shanghai).
—— 1935c, *Shanghai mishi diaocha* 上海米市調查 (An Investigation into the
Rice Market of Shanghai), (Shanghai), Japanese translation, 1940.
Shen Shike 沈時可 , 1934, *Haimen, Qidong xian zhi zudian zhidu* 海門啓東縣之
租佃制度 (The Tenancy System of Haimen and Qidong Counties),
Vol. 60, in Xiao Zheng (1977).
Shen, N.C., 1936, 'The local government of China', *Chinese Social and
Political Science Review*, pp. 163–201.
Shim, Edward, 1925, 'Report of a fertilizer survey in the mulberry districts
of Kwangtung,' *Lingnaam Agricultural Review*, Vol. 2, No. 2,
pp. 74–89.
Shiyebu guoji maoyiju 實業部國際貿易局 , 1933, *Zhongguo shiyezhi: Jiangsu
sheng* 中國實業志：江蘇省 (A Record of Chinese Enterprises: Jiangsu
Province), (Shanghai).

Shiyebu yinjia wujia taolun weiyuanhui 實業部銀價物價討論委員會 , 1936, *Zhongguo yinjia wujia wenti* 中國銀價物價問題 (Problems concerning the Price of Silver and Commodity Prices in China), (Shanghai).

Shiyebu Zhongguo jingji nianjian bianzhuan weiyuanhui 實業部中國經濟年鑑編纂委員會 1934, *Zhongguo jingji nianjian* 中國經濟年鑑 (The Economic Yearbook of China), (Shanghai).

—— 1936, *Zhongguo jingji nianjian xubian* 中國經濟年鑑續編 (Supplement to the Economic Yearbook of China), (Shanghai).

—— 1937, *Zhongguo jingji nianjian disanbian* 中國經濟年鑑第三編 (Third Edition of the Economic Yearbook of China), (Shanghai).

Shunde Longjiang xiangzhi 順德龍江鄉志 (A Record of Longjiang District in Shunde), 1926.

Shunde xianzhi 順德縣志 (A Record of Shunde County), 1929.

Sichuan sheng Zhongguo jingjishi xuehui 四川省中國經濟史學會 (ed.), 1986, *Zhongguo jingjishi yanjiu luncong* 中國經濟史研究論叢 (Essays on Chinese Economic History), (Chengdu, Sichuan daxue chubanshe).

Skinner, G. William, 1964–5, 'Marketing and social structure in rural China', *Journal of Asian Studies*, Vol. 24, pp. 3–43, Vol. 24, No. 2, pp. 195–228, and Vol 24, No. 3, pp 363–99.

Skinner, G. William, Hsieh, Winston, and Tomika Shigeaki, 1973, *Modern Chinese Society, An Analytical Bibliography* (Stanford, Stanford University Press).

So, Alvin Y., 1986, *The South China Silk District: Local Historical Transformation and the World System Theory* (New York, State University of New York Press).

SP: Shenbao

Spalding, W.F., 1920, *Eastern Exchange, Currency and Finance* (London, Sir Isaac Pitman and Sons, Ltd).

Stauffer, Milton T. (ed.), 1922, *The Christian Occupation of China* (Shanghai).

Stockard, Janice E., 1985, 'Marriage and marriage resistance in the Canton delta, 1860–1930' (unpublished Ph.D. dissertation, Stanford University).

Stross, Randall, 1982, 'A hard row to hoe: the political economy of Chinese agriculture in western Jiangsu, 1911–1937' (unpublished dissertation, Stanford University).

—— 1984, 'Marketing and modernizing in Republican China's countryside: the puzzling case of Western Jiangsu', *Republican China*, No. 2, pp. 1–7.

—— 1985, 'Number games rejected: the misleading allure of tenancy estimates', *Republican China*, Vol. 10, No. 3, pp. 1–17.

Sun Jiashan 孫家山 , 1984, *Subei yankenshi chugao* 蘇北鹽墾史初稿 (A First History of the Reclamation of Salt Land in Northern Jiangsu) (Beijing, Nongye chubanshe).

Sun Tangyue 孫宕越, 1937, 'Yuebei yu Gongnan Xiangnan zhi jiaotong yu yunshu' 粤北與贛南湘南之交通運輸 (Traffic and transport between northern Guangdong and southern Jiangxi and southern Hunan), *Dili xuebao* 地理學報, Vol. 4, No. 1, pp. 867–87.

Suzuki Tomoo 鈴木智夫, 1967, 'Shinmatsu gensoron no tenkai — 'Sokaku' no kenkyū' 清末減租論の展開——「租覈」の研究 (The beginning of the rent-reduction argument in the late Qing — a study of the *zuhe*), in Tōkyō Kyōiku Daigaku Tōyōshigaku Kenkyūshitsu and Ajiashi Kenkyūkai Chūgoku Kindaishi Kenkyūkai, 1967, pp. 199–246.

Tang Wenqi 唐文起, 1985, 'Yingkou tubu shichang de xingshuai jiqi dui Nantong tubuye de yingxiang' 營口土布市場的興衰及其對南通土布業的影響 (The rise and decline of the native cloth market in Yingkou and its impact on the native cloth industry in Nantong), Sichuansheng Zhongguo jingjishi xuehui, 1986, pp. 312–25.

Tao Xu 陶煦, n.d. (*c*.1884), *Zuhe* 租覈 (Inquiry into Rents), 1927, reproduced in Tōkyō Kyōiku Daigaku Tōyōshigaku Kenkyūshitsu and Ajiashi Kenkyūkai Chūgoku Kindaishi Kenkyūkai, 1967.

Taylor, F.E., 1896–7, 'Scarcity of copper cash and the rise in prices', *Journal of the North China Branch of the Royal Asiatic Society*, Vol. 31, pp. 75–80.

Thaxton, Ralph, 1983, *China Turned Rightside Up: Revolutionary Legitimacy in the Peasant World* (New Haven, Yale University Press).

Thompson, E.P., 1971, 'The moral economy of the English crowd in the eighteenth century', *Past and Present*, Vol. 50, pp. 70–136.

Tōa Dōbunkai 東亞同文會 1920, *Shina shōbetsu zenshi* 支那省別全誌 (A Complete Record of China's Provinces), Vol. 16 (Tokyo).

'Tobacco production in Kwangtung', 1926, *Chinese Economic Monthly*, pp. 526–30.

Tōkyō chigaku kyōkai 東京地學協會 1917, *Chūshina oyobi Minami-Shina* 中支那及南支那 (Central China and South China), (Tokyo).

Tōkyō Kyōiku Daigaku Tōyōshigaku Kenkyūshitsu 東京教育大學東洋史學研究室 and Ajiashi Kenkyūkai Chūgoku Kindaishi Kenyūkai アジア史研究會中國近代史研究會, 1967, *Kindai Chūgoku nōson shakaishi kenkyū*, 近代中國農村社會史研究 (Studies of Modern Chinese Rural Social History), (Tokyo, Kyūkō shoin).

Topley, Marjorie, 1975, 'Marriage resistance in rural Kwangtung', in Margery Wolf and Roxann Witke (eds.), *Women in Chinese Society* (Stanford, Stanford University Press).

Touzet, Andre, 1939, *Le régime monétaire indochine* (Paris, Librairie du Recueil Sirey).

Trewartha, Glenn T., 1939, 'Field observations on the Canton delta of South China', *Economic Geography*, pp. 1–10.

Tsu Chwan-hwa, 1939, 'Retail prices in Nanking since the withdrawal of the Chinese forces', *Economic Facts*, No. 12, pp. 608–17.

Ukers, William H., 1935, *All About Tea* (New York).

Viraphol, Sarasin, 1977, *Tribute and Profit: Sino-Siamese Trade, 1652–1853* (Cambridge, Mass., Harvard University Press).

Wakeman, Frederic, and Grant, Carolyn, (eds), 1975, *Conflict and Control in Late Imperial China* (Berkeley, University of California Press).

Walker, Kathy Le Mons, 1986, 'Merchants, peasants, and industry: the political economy of cotton textiles, Nantong County, 1895–1935' (unpublished Ph.D. dissertation, University of California, Los Angeles).

Walker, Kenneth R., 1984, *Food Grain Procurement and Consumption in China* (Cambridge, Cambridge University Press).

Wang Chengyin 汪呈因, 1946, *Tezhong daozuoxue* 特種稻作學 (Studies of Special Varieties of Rice), 1946 (Shanghai, Zhonghua shudian) first edition, 1944.

Wang Di 王笛, 1987, 'Qingmo minchu woguo nongye jiaoyu de xingqi he fazhan' 清末民初我國農業教育的興起和發展 *Zhongguo nongshi* 中國農史 (The rise and development of agricultural education in our country in the late Qing and early Republic), Vol. 1, pp. 65–81.

Wang Jingyu 汪敬虞, 1957, *Zhongguo jindai gongyeshi ziliao* 中國近代工業史資 (Source Materials on Modern Chinese Industrial History), (Beijing, kexue chubanshe).

—— 1962, 'Guanyu Jichanglong sichang di ruogan shiliao ji zhide yanjiu di jige wenti' 關於繼昌隆絲廠的若干史料及值得研究的幾個問題 (On certain source materials on the Jichanglong silk factory and several problems that are worth studying), *Xueshu yanjiu*, No. 6, rep. in Huang Yiping 黃逸平 (ed.), *Zhongguo jindai jingjishi lunwenxuan* 中國近代經濟史論文選 (A Selection of Essays on Modern Chinese Economic History), (Shanghai, Renmin chubanshe, 1985, pp. 671–91).

Wang Nanping 王南屏, 1936, 'Jiangbei nongcun shikuang', 江北農村實況 (Actual conditions in the villages of northern Jiangsu), in Qian Jiaju, 1936, pp. 610–19.

Wang Peitang 王培棠, 1938, *Jiangsu sheng xiangtu zhi* 江蘇省鄉土誌 (A Record of Local Conditions in Jiangsu Province), (Changsha).

Wang Shuhuai 王樹槐, 1984, 'Mianye tongzhi weiyuanhui de gongzuo chengxiao, 1933–1937' 棉業統制委員會的工作成效, 1933–1937 (The achievements of the Cotton Goods Centralisation Committee, 1933–1927), Zhongyang yanjiuyuan jindaishi yanjiusuo, (ed.), *Kangzhanqian shinian guojia jiansheshi yantaohui lunwenji* 抗戰前十年國家建設史研討會論文集 (Essays from the Symposium on the History of National Construction in the Ten Years Before the War), pp. 713–63.

—— 1985, 'Jiangsu Huainan yanken gongsi de kenzhi shiye (1901–1937)', 江蘇淮南鹽墾公司的墾殖事業 (1901–1937) (The reclamation activites of the Huainan Salt-Fields Reclamation Co. in Jiangsu (1901–1937)), *Zhongyang yanjiuyuan jindaishi yanjiusuo jikan*, Vol. 14, pp. 191–266.

—— 1986, 'Jiangsusheng de tudi chenbao, 1933–1936', 江蘇省的土地陳報 1933–1936 (Land reports in Jiangsu Province, 1933–1936), Zhongyang yanjiuyuan jindaishi yanjiusuo, (ed.), *Jindai Zhongguo quyushi yantaohui* 近代中國區域史研討會 (Symposium on Modern Chinese Regional History), pp. 519–57.

Wang Weiping 王維屏, 1956, *Shuixiang Jiangsu* 水鄉江蘇 (Jiangsu, the Water District), (Shanghai).

Wang Yeh-chien, 1973, *Land Taxation in Imperial China, 1750–1911* (Cambridge, Mass., Harvard University Press).

Wang Yejian 王業鍵 (Yeh-chien Wang), 1981, *Zhongguo jindai huobi yu yinhang de yanjin* 中國近代貨幣與銀行的演進 (The Evolution of Currency and Banking in Modern China), (Taibei).

Watson, Rubie S, 1985, *Inequality Among Brothers, Class and Kinship in South China* (Cambridge, Cambridge University Press).

Watt, John, 1972, *The District Magistrate in Late Imperial China* (New York, Columbia University Press).

Wei Jianxiong 韋健雄, 1935, 'Wuxi sange nongcun de nongye jingying diaocha' 無錫三個農村的農業經營 (Rural enterprises in three villages in Wuxi), *Zhongguo nongcun*, Vol. 1, No. 9, rep. in Feng Hefa, 1935, pp. 674–91.

Wei Jianyou 魏建猷, 1955, *Zhongguo jindai huobishi* 中國近代貨幣史 (A Monetary History of Modern China), (Shanghai, Qunlian chubanshe).

Weng Zushan 翁祖善, 1937, 'Wuxi Beixia nongmin shenghuo mantan 無錫北夏農民生活漫談 (Rambling Discussions on Peasant Livelihood in Beixia, Wuxi), in Yu Qingtang, 1937, pp. 79–86.

'Wholesale price indexes in Canton', 1935, *Chinese Economic Journal*, Vol. 26, No. 14, p. 217.

Wickberg, Edgar, 1981a, 'Continuities in land tenure, 1900–1940', in Emily Martin Ahern and Hill Gates, 1981, pp. 212–38.

—— 1981b, 'Another look at land and lineage in the New Territories c.1900', *Journal of the Hong Kong Branch of the Royal Asiatic Society*, Vol. 21, pp. 25–42.

Wolf, Arthur P., and Huang Chieh-shan, 1980, *Marriage and Adoption in China, 1845–1945* (Stanford, Stanford University Press).

Wong Yin-seng, Chang Hsi-chang, and others, 1939, 'Change in land ownership and the fate of permanent tenancy', in Institute of Pacific Relations.

Wong, R. Bin, 1982, 'Food riots in the Qing dynasty', *Journal of Asian Studies*, Vol. 41, No. 4, pp. 767–88.

Wright, Stanley F., 1935, *China's Customs Revenue Since the Revolution of 1911* (Shanghai, Statistical Department of the Inspectorate General of Customs).

Wu Chengluo 吳承洛, 1957, *Zhongguo dualiangheng shi* 中國度量衡史 (A History of Measures of Length, Capacity, and Weight in China), (first edition, Shanghai, 1937).

Wu Huabao 吳華寶, 1936, 'Zhongguo zhi nongye hezuo' 中國之農業合作 (Agricultrual cooperatives in China), in Fang Xianting, 1938, pp. 433–50.

Wu Hui 吳慧, 1985, *Zhongguo lidai liangshi muchan yanjiu* 中國歷代糧食畝產研究 (Studies into Per *Mu* Yields of Food Crops in Each Dynasty in China), (Beijing, Nongye Chubanshe).

Wu Ruilin 伍銳麟, 1937, 'Guangzhoushi Henandao Xiaducun qishiliu jia diaocha' 廣州市河南島下渡村七十六家調查 (An investigation into 76 households in Xiadu Village, Henan Island, Guangzhou City), *Lingnan xuebao* 嶺南學報 Vol. 6, No. 4, pp. 236–303.

Wu Shoupeng 吳壽彭, 1930, 'Douliu yu nongcun jingji shidai de Xuhai geshu' 逗留於農村經濟時代的徐海各屬 (Districts that have remained in the stage of the rural economy in Xuzhou and Haizhou), *Dongfang zazhi*, Vol. 27, Nos. 6 and 7, rep. in Feng Hefa, 1933, pp. 330–61.

Wu Yannan 吳雁南, 1958, 'Shilun Taiping tianguo de tudi zhidu' 試論太平天國的土地制度 (Preliminary discussion of the land system of the Taiping Heavenly Kingdom), *Lishi yanjiu*, Vol. 10, pp. 17–34.

Wu Zhihua 吳致華, 1935, *Jiangdu kengdi fenpei* 江都耕地分配 (The distribution of farmland in Jiangsu), Vol. 66, in Xiao Zheng, 1977.

'Wuxi mishi diaocha' 無錫米市調查 (An Investigation into the rice market of Wuxi), 1936, *Shehui jingji yuebao* 社會經濟月報, Vol. 3, No. 7, pp. 43–66, and No. 8, pp. 21–58.

Xia Lingen 夏林根, 1984, 'Lun jindai Shanghai diqu mianfangzhi shougongye de bianhua' 論近代上海地區棉紡織手工業的變化 (On the changes in the cotton spinning and weaving handicraft industries in the Shanghai region in the modern period), *Zhongguo shehui jingjishi yanjiu*, No. 3, pp. 24–31.

Xiangshan xianzhi 香山縣志 (A Record of Xiangshan County), 1920.

Xiao Yizhang 蕭奕璋 (comp.), n.d., *Tianxia shuilu lucheng xinbian* 天下水陸路程新編 (A New Compilation of Water and Land Routes Under Heaven), n.p.

Xiao Zheng 蕭錚, 1977, *Minguo ershi niandai Zhongguo dalu tudi wenti ziliao* 民國二十年代中國大陸土地問題資料 (Source Materials on Land Problems in Mainland China in the 1930s), (Taibei, Chengwen).

Xie Xueying 謝雪影, 1935, *Chaomei xianxiang* 潮梅現象 (Current Scenes in Chaozhou and Mei County), (Shantou, Shishi tongxunshe).

Xinhui Tanjiang xingzu zizhihui guizhang 新會淡江興族自治會規章 (Regulations for the Self-Government Association for Advancing the Lineage at Tanjiang, Xinhui), (n.d., n.p.).

Xu Daofu 許道夫, 1983, *Zhongguo jindai nongye shengchan ji maoyi tongji ziliao* 中國近代農業生產及貿易統計資料 (Statistical Source Materials on Agricultural Production and Trade in Modern China), (Shanghai, Renmin chubanshe).

Xu Dixin 許滌新, 1935, 'Nongcun pochan zhong di nongmin shengji wenti' 農村破產中底農民生計問題 (The problem of peasant livelihood under rural bankruptcy), *Dongfang zazhi*, Vol. 32, No. 1, pp. *nong* 45–56.

Xu Hongkui 徐洪奎, 1934, *Yixing xian xiangcun xinyong zhi gaikuang jiqi yu diquan yidong zhi guanxi* 宜興縣鄉村信用之概況及其與地權異動之關係 (General Conditions of Rural Credit and Its Relationships to Changes in Land Rights in Yixing County), (Taibei), Vol. 88, in Xiao Zheng (1977).

Xu Xinwu, 'The struggle of the handicraft cotton industry against machine textiles in China', *Modern China*, pp. 31–49.

Xu Xinwu 徐新吾, Shen Jianhua 沈劍華, and Tang Kentang 湯肯堂, 1986, 'Zhongguo jindai saosi gongye de youxian fazhan yu zouxiang pochan' 中國近代繰絲工業的有限發展與走向破產 (Limited Development in the Silk-Reeling Industry and its Progress to Bankruptcy in Modern China), in Sichuansheng Zhongguo jingjishi xuehui, 1986, pp. 42–54.

Xu Xinwu and Wei Tefu 韋特孚, 1983, 'Zhongri liangguo saosi shougongye ziben zhuyi mengya bijiao yanjiu' 中日兩國繰絲手工業資本主義萌芽比較 (A comparison of nascent capitalism in the silk-reeling handicraft industry in China and Japan), *Lishi yanjiu*, No. 6, pp. 135–47.

Xuxiu Jiangdu xianzhi 續修江都縣志 (Supplement to the Records of Jiangdu County), 1926.

Xuxiu Nanhai xianzhi 續修南海縣志 (Supplement to the Records of Nanhai County), 1910.

Xuxiu sangyuanwei zhi 續修桑園圍志 (Supplement to the Records of the Mulberry Farm Dyke), n.d. (1923), Jiujiang, Guangdong.

Yan Xinzhe 嚴學熙, 1935, *Nongcun jiating diaocha* 農村家庭調查 (A Survey of Rural Families), Shanghai.

Yan Xuexi 言心哲, 1985, 'Lin Jubai *Jindai Nantong tubushi* jianjie' 林學百《近代南通土布史》簡介 (Introducing Lin Jubai, *A History of the Native Cloth of Modern Nantong*), *Jindaishi yanjiu*, No. 4, pp. 302–4.

—— 1986, 'Cansang shengchan yu Wuxi jindai nongcun jingji' 蠶桑生產與無錫近代農村經濟, *Jindaishi yanjiu*, No. 4, pp. 24–58.

Yan Zhongping 嚴中平, 1963, *Zhongguo mian fangji shigao* 中國綿紡織史稿 (A Draft History of Cotton Spinning and Weaving in China), (Beijing, Kexue chubanshe).

Yang, C.K., 1944, *A North China Local Market Economy, a Summary of a Study of Periodic Markets in Chowping Hsien, Shantung* (New York, Institute of Pacific Relations), mimeo.

—— 1959, *A Chinese Village in Early Communist Transition* (Cambridge, Mass., the M.I.T. Press, second printing, 1966).

Yang Duanliu 楊端六, 1962, *Qingdai huobi jinrong shigao* 清代貨幣金融史稿 (A Draft History of the Currency in the Qing), (Beijing, Sanlian shudian).

Yang Jicheng 羊冀成, 1936, *Songjiang mishi diaocha* 松江米市調查 (An Investigation into the Rice Market of Songjiang), (Shanghai).

Yang Ruxiong 楊汝熊, 1937, 'Xushu de Huaishui' 徐屬的淮水 (The Huai River at Xuzhou), in Yu Qingtang, 1937, pp. 209–16.

Yang, W.Y., and Lu Sheng-hwai, 1938, 'Price changes in Chinese rural market towns, September, 1935 to October 1937', *Economic Facts*, No. 9, pp. 378–93.

Yang Yinpu 楊蔭溥, 1930, *Zhongguo Jiaoyisuo lun* 中國交易所論 (A Discussion on Commodity Exchanges in China), (Shanghai, Shangwu).

Yao Enrong 姚恩榮 and Zou Yingxi 鄒迎曦, 1983, '1917–1937 nian Dafeng deng liu yanken gongsi zhimian jiankuang' 1917–1937 年大豐等六鹽墾公司植棉簡況 (A general overview of the cultivation of cotton by six salt-field reclamation companies, including Dafeng, 1917–1937), *Lishi yanjiu*, No. 3, pp. 113–21.

Ye Duzhuang 葉篤莊, 1948, *Huabei mianhua jiqi zengchan wenti* 華北棉花及其增產問題 (The Cotton of North China and Problems Relating to Increasing its Yield), (Nanjing).

Ye Qianji 葉謙吉, 1935, 'Zhongguo mianhua yunxiao hezuo de zuzhi wenti' 中國棉花運銷合作的組織問題 (Problems in the organization of distribution co-operatives for cotton in China), in Fang Xianting, 1938, pp. 528–37.

Yinxian tongzhi 鄞縣通志 (A Record of Yin County), 1935.

Yu Lin 余霖, 1932, 'Jiangnan nongcun shuailuo di yige suoyin' 江南農村衰落的一個索引 (An index to rural decline in southern Jiangsu), *Xin chuangzao*, Vol. 2, Nos. 1 and 2, rep. in Feng Hefa, 1933, pp. 400–21.

Yu Qingtang 俞慶棠, 1937, *Nongcun shenghuo congtan* 農村生活叢談 (Rambling Discussions on Village Life), (Shanghai, Shenbaoguan).

Yuan Yinhuai 阮蔭槐, 1935, *Wuxi zhi tudi zhengli* 無錫之土地整理 (The Reorganization of Land Records in Wuxi), Vols. 35 and 36, in Xiao Zheng, 1977.

Zhan Ran 湛然, 1934, 'Nantong de nongcun' 南通的農村 (The villages of Nantong), *Zhongguo nongcun jingji yanjiuhui huibao* 中國農村經濟研究會會報 rep. in Feng Hefa, 1935, pp. 24–6.

Zhang Diken 張廸懇, 1985, 'Guanyu Wuxi saosi gongye fazhan de jige wenti' 關於無錫繅絲工業發展的幾個問題 (Several problems concerning the development of the silk-reeling industry in Wuxi), *Zhongguo shehui jingjishi yanjiu*, No. 4, pp. 79–86.

Zhang Hanlin 張漢林, 1930, *Danyang nongcun jingji diaocha* 丹陽農村經濟調查 (An Investigation into the Rural Economy of Danyang), n.p.

Zhang Huiqun 張惠羣 n.d. (1930s), *Yanken quyu zudian zhi yanjiu* 鹽墾區域租佃制度之研究 (A Study of the Tenancy System in the Salt-field Reclamation Districts), Taibei, Vol. 61, in Xiao Zheng, 1977.

Zhang Kai 章階, 1984, 'Xinzhongguo chengli qian bangeduo shiji zhong woguo zuowu yuzhong shiye gaishu' 新中國成立前半個多世紀中我國作物

育種事業概述 (A general account of the development of new varieties of seeds in our country in the half century or more before the establishment of New China), *Zhongguo nongshi*, No. 2, pp. 51–60.

Zhang Liluan 張履鸞, 1933, 'Jiangsu Wujin wujia zhi yanjiu' 江蘇武進物價之研究 (A study of prices in Wujin, Jiangsu), *Jinling xuebao*, Vol. 3, No. 1, pp. 153–216.

Zhang Qianjiu 張潛九, 1935, 'Dong Taihu weitian shimo ji' 東太湖圍田始末記 (An account from beginning to end of the dyked fields on the eastern banks of Lake Tai), *Zhongguo nongcun*, Vol. 1, No. 10, pp. 92–9.

Zhang Shantu 張善圖, 1930, 'Minguo yilai Guangzhoushi mijia biandong zhi yanjiu' 民國以來廣州市米價變動之研究 (A study of the changes in the price of rice in Guangzhou city since the beginning of the Republic), *Shehui kexue luncong* 社會科學論叢, Vol 2, No. 10, pp. 101–18.

Zhang Xinyi 張心一, 1932, *Zhongguo nongye gaikuang guji* 中國農業概況估計 (An Estimate of Agricultural Conditions in China), (Nanjing).

Zhang Xinyi, Tao Huanfen 陶桓棻, and Zhuang Jiceng 莊繼曾 1934, *Shiban Jurong xian renkou nongye zongdiaocha baogao* 試辦勾容縣人口農業總調查報告 (Report on the Attempt to Survey the Population and Agriculture of Jurong County), (n.p., Taibei, rep. 1971).

Zhang Yifan 張一凡, 1948, *Fenmaiye xuzhi* 粉麥業須知 (Essentials in the Flour and Wheat Industries), (Shanghai).

Zhang Youyi 章有義, 1957, *Zhongguo jindai nongyeshi ziliao* 中國近代農業史資料 (Source Materials on Modern China's Agriculture), Vols. 2 and 3 (Beijing).

Zhao Chengxin 趙承信, 1929, 'Xinhui Ciqi tudi fenpei diaocha' 新會慈溪土地分配調查 (An Investigation into Land Distribution in Ciqi in Xinhui), *Shehui xuejie* 社會學界, Vol. 5, rep. in Feng Hefa, 1933, pp. 936–51.

Zhao Zongxu 趙宗煦, 1936, *Jiangsu sheng nongye jinrong yu diquan yidong zhi guangxi* 江蘇省農業金融與地權異動之關係 (Rural Finance and Its Relationships to Changes in Land Rights in Jiangsu Province), Taibei, Vol. 87, in Xiao Zheng, 1977.

Zhong Gongfu 鍾功甫, 1958, 'Zhujiang sanjiaozhou di sangji yutang ji zheji yutang' 珠江三角洲的桑基魚塘及蔗基魚塘 (The mulberry dykes and fishponds and the sugar-cane dykes and fishponds of the Zhujiang delta), *Dili xuebao*, pp. 257–72.

Zhongguo diyi lishi danganguan 中國第一歷史檔案館, Zhongguo shehui kexue yuan lishi yanjiusuo 中國社會科學院歷史研究所 comps., *Qingdai dizu boxue xingtai* 清代地租剝削形態 (Features of Rent Exploitation in the Qing), (Beijing, Zhonghua shuju).

Zhongguo kexueyuan Shanghai jingji yanjiusuo 中國科學院上海經濟研究所 Shanghai shehui kexueyuan jingji yanjiusuo 上海社會科學院經濟研究所 1958, *Shanghai jiefang qianhou wujia ziliao huibian, 1921–1957* 上海解放前後物價資料彙編, 1921–1957 (Source Materials on Prices in Shanghai

Before and After the Liberation, 1921–1957), (Shanghai).

Zhongguo jingji nianjian 1934, see: Shiyebu Zhongguo jingji nianjian bianzhuan weiyuanhui, 1934.

Zhongguo jingji nianjian 1936, see: Shiyebu Zhongguo jingji nianjian bianzhuan weiyuanhui, 1936.

Zhongguo jingji nianjian, 1937, see: Shiyebu Zhongguo jingji nianjian bianzhuan weiyuanhui, 1937.

Zhongguo mianye tongjihui 中國棉業統計會 , 1935, *Zhongguo mianye tongji* 中國棉業統計 (Statistics on the Cotton Industry in China), n.p.

Zhongguo nianjian 中國年鑑 (The China Yearbook), 1924 (Shanghai).

Zhongguo renmin daxue Qingshi yanjiusuo, danganxi, Zhongguo zhengzhi zhidushi jiaoyanshi 中國人民大學清史研究所，檔案系‧中國政治制度史教研室 comps., *Kang, Yong, Qian shiqi chengxiang renmin fankang douzheng ziliao* 康、雍、乾時期城鄉人民反抗鬥爭資料(Source Materials on Rebellious Struggles by Urban and Rural People in the Kangxi, Yongzheng, and Qianlong Periods), (Beijing, Zhonghua shuju).

Zhongguo renmin yinhang zonghang canshishi jinrong shiliaozu 中國人民銀行總行參事室金融史料組 , 1964, *Zhongguo jindai huobishi ziliao* 中國近代貨幣史資料 (Source Materials on the History of Modern China's Currencies), (Beijing, Zhonghua shuju).

Zhongguo renmin yinhang Shanghaishi fenhang 中國人民銀行上海市分行 1960, *Shanghai qianzhuang shiliao* 上海錢莊史料 (Source Materials on Native Banks in Shanghai), (Shanghai, Renmin chubanshe).

Zhongyang dangbu guomin jingji jihua weiyuanhui 中央黨部國民經濟計劃委員會 , 1937, *Shinian lai zhi Zhongguo jingji jianshe* 十年來之中國經濟建設 (Ten Years of Economic Construction in China), (Nanjing).

Zhongyang daxue jingji ziliaoshi 中央大學經濟資料室 , 1935, *Tianfu fujiashui diaocha* 田賦附加稅調查 (An Investigation into Supplementary Taxes Added onto the Land Tax), (n.p., 1971, Taibei rep.).

Zhongyang qixiangju kexue yanjiuyuan 中央氣象局科學研究院 , 1981, *Zhongguo jinwubai nianlai hanlao fenbu tuji* 中國近五百年來旱澇分佈圖集 (An Atlas of Droughts and Floods in China in the Last Five Hundred Years), (Beijing).

Zhongyang yinhang jingji yanjiuchu 中央銀行經濟研究處 , 1936, *Zhongguo nongye jinrong gaiyao* 中國農業金融概要 (An Overview of Chinese Agricultural Finance), (Shanghai).

Zhou Gucheng 周谷城 , 1931, *Zhongguo shehui zhi bianhua* 中國社會之變化 (Social Changes in China), (Shanghai, Xinshengming shuju).

Zhou Tingdong 周廷棟 , 1927, 'Taicang (Jiangsu sheng)' 太倉（江蘇省）(Taicang (Jiangsu Province)), in 'Gedi nongmin zhuangkuang diaocha' 各地農民狀況調查 (Investigation into the conditions of the peasantry of various places), *Dongfang zazhi*, Vol. 24, No. 16, 122–24.

Zhou Yishi 周一士 1957, *Zhongguo gonglu shi* 中國公路史 (A History of China's Motor Roads), (Taibei).

Zhu Fucheng朱福成, n.d. (1930s), *Jiangsu shatian zhi yanjiu* 江蘇沙田之研究 (A Study of 'Sandy Land' in Jiangsu), Vol. 69, in Xiao Zheng, 1977 (Taibei).

Zhu Guanghua朱光華, 1985, 'Qingdai de jiqi mianfen gongye' 清代的機器麵粉工業 (The machine flour-milling industry in the Qing), *Zhongguo shehui jingjishi yanjiu*, No. 2, pp. 58–62.

Zhu Kezhen竺可楨, 1926, 'Lun Jiangzhe liangsheng renkou zhi midu' 論江浙兩省人口之密度 (On the density of population in the two provinces of Jiangsu and Zhejiang), *Dongfang zazhi*, Vol. 23, No. 1, pp. 91–112.

Zhu Side 朱嗣德, 1980, *Minguo ershi nian zhi sanshi niandai Zhongguo nongcun jingji wenti* 民國二十年至三十年代中國農村經濟問題 (Problems in the Rural Economy in the 1930s and 1940s) (Taibei, Zhongguo dizheng yanjiusuo).

Zou Dafan鄒大凡, Wu Zhiwei 吳智偉, Xu Wenhui 徐雯惠, 1965, 'Jin bainian lai jiu Zhongguo liangshi jiage de biandong qushi' 近百年來舊中國糧食價格的變動趨勢 (Trends in Food Prices in Old China in the Last One Hundred Years), *Xueshu yuekan* 學術月刊, rep. in Cuncui xueshe 荐萃學社 (ed.), 1979, *Zhongguo jinsanbainian shehui jingji shilunji* 中國近三百年社會經濟史論集 (Essays on the Last Three Hundred Years' Economic History in China), (Hong Kong).

Zou Yiren 鄒依仁, 1980, *Jiu Shanghai renkou bianqian de yanjiu* 舊上海人口變遷的研究 (Studies of Population Changes in Old Shanghai), (Shanghai, Shanghai renmin chubanshe).

Glossary

bangshou 幫手
Bao'an 寶安
Beijiang 北江
bu 步
buji buhan 不飢不寒
caizheng ting 財政廳
cansha 蠶沙
chan 産
Chang'ancun 長安村
Changjiang 長江
Changsheng shoushe 長生壽社
Changshu 常熟
Changzhou 常州
Chao'an 潮安
Chaozhou 潮州
Chen Jiongming 陳炯明
chonghua tian 崇劃田
Chongming 崇明
Chuanchanghe 串場河
Chuansha 川沙
Chunhua zhen 淳化鎮
ci 祠
cien [jin] 瑾
Dabu (Tai Po) 大埔
dan 担
daxing 大姓
Deqing 德慶
Dianbai 電白
Dongguan 東莞
Donghai husha gongyue 東海護沙公約
Donghai hushaju 東海護沙局
Dongjiang 東江
Dongtai 東台
dou 斗
Enping 恩平
fabi 法幣
Fengxian 豐縣
Foshan 佛山
Funing 阜寧
fu 府
Fushan tang 福善堂
Gaoyao 高要
Gaozhou 高州
geju 攔具
Gongbei 拱北
gongci 公祠
gongliang 工糧
gongsi 公司
Guangdong 廣東
guanggun 光棍
Guangning 廣寧
Guanyun 灌雲
Guizhou 桂州
Guoyang 渦陽
haiguan liang 海關兩
haihu 海斛
Haimen 海門
Haizhou 海州
Hanjiang 韓江
Haoyin 毫銀
Haozhuan 毫券
Henan 河南
Hengtou xiang 亨頭鄉
Heyuan 河源
Huai 淮
Huai'an 淮安
Huaxian 花縣
Huizhou 惠州
ji 集
jia 家
Jiangdu 江都
Jiangmen 江門
Jiangnan 江南
Jiangning 江寧
Jiangsu 江蘇
Jiangyin 江陰
Jiaying 嘉應

Jieyang 揭陽
Jingjiang 靖江
Jintan 金壇
Jiulong 九龍
Juyong 句容
Kaixiangong 開弦弓
Kunshan 昆山
Leizhou 雷州
li 里
Liangchuanwan (Leung Shuen Wan) 糧船灣
Lianzhou 連州
Lihe 裏河
lijin 厘金
Lishe 禮社
liudong 流動
lixiahe 裏下河
Liyang 溧陽
Liyunhe 裏運河
Long-Hai 隴海
lougui 陋規
Luzhou *fu* 廬州府
Maoming 茂明
Minglun *tang* 明倫堂
mu 畝
neisha 内沙
Nan'ao 南澳
Nanhai 南海
Nanhui 南匯
Nantong 南通
Nantou 南頭
Nanxiong 南雄
Ningguo *fu* 寧國府
nongshe 農舍
Panyu 番禺
Peixian 沛縣
piantang 片糖
Pukou 浦口
putong de tian 普通的田
Qidong 啓東
Qing 青
qing 頃
Qingjiangpu 清江浦
Qingyuan 清遠

Qinzhou 欽州
Qiongzhou 瓊州
Rong 榮
Rong Desheng 榮德生
Rong Zongjing 榮宗敬
Rongxiang 榮巷
Rugao 如皋
Sanshui 三水
Shajing 沙井
Shantou 汕頭
Shaozhou 韶州
shatian 沙田
she 社
Shengze 盛澤
shi 石
shice 實測
shimu 市畝
Shiqi 石岐
shishi 市石
Shunde 順德
Shuyang 沭陽
Sihui 四會
Songjiang 松江
Suqian 宿遷
Suzhou 蘇州
Taicang 太倉
Taishan 台山
tang 堂
Tanjiang 淡江
tianye gonghui 田業公會
Tonghai 通海
tongjishi 統計室
Tongshan 銅山
Tongzhou 通州
tuanlian 團練
tuweizi 土圍子
waisha 外沙
Wanqingsha 萬頃沙
Wujiang 吳江
Wujin 武進
Wuxi 無錫
Wuzhou 梧州
Xiahe 下河
xian 縣

xiang 鄉
xiangshen 鄉紳
xiangshao 鄉稍
Xiao 蕭
Xiaodingxiang 小丁巷
xiaokang 小康
Xigong (Saikung) 西貢
Xijiang 西江
Xin'an 新安
xing 升
Xinhui 新會
Xinning 新寧
Xue 薛
Xue Fucheng 薛福成
Xue Nanming 薛南溟
Xui Shouxuan 薛壽萱
xuli 胥吏
Xuzhou 徐州
yamen 衙門
Yancheng 鹽城
Yangchun 陽春
Yangmuqiao 楊木橋
Yangshan 陽山
Yangzhou 楊州
Yantian 鹽田
yazu 押租

yibao sandan 一包三担
Yingde 英德
yitu 義圖
Yixing 宜興
Yizheng 儀徵
Yong-Gui gongyue 容桂公約
Yongqi 容奇
Zengcheng 增城
zhai 寨
Zhang Jian 張謇
Zhang Lixiang 張履祥
Zhang Xun 張勳
Zhang Zhidong 張之洞
zhangfang 賬房
zhen 鎮
Zhengxiang 鄭巷
Zhenjiang 鎮江
Zhenze 震澤
Zhongshan 中山
zhou 州
Zhujiang 珠江
zhuang 莊
zhuizu weiyuanhui 追租委員會
zhuizuju 追租局
zongcangting 總倉廳

Index